Aging

VOLUME 34

Human Aging Research

Concepts and Techniques

Aging Series

Aging
VOLUME 34

Human Aging Research
Concepts and Techniques

Editors

Barbara Kent, Ph.D.
Associate Professor
Physiology and Biophysics and
Geriatrics and Adult Development
Mount Sinai School of Medicine
New York, New York

Robert Butler, M.D.
Brookdale Professor
Chairman, Gerald and May Ritter
Department of Geriatrics and
Adult Development
Mount Sinai Medical Center
New York, New York

Raven Press  New York

Raven Press, 1185 Avenue of the Americas, New York, New York 10036

Made in the United States of America

Library of Congress Cataloging-in-Publication Data

Human aging research.

  (Aging ; v. 34)
  Includes bibliographies and index.
  1. Aging—Research—Methodology. 2. Geriatrics—
Research—Methodology. I. Kent, Barbara, 1940–
II. Butler, Robert N., 1927–   . III. Series.
[DNLM: 1. Aging. 2. Research—methods. W1 AG342E v.34 /
WT 20 H918]
QP86.H753   1988   612′.67′072   85–43149
ISBN 0–88167–372–2

9 8 7 6 5 4 3 2 1

Preface

This volume introduces concepts and techniques in human aging research to students, postgraduate fellows, and medical and other specialists who are interested in the critical questions of gerontology and geriatrics—disciplines that study the role of aging in human affairs, generally, and in health and disease, specifically. The focus of the book is on the biomedical aspect of human aging research.

In 1982 the Mount Sinai Medical Center in New York City established the nation's first medical school department of geriatrics, the Gerald and May Ellen Ritter Department of Geriatrics and Adult Development. By 1983 a sizeable group of young physicians had joined the fellowship program for training in the emerging role of academic geriatrician, a role for which there is ever-increasing demand. To equip Fellows with the knowledge and tools necessary to approach research questions in geriatrics and gerontology, we introduced a 24-session summer intensive in human aging research. The course is broadly based, with special consideration given to techniques and concepts particularly applicable to the study of aging populations. Statistical and epidemiological methods are highlighted as are problems that are salient, if not unique, to research in aging systems. The lectures and discussions from the seminar form the basis of this volume. The essays included here are not intended to be reviews of the state of knowledge of each topic, but rather approaches to how one would go about studying questions in human aging. We believe that the reader of this text will gain a greater appreciation of how to review critically the literature in the field of aging, develop a sense of the special requirements for conducting human aging research, and be able to design and conduct research in gerontology and geriatrics.

The demographic imperative of the 1980s and the coming decades points to the growing need for research in human aging, which, by virtue of the fact that it emerged relatively recently, has received less attention than other fields with longer histories. Aging research, then, is a vast and fertile field offering unlimited opportunities for exciting and innovative contributions. Now and in the coming years we will need many more excellent researchers to meet the new challenges in this field. It is with this in mind that we present *Human Aging Research: Concepts and Techniques*. Our aim is to stimulate readers to make their own contributions to aging research, from increasing their observational powers, to participating in clinical and basic investigations that will enhance the care of older people, and, ultimately, to understanding human aging.

We assume that this effort is not perfect. We hope our readers will send us

their comments and suggestions so that we may improve future editions to better serve graduate, postgraduate, and continuing medical and related education.

BARBARA KENT, PH.D.
ROBERT N. BUTLER, M.D.

Contents

Contributors

William H. Adler, M.D.
Clinical Immunology Section
Gerontology Research Center
National Institute on Aging
National Institutes of Health
Baltimore, Maryland 21224

Diana S. Beattie, Ph.D.
Department of Biochemistry
West Virginia University
School of Medicine
Morgantown, West Virginia 26506

Samuel W. Bloom, Ph.D.
Department of Community Medicine
Mount Sinai Medical Center
One Gustave Levy Place
New York, New York 10029

W. Ted Brown, M.D., Ph.D.
Department of Human Genetics
New York State Office of Mental
  Retardation and Developmental
  Disabilities
Institute for Basic Research in
  Developmental Disabilities
1050 Forest Hill Road
Staten Island, New York 10314

Robert N. Butler, M.D.
Department of Geriatrics and Adult
  Development
Mount Sinai Medical Center
One Gustave Levy Place
New York, New York 10029

Christine K. Cassel, M.D.
Department of Medicine
Section of General Internal Medicine
The University of Chicago
Pritzker School of Medicine
5841 South Maryland Avenue
Chicago, Illinois 60637

Thomas C. Chalmers, M.D.
Department of Health Policy Management
Harvard School of Public Health
677 Huntington Avenue, Room 405
Boston, Massachusetts 02115

Peter Davies, Ph.D.
Departments of Pathology and
  Neuroscience
Albert Einstein College of Medicine
1165 Morris Park Avenue
Bronx, New York 10461

Richard M. Fagerstrom, Jr., Ph.D.
Biomathematical Science Department
Mount Sinai Medical Center
One Gustave Levy Place
New York, New York 10029

Nancy S. Foldi, Ph.D.
Department of Geriatrics and Adult
  Development
Mount Sinai Medical Center
One Gustave Levy Place
New York, New York 10029

Jeffrey B. Halter, M.D.
Department of Internal Medicine
Division of Geriatric Medicine
University of Michigan Medical School
1010 Wall Street
ST1508 Turner Building
Ann Arbor, Michigan 48109

Leonard Hayflick, Ph.D.
School of Medicine
University of California, San Francisco,
  and
Cell Biology and Aging Section (151E)
VAMC
4150 Clement Street
San Francisco, California 94143

Dorothy R. Hill, M.S.
Gustave L. and Janet W. Levy Library
Mount Sinai School of Medicine
One Gustave Levy Place
New York, New York 10029

Barbara Kent, Ph.D.
Geriatrics and Adult Development
Department of Physiology and Biophysics
One Gustave Levy Place
New York, New York 10029

Donald West King, Jr., M.D.
Department of Pathology
Division of Biological Sciences
The University of Chicago
Box 417
950 East 59th Street
Chicago, Illinois 60637

Edward G. Lakatta, M.D.
Laboratory of Cardiovascular Sciences
Gerontological Research Center
National Institute on Aging
National Institutes of Health
Baltimore, Maryland 21224

Michael D. Lebowitz, M.D., Ph.D.
Department of Internal Medicine
Pulmonary Disease Section
Division of Respiratory Sciences
University of Arizona College of Medicine
Tucson, Arizona 85724

Leslie S. Libow, M.D.
The Jewish Home and Hospital for Aged
120 West 106th Street
New York, New York 10025, and
Mount Sinai School of Medicine
One Gustave Levy Place
New York, New York 10029

Diane E. Meier, M.D.
Department of Geriatrics and Adult
  Development
Mount Sinai Medical Center
One Gustave Levy Place
New York, New York 10029

Michael N. Mulvihill, Ph.D.
Department of Community Medicine
Mount Sinai Medical Center
One Gustave Levy Place
New York, New York 10029

James E. Nagel, M.D.
Clinical Immunology Section
Gerontology Research Center
National Institute on Aging
National Institutes of Health
Baltimore, Maryland 21224

Richard R. Neufeld, M.D.
The Jewish Home and Hospital for Aged
120 West 106th Street
New York, New York 10025, and
Mount Sinai School of Medicine
One Gustave Levy Place
New York, New York 10029

Monte Peterson, M.D.
Department of Geriatrics and Adult
  Development
Mount Sinai Medical Center
One Gustave Levy Place
New York, New York 10029

Hans Popper, M.D.
Mount Sinai School of Medicine
One Gustave Levy Place
New York, New York 10029

Irene C. Rayman, Ph.D.
Department of Community Medicine
Mount Sinai School of Medicine
New York, New York 10029

John C. Thornton, Ph.D.
Biomathematical Science Department
Mount Sinai Medical Center
One Gustave Levy Place
New York, New York 10029

Aging
VOLUME 34

Human Aging Research
Concepts and Techniques

Human Aging Research: Concepts and Techniques,
edited by B. Kent and R. N. Butler.
Raven Press, Ltd., New York © 1988.

Excellence, Efficiency, and Economy Through Aging Research

Robert N. Butler

Department of Geriatrics and Adult Development, Mount Sinai Medical Center,
New York, New York 10029

Elderly populations around the world are growing rapidly, a triumph of productivity, science, public health and sanitation measures, and individual health care. The aging of the population, however, has financial implications for individuals and governments; and in trying to relieve strained budgets by economizing on spending for health, governments are tempted to reduce support for biomedical and other health-related research.

Paradoxically, the "savings" may represent foregone economies over the long run. One function of basic, clinical, and service-oriented research is to produce more effective treatments and preventive measures, to make services more efficient, and to help more people to function on their own, as productively as possible, despite handicaps. An outstanding example of the economies achievable through research is the antipolio vaccination, which obviated resort to costly acute care, rehabilitation, and other services. Basic research into the nature of viruses and the immune system preceded the achievement; the investment in this research yielded many times its dollar value in savings, the promotion of productivity, and the quality of human life.

Given population aging and the rising costs of care of the elderly, we need to establish a proactive research agenda for understanding and intervening in age-related diseases and for promoting health and functional capacity (2). The agenda may cover basic and clinical studies with room to capitalize on new opportunities. For example, explorations in the molecular biology of aging may lead logically to clinical studies of pharmacokinetics in older people and then to the design and testing of new drugs for efficacy and safety.

This line of thought is worth pursuing, in terms of pharmacology, for a pragmatic perspective on the need for developing a research agenda adapted to the longevity revolution. Among pharmacologically relevant characteristics frequently observed in older persons are a decrease in renal function with age, including decreases in blood flow, glomerular filtration rate, and tubular secretion; oversecretion of antidiuretic hormone (ADH) and increased potential for water intoxication; reduced renin–aldosterone responses, yielding an altered response to diuretic and antihyper-

1

tensive drugs; and decreased baroreceptor sensitivity, tending toward orthostatic hypotension. These conditions must be taken into account when designing drugs in order to avoid or minimize adverse reactions, especially in the frail elderly who may need these agents the most. Equally important is research to explain why these decrements occur, how they may be linked among themselves and with other characteristics of the aging human being, why they are not universal among older persons, and the nature of interindividual variation in renal capacity. For example, significant subsets of the older population do not display the renal changes described above. There are longitudinal data to show increments in renal function as individuals age, e.g., increased blood flow. The study of interindividual variation bears on the issue of adjusting dosages for individual needs. (I am indebted to William Abrams, M.D., of Merck, Sharpe and Dohme for much of the foregoing discussion).

The kidney is but one organ system displaying age-related functional changes of pharmacological significance. Older people tend to have an increasing sensitivity to central nervous system (CNS) drugs. One that is generally benign in the young adult may be potent in the older adult; it may achieve greater pain relief but at the risk of severe CNS effects.

Our pharmacological knowledge of older persons must be deepened in order to meet their diverse and conflicting clinical needs safely and effectively. Among the products to be created out of basic research understandings are the following.

1. An antiarthritic agent that does not affect renal prostaglandin mechanisms or interact adversely with drugs commonly used in the elderly
2. A sleeping pill based on modern concepts of sleep patterns in the elderly
3. An antidepressant that circumvents age-related changes in receptor populations
4. An oral broad-spectrum antibiotic whose safety and efficacy is not compromised by altered renal function
5. Vaccines tailored to the altered immune status of the elderly

Aging research also may have practical public policy implications. In 1978 Congress passed the Experienced Pilots Act to resolve issues concerning mandatory retirement. A group of pilots who had turned 60 and did not want to stop flying, the Gray Eagles, lobbied for legislation and conducted court cases to overturn a 1959 federal regulation requiring retirement from piloting commercial passenger airliners at age 60. In the Act, Congress ordered the National Institute on Aging to study the following questions.

1. Is the age 60 requirement medically justified?
2. Is mandatory retirement at any age medically justified?
3. Are required medical examinations of pilots given often enough?
4. What is the impact of aging on human performance?

The Institute was forbidden to return to Congress with a conclusion that funding for longitudinal studies should be increased. Yet that was (and still is) necessary. No pilot over age 60 had flown commercial airliners since 1959. There was no way to undertake a direct comparative study of pre- and post-60 performance of pilots in airliners. Information on reaction time was available through the technology of cockpit simulations, but we had neither the necessary data nor techniques for measuring individual functions that are predictive. We did propose a modified longitudinal study in which the Federal Aviation Agency would invite pilots at age 55 to join a program permitting them to fly until 65, provided they participated in an intensive longitudinal investigation. This proposed study had not been approved at the time of this writing.

A similar challenge for research emerged from the National Commission on Social Security Reform in 1982. Fifty years earlier the average life expectancy at birth was 58 for men and 62 for women. Today it is 71 for men and 78 for women. The Commission asked this question: Had "work ability" increased in proportion to the increase in life expectancy since passage of the 1935 Social Security Act? If so, did it justify an increase in the age of eligibility for full retirement benefits?

These apparently simple questions had no clear answer. There is no established relation between average life expectancy and disability-free life expectancy, average health expectancy, or active life expectancy. The National Center for Health Statistics has found an increasing proportion of disability for every decade of life. We do not have specific age-linked measures of individual functioning. What applies in the aggregate does not necessarily predict this or that individual's longevity or functioning. Blacks and Hispanics do not enjoy the same average life expectancy as most Americans. They contribute to Social Security throughout their lives, yet many die before becoming eligible for benefits. If one raised the age for full benefits from 65 to 67, the impact would be severe for minorities and for individuals needing to retire because of inability to obtain work or continue work. The Commission voted for retirement at age 67 as a matter of program economics, not gerontological science, and Congress passed the proposal into law.

In the health-services realm, aging research is needed to answer a variety of practical questions.

1. Does the prospective payment system in Medicare, based on diagnosis-related groups (DRGs), fit well with scientifically accurate concepts of the older patient? The DRGs proceed from the outlook of acute, organ-specific medicine, not the geriatric orientation toward the functional performance of the individual in daily activities of life in his or her physical and social environment. The difference in concept leads to a difference in plan of care. Moreover, the DRG approach appears incomplete without an index of severity/complexity to capture all the factors relevant to the care of the very old, frail, and poor. The omission may have disastrous effects.

2. How can we evaluate service and treatment modalities for best results with older patients? How do we assure ourselves that "soft" and "hard" technologies really are effective? Does "too much" social service weaken the survivability of older persons, as observed by Blenkner et al. (3)?

Arguments for the practicality of aging research are necessary to overcome resistance to its funding. This resistance is rooted in a traditional repulsion to old age in Western culture. The view of human aging as implacable dates back to antiquity: Aurora, the goddess of dawn who loved Tithonus, a mortal, persuaded Zeus to let Tithonus live forever. She failed to ask Zeus to preserve Tithonus as a vital being, however, and so was left with an increasingly decrepit lover for eternity. Images expressing fear of growing decrepit as one grows old can be found in many other examples of Western literature.

These negative images have undermined support for aging research. Many thoughtful members of Congress, contemplating fiscal initiatives, have wondered if extending life would be socially disastrous. Yet research itself can help erase these images. The wisdom of the Research on Aging Act of 1974, which created the National Institute on Aging (NIA), was in declaring the NIA goal as maintaining and promoting the middle, prime years of life. At its outset, NIA gave leading priorities to research on senile dementia of the Alzheimer's type, other matters affecting the fast-growing 85-plus age group, and the molecular biology of aging. In my opinion, when senility in its manifold forms (especially Alzheimer's disease) is solved, there will be a dramatic increase in funding for research on aging and longevity.

DEVELOPMENT OF GERONTOLOGY

When setting the stage for an effective agenda, questions about the productivity of aging research should be welcomed. They provide the opportunity for pointing out that gerontology is a relatively new scientific enterprise. "Gerontology" is a twentieth century term that Eli Metchnikoff, the 1903 Nobel Prize winner, used for the first time in his book *The Nature of Man: Studies in Optimistic Philosophy* (15). Gerontology may be broadly defined as the study of aging in its biological, psychological, and social dimensions. Part of gerontology is developmental biology. It seeks a fundamental understanding of the mechanisms of senescence and longevity as well as the continuum of growth and differentiation. Gerontology is a critical component of the biology of the human life cycle.

As this broad definition may suggest, gerontology is derivative of other sciences, and it is interdisciplinary. It is the nature of gerontology to break down barriers between fields and departments in seeking fundamental and holistic understanding. It is ready to prosper from the "new biology" (which includes recombinant DNA and hybridoma technology), the flourishing neurosciences, and new instrumentation (e.g., positron emission tomography and magnetic resonance imaging). Some scientists, unable to grasp the holistic nature of gerontology, have scorned it as a nonscience.

The development of modern gerontological science offers a contrast to traditional passivity. The signal event came in 1941 when the Josiah Macy Jr. Foundation gave $10,000 to an activist Public Health Service to establish a program for the study of human aging. The grant supported the recruitment and work of Nathan Shock, the pioneer gerontologist in the United States, who has marked his 80th birthday and continues in the role of scientist emeritus. A psychologist by training and a physiologist by instinct, Shock surveyed various facets of aging, from the physiological to the sociopsychological. He emphasized the need for solid scientific approaches; and from the laboratories and programs he and colleagues initiated have come a cadre of basic and clinical researchers and a flow of respected scientific studies. It took years to obtain funds, facilities, and staff through the National Institutes of Health; and the gerontology program was transferred among Institutes until it found its place in the newest, the National Institute on Aging, in 1975. By then, a human aging study in Shock's laboratories—unique in its breadth, depth, and duration of research—reached its 25th year. The Baltimore Longitudinal Study of Aging is a landmark in gerontology and bioscience (21). Yet it is in many ways a pilot effort and, with other longitudinal studies, a foundation on which to organize and expand research on aging.

RESEARCH PRIORITIES

Building a national research agenda on aging requires choices. What considerations are paramount in establishing priorities? Where do we start? Certainly, we must consider impacts: the burden of illness as it falls on individuals and families, and the social and economic costs. We must see if the questions posed are answerable in terms of contemporary concepts and technologies. We must consider resource limitations. For example, are there enough qualified scientists available to pursue a topic to a conclusion? How do we apportion resources among basic and health and social services delivery issues?

We already have a head start on forming priorities and can draw from superb sourcebooks. Research on aging is well served by the second editions of the *Handbooks on Aging* (Van Nostrand Reinhold, New York), covering biology, psychology, and the social sciences under the general editorship of James E. Birren.

Key documents for those engaging in aging research are also available from the NIA. *Mammalian Models for Research on Aging* (6) was created by the NIA and the Institute of Laboratory Animal Resources of the National Academy of Sciences. This book offers a quick path to animal models that may be relevant to specific aging research. Because of progress in animal models since 1981, the book deserves to be updated. The use of species well defined for youth and old age is particularly important in pharmacological studies. About 30% of all medications are consumed by the 11.6% of the U.S. population over age 65; yet there is little drug testing in aging animal models. Most of the work is done in young animals.

The second book is *Biological Markers of Aging* (17). It reports on efforts to find nonlethal markers of aging. Vital capacity is an example. The search for biological markers has been elusive. Comfort (5) looked in vain for a single measure of biological age. Now the pursuit is for a pattern profile of variables related to biological aging. As the discussion of the Experienced Pilots Act and Social Security reform suggests, we need measures of functional aging different from measures of chronological aging. We must measure individual variation. The NIA is sponsoring a 10-year project on biological markers. There are techniques that measure time. Masters et al. of the Scripps Institute of Oceanography, looking at the dentine of the teeth as well as the lens of the eye, measured the racemization of aspartic acid and found it possible to gain a measure of the passage of time since birth rather than of biological aging (14).

The third book, *Biological Mechanisms of Aging* (20), is already outdated, which is good news, for it reflects scientific process. Yet the book provides a useful historical review under these major rubrics: (a) genetic theories of aging; (b) DNA repair (e.g., Hart and Setlow found the rate of DNA repair is directly related to species longevity); (c) protein synthesis (the work of Orgel regarding errors in protein synthesis that lead to catastrophe and cell aging and death); (d) posttranslational changes; (e) role of the immune system; and (f) role of the neuroendocrine system. Hayflick found a limit of some 50 cell doublings to the longevity of a cell line. There is no single, universal aging process, even at the cellular level. Mutant models with certain biochemical defects have a hypothesized relation to aging, e.g., altered superoxide dismutase. These models are useful for experimentation.

Aging in Society (18) summarized much of the contemporary sociohistorical aspects of aging and points the way to new hypotheses. Other progress in biological theories of aging are summarized in *Modern Biological Theories of Aging* (23).

PROMISING THEORIES AS RESEARCH WEATHERVANES

Two promising theories of aging—somatic mutations and programmed aging and death—suggest that the same kind of interactions between the environment and intrinsic factors provided a role for oncogenes. Perhaps we should conceptualize "gerontogenes" prepared to transform normal cells into aging cells.

Work on CNS redundancy and neuroplasticity is at the cutting edge of neuroscience. Cotman and Holet's (8) work at the University of California at Irvine reveals that experimental rodents can develop new nerve circuits (reactive synaptogenesis). Healthy cells surrounding the severed portions of the hippocampus have been found to reconnect. The work of Diamond et al. (11) showed that increasing the stimuli in the environment of various animals leads to continuing dendritic arborization and new connections even in older adults.

The senile dementia story is an intriguing one. One of the key points is the excitement that resulted from identification of a gene in the fourth chromosome for Huntington's disease (7). Progress has also been made in identifying a genetic defect responsible for Alzheimer's disease (19) and in possible treatment (22).

Certainly, the prospect of genetic engineering to introduce treatment or to find ways of prevention is extraordinarily exciting.

Davies and Maloney (10) found a reduction of enzymes in Alzheimer's disease. It seems unlikely that there is only one neurotransmitter deficit in a disease that is as complex as Alzheimer's disease. Would human evolution be sustained by dependence on one transmitter system? Some other neurotransmitters have also been found to be reduced in Alzheimer's disease, as reported by Carlsson and Windblad (4). L-DOPA is certainly not a solution to the problem of Parkinson's disease, but it has helped. A similar modest development of a means by which to improve memory in the Alzheimer's patient would help maintain people at home.

Given high personal and social costs, it becomes important to continue to understand the cholinergic neuron hypothesis. The Johns Hopkins group found damage in the nucleus basalis of Meynert in the forebrain of Alzheimer's patients on postmortem examination (9).

The impact of individual and population aging on societal and industrial productivity—already a concern in Japan, which is experiencing rapid population aging—will soon be one of the most potent scientific and political issues of our time. The goal of gerontology is to maintain the maximum integrity and efficiency of the organism over time, or, as one of the NIA's publications (16) put it, to promote "health and well-being by extending the vigorous and productive years of life." Research on aging must therefore address the age-related progressive loss of reserve function and the decrease in homeostasis or homeostatic competence or, to put it differently, the increasing vulnerability to diseases and disabilities.

GOALS OF THE NIA RESEARCH PLAN

Work on the NIA research plan began in 1980. To develop a long-range plan for promoting health and well-being by extending the vigorous and productive years of life through research on age, expert panels were asked to review past and current research on aging, assess and consolidate the current state of knowledge including an analysis of progress and barriers, define the needs and promising opportunities in research on aging, and make recommendations to the NIA for future action.

The goals are to (a) understand the basic processes of aging; (b) understand, prevent, and control the clinical manifestations of age-related disorders; (c) understand the interactions between older people and a dynamic society; and (d) increase the opportunity, motivation, and support older people require in order to contribute productively to society. The resulting plan was accordingly divided into four parts, but it has never been "priced" and elaborated with a full-scale plan of implementation, including a timetable, administrative personnel, and training needs.

Because of restraints by the Executive branch of government, it is virtually impossible for the NIA leadership to put a price tag on such a plan. Such an evaluation must be done by an external group, which also must encourage the executive and legislative branches of the federal government to support a vastly expanded program of aging research. It is justified because of the challenge posed by the extraordinary increase in the absolute number and relative proportion of older persons in the U.S. population and the need to effectively meet the associated health and social costs.

CONCLUSION

It is possible to say that gerontology is practical and potentially cost-effective in its application. It offers more payoffs than, for example, examination of one disease at a time. Consider the immune system. It is my contention that the understanding necessary to control immune senescence and the autoimmune phenomena that develop with age will allow us to control multiple diseases.

Longitudinal studies are of critical importance to more than gerontology. Our society invests substantial sums in studies of disease but relatively little to understanding health status over time. We need comprehensive longitudinal studies of community-living people in various social, economic, and ethnic groups. A national population "laboratory" program would provide opportunities to identify and measure changes over time in various aspects of human performance, gather insights into the personal experience of aging, study factors critical to adaptation and survival in old age, and mount normative longitudinal studies of such variables as bone mass, which is essential to the understanding of osteoporosis.

To approach goals and address issues, the gerontologist must straddle the gray area between normal aging and disease. The excellent work of Andres and Tobin (1) on glucose metabolism has helped reshape our view of diabetes and old age. One can make similar points about the borderline between aging and disease in connection with osteoporosis, hypertension, and other conditions.

Aging differs from disease, but this fact does not mean that aging is not related to disease. Indeed, age is critical to pathogenesis, along with genetic predisposition and environmental experience. Thus we need conventional biomedical research supplemented by both the perspective of aging variables and the direct conduct of aging research. We must systematically build the relations between the clinical situation and the basic sciences. Holliday (13) of the National Institute for Medical Research in London stated, "The fundamental strategy adopted by many research foundations and others responsible for the direction of medical research is that each disease should be studied separately. What is needed is a concentration of effort on the study of molecular and cellular causes of aging. This type of research should have a central position in the strategies for biomedical research and receive far more support than it does at the present time."

Gruman (12), physician and historian, introduced the term "prolongevity" and defined it as "the belief that it is possible and desirable to extend life significantly by human action." George Bernard Shaw wrote in "Back to Methuselah" that "men do not live long enough. They are, for all purposes of high civilization, mere children when they die."

REFERENCES

1. Andres, R., and Tobin, J. D. (1977): Endocrine systems. In: *Handbook of Biology of Aging,* edited by C. E. Finch and L. Hayflick, pp. 357–378. Van Nostrand Reinhold, New York.
2. Birren, J. E., Butler, R. N., Greenhouse, S. W., Sokoloff, L., and Yarrow, M. R. (1963): *Human Aging: A Biological and Behavioral Study.* Public Health Service Publication 986, Washington, DC.
3. Blenkner, M., Bloom, M., Wasser, E., and Nielsen, M. (1981): Protective services for old people: findings from the Benjamin Rose Institute Study. *Social Casework,* 52:483–522.
4. Carlsson, A., and Winblad, B. (1976): Influence of age and time interval between death and autopsy on dopamine and 3-methoxytyramine levels in human basal ganglia. *J. Neural Transm.,* 38:271–276.
5. Comfort, A. (1979): *Aging, the Biology of Senescence.* Elsevier/North Holland, New York.
6. Committee on Animal Models for Research on Aging, Institute of Laboratory Animal Resources, National Academy of Sciences (1981): *Mammalian Models for Research on Aging.* National Academy Press, Washington, DC.
7. Conneally, P. M., Gusella, J. F., and Wexler, N. S. (1985): Huntington's disease: linkage with G8 on chromosome 4 and its consequences. *Prog. Clin. Biol. Res.,* 177:53–60.
8. Cotman, C. W., and Holets, V. R. (1985): Structural change at synapses with age: plasticity and regeneration. In: *Handbook of the Biology of Aging,* 2nd ed., edited by C. E. Finch and E. L. Schneider. Van Nostrand Reinhold, New York.
9. Coyle, J. T., McKinney, M., and Johnston, M. V. (1981): Cholinergic innervation of the cerebral cortex: implications for the pathophysiology of senile dementia of the Alzheimer's type. In: *Brain Neurotransmitters and Receptors in Aging and Age-Related Disorders,* edited by S. J. Enna, T. Samorajski, and B. Beer, pp. 149–161. Rover Press, New York.
10. Davies, P., and Maloney, A. J. F. (1976): Selective loss of central cholinergic neurons in Alzheimer's disease. *Lancet,* 2:1403.
11. Diamond, M. C., Krech, S., and Rosenzweig, M. R. (1964): The effects of an enriched environment on the histology of the rat cerebral cortex. *J. Comp. Neurol.,* 123:111–120.
12. Gruman, G. J. A. (1966): *History of Ideas About the Prolongation of Life: The Evolution of Prolongevity Hypotheses to 1800.* American Philosophical Society, Philadelphia.
13. Holliday, R. H. (1984): The aging process is a key problem in biomedical research. *Lancet,* 2:1386–1387.
14. Masters, P. M., Bada, J. L., and Zigler, J. S., Jr. (1977): Aspartic acid racemization in the human lens during aging and in cataract formation. *Nature,* 268:71–73.
15. Metchnikoff, E. (1901): *The Nature of Man: Studies in Optimistic Philosophy.* Putnam, New York.
16. National Institute on Aging, Report of the National Research on Aging Planning Panel (1982): *A National Plan for Research on Aging. Toward an Independent Old Age.* NIH Publ. 82–2453, Washington, DC.
17. Reff, M. E., and Schneider, E. L. (1982): *Biological Markers of Aging.* NIH Publ. 82–2221, Washington, DC.
18. Riley, M. E., Hess, B. B., and Bond, K. (1983): *Aging in Society: Selected Reviews of Recent Research.* Lawrence Erlbaum, Hillsdale, NJ.
19. St. George-Hyslop, P. H., Tanzi, R. E., Polinsky, R. J., Haines, J. L., Nee, L., Watkins, P. C., Myers, R. H., Feldman, R. G., Pollen, D., and Drachman, D. (1987): The genetic defect causing familial Alzheimer's disease maps on chromosome 21. *Science,* 235:885–890.
20. Schimke, R. T. (1981): *Biological Mechanisms of Aging.* NIH Publ. 82–2194, Washington, DC.
21. Shock, N. W., Greulich, R. C., Andres, R., Arenberg, D., Costa, P. T., Jr., Lakatta, E., and

Tobin, J. D. (1984): *Normal Human Aging: The Baltimore Longitudinal Study of Aging.* NIH Publ. 84–2450, Washington, DC.
22. Summers, W. K., Majorski, L. W., Marsh, G. M., Tachiki, K., and Kling, A. (1986): Oral tetrahydroaminoacridine in long-term treatment of senile dementia, Alzheimer's type. *N. Engl. J. Med.,* 315:1241–1287.
23. Warner, H., Butler, R. N., Sprott, R., and Schneider, E. (1987): *Modern Biological Theories of Aging.* Raven Press, New York.

Human Aging Research: Concepts and Techniques,
edited by B. Kent and R. N. Butler.
Raven Press, Ltd., New York © 1988.

Epidemiology and Experimental Design in Aging Research

Michael N. Mulvihill

Department of Community Medicine, Mount Sinai School of Medicine,
New York, New York 10029

Epidemiology has been defined as "the study of the distribution and determinants of disease frequency in man" (1). Although the definition refers to "disease" as its focus, we can consider it in its broadest context to include any health or social problem. It may even include undesirable behaviors, e.g., patient noncompliance, or other nondisease events or states such as accidents or dissatisfaction with health care services. What makes epidemiology stand apart from other health sciences is that it focuses on population groups rather than on individuals. The epidemiologist seeks to describe patterns of disease and investigates the types of people who are most likely to have or develop disease. As the patterns of a particular disease become understood in terms of who is more likely to develop the disease or under which circumstances, knowledge of these characteristics can be used to target or direct health services to those most likely to be at risk. In order to clearly understand this epidemiologic process, certain definitions and concepts are necessary.

RATES

The epidemiologic approach focuses on the frequency of health problems. In order to describe these frequencies, we use *rates* of occurrence. This method is in contrast to the simple counting of events. For example, consider the following statement: "Last year there were 250 patients discharged from the hospital with excessive length-of-stays." (We would have to define carefully what we mean by "excessive length-of-stay.") If "the hospital" were a small community hospital with only 50 beds and 3,000 admissions per year, the magnitude of the problem would be quite different than if "the hospital" were a large teaching hospital with 400 beds and 24,000 admissions per year. In other words, we need to know the proper context of the count. We should ask ourselves: These 250 patients with excessive length-of-stays occurred among how many patients who could have had an excessive length-of-stay? For the rate, the count (the 250) represents the

11

numerator, and the potential population giving rise to these 250 is the denominator.

The denominator is frequently called the "population at risk," because they are the group at risk of being counted in the numerator. In this case it might be the total number of admissions to that hospital for the same year. Let us suppose the hospital had 5,000 admissions during the year. The rate of excessive length-of-stay would be 250 per 5,000 admissions. We usually divide this fraction ($^{250}/_{5,000}$) = 0.05 and multiply by some multiple of 10 (i.e., 10, 1,000, 10,000, etc.) to get rid of the decimal point. It is then expressed as 5 per 100 admissions or 50 per 1,000 admissions. We do this computation to facilitate the comparison of rates by creating a common denominator.

There are two major rates that need to be clearly understood and distinguished: the *incidence rate* and the *prevalence rate*. The incidence rate refers to the frequency of coming down with (contracting) the disease. The prevalence rate refers to the rate of having the disease at any point in time irrespective of when the disease was contracted. Both rates are expressed as per 100 or 10,000, etc. persons at risk.

Consider the following hypothetical example, which might make these two rates, and particularly their difference, more clear. Suppose we have a community of 10,000 people. In Fig. 1 each line represents an individual who has contracted the disease of interest. The length of the line corresponds to the time period or duration the individual has this disease. In this example, the annual incidence rate for the year depicted is 7 per 10,000 persons at risk. This rate corresponds to the number of X's that occur during the study year. Those who entered the year with preexisting disease (who were diagnosed during the previous year) are not counted. Prevalence is usually reported for a single point in time and refers to the rate at which the disease affected the population at any instant in time. In the example, the prevalence rate on January 1 was 10 per 10,000 population and on December 31 it was 12 per 10,000. Note that for prevalence it does not matter when the person was diagnosed, only if the individual had the disease at the specified time.

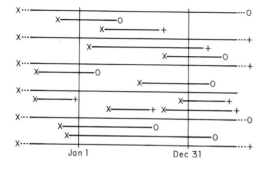

FIG. 1. Comparison of incidence rate and prevalence rate. Each line represents an individual who has contracted the disease of interest. X = the date of diagnosis. + = the date of cure. O indicates that the individual died.

RELATION BETWEEN INCIDENCE AND PREVALENCE

Imagine that the disease is one of short duration, e.g., the common cold. The diagram would simply contain a series of X's with short duration lines. The annual incidence rate would be large relative to the prevalence at any particular point in time. Conversely, if the disease is of long duration, e.g., diabetes or hypertension, the prevalence rate would be high relative to the annual incidence because one would have a large number of cases on hand diagnosed in previous years relative to the number of newly diagnosed cases for a single year.

The relation between incidence and prevalence can be algebraically depicted as follows:

Prevalence rate at a point in time = annual incidence rate × average duration

This relation holds if the duration of the disease is stable and if there is little variation from one time period to another in the incidence rate (e.g., seasonal variation). If the annual incidence rate for a condition is about 36 per 100,000 population and the average duration is approximately 1 month ($\frac{1}{12}$ year), the expected prevalence at any point in time would be 3 per 100,000 population.

One can see that prevalence is a useful concept for planning health care services in that it reflects the health care needs of the population at any given time. Incidence is more useful for studying the causes of disease, as we are interested in which factors make people more likely to contract the disease (become "new cases").

BASIC STUDY DESIGNS

The basic strategy of epidemiology is to compare two or more groups of people. We are trying to compare, in every instance, the attributes or characteristics of people who have or develop a condition or disease with those who do not in order to determine if there is a relation between possessing a certain set of characteristics and having the condition or disease. As an example, we might be interested in knowing if people who have a particular characteristic, e.g., cigarette smoking, have a different risk of developing a condition, e.g., lung cancer, than those who do not smoke cigarettes. We might be interested in finding out if people who have a first degree relative with Down's syndrome (their characteristic) have a different risk of developing Alzheimer's disease (the condition) than people who do not have a relative with Down's syndrome. So the basic strategy is to compare two or more groups—compare them in terms of their characteristics and in terms of the occurrence of the condition being studied. The condition can be a disease or it can be a behavior, e.g., the response to a health program, or it might be combinations of the two.

The unit of study, which is the second point of the strategy, is never a single individual but, rather, a population, a group, or an aggregate of people. For this reason the findings of epidemiologic studies are expressed in terms of the probabilities of the people with the characteristic having a greater or lesser chance of developing the condition than people without the characteristic. Thus the results may or may not be applicable to any given individual but, rather, are applicable to classes or types of people.

Third, the techniques used are usually those of an observational science in contrast to those of an experimental science such as a clinical trial. It is necessary to spend a little time at this point discussing the fundamental differences between an observational and an experimental science.

The first difference between the experimental and observational approaches is that in an experimental science the factor(s) of interest to the investigator is under the control of the investigator and can be manipulated by him. If one wishes to investigate if diets with little calcium cause osteoporosis, for example, it is possible under experimental conditions to collect a group of animals free of bone disease with the same nutritional state at the beginning of the study. By changing the diet in some of them while keeping everything else constant, it is then possible to see if those of the deficient diet develop more osteoporosis than the others. In the observational sciences, on the other hand, the variables of interest are not under the investigator's control, and they cannot be manipulated. All that can be done is to observe what happens to people under different circumstances, e.g., if people who happen to consume less calcium do have more osteoporosis than those who are well nourished.

That these factors are or are not under the investigator's control has a number of important implications. The first of these implications is that in an experimental situation all other factors that might influence the condition being studied are under the control of the investigator. He or she can make the experimental and comparison groups comparable for the other factors by assigning individuals to one group or the other at random to ensure that the two groups are similar with respect to the other factors that may influence the outcome. (This strategy is discussed more completely in the chapter by Chalmers.) It is not possible in the observational sciences because it is not possible to hold all other factors constant, as they are not under the control of the investigator. It is sometimes possible by statistical means to adjust for the effect of the other factors, but the investigator does not have the power to allocate them or to prevent their operation.

The third point is that in many observational studies it is not possible to determine which finding is antecedent and which is consequent, i.e., which is cause and which is effect. As an example, consider the question of early retirement leading to depression. If it were found that more depressed people had taken early retirement than individuals who show no signs of depression and that there was a reasonable assurance that other factors (e.g., physical health status) were not influencing this relation, it still could not be said whether early retirement caused the depression or the depression caused the early retirement. From this type of study it is not possible to say with a great deal of certainty which came first—the choice of early retirement or the depression.

By contrast, in the experimental situation the relation is quite clear. It has been determined in the experimental situation, in advance, what is to be manipulated and what is to be kept constant in order to tell which is first, i.e., which is the cause and which is the effect. There are, however, some types of observational studies, discussed later, in which it is possible to determine these antecedent–consequent relations.

Steps Involved in Observational Science

The steps involved in any observation (Fig. 2) start by posing a question. The objective may be to reduce the occurrence of a particular disease. The question, then, is what changes in the behavior of people or the environment in which they live must be instituted in order to accomplish the reduction. These theories then lead to a set of observations that include the occurrence of the condition being studied and the various characteristics of the people with and without the condition. The observations then must be classified (i.e., clearly defined and categorized) in order that they can be compared eventually. Having determined the classification scheme, it is then necessary to gather and record the data; these data must be processed and reduced to a form in which they can be interpreted (i.e., by creating tables that compare one group to another), as it would be impossible to interpret each individual item of datum separately. In other words, it is necessary to get some measurement of the experience of the total groups. Once this task has been done, it is now possible to start the analysis phase and the interpretation of findings. The next question to be asked is how generalizable are these data? Do they apply only to the particular situation that has been studied, or can they be applied more widely and lead to further hypothesis formation? Do they lead to modification of the original set of ideas? This set of questions then leads to further theory building.

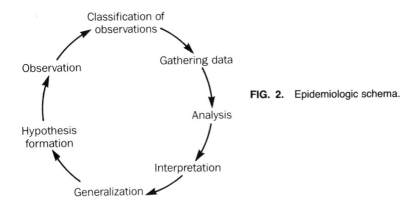

FIG. 2. Epidemiologic schema.

It can be a circular process and may be started at many places. Some people start with the observations of what has happened. From these observations they derive a tentative theory. Others start with a theory, attempt to confirm it, and then modify the theory. Wherever the process starts, these steps are essentially the major ones that are taken in the application of epidemiologic principles.

Cohort Method

There are two and possibly three ways in which epidemiology tends to classify the initial observations. We can start by classifying people into groups with and without a particular characteristic, which is thought to be causal, and determine the occurrence or development of the condition or disease in such groups. This particular method is called the *cohort study method,* (The term *cohort* refers to groups of individuals who share a common characteristic. Birth cohorts, a commonly used cohort type, refers to individuals born at about the same time.) With this method subjects are followed forward in time to see in whom the condition develops. For example, a characteristic might be employment status, and the condition of interest might be depression. According to this method, then, it would be necessary to classify people into employed and unemployed categories (none with evidence of depression) and then follow them over time in order to see how many in each category develop depressive symptoms. In the same way, people exposed and those not exposed to atmospheric pollution may be followed to observe the occurrence of respiratory disease. In each instance, groups of people free of the condition who do and who do not possess a characteristic or set of characteristics are compared. These characteristics may be personal characteristics of the individuals or they may be habits or behavior, e.g., cigarette smoking. They might be characteristics of the group to which they belong, e.g., employment status, or they might be the characteristics of the environment to which they are exposed, e.g., atmospheric pollution. The groups are differentiated only in being exposed or not exposed or having or not having a particular set of characteristics.

Essentially, with this type of study we ask two major questions. The first can be phrased something like this: "In those groups that we have studied, do a greater proportion of the individuals with the characteristic develop the condition than those without the characteristic?" With this question we are comparing two proportions or two rates.

The second question to ask is "Would these results also occur in groups we have not studied but who also have or do not have these characteristics?" In other words, rarely in these investigations or applications of the methods are we interested only in the particular group that is being studied. We want to know how widespread (i.e., how generalizable) the problem is. When considering the second question, the answers depend on how representative of some larger group of people is the group that is being studied (the sample). These larger groups are called the *reference population* and sometimes the *population at risk*. The degree

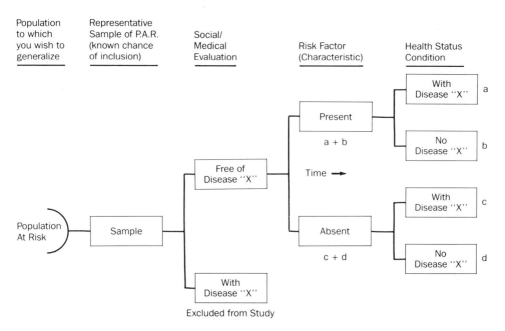

FIG. 3. Cohort method. P.A.R. = population at risk.

to which the sample (the group studied) is representative of some larger population depends on the adequacy of the sampling techniques. Sampling becomes necessary because it is usually impossible to study all of the people of interest. One could not study all inhabitants of a state or all the people more than 60 years old in the country. It would not be possible to observe and classify all those people, so as an alternative it becomes necessary to draw a *sample* of such people for study.

Returning then to the first question, let us take a look at what happens when you use the cohort method (Fig. 3). Essentially, we start by defining the population at risk or the people in whom we are interested. A sample is drawn in such a way that the probabilities of any person being included are known in order that the results may eventually be referred back to the population at risk. After excluding people who already have the outcome condition (depression), the people in the sample are classified into two or more groups. For simplicity in this example, consider just two groups: those with the characteristic (i.e., those who opt for early retirement) and those without the characteristic (i.e., those who do not). Over the course of time for each of these two groups, we want to know how many develop the condition, i.e., how many of those who elect early retirement develop depressive symptoms (a) and how many do not (b). Similarly, among those who did not have that particular characteristic to start with (they worked until a mandatory retirement age), how many developed the condition (c) and how many did not (d). One must then compare the proportion of individuals with the characteristic who developed the condition with the proportion of people without the characteristic who developed the condition. In other words, compare the proportion $a/(a + b)$ (i.e., the proportion of people who have the characteristic who developed the condition) with $c/(c + d)$ (i.e., the proportion of people without the characteristic who developed the condition).

Case–Control Method

Contrast the cohort method of classifying people with the second way of classifying people. Here, instead of starting with the individuals who have and do not have the characteristic, we start with those individuals who have and do not have the condition and then examine their characteristics. With this method (Fig. 4) we start with a group of elderly people who have clinical depression and a group of elderly people who do not and determine if they differ in their past employment status. This particular type of study is called a *case comparison* or *case–control study* because we wish to see if a group of cases differ from noncases with respect to some characteristic prior to the occurrence of the condition.

The case–control approach differs logically from the cohort approach. With the case–control study we do not know what the reference population is. We start with cases, or people with the condition, and select another group of similar people (the control group) in which the condition is absent, the noncases. We then compute the proportion of cases and noncases that have the characteristic. That is, we would compare $a/(a+b)$ with $c/(c+d)$.

Examining these proportions, it can be seen that with these two approaches we have asked two fundamentally different questions. With the first approach (cohort study) we have asked: "Do a greater proportion of the individuals with the characteristic develop the condition?" With the second approach (case–control), we are asking: "Do a greater proportion of the people with the condition have the characteristic?" They are different questions. We are not as interested in the second question as in the first for a logical reason. Although one might find that most of the elderly who are depressed had taken early retirement, it does not mean that most of those retiring early experience depression.

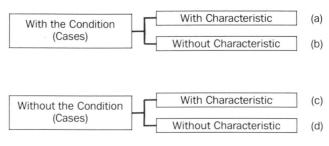

FIG. 4. Case–control method.

As another example, one might say that most people with elevated blood pressure are overweight, but it does not mean that most obese people have elevated blood pressure. It is one thing to say that most typhoid patients come from poor homes, but it does not mean that most individuals from poor homes have typhoid fever. The case–control approach, by way of its design, tells us if most typhoid fever cases come from poor homes.

Why then with the case–control approach are we unable to ask the first type of question? Why is it not possible with the case–control approach to ask by just recombining the figures? The reason is because *we have started without a reference population,* the population at risk. In particular, we cannot be sure that those people with the characteristic in the group studied are truly representative of the extent of the characteristic in the population.

Advantages and Disadvantages of Cohort and Case–Control Methods

The main advantages of the case–control method are that it is feasible, short term, and economical, particularly if the condition being studied occurs infrequently. If the number of cases that occur is small, it is still possible to collect most of all existing cases for study, whereas with a cohort study it may be necessary for many years to pass before such a group can be accumulated. The more frequent the condition, the easier and more feasible it is to do a cohort study; the more infrequent, the greater is the reliance on case–control designs.

Cohort studies are vexed by one particular type of problem: the loss of follow-up (attrition) for various reasons. If a study started with a large group of people who are smokers and nonsmokers and followed these people for 5 years to determine whether they did or did not get lung cancer, some of those people would die from other causes, some would migrate, some would refuse to cooperate, and some, for various other reasons, would get lost from the study. If this attrition rate, for causes other than the occurrence of the condition, is different for those with the characteristic compared to those without the characteristic, it would be difficult to draw conclusions because the two groups would have been exposed to observation for different periods of time during which they could develop the condition.

The major disadvantage of the case–control method is the difficulty experienced when answering the appropriate question. At best, the risk the characteristic confers can only be estimated. Second, with the case–control method there is often difficulty deciding which came first, the cause or the effect. For example, when studying the relation of physical activity to heart disease, suppose it is found that those people who are free of heart disease were more active than the people who had heart disease. It would be difficult to ascertain if people with heart disease selected a more sedentary type of job than did the healthy, or if physical activity protects against heart disease. This problem does not apply to the cohort method, where the study starts with a group of people free of the condition but who do or do not have the risk factor (sedentary life style) and who are then observed over time for development of the condition (heart disease).

Cross-Sectional Studies

The third method by which studies may be conducted is called a *cross-sectional survey* or *prevalence study*. With this approach a representative sample of a population is selected and examined for the occurrence of the condition; and at the same time the occurrence of the characteristics is determined. In other words, a population is chosen, e.g., a particular geographic district; then a sample is selected that is representative of the area. At this point the investigation determines who has cancer and who does not and what their smoking histories are. This approach, which is one of the most common, is intermediate between a case–control and a cohort study. It has in common with the cohort study the fact that there is a reference population to which we can refer the data; i.e., a representative sample of some larger group is being studied. The cases are not matched with the controls, as with the case–control method, but are compared to noncases drawn from the same population. As we are now dealing with a representative sample, it is possible to analyze the data in the same form as the cohort study. In other words, with a cross-sectional study one can talk about the proportion of smokers who have lung cancer because the smokers in the sample are representative of a larger population of smokers.

Although cross-sectional studies resemble cohort studies in this respect, they also resemble case–control studies in that there can be a problem of the antecedent-consequent relations. In summary, the cross-sectional or prevalence study has a representative sample, which is an advantage over the case–control study in that it is possible to compare (a) the proportion of those with the characteristic who have the condition with (b) those without the characteristic who have the condition. It is therefore possible to perform the same type of computation as in a cohort study. However, cross-sectional data must be interpreted with caution because we are dealing with problems of untangling the antecedent versus consequent relation. This problem does not occur with a cohort study, as there the study has started out with people free of the condition who have been followed through time to determine who develops the condition.

COLLECTION AND STORAGE OF DATA

Having decided on the particular strategy to be employed, the particular method in which cases and noncases are to be counted and classified, the next question is how the data are to be gathered and recorded. There are a number of important points here. For any characteristic or for any condition to be recorded, it is necessary first to have agreed on the *definition* of the condition or characteristic to be studied.

Second, separate from the definition, a set of *criteria* by which the condition or characteristic is ascertained is needed. It is important to distinguish between the definitions and the criteria for ascertainment.

In many instances the definition alone is quite unsatisfactory, for practical purposes, for any kind of epidemiologic study. For example, if a study is to be done on the occurrence of home accidents in different types of homes and the *definition* of an accident chosen was "an unforeseen occurrence, especially one of injurious character," it might well be a good definition of an accident, but it does not indicate specifically what is to be counted. Are cut fingers or any break in the skin to be counted or only fractures or injuries leading to disability? If so, what is going to be the degree of severity that is accepted before it is to be counted as an accident? Would poisoning count as an accident? These items are some of the *criteria* that would have to be applied to make the definition operational.

As another example, suppose one is interested in the concept of social class. Social class is defined by sociologists as groups of people evaluated differently by members of their community in terms of power, prestige, and status. Some people are valued as having much power, prestige, and status, whereas others are valued as having little, with a range between them. How does one operationalize the definition? How does one assess whether a person belongs to one social class or another? What are the criteria to be used? It has been found that two measurements—the occupation and the education of the head of the household—correlate highly with the way people are evaluated by the members of their community and can be used to classify people into social classes.

When developing criteria it must be borne in mind that they determine the completeness with which the conditions or the characteristics are ascertained. When measuring the distribution of a disease in a population, one must recognize that the disease exists in varying degrees of severity. The criteria determine what proportion of this disease is counted and measured, and what proportion is not. It is important, then, to realize that if two or more populations are to be compared for the occurrence of disease the same criteria must be used for each. In other words, the criteria must be standardized.

The individual designing a study must be sensitive to and try to avoid observer bias. This problem relates to the situation when the individual collecting the data on one variable is aware of the study subject's status on the other. Take, for example, a case–control study of cancer of the lung and smoking. If the interviewer knows that the study subject being questioned about smoking history is a "case" (i.e., has lung cancer and is not a control), he may overemphasize the extent of the smoking history. This problem can crop up with any study design, and the best way to avoid it is to try to keep the data gatherer "blind," or unaware of the study subject's status on one variable as he is evaluating the other.

Another type of bias may be problematic in the case–control study: biased recall. When study subjects are asked to recall past events or describe their behavior over the course of many years, their memories may be selectively altered by the knowledge of their diagnosis. For example, a lung cancer victim may exaggerate his smoking history, a coronary victim may overestimate his sedentary life style, etc. unconsciously as a means of explaining the disease. This situation may be unavoidable in case–control studies, as in most situations the subject is aware of the diagnosis.

RISK ASSESSMENT

Earlier we discussed the need to compare the rates of disease occurrence among the exposed (with the risk factor) to the unexposed (those without the risk factor, i.e., the control group). Here we turn our attention to various ways of making this comparison. We try to measure the degree to which the exposure (risk factor, characteristic) is associated with the disease (condition). In other words, we desire a quantitative way of describing the *strength of the association* between the exposure and the resulting condition.

One means of describing the strength of an association between an exposure and a disease is by calculating the *relative risk*. The relative risk tells us the chances of developing the disease if one is exposed to the supposed causal factor relative to the chances of developing the disease if one is not exposed. Because we are referring to developing the condition, we must use an incidence rate as the basis for this calculation.

$$\text{Relative risk} = \frac{\text{incidence rate among those exposed}}{\text{incidence rate among those not exposed}}$$

For example, if the incidence rate of clinical depression following early retirement is 166 per 1,000 and 7 per 1,000 among those who retire at the mandatory age, the realtive risk is

$$\frac{166/1,000}{7/1,000} = 23.7$$

This number (it has no denominator) is interpreted as follows: Those who retire early are 23.7 times more likely to develop clinical depression than are those who do not retire early.

Relative risk calculations may be performed on mortality rates (they are a kind of incidence rate in that they are events) but should be interpreted as the relative risk of dying from disease, not of contracting the disease.

Relative risk statements are sometimes based on cross-sectional studies, i.e., using prevalence rates in place of incidence rates. When relative risk is based on prevalence data, one is really talking about "the relative risk of *having* the particular condition," rather than of getting it, which would necessitate an incidence rate.

Data from case–control studies cannot be used to calculate relative risk, as we do not obtain disease rates because we do not start with a reference population. However, it is possible to obtain an estimate of relative risk provided the following two conditions are met: (a) The disease or condition has a low incidence in the general population. This statement is true for most chronic diseases. (b) The control and case groups are representative of their respective population with regard to the frequency of the attribute (causal factor).

The estimate of relative risk based on case–control data is sometimes called the *odds ratio* and is derived as follows.

	Cases	*Controls*
With characteristic	*a*	*b*
Without characteristic	*c*	*d*
Total	*a + c*	*b + d*

This table would be generated from a case–control study in which a sample of cases (*a* + *c*) were studied and classified in terms of having the suspected risk factor or exposure (*a*) or not (*c*). A sample of noncases (controls), which are similar to the cases with regard to other attributes (e.g., age, sex), are similarly classified (*b* + *d*). The odds ratio is simply *ad/bc*, or the cross-product ratio. The interpretation of this estimate of relative risk is similar to that of the relative risk derived from incidence rates. However, remember that this method is *indirect* and is only an estimate.

Another method of calculating the odds ratio from case–control studies is possible when the controls are selected in a different manner. With what is called *matched-pair design,* an individual control is selected for each case (matched for attributes such as age and sex). In this situation a series of pairs is developed, and the analysis takes it into account. The resulting table now looks like:

Controls	*Cases with characteristic*	*Cases without characteristic*
With characteristic	*a*	*b*
Without characteristic	*c*	*d*

The values in the table (*a, b, c, d*) refer not to the number of individuals but, rather, to the number of pairs. The *c* items, for example, refer to the number of pairs in which the case member of the pair has the characteristic but the control member does not. The estimate of relative risk (odds ratio) is the ratio of the discordant pairs = *c/b*. Note that the *a* and *d* items are not used in the analysis because the pairs are alike with respect to the characteristic and thus do not help discriminate cases from controls.

Another kind of risk is the *attributable risk*. In this situation one examines the incidence of disease among those with the risk factor (e.g., incidence rate of lung cancer among smokers) and asks the questions, "How much of that rate can be attributed to the factor of smoking itself, as the disease also occurs in individuals without that specific risk factor?" (For example, lung cancer does occur among individuals who never smoked.) The attributable risk is derived simply by subtracting the incidence rates. For example, if the annual incidence rate of chronic bronchitis among smokers is 106 per 100,000 and 5 per 100,000 for nonsmokers, the attributable risk is 101 cases per 100,000 smokers. That is, 101 of the 106 cases per 100,000 smokers can be attributed to (or explained by) the fact that they were smokers. These data are sometimes expressed as a percentage: $101/106 = 95\%$ of cases with chronic bronchitis among smokers can be attributed to their smoking.

This risk is useful when assessing the impact of the risk factor in terms of producing disease in the population and the potential benefits of trying to reduce disease (number of cases preventable) by eliminating the factor. On the other hand, relative risk is a better measure of assessing an etiologic relation between the disease and the characteristic.

REFERENCES

1. MacMahon, B., and Pugh, T. F. (1970): *Epidemiology: Principles and Methods.* Little, Brown, Boston.

Human Aging Research: Concepts and Techniques,
edited by B. Kent and R. N. Butler.
Raven Press, Ltd., New York © 1988.

Basic Statistics and Their Use in Aging Research

John C. Thornton and Richard Fagerstrom

*Biomathematical Science Department, Mt. Sinai Medical Center,
New York, New York 10029*

In aging research (indeed in all clinical research) measurements on a variety of variables are taken on each patient. The information so gathered may serve two purposes: (a) hypothesis generation (suggestion of structure), and (b) hypothesis testing (evaluation of structure). We are concerned first with hypothesis generation, turning to hypothesis testing later.

HYPOTHESIS GENERATION

By hypothesis generation is meant the development of explanations for the observed structure of the data. Perception of structure entails a reduction or summary of the data. A smattering of numbers rarely presents a recognizable pattern. The essence of the data must be distilled.

A first step in this process involves determining the frequencies with which values occur. Some variables have a limited range of "value." Sex (male or female), eye color (brown, blue, green, or other), health status (normal or abnormal), and disease status (present or absent) are examples. In this case a distribution of frequencies is obtained by simply counting the number of times each value is encountered in the data set. These frequencies may be expressed as proportions upon division by the total number of observations, yielding relative frequencies. However, this procedure is not immediately of use in the description of data on variables with a large range of values. Any particular value is sufficiently rare that few realizations of it occur, and the frequency distribution thereby constructed is not informative. The usefulness of the frequency distribution can be enhanced by grouping the data into categories and constructing the frequency distribution of the categories.

Stem and Leaf Design

The structure of the data is better communicated by a graphic display of the frequency distribution. A traditional display technique involves construction of a

25

histogram. However, the stem and leaf diagram conveys more information than a histogram and is as easy to construct. The technique is illustrated by example.

Example 1. The weight in pounds of a 77-year-old man was recorded each day for a month. The following data were obtained (listed in the order that they were recorded): 186, 184, 180, 175, 177, 176, 176, 176, 175, 174, 174, 175, 175, 175, 175, 175, 173, 170, 170, 170, 171, 170, 170, 169, 170, 167, 166, 169, 168, 169, 165.

To construct a stem and leaf diagram each value is split into two segments. The leading digits form the stem. The leaf is the leading digit of the remaining digits. For example, the rule may indicate that the number 20763 is to be split as follows.

Leading digits: 20
Trailing digits: 763

The stem is 20 and the leaf is 7.

The stem and leaf diagram is constructed as follows:

1. Choose a suitable pair of adjacent digit positions to split the values. We chose to split the weights between the 10 and unit positions; i.e., 186 is split as 18 6.
2. Write down a column of all possible leading digits in order from the lowest to the highest. These are the stems.
   16 |
   17 |
   18 |
3. For each weight, write down the leaf in the row corresponding to its stem.
   16 | 9 7 6 9 8 9 5
   17 | 5 7 6 6 6 5 4 4 5 5 5 5 5 3 0 0 0 1 0 0 0
   18 | 6 4 0
4. Rank the leaves in each row in ascending order.
   16 | 5 6 7 8 9 9 9
   17 | 0 0 0 0 0 0 1 3 4 4 5 5 5 5 5 5 5 5 6 6 6 7
   18 | 0 4 6
   Unit = 1 lb.
   The unit gives the decimal position for the leaf.
5. This diagram can be improved by stretching it out. We split each stem into two groups. The first group gets digits 0, 1, 2, 3, and 4. The second group gets digits 5, 6, 7, 8, and 9.
   16 |
   16 | 5 6 7 8 9 9 9
   17 | 0 0 0 0 0 0 1 3 4 4
   17 | 5 5 5 5 5 5 5 6 6 6 7
   18 | 0 4
   18 | 6
   Unit = 1 lb.
   Stem and leaf diagram for daily weights of a 77-year-old man.

Note that the stem and leaf diagram presents not only the frequency distribution but also the data set, making it a clever way to list observations.

Often an entire frequency distribution contains more information than is wanted or can be assimilated. Of most interest are certain global features of the distribution. These features are expressed by summary statistics. A few such statistics are described.

An important feature of a distribution is its location. By location is meant the center (in some sense) of a distribution, a value about which all others cluster. The two most frequently employed measures of location are the arithmetic mean and the median.

Mean

The arithmetic *mean* is the simple average.

Example 2. The ages of five patients are 55, 54, 56, 53, and 57 years. Their mean age is

$$(55 + 54 + 56 + 53 + 57)/5 = 55 \text{ years.}$$

In mechanical terms the arithmetic mean is the center of mass. Viewing the values of the variable as distances along a beam and the frequencies of these values as weights placed on the beam at the corresponding distances, it is seen that the arithmetic mean indicates the distance at which a wedge may be positioned under the beam to balance it. Naturally, if a weight is placed far out on the beam, the wedge must be moved to compensate for it. The farther away the weight is placed, the more the wedge must be moved, which is just another way of saying that the arithmetic mean is greatly influenced by extreme (outlying) values.

Example 3. Assume that the oldest patient in example 2 was not 57 years but was actually 97 years. Now the patients' average age is

$$(55 + 54 + 56 + 53 + 97)/5 = 63 \text{ years.}$$

Median

The *median* does not take into account how extreme the outermost observations are. It is the value below which half of the remaining observations lie. The median corresponds not to the average of the observations but to the average of their ranks. If the observations are ordered from least to greatest and assigned ranks, the median is the value of average rank.

Example 4. The median age of the patients in example 2 is calculated as follows:

1. Order the data from least to greatest and assign each a rank.

Age	53	54	55	56	57
Rank	1	2	3	4	5

2. Calculate the average rank.

$$(1 + 2 + 3 + 4 + 5)/5 = 3$$

3. The median is the value of average rank. The average rank is 3; therefore the median age is 55 years.

Example 5. The median age of the patients in example 3 is 55 years. As seen in the last example, the median is not influenced by how large the largest observation is. In practice, both the mean and the median should be computed, as they measure different aspects of location. The median depends on order and frequency. The mean depends on magnitude and frequency.

Dispersion

Another global feature of a frequency distribution is its *dispersion* or *variability.* The two distributions shown in Fig. 1 appear to have the same location; however, one is wider, more dispersed, than the other. When measuring dispersion we determine in various ways how far apart the values are from each other. Four measures are considered: (a) range, (b) variance, (c) standard deviation, and (d) coefficient of variation.

The simplest measure of dispersion is the *range,* which is the difference between the largest and smallest values. Much information about variability is not used

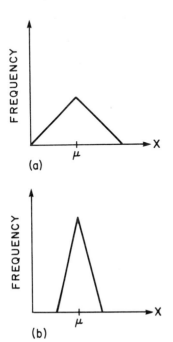

(a)

(b)

FIG. 1. Frequency distribution of two variables. Although both distributions have identical means, μ, distribution **a** exhibits more variability (spread) than does distribution **b.**

by this measure, as only two values enter into its computation. Therefore the value of the range may not correspond to one's impression of variability.

To use all values in its computation, variability may be expressed as an average distance from a designated point. For the sake of mathematical convenience, this point is taken to be the mean. Distance is expressed as a squared deviation (again for mathematical convenience). When computing the average, it is customary to divide by the number of observations minus 1. The measure so derived is known as the *variance*.

Example 6 (variance). The variance of the ages given in example 2 is

$$[(55 - 55)^2 + (54 - 55)^2 + (56 - 55)^2 + (53 - 55)^2 + (57 - 55)^2]/(5 - 1)$$
$$= [(0)^2 + (-1)^2 + (1)^2 + (-2)^2 + (2)^2]/4 = 2.5 \text{ years}^2.$$

One disadvantage of the variance as a measure of dispersion is that its units are the square of those of the data. For example, age is measured in years, but variance is measured in square years. To correct this problem, the square root of the variance, called the *standard deviation*, is often used.

Example 7 (standard deviation). The standard deviation of the ages given in example 2 is

$$\sqrt{2.5} = 1.58 \text{ years}$$

It is frequently of interest (especially when comparing data from different groups) to express dispersion relative to location. For instance, within a population of elephants a standard deviation in weight of a pound is negligible, whereas in a population of mice it is huge. One has the impression that the variability in weights should be expressed relative to animal size before comparisons can be made. It leads to consideration of the *coefficient of variation*, which is the ratio of the standard deviation to the mean.

Example 8 (coefficient of variation). The coefficient of variation of the ages given in example 2 is

$$1.58/55 = 0.0287 \ (2.87\%).$$

(Sometimes it is multiplied by 100 and expressed as a percent.)

Multivariate Statistics

Thus far, summary statistics have involved only one variable. Such statistics are said to be univariate. However, in many situations a relation among different variables is of interest. For the sake of simplicity, let us consider the case of two variables (call them x and y). First suppose that both variables are measured on a continuous scale. (A scale is continuous if for every pair of feasible values on it another feasible value lies between them.) A visual impression of association is obtained by constructing a *scatter diagram* in which y is plotted versus x.

Example 9 (*scatter diagram*). The forced vital capacity (FVC) and forced expiratory volume in 1 second (FEV_1) were measured for five men. The following data were obtained:

	Pt. 1	Pt. 2	Pt. 3	Pt. 4	Pt. 5
FVC	3.5	3.2	3.4	3.4	3.3
FEV_1	2.8	2.4	2.7	2.5	2.6

The scatter diagram for FEV_1 versus FVC is given in Fig. 2.

On inspection of a scatter diagram, one may inquire about the extent to which the relation between y and x is linear. A statistic that allows one to make the assessment is the Pearson correlation coefficient. It measures the degree to which two variables covary after adjusting for their individual variabilities. To express covariance it is necessary to introduce some mathematical notation. Suppose that x and y have been measured on each of n subjects, so that we have the measurements x_1 and y_1 on the first subject, x_2 and y_2 on the second subject, and so forth through x_n and y_n on the nth subject. The covariance (Cov) of x and y is

$$\text{Cov}(x,y) = ((x_1 - \bar{x})(y_1 - \bar{y}) + (x_2 - \bar{x})(y_2 - \bar{y}) + \ldots + (x_n - \bar{x})(y_n - \bar{y}))/$$
$$(n - 1)$$

where $\bar{x}$ and $\bar{y}$ are the arithmetic means of x and y, respectively. If deviations from the mean in x are accompanied by deviations in the same direction from the mean in y, the covariance is positive. If the deviations in y are in the opposite direction, it is negative.

One difficulty with covariance as a measure of linear association is that two relations may be equally linear when viewed on a scatter diagram, but one may have a larger covariance due merely to the wider range of values involved. To

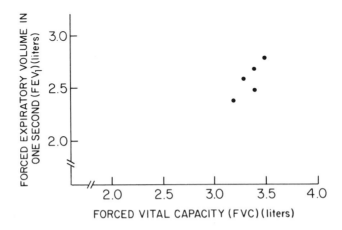

FIG. 2. Scatter diagram: FEV_1 versus FVC for five men.

circumvent this difficulty, all deviations are measured relative to their standard deviations. The Pearson correlation coefficient (r) is obtained. Therefore

$$r = \text{Cov}(x,y)/(S_x S_y)$$

where S_x and S_y are the standard deviations of x and y, respectively. Possible values of r range from -1 to $+1$. A value of $+1$ indicates a perfect positive linear association, whereas a value of -1 is indicative of a perfect negative linear association. If r is zero, x and y do not covary in a linear sense (Fig. 3).

Example 10 (Pearson correlation). Calculate the Pearson correlation for FVC and FEV_1 given in example 9.

	FVC	FEV_1	$(FVC - \overline{FVC})^2$	$(FEV_1 - \overline{FEV_1})^2$	$(FVC - \overline{FVC}) \times (FEV_1 - \overline{FEV_1})$
	3.5	2.8	0.0196	0.0400	0.028
	3.2	2.4	0.0256	0.0400	0.032
	3.4	2.7	0.0016	0.0100	0.004
	3.4	2.5	0.0016	0.0100	0.004
	3.3	2.6	0.0036	0.0000	0.000
Total	16.8	13.0	0.0520	0.1000	0.068
Mean	3.36	2.6			

$$r = 0.068/\sqrt{(0.0520)(0.1000)}$$
$$r = 0.94$$

Frequently it is of interest to evaluate more than just the linearity of an association, especially if the evidence of linearity is good. One may wish to develop an equation describing how y varies with x. If the relation of y and x appears to be linear, it can be described in equation form provided three quantities are known: $\bar{x}$ (the mean of the x values), $\bar{y}$ (the mean of the y values), and the slope of the line.

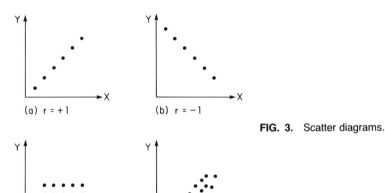

(a) r = +1   (b) r = −1   (c) r = 0   (d) 0 < r < 1

FIG. 3. Scatter diagrams.

(This line is known as the regression of y on x.) When estimating the slope we want a line that best fits the data according to some criterion. The most commonly used criterion is that of *least squares*. By the least squares criterion a line is fitted that has the smallest variance of the points about it. The technique is illustrated in example 11.

Example 11 (linear regression). Suppose for the sake of simplicity that we wish to fit a line to four points using the least-squares criterion. The scatter diagram with a candidate line is presented in Fig. 4. The variance of the points about the line is obtained from the sum of the squared distances between the point and the line denoted by the double arrows in Fig. 4. The variance conforms with the definition given earlier if each point on the line represents the mean value of y for that particular value of x. We have here designated a variable (y) whose values are dependent on the value of x, called the independent variable. Frequently x is a variable (e.g., age) that is easily measured with precision; y is a variable whose value is to be predicted knowing the value of x. The least squares estimate for the slope of the regression line is

$$b = \frac{(x_1 - \bar{x})(y_1 - \bar{y}) + (x_2 - \bar{x})(y_2 - \bar{y}) + \cdots + (x_n - \bar{x})(y_n - \bar{y})}{(x_1 - \bar{x})^2 + (x_2 - \bar{x})^2 + \cdots + (x_n - \bar{x})^2}.$$

In terms of the Pearson correlation coefficient (r), the standard deviation of x (S_x) and the standard deviation of y (S_y), the slope is

$$b = r\, S_y/S_x.$$

The regression equation of y on x is

$$y = \bar{y} + b(x - \bar{x}).$$

Example 12 (linear regression). FVC and age are measured on four patients. Calculate the linear regression equation of FVC on age.

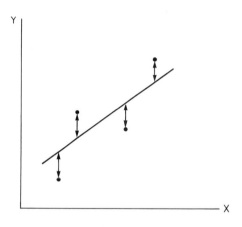

FIG. 4. Scatter diagram.

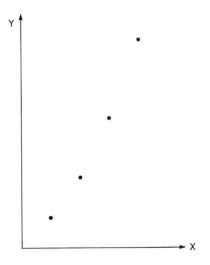

FIG. 5. Scatter diagram.

Patient	FVC	Age	$FVC - \overline{FVC}$	$Age - \overline{Age}$	$(FVC - \overline{FVC}) \times (Age - \overline{Age})$	$(Age - \overline{Age})^2$
1	3.4	70	−0.10	2.5	−0.25	6.25
2	4.0	60	0.50	−7.5	−3.75	56.25
3	3.0	75	−0.50	7.5	−3.75	56.25
4	3.6	65	0.10	−2.5	−0.25	6.25
Total	14.0	270	0.00	0.00	−8.00	125.00
Mean	3.5	67.5				

$$b = -8.00/125 = -0.064$$

The regression equation is

$$FVC = 3.5 - 0.064(age - 67.5).$$

The method of least squares may be used to fit any curve to the data. For example, the scatter diagram may be like the one in Fig. 5, which suggests that the rate of increase of y with x is not constant but is greater for larger values of x, indicating a quadratic component (one in x^2) to the relation between y and x. The relevant equation is

$$y = \bar{y} + b_1(x - \bar{x}) + b_2(x - \bar{x})^2$$

where b_1 and b_2 are estimates obtained by the method of least squares.

HYPOTHESIS TESTING

We have been discussing methods that are useful for generating hypotheses to explain the observed structure of a data set. Now we discuss hypothesis testing. Our hypothesis represents a model or an idea that we believe can explain a phenomenon of interest to us. It may be a theoretical model or an empirical model. Because an empirical model is derived from a specific data set, we expect it to predict the observed structure for that data set. However, we need to know if it can predict the structure that would be observed in other data sets. That is, does our hypothesis have applicability beyond the data set that generated it? The ability of a theoretical model to predict observed structure must also be evaluated. In either case, we need to design experiments to test our hypotheses.

Hypothesis testing involves two components: (a) expected or predicted values and (b) observed or actual values. The expected values are derived from the hypothesis being tested; i.e., the hypothesis predicts what should happen when we conduct our study. The actual values are obtained from our study; i.e., observation tells us what happened when we performed the study. The decision to reject or not to reject the hypothesis is based on a comparison of these two components. If the observed values are not consistent with the predicted values, we reject the hypothesis and formulate a new one. The hypothesis being tested is usually referred to as the *null hypothesis*.

The *test statistic* is the rule or formula used to compare the expected values with the observed values. The magnitude (numerical value) of the statistic is used as a measure of the discrepancy between what we predicted from our hypothesis and what we observed from our study. Its value is the basis for rejecting or not rejecting the hypothesis.

For a specified hypothesis, the magnitude of a statistic is determined by the actual data obtained from the study. Each replication of the study produces its own data set, which is used to calculate a numerical value for the statistic. For all possible replications of the study, we produce all possible data sets for the specified hypothesis. We can calculate the numerical value for the statistic for each data set and hence obtain all possible values of the statistic for the specified hypothesis. This collection of numerical values for the statistic determines the distribution of the statistic.

The *critical region* for the test is the set of numerical values for the statistic that results in the decision to reject the hypothesis. The distribution is used to calculate the probability that the statistic can assume a value assigned to the critical region. This probability is called the *level of significance* of the test and is usually denoted by the Greek letter alpha. The level of significance of the test is the probability of rejecting the hypothesis when the hypothesis is true.

We use two examples to illustrate the concepts associated with hypothesis testing: the chi-square test and Student's *t*-test.

Chi-Square Test

Example 13 (*chi-square test*). The patients are divided into two age groups. Patients who are less than 65 years old belong to group A. Patients who are 65 years and older are assigned to group B.

We have noticed that pneumonia patients frequently have chills. Our clinical observations suggest that there is no relation between a patient's age group and the presence of chills. Based on these observations, we state the following hypothesis:

The probabilities of pneumonia patients having chills are identical for both age groups.

After formulating our hypothesis, we conduct a study to test its validity. We take a random sample of pneumonia patients from each age group. (It is not practical or feasible to observe every patient in both age groups.) Each patient selected for the study is examined for the presence or absence of chills.

We examined 60 patients from group A and 120 patients from group B. The data obtained from our study are given below.

	Chills present		
	Yes	*No*	*Total sample*
Group A	30	30	60
Group B	30	90	120

To test our hypothesis we need to compare these observed values with our predicted values. Our hypothesis specifies that the proportion of patients with chills is the same for both groups; therefore we expect the same percentage of both groups to have chills. The actual percentage is not specified by our hypothesis. However, we can use our data to estimate the proportion of patients with chills. Assuming the hypothesis is true, the probability of a pneumonia patient having chills can be estimated by the total number of patients with chills $(30 + 30 = 60)$ divided by the total number of patients $(60 + 120 = 180)$. We expect one-third $(60/180 = 1/3)$ of the patients to experience chills. Therefore we predict that 20 $[60 \times (1/3) = 20]$ patients in group A and 40 $[120 \times (1/3) = 40]$ patients in group B will have chills. For the sample sizes used in our study, our hypothesis predicts the results displayed below.

	Chills present		
	Yes	*No*	*Total sample*
Group A	20	40	60
Group B	40	80	120

We need a statistic to compare the observed results with the expected results. As a basis for the comparison, let us use the sum of the differences between the observed and expected values.

$$\text{Sum of differences} = (30 - 20) + (30 - 40) + (30 - 40) + (90 - 80)$$

$$= (10) + (-10) + (-10) + (10) = 0$$

The differences sum to zero. Negative differences are canceled by positive differences. We can overcome this difficulty by summing the squares of the differences. (The squares of both positive numbers and negative numbers are positive.)

$$\text{Sum of differences squared} = (30 - 20)^2 + (30 - 40)^2 + (30 - 40)^2 + (90 - 80)^2$$
$$= (10)^2 + (-10)^2 + (-10)^2 + (10)^2$$
$$= 100 + 100 + 100 + 100 = 400$$

However, the difference of 10 contributes the same value when the expected value is 20 as when the expected value is 80. Although these differences are identical, the first 10 represents 50% of its expected value, and the second 10 is 13% of its expected value. It seems reasonable to assign more importance, or weight, to the first case. Therefore we need to make an adjustment for the magnitude to the expected value. This adjustment is accomplished by dividing the square of the difference by the expected value. (For a given difference, this ratio increases as the magnitude of the expected value decreases.) Our statistic is as follows.

$$\chi^2 \text{ calc.} = (30 - 20)^2/20 + (30 - 40)^2/40 + (30 - 40)^2/40 + (90 - 80)^2/80$$
$$= 5.00 + 2.50 + 2.50 + 1.25 = 11.25$$

The statistic provides us with a measure of the disagreement between the expected values (hypothesis) and the observed values (observation). If there were no differences between the observed and expected results, the value of the statistic would equal zero. Any difference between predicted and observed outcomes results in a positive value for our statistic. This fact may suggest that we reject our hypothesis if the statistic is more than zero. However, we must remember that we have observed only a small sample of pneumonia patients. Because patient characteristics do vary, we expect our study results (observations) to vary from sample to sample. Because some disagreement is anticipated, we need to know when the statistic is large enough to justify rejecting our hypothesis, i.e., when more disagreement is indicated than would be expected by chance (random sampling) alone. We must study the set of all possible values for the statistic that could be obtained from our hypothesis by replicating our study; i.e., we need to know the distribution of our statistic. The distribution of values is due to random sampling and is not the result of any failure of our hypothesis.

The distribution is used to define the critical region. (The critical region is the set of values for the statistic that suggests a large discrepancy between our observed and expected results. We reject the hypothesis if the calculated value of the statistic belongs to the critical region.) The distribution for our statistic is known as the chi-square distribution with one degree of freedom. Some selected values from it are

Probability 100α	50%	40%	30%	20%	10%	5%
Value of χ^2	0.45	0.71	1.07	1.64	2.71	3.84

where 100α represents the probability, expressed as a percent, that the statistic will be equal to or larger than the corresponding value. Fifty percent of the values for the statistic are equal to or more than 0.45. We decide to use as our definition of a large value that value which is exceeded no more than 5%. Five percent of the statistic's distribution lies beyond 3.84; therefore the critical region for our test is the set of all values more than 3.84. It corresponds to a level of significance equal to 0.05.

Because the calculated value of the statistic is 11.25 and is more than 3.84, we reject our hypothesis. We conclude that our results are not consistent with the hypothesis that the probabilities of chills are the same for both groups. Comparing the calculated value, 11.25, with the distribution of possible values, it or a larger value would be expected fewer than once in a thousand times; i.e., the probability of obtaining a measure of disagreement equal to or larger than 11.25 is less than 0.001.

These data suggest that there is a statistically significant difference ($p<0.001$) in the proportion of pneumonia patients having chills between the two groups. Fifty percent of group A (younger group) and 25% of group B (older group) have chills.

Student's t-Test

Example 14. The mean expiratory anteroposterier (AP) diameter of the chest for normal men (ages 50–70 years) is 20 cm. Our clinical observations suggest that the expiratory AP diameter is identical for patients with advanced pulmonary emphysema. We conduct a study to test the following hypothesis.

The mean expiratory AP diameter for patients with advanced pulmonary emphysema is equal to 20 cm.

A random sample of 25 patients was selected. Their AP diameters were measured. The following summary statistics were calculated from these data.

$$\bar{x} = 24 \text{ cm (mean)}$$

$$s = 2 \text{ cm (standard deviation)}$$

To test our hypothesis, we need a statistic to compare our observed result (mean 24) with our predicted result (mean 20). The statistic could be defined as the difference between the observed value and the predicted value.

$$\text{Difference} = \text{observed} - \text{expected}$$

$$= 24 - 20 = 4 \text{ cm}$$

However, the difference is difficult to evaluate. It does not take into consideration the variability among the readings. If there is no variation, the 4-cm difference is large. As the variability increases, however, the importance of a 4-cm difference decreases. This difficulty can be circumvented by dividing the difference by its standard deviation (which provides a standardized variable with a variance equal to one). The standard deviation of the difference is called the *standard error of the mean* and is equal to

$$s/\sqrt{n} = 2/\sqrt{25} = 2/5 = 0.4$$

where s is the sample standard deviation, and n is the sample size. The statistic is

$$T_{cal} = \frac{x - \mu}{s/\sqrt{n}} = \frac{24 - 20}{2/\sqrt{25}} = 10.00$$

where μ is the value specified by our hypothesis. The distribution of this statistic is called the *t*-distribution with $n - 1$ degrees of freedom. Some selected results from it are as follows.

Probability 100α	50%	20%	10%	5%	1%
Value t_{24}	0.68	1.32	1.71	2.06	2.49

Using a level of significance equal to 0.05, the critical region corresponds to absolute values of the statistic more than 2.06. Because the calculated value equals 10 and is larger than 2.06, we reject our hypothesis. The probability of the absolute value of the statistic exceeding the observed value (10.0) is less than 0.001.

These data suggest that the mean expiratory AP diameter is more than 20 cm in patients with advanced pulmonary emphysema ($p < 0.001$). We estimate their mean AP diameter to be 24 cm.

When testing a hypothesis there are two possible errors that we can make. The first error is called the *type I error*. A type I error occurs when we incorrectly reject our hypothesis. The level of significance (α) is the probability of making a type I error. The second error is called the *type II error*. This error occurs when we falsely accept our hypothesis. The probability of making a type II error is denoted by the Greek letter beta. (An alternative hypothesis must be specified before we can calculate beta.)

When the data suggest that we reject our hypothesis, the type I error is our only concern. The probability of making this error was established by the level of significance of the test. We select a level of significance that will result in an acceptable risk and design our study accordingly.

When the data are consistent with the hypothesis, the type II error is a concern. The probability of making this error depends on the *alternative hypothesis*. (The alternative hypothesis is the hypothesis that is accepted when we reject the null hypothesis.) Because there are usually many alternatives to the hypothesis being tested, it is difficult to specify beta. (Different alternative hypotheses can yield different betas.) Although it is difficult to evaluate the type II error, we need to recognize that many alternative hypotheses usually exist that could produce results consistent with our hypothesis.

CONCLUSION

We have discussed hypothesis generation and hypothesis testing. We should remember that we cannot test a hypothesis with the data set used to generate it. While analyzing and interpreting data, we must understand the objective of the study: to develop a hypothesis or to test a hypothesis.

When testing a hypothesis, we must adhere to the specifications of the protocol. We cannot allow the data to influence us in any manner that would result in violating the protocol. Any deviations or alterations could seriously affect the probabilities of making type I and type II errors.

We have more freedom to react to the data when we are generating a hypothesis. We can do whatever is necessary to develop an understanding of our data. However, the observation that our (derived) hypothesis is consistent with this data set does not constitute a test (proof) of the hypothesis. We need to perform additional studies designed to test the hypothesis.

SELECTED READING

We have provided the following list of references. The first five references are introductory textbooks and are recommended for people with limited backgrounds. Reference 6 discusses exploratory data analysis and requires only a minimal background.

References 7 and 8 are also introductory textbooks. They cover more material than is covered in the first five references. The remaining ones are considered intermediate or advanced references. We suggest that someone with no statistical background use the following sequence for study.

1. Read any textbook from references 1 to 5.
2. Read either reference 7 or 8.
3. Read reference 6.
4. Read any of the additional references as required.

1. Kuebler, R. R., and Smith, H., Jr. (1976): *Statistics: A Beginning.* Wiley, New York.
2. Remington, R. D., and Schork, M. A. (1970): *Statistics with Applications to the Biological and Health Sciences.* Prentice-Hall, Englewood Cliffs, NJ.
3. Kuzma, J. W. (1984): *Basic Statistics for the Health Sciences.* Mayfield, Palo Alto, CA.
4. Glantz, S. A. (1981): *Primer of Biostatistics.* McGraw-Hill, New York.
5. Ingelfinger, J. A., Mosteller, F., Thibodeau, L. A., and Ware, J. H. (1983): *Biostatistics in Clinical Medicine.* Macmillan, New York.
6. Velleman, P. F., and Hoaglin, D. C. (1981): *Applications, Basics, and Computing of Exploratory Data Analysis.* Daxbury Press, Boston.

7. Zar, J. H. (1984): *Biostatistical Analysis,* 2nd ed. Prentice-Hall, Englewood Cliffs, NJ.
8. Armitage, P. (1974): *Statistical Methods in Medical Research,* 3rd printing. Wiley, New York.
9. Kirk, R. E. (1982): *Experimental Design,* 2nd ed. Brooks/Cole, Monterey, CA.
10. Winer, B. J. (1971): *Statistical Principles in Experimental Design,* 2nd ed. McGraw-Hill, New York.
11. Kleinbaum, D. G., and Kupper, L. L. (1978): *Applied Regression Analysis and Other Multivariable Methods.* Duxbury Press, North Scituate, MA.
12. Draper, N., and Smith, H., Jr. (1981): *Applied Regression Analysis,* 2nd ed. Wiley, New York.
13. Daniel, C., and Wood, F. S. (1980): *Fitting Equations to Data.* Wiley, New York.
14. Mosteller, F., and Tukey, J. W. (1977): *Data Analysis and Regression.* Addison-Wesley, Reading, PA.
15. Morrison, D. F. (1976): *Multivariate Statistical Methods,* 2nd ed. McGraw-Hill, New York.
16. Upton, G. J. G. (1978): *The Analysis of Cross-Tabulated Data.* Wiley, New York.
17. Everitt, B. S. (1977): *The Analysis of Contingency Tables.* Wiley, New York.
18. Siegel, S. (1956): *Nonparametric Statistics for the Behavioral Sciences.* MeGraw-Hill, New York.
19. Kleinbaum, D., Kupper, L., and Morgenstern, H. (1982): *Epidemiologic Research,* Lifetime Learning Publications, Belmont, CA.
20. Friedman, L. M., Furberg, C. D., and DeMets, D. L. (1982): *Fundamentals of Clinical Trials.* John Wright, Boston.
21. Schlesselman, J. J. (1982). *Case-Control Studies.* Oxford University Press, New York.
22. Whitehead, J. (1983). *The Design and Analysis of Sequential Clinical Trials.* Wiley, New York.

Human Aging Research: Concepts and Techniques,
edited by B. Kent and R. N. Butler.
Raven Press, Ltd., New York © 1988.

Computers in Geriatrics Research: Uses and Applications

Monte Peterson

*Department of Geriatrics and Adult Development, Mount Sinai Medical Center,
New York, New York 10029*

The skills and knowledge necessary for planning and carrying out a research project are not always easily acquired. Without discounting the value of actual experience, it may also be helpful to have a more didactic introduction (7,8). Relatively few trainees in the health professions currently receive any formal training in research design, statistics, etc. Likewise, opportunities for exploring the applications of computers in medicine usually depend on local resources and interest.

The purpose of this chapter is to give the reader an overview of computer applications in geriatrics, with the focus on clinical research. The remainder of the chapter is organized as follows:

1. Definition of some basic terms, with the emphasis on databases
2. A review of examples of computerized databases that have been implemented in geriatrics and long-term care
3. A brief differentiation of two classes of available software: clinical research software and general ("off-the-shelf") software
4. An exposition of one paradigm for the steps of a research project, with examples of computer applications at each step

Before proceeding, it should be noted that computers are proving to be invaluable in health services research related to aging. As an example, Davis (4) studied demographic trends in the elderly population using the CAPAS (computer assisted policy analysis and simulation) model on a microcomputer.

DEFINITIONS

The field of medical informatics or medical information science is concerned with all things related to biomedical information, including the meaning of commonly used terms. Definitions of the following terms have therefore been derived from the medical informatics literature.

Data and Information

Let us start by differentiating the terms data and information. The relation has perhaps best been stated by Wiederhold (14): "Information is generated from data through processing."

Database

Consideration of what a database is logically follows. Wiederhold defines a database as "a collection of related data, with facilities that process these data to yield information." Note that the second half of the definition expands the definition beyond that of just a collection of data.

Perhaps the main obstacle to the understanding of what a database is all about has been the use of the term database to refer to different applications. Two examples are clinical databases and online databases:

1. A *clinical database* implies a collection of data on patients. Blois (1) has pointed out how it differs from a computerized medical record: A clinical database is "usually designed for purposes other than patient care." In its most basic version, a computerized medical record is an electronic equivalent of the paper record.

2. An *online database* might (using the above distinction between data and information) better be called an information system. Online databases (e.g., MEDLINE) aid in the selection and retrieval of information instead of its generation.

Database Services

Database services (also referred to as information services) offer the subscriber access to a collection of online databases.

Database Management and File Management Systems

Database management systems, sometimes referred to as data managers, facilitate the collection, organization, storage, and processing of data. There are several categories of database management systems; we review the relational, hierarchical, and network models.

Relational DBMS

The basic components of a relational DBMS are records, fields, and files.

1. *Records.* A record holds the data items for a single entry. An example of a record is as follows:

Smith, Grace   1/1/03   Diabetes

2. *Fields.* A field is a storage unit holding a single data item within a data record. Using the same example (Smith, Grace), 1/1/03 and Diabetes are the *values* of the fields; Name, Birthdate, and Diagnoses are the *names* of the fields:

Name	*Birth date*	*Diagnoses*
Smith, Grace	1/1/03	Diabetes

3. *Files.* A file is a collection of records. Continuing the above example, the Diagnoses file would also contain names and diagnoses of other patients. Each file can be considered a two-dimensional table; each record then becomes a row and each field a column.

A relational DBMS derives its name from the ability to *relate* files based on common data. For example, if there were a Medications file with Name and Medications as the field names, this file could be joined with the Diagnoses file to make a new file:

Name	*Diagnoses*	*Medications*
Smith, Grace	Diabetes	Insulin

Hierarchical DBMS

The structure of a hierarchical DBMS is like an upside-down tree. Similar to a relational database, a hierarchical database is also made up of records. However, the connections between files depend on the structure of the database, not on the contents of the files. This type of structure is known as *one-to-many* (the file at the top of the structure is connected to many files beneath it).

Network DBMS

The structure of a network database is basically hierarchical, but the model allows for *many-to-many* connections.

Computer Hardware

Before moving on to the examples, a review of computing hardware terminology may be useful.

1. *Computers.* The categories of mainframe, minicomputer, and microcomputer still generally hold: mainframe computers are the largest type available, minicomputers are mid-sized, and microcomputers are also known as personal or desktop computers.

2. *Peripheral devices* (input/output, or I/O, devices). Peripheral devices encompass everything but the central processing unit itself. Therefore the keyboard and monitor are actually peripheral devices. Another important peripheral device is the modem, a device (modulator/demodulator) that enables data to be transmitted between computers, usually over telephone lines.

COMPUTERIZED DATABASES: EXAMPLES

Geriatrics/Long-Term Care

Each of the databases cited in this section was created for a given clinical population, not just to facilitate a given research study.

1. *On Lok Senior Health Services.* Perhaps the earliest computerized information management system in the area of long-term care is that developed by the On Lok Institute in San Francisco (3). This system is microcomputer-based, with the software system divided into Fiscal Management and Client Management components.

2. *Philadelphia Gerontology Research Consortium* (6). As part of a Teaching Nursing Home award from the National Institute on Aging, the Philadelphia Gerontology Research Consortium established a clinical research database and subject registry. At the time of reporting, more than 200 variables were being collected on the database members, drawn from the health care facilities and life care communities making up the consortium. Because of concerns over privacy and confidentiality, consent for inclusion into the clinical database was obtained separately from consent for participation in any of the research studies. The subject registry lists demographic and location information, and it is easily linked to the database files where clinical information is stored.

3. *Massachusetts General Hospital Coordinated Care Program* (16). This program began as a demonstration project funded by the Robert Wood Johnson Program for Hospital Initiatives in Long Term Care. Its goal is to maintain or improve the functional status of clients while reducing unnecessary utilization of hospitals, nursing homes, and emergency rooms. Care for an individual client is managed and coordinated by an interdisciplinary project team based at Massachusetts General Hospital (MGH). The medical record system is a version of COSTAR (Computer-Stored Ambulatory Record), which has been enhanced for long-term care purposes by the addition of special divisions for nonphysician team members. The system is based on an MGH mainframe computer, with direct-line modem connection to three MGH satellite community health centers.

4. *Geriatric Research, Education, and Clinical Center (GRECC), Minneapolis Veterans Administration Medical Center (VAMC)* (9). Another hospital-based mainframe database that takes into account the needs of nursing is that established by the GRECC at the Minneapolis VAMC. In addition to demographic information, the database includes a patient care section that primarily includes functional status and behavior status for nursing management. Another section of the database is reserved for medical test information, with a particular emphasis on evaluations for dementia.

5. *Baylor Veterans Administration Medical Center* (VAMC) (12). In contrast to most of the above applications, the clinical information system in use on the Geriatric Evaluation Unit (GEU) at the Baylor VAMC utilizes microcomputers. The software is a general database management system, dBase III, augmented by an operating shell. In addition to containing inpatient and outpatient data, the system has other capabilities, including statistical analysis, data onsets, online database searching, and word processing.

Disease-Specific Databases

One example of a database consisting of a specific population is that established by the Dementia Clinic at Burke Rehabilitation Center. At the time of publication (15), this database consisted of data on more than 600 patients who had been evaluated for cognitive impairment. (This reference is significant in that it includes copies of the actual evaluation forms.)

COMPUTER APPLICATIONS IN RESEARCH: GENERAL

One way to classify software programs that might be useful in clinical research is by the specificity of the software: clinical software and general (''off-the-shelf'') software.

Clinical Software

There is an ever-increasing variety of software programs variably billed as clinical research software, clinical database management systems, etc. As is shown by the following examples, many of these programs are versatile and can be used for a variety of purposes: patient care, education, administration, and research. For this review, two programs are briefly mentioned that were originally developed for minicomputers but for which microcomputer versions have recently become available.

1. *CLINFO* (13). A data management system and analysis system for clinical research, CLINFO was developed under sponsorship of the National Institutes of

Health and has been used in more than 40 academic medical centers across the country. Strain et al. (11) have described their applications of CLINFO on a consultation liaison psychiatry service.

2. *Clinical Data Manager* (CDM). McCormick and McQueen (10) reported their use of this program for an incontinence study at the Francis Scott Key Medical Center in Baltimore. Neither purely relational nor hierarchical, CDM produces a "relational hierarchical" structure. Also significant in this application is built-in computerized instruction and a protocol to evaluate the use of this system.

General Software

One does not need a clinical research software program in order to do research. For example, Clapp-Channing and Bobula (2) utilized dBase II, one of the most widely used relational database management systems, in their study of the effect of hospitalization on functional capacity of elderly persons.

COMPUTER APPLICATIONS THROUGHOUT A RESEARCH PROJECT

In addition to database management systems, other software programs can be used to facilitate a research project. In this section, one paradigm (5) is reviewed for the steps involved in the research project and examples of software given that might be appropriate at each step (Table 1).

Development of a Study

1. *Identify research idea; develop preliminary outline.* It is often helpful to get ideas down on paper to review and revise; a word processor is the class of software for this purpose. Some word processors have built-in outline capabilities; another group of programs (variably called outliners, idea processors, or thought processors) are specifically designed for this purpose, and most can work within a word processor.

2. *Conduct bibliographic search.* In the section on databases, we introduced the term online databases, also referred to as information retrieval systems. MEDLINE is the database most commonly used by biomedical researchers, and it is the equivalent of Index Medicus online. MEDLINE can be accessed either directly from the National Library of Medicine or through a variety of commercial information retrieval services, such as BRS/Saunders Colleague or Knowledge Index. All that is necessary to access oneline databases is (a) a personal computer; (b) a modem (a type of computer hardware that transmits and receives information over phone lines); (c) a communication software program; and (d) a subscription to a particular service. For researchers in geriatrics/gerontology, AGELINE is a

TABLE 1. *Steps in the research process and potential computer applications*

Steps	Applications
Development of a study	
1. Identify research idea; develop preliminary outline.	Word processing software Idea/thought processor (outliner)
2. Conduct bibliographic search.	Online database Communications software
3. Compile personal reference files.	Bibliographic retrieval software
4. Formulate conceptual and theoretical context.	—
5. Formulate operational questions and hypotheses.	—
6. Develop research design, including analytic design.	Project managers
7. Design or obtain data collection instruments.	Database management software Forms design software
Implementation of study procedures	
1. Collect data.	Digital/analog converters Consoles (direct access) Electronic mail
2. Process data: coding, data entry, editing.	Voice recognition software Classification software
3. Analyze data: summaries, tabulation, statistical analyses.	Database management systems Statistical software
Communication of research findings	
1. Present results in graphic form.	Graphics software
2. Prepare written report.	Stand-alone programs vs. integrated programs
3. Disseminate results by means of publication or presentation.	Electronic mail

Adapted from Gilchrist (5).

database compiled by the National Gerontology Resource Center of the American Association of Retired Persons.

3. *Compile personal reference files.* There are numerous programs available, referred to as bibliographic assistance software, that can be helpful in organizing one's reference files. Some of these programs, known as bibliographic *retrieval* software, enable one to ''download'' references obtained from online searching.

4. *Formulate conceptual and theoretical context.*

5. *Formulate operational questions and hypotheses.*

6. *Develop a research design, including an analytical design.* Any programs that can produce flow charts (some graphics programs, ''organizational'' software) may be useful in visualizing, for example, how subjects are going to be selected for a given project. When planning the logistics of carrying out a project, project management software can be useful in mapping out the time frame and necessary resources (personnel and equipment).

7. *Design or obtain data collection instruments.* Ideally, any instruments for data *collection* can be also used for data *entry.* Many database management systems can generate forms that are hard copies of computer files. In addition, there are several forms of design software programs that can be used to "custom make" well-designed forms.

Implementation of Study Procedures

1. *Collect data.* Computer applications at this step obviously depend on the type of data to be collected. Physiological parameters such as blood pressure, temperature, etc. are increasingly being recorded directly into automated devices. Some research studies may allow the direct entry of historical data (e.g., medical history) by either a staff member or the research subject.

2. *Process data: coding, data entry, and editing.* With the increasing sophistication and decreasing price of text scanners and voice recognition systems, these means of data entry may improve the traditionally time-intensive task of data entry. Any study that produces classifiable data may benefit from the classification or coding software (e.g., diagnosis-related groups).

3. *Analyze data: summaries, tabulation, statistical analyses.* Data management systems have the varying capabilities to produce data summaries in the form of reports, and some have basic statistical functions built in. Usually, however, one requires additional statistical support in the form of statistical software. Until recently one needed access to a mainframe computer in order to "run statistics." It is still often necessary, especially for certain statistical tests and with data sets of a certain size. Some projects can be done without resorting to a mainframe, thanks to statistical software developed for personal computers.

Communication of Research Findings

1. *Present results in graphic form.* Presentation graphics software refers to professional graphics that one can produce on a personal computer. A variety of specialized hardware (screen cameras, plotters, laser printers, etc.) provide numerous options in the presentation.

2. *Prepare written report.* Word processors are the mainstay for this application. Tables or graphs may be imported from database management systems or spreadsheets may be used, utilizing either a function of the word processor itself or a special utility program. Another option is to set up a given project on an integrated package, one that has word processing, database, and spreadsheet functions built into one program. For most research applications, the "standalone" approach is probably preferable.

3. *Disseminate results by means of publication or presentation.* Another means of disseminating results that may become more common in the future is through

telecommunications. There are a number of electronic bulletin boards dealing with medical subjects. Some multisite studies have relied on the transmission of data electronically. Some of the previously mentioned online databases have libraries comprised of complete text books and medical journals.

COMPUTER APPLICATIONS IN GERIATRICS/LONG-TERM CARE: PROFESSIONAL ACTIVITIES

Geriatrics/Gerontology

The American Geriatrics Society now offers workshops at their annual meetings. The Gerontological Society of America similarly has special sessions of its annual meeting devoted to microcomputer applications.

Medical Informatics

The largest professional organization in medical informatics is the American Association of Medical Systems and Informatics (AAMSI). AAMSI is one of the primary sponsors each year of the Symposium on Computer Applications in Medical Care (SCAMC). Most of the examples of computerized databases cited earlier were originally presented at this forum. In addition, AAMSI has a Professional Specialty Group program, with one of the professional speciality groups being Geriatrics/Long-Term Care.

SUMMARY

There are many options available for data management in research. The following suggestions are offered.

1. Start thinking about data collection and management from the start.
2. Seek out existing resources (hardware, software, personnel) in your department and institution.
3. Always consider the above resources in the preparation of a grant proposal.
4. When embarking on a new clinical activity (e.g., geriatric inpatient unit), start building a clinical database from the outset.

ACKNOWLEDGMENTS

The author thanks Rajendra Jutagir, Ph.D., for his comments during the preparation of this manuscript.

REFERENCES

1. Blois, M. (1984): Medical records and clinical databases: What is the difference? *M.D. Comput.,* 1:24–28.
2. Clapp-Channing, N. E., and Bobula, J. A. (1984): Microcomputer-based management of a longitudinal geriatric research study. In: *Proceedings of the Eighth Annual Symposium on Computer Applications in Medical Care,* edited by G. S. Cohen, pp. 348–351. IEEE Computer Society Press, Washington, DC.
3. *Computerized Information Management in Long-Term Care: A Case Study.* On Lok Institute, San Francisco, 1983.
4. Davis, K. (1983): Health implications of aging in America. In: *Proceedings of the Seventh Annual Symposium on Computer Applications in Medical Care,* edited by R. Dayhoff, pp. 625–631. IEEE Computer Society Press, Washington, DC.
5. Gilchrist, P. (1986): Research data management. In: *Handbook for the Academic Physician,* edited by W. C. McFaghie and J. J. Frey, pp. 251–278. Springer-Verlag, New York.
6. Green, R. S., Steinmann, W., Ellis, N., O'Brien, L., Pack, A., Lawton, M. P., Pfohl, D., Stein, A., and Abrutyn, E. (1985): A registry and database for gerontology research: the teaching nursing home approach to medical services for the elderly. In: *Proceedings of the Ninth Annual Symposium on Computer Applications in Medical Care,* edited by M. J. Ackerman, pp. 624–628. IEEE Computer Society Press, Washington, DC.
7. Katz, B. (1986): Clinical research system (review). *M.D. Comput.,* 3:53–61.
8. King, C., Manire, L., Strong, R. M., and Goldstein, L. (1984): Data management systems in clinical research. In: *Information Systems for Patient Care,* edited by B. Blum, pp. 404–415. Springer-Verlag, New York.
9. Kuskowski, M. (1984): A computerized database for geriatric research and patient care. In: *Proceedings of the Eighth Annual Symposium on Computer Applications in Medical Care,* edited by G. S. Cohen, pp. 352–353. IEEE Computer Society Press, Washington, DC.
10. McCormick, K., and McQueen, L. (1986): The development and use of a database management system for clinical geriatric research. In: *Proceedings of the Fifth World Conference on Medical Informatics, MEDINFO 86,* edited by R. Salamon, B. Blum, and M. Jorgensen, pp. 527–531. North Holland, Amsterdam.
11. Strain, J. J., Norvell, C. M., Strain, J. J., Mueenuddin, T., and Strain, J. W. (1985): A microcomputer approach to consultation liaison data basing: Pedagog-Admin-Clinfo. *Gen. Hosp. Psychiatry,* 7:113–118.
12. Teasdale, T. A., Snow, E., Carpenter, D., and Luchi, R. J. (1986): A geriatric evaluation unit's use of a microcomputer for patient care and research. *Gerontologist,* 26:4–7.
13. Whitehead, S. F., and Streeter, M. (1984): CLINFO—a successful technology transfer. In: *Proceedings of the Eighth Annual Symposium on Computer Applications in Medical Care,* edited by G. S. Cohen, pp. 557–560. IEEE Computer Society Press, Washington, DC.
14. Wiederhold, G. (1981): *Databases for Health Care, Vol. 12: Lecture Notes in Medical Informatics.* Springer-Verlag, New York.
15. Zemcov, A., Barclay, L. L., Brush, D., and Blass, J. P. (1984): Computerized data base for evaluation and follow-up of demented outpatients. *J. Am. Geriatr. Soc.,* 32:801–842.
16. Zielstorff, R. D., Jette, A. M., Barnett, G. O., Schaumburg, D., Piggins, J., Weidman-Dahl, F., Gross, H., and Webster, S. (1985): A COSTAR system for hospital-based coordination of long term care for the elderly. In: *Proceedings of the Ninth Annual Symposium on Computer Applications in Medical Care,* edited by M. J. Ackerman, pp. 17–21. IEEE Computer Society Press, Washington, DC.

Human Aging Research: Concepts and Techniques,
edited by B. Kent and R. N. Butler.
Raven Press, Ltd., New York © 1988.

Survey Research as a Tool for Studying Problems in the Elderly*

Irene C. Rayman and Samuel W. Bloom

Department of Community Medicine, Mount Sinai School of Medicine,
New York, New York 10029

How many persons aged 60 or above live in Typicaltown, USA? What proportion of the town's population do they represent? Is Typicaltown unique in this respect, compared with American towns of the same size? Is the distribution by sex the same in this population group as in Typicaltown's general population? Does it change when the cohort reaches 75? How do the individuals in this group feel about themselves? Are their attitudes similar or different from those of other age groups? How do the town's younger citizens perceive the older ones?

These kinds of questions are best answered by survey data. Sometimes they are answerable by large data banks regularly collected and available either directly upon inquiry (e.g., the Census Bureau) or are in raw data form that can be purchased and analyzed. Others require the full process—from the preparation of survey instruments through data collection, processing, and analysis.

This chapter presents the social survey as one approach to studying aging and the aged. It provides an overview of the factors involved in planning and implementing a survey, with two objectives: (a) to enable the reader to assess the appropriateness of the survey method for a proposed research topic, and (b) to enable the reader to better understand and critically examine survey research as reported by others. It is not intended as a ''how-to-do-it'' guide. For more detailed information on survey research, a list of references is included in the Selected Reading list at the end of the chapter.

WHAT A SURVEY IS AND WHAT IT IS NOT

Survey research has become a major tool of all the social sciences. That this chapter is written by sociologists simply reflects the fact that sociology as a discipline

---

*Portions of this chapter are based on Rayman, I. (1975): Survey techniques for planning and evaluation. In: *Program Planning and Evaluation: Selected Topics for Vocational Rehabilitation*, edited by I. Robinault and M. Weisinger. ICD Rehabilitation Research Center, New York.

has adopted the survey method perhaps more enthusiastically than any other, used it, and developed it most extensively. Nevertheless, a survey is the same whether used by an epidemiologist, a physician, or a sociologist. It is a tool to accomplish two main purposes:

1. *Description:* finding out how one or more characteristics are distributed in a population. For example, how many individuals over the age of 70 are living alone in the population of a given community?

2. *Explanation:* to find out why a distribution takes the form it does. Let us say that the survey finds that a disproportionate number of women of lower socioeconomic class status and who are over 70 are living alone. Why? Survey analysis provides methods for answering such a question.

The *census* of the United States is a special case. Although it collects data in the same way as the social survey, the census *enumerates* an entire population, determining the actual distribution of characteristics. The survey *estimates* such distributions on the basis of data from samples of the population. The statistical information from the census is valuable, sometimes essential for much of survey research, especially as a basis for sampling. It provides the vital statistics of the general population on which the probability sampling techniques of many surveys are based.

The federal government, apart from the Census Bureau, conducts a variety of continuing surveys. One example is the National Health Survey of the Department of Health and Human Services (DHHS). In a later section on how to plan a survey, such sources are described in more detail.

A survey, though a rigorous scientific tool, is *not* an experiment. Like the experimental method, a survey is designed to collect data about *dependent* and *independent* variables. Furthermore, it seeks to explain the sources of variation in the dependent variable. In the experimental method, however, the investigator controls the effects of "extraneous causal factors" on the dependent variable, whereas survey analysis uses procedures of statistical inference to arrive at conclusions about the relation between independent and dependent variables. Stated another way, the experimental method manipulates the situation of inquiry *before* the data are gathered; the survey method manipulates observational data *after* they have been gathered.

Surveys, of course, use only human subjects. With medical experimentation, when human subjects (in contrast, for example, to animals) are used, ethical questions are critically important. Some of the most oft-cited examples are the following.

1. The Tuskegee experimental study of syphilis among men with the disease, 400 of whom were given placebos for "bad blood" and never told about the correct diagnosis (4).
2. The Willowbrook study in which institutionalized mentally retarded children were deliberately infected with hepatitis, again without informing them or their guardians.

For the survey method, the major ethical issues are the protection of the *confidentiality* of collected information, the right of informants to *privacy,* and the concept of *informed consent.*

The survey method also should be differentiated from *demographic studies.* Demographic studies rely heavily on data from the census and other records of age, sex, death, etc. of total populations. Surveys rely mainly on their own data from questionnaires and interviews, dealing with samples of populations.

Epidemiology is a discipline that relies heavily on the survey method. It studies disease from the point of view of the mutual interaction and balance of three main sets of factors: the *host,* varying in genetic resistance, susceptibility, and degree of immunity to the disease; the *agent,* or carrier, of the disease; and the *environment,* social as well as physical, which affects the susceptibility of the host, the virulence of the agent, and the quantity and quality of the contact between host and agent. Like surveys in general, it is concerned with variations in some phenomenon according to different social characteristics.

For example, let us say that a difference would be observed in the frequency of Alzheimer's disease among Japanese men compared to non-Japanese men. The question for the epidemiologist now becomes one of determining why this difference occurs. Some characteristics of Japanese men are hypothetically causal to the disease. If one controls for those characteristics in the two groups of men, a change in the original correlation should be produced. To be more specific, the different rate among Japanese might be explained logically by a genetic inheritance factor, cultural influences on life style or diet, or environmental factors. The epidemiological research must be designed to account for such hypothetical possibilities. To answer the genetic hypothesis, the incidence rates of Alzheimer's could be compared among native Japanese men, Hawaiian Japanese men, and mainland Japanese-Americans. If the rates prove to be similar, further analysis of the genetic hypothesis would be indicated. Similar investigations of cardiovascular disease have proved useful.

What a social survey is may be best conveyed by its uses. The term "social survey" and the techniques associated with it, have been applied to a wide variety of investigations, including public opinion polls, market research studies, epidemiological studies, and, perhaps the most well known, the census of the population. Most generally, the survey is the best method for collecting original data for purposes of studying a population that cannot be observed directly (see Note 1, below).

---

1. Another approach is to observe behavior directly. The researcher may observe behavior as a participant in the group under study or as a nonparticipant. That is, the observer may observe with or without "becoming a functioning member of the group and taking part in its activities" (Theodorson, G. A., and Theodorson, A. G.: *A Modern Dictionary of Sociology,* pp. 279–280. Thomas Y. Crowell Company, New York, 1969). For information on observation as a method, see, for example, *Analyzing Social Settings: A Guide to Qualitative Observation and Analysis,* edited by J. L. Lofland. (Wadsworth, California, 1971). See also Trow, M.: Comment on participant observation and interviewing: a comparison; and Becker, H. S., and Geer, B.: Participant observation and interviewing, a rejoinder. In: *Qualitative Methodology,* edited by Filstead, W. J. (Markham, Chicago, 1970). Other means of obtaining information have been classified and described by several social scientists as (a) the use of precollected

A population may be too large; perceptions, beliefs, or attitudes are not observable; some behavior is private. With a survey, information is obtained indirectly, through reports of attitudes or behavior from the respondent. Respondents may report about themselves or, acting as informants, about others. They may report on attitudes or behavior that is past, current, or prospective. The approach used to gain such information is the asking of questions in two ways: interviews and questionnaires.

HISTORY OF SURVEY RESEARCH

When speaking of classic examples of the social survey, the most frequently mentioned are (a) Durkheim's attempt to explain variations in suicide rates by differences in the social structure (2); (b) the studies of soldiers' attitudes conducted by the Research Branch of the U.S. Army during World War II and reanalyzed afterward in *The American Soldier* (12); and (c) the series of voting behavior studies that began with *The People's Choice* (5). The use of the method, however, is much older.

The modern social survey can be distinguished by two basic elements: (a) the use of rates as dependent variables; and (b) the explanation of differences in rates by means of their associations with other social phenomena. The use of these features has been dated to 1662, when Graunt published the first data on urban and rural death rates (3,11).

Not until the nineteenth century, however, did the study of *voluntary acts* begin with the recognition that suicide showed the same constancy of rates that had been observed for the excess of male births over female births. Thus was born the field that was called "moral statistics." Especially in France, and used by the Belgian astronomer Adolphe Quetelet, moral statistics during the early nineteenth century reached a level of development that resembled modern sociology. Quetelet's contributions included: (a) the use of multivariate tables to explore the relations between rates of crime and marriage with demographic factors such as age and sex; (b) the application of the calculus of probability to explaining the constancy of social rates over time; and (c) the establishment of a professional association, The Statistical Society of London, which later became the Royal Statistical Society (11).

By the late nineteenth century, methods of survey data analysis had reached a high stage of development. Tables for causal analysis were used by Charles Booth in his monumental study of the London poor and by Emile Durkheim in his

---

or preexisting data, including personal and public documents, published volumes; and (b) the use of experiments in laboratories on natural settings. See Leik, R. L.: *Methods, Logic and Research of Sociology,* pp. 33–41 (Bobbs-Merrill, New York, 1972); Babbie, E. R.: *The Practice of Social Research,* p. 257. (Wadsworth, California, 1975); Thomlinson, R.: *Sociological Concepts and Research,* pp. 40–60 (Random House, New York, 1965); Cole, S.: *The Sociological Method,* pp. 37–40 (Markham, Chicago, 1972).

study of suicide. In the meantime, statistical analysis developed new dimensions through the work of Galton, Pearson, and Yule on correlation coefficients and the statistics of the significance of difference (11).

Between the two world wars, the technology of data recording, recovery, and analysis took a quantum leap with the introduction of punch card machines. Survey research became large-scale, and commercial. Examples included market research, opinion polling, and communications research. Elmo Roper and George Gallup introduced the periodic national sample opinion polling that is now a standard part of American life. When World War II began, particularly through Stouffer et al.'s Information and Education Research Branch, but also in most other areas of the military effort, survey research became an important tool (12).

Survey research was now so elaborately quantitative that teams of researchers were required for its effective utilization. Responding to the need, a group of university-based organizations were created:

1. Bureau of Applied Social Research at Columbia University
2. Survey Research Center at the University of Michigan
3. National Opinion Research Center (NORC) at Chicago
4. Washington Public Opinion Research Center at the University of Washington

Today there are many more, signifying the full-scale institutionalization of the social survey.

RESEARCH ON AGING: IMPLICATIONS FOR SURVEY TECHNIQUES

The National Research on Aging Panel was organized in late 1980 to assist the National Institute on Aging (NIA) in the development of a long-range plan "for promoting health and well-being by extending the vigorous and productive years of life through research on aging" (8).

Physiological aging is viewed as only one of the many factors determining the condition and status of older people. Hence the Panel recommended that research on the "basic mechanisms of aging" and the "clinical manifestations of aging" be supplemented by research in the social and behavioral sciences (including demography, epidemiology, sociology, anthropology, economics, psychology) in order to examine how social, cultural, economic, and psychological factors influence the health and well-being of older people.

More specifically, the Panel identified 14 research areas:

. . . longevity; health and health care systems; household, family, and kin; social networks, voluntary associations, and nonkin systems; labor force participation; the future of income, assets, and consumption; emerging roles and lifestyles; social stratification; political systems and aging; legal systems; living arrangements; housing and residential mobility; methodological research; societal values and attitudes toward aging and the aged; and cross-national and comparative studies.

A review of the Panel's findings and recommendations suggest that there are current implications for the role of survey techniques in such research on aging (8).

PLANNING THE SURVEY

When planning a survey, existing information is examined to help formulate or clarify the research problem as well as provide background information for designing the survey and survey instruments. To start, it is useful to consult the usual reference literature, such as the Cumulative Index Medicus (see Note 2, below). There are also periodicals that are specifically concerned with the problems of aging (see Note 3, below). Government publications can also be helpful, from local and state as well as federal agencies. As indicated above, probably the best known and most commonly used source is the United States Census of Population and Housing conducted by the Department of Commerce every 10 years. The results are issued in the form of printed reports, microfiche, microfilm, and computer tapes. The data include general population characteristics, e.g., age, sex, race, marital status; general social and economic characteristics, e.g., nativity and parentage, school enrollment, vocational training, disability, employment status, vocational group; and housing characteristics for states, cities, and counties, including facilities, number of rooms, persons per room. In addition, the Bureau of the Census publishes a number of special reports during noncensus years. The Social and Economic Statistics Administration of the Bureau of the Census publishes quarterly reports. To help individuals utilize the enormous amount of material, the Bureau provides a number of guides (see Note 4, below).

Another source of statistical information dealing with the general population, but of particular use in aging research, is the National Health Survey. It is a continuing program of surveys of the United States, using a representative sample, to obtain information about the health conditions of the general population. It comprises three parts: (a) the Health Interview Survey, a continuing nationwide sampling and interviewing of households; (b) the Health Examination Survey, a

---

2. See also *Index to Hospital Literature, Index to Nursing Literature, ARECO's Index to Periodical Literature on Aging, Gerontological abstracts, Psychological Abstracts.*

3. See, for example, *Experimental Aging Research, Experimental Gerontology, Geriatric Medicine, Gerontologist, Gerontology, Gerontology and Geriatric Education, Journal of the American Geriatric Society, Journal of Clinical and Experimental Gerontology, Journal of Gerontology.*

4. See, for example, *1980 Census of Population and Housing Users' Guide,* U.S. Department of Commerce (November 1982). See also *Census Catalogue and Guide,* 1987 Annual, Washington, DC (June 1987); Shryock, H. S., et al.: *The Methods and Materials of Demography,* Vols. I and II (U.S. Department of Commerce, Bureau of the Census, U.S. Government Printing Office, Washington, DC, May 1973), which provides a description of methods used by technicians or research workers when dealing with demographic data. It offers instruction in how to use population data appropriately by knowing their sources, limitations, and underlying definitions.

physical examination and testing of samples of individuals; and (c) the Health Records Survey, another series of sample surveys in which the sources of information are establishments that provide hospital and other medical, dental, and nursing types of health-related care to the general population.

The National Center for Health Statistics, another source of data, conducts three health care utilization surveys that provide estimates of utilization of health care in a particular setting (see Note 5, below). The National Ambulatory Medical Care Survey examines health care provided in physicians' offices; the National Discharge Survey, on the health care provided in short-stay, nonfederal hospitals; and the National Nursing Home Survey, on the health care provided in nursing homes.

Other agencies include the U.S. Department of Health and Human Services, the National Center for Health Services Research, and the Special Committee on Aging, U.S. Senate. The *Monthly Catalogue of Government Publications* indexes many of these reports.

Consultation with Community Groups or Individuals

Much can be gained from talks or correspondence with selected individuals or groups who are believed to have special information about the subject matter of the intended research. They may include civic leaders, newspaper editors, managers of radio and television stations, elected officials, representatives of community organizations, hospitals, etc. This procedure is referred to as the "experience survey." Contacts with such informants need not be of a formal nature; much can be gained from informal conversations and meetings. For instance, the director of a long-term care facility and the staff workers may have insights into the characteristics of aged persons and their needs, as well as the probable effectiveness of various approaches in meeting their needs. Such an "experience survey" can provide information about practical possibilities for doing different types of research and a summary of the knowledge of skilled practitioners about the effectiveness of various methods and procedures in achieving specific goals (10).

Review of Existing Facilities

In order to plan for services for the elderly, for example, it may be worthwhile to identify the resources that are available within a given community (see Note

---

5. See *Origin, Program and Operation of the United States National Health Survey,* National Center for Health Statistics, Series 1, No. 1, (U.S. Department of Health, Education and Welfare, Washington, DC, August 1963) for a detailed description of the developments leading to the enactment of the National Health Survey Act and a summary of the policies, initial program, and operation of the survey.

6, below). A first step would be to obtain a list of the facilities providing the services in question, which might be accomplished by so simple a step as consulting the Yellow Pages of the telephone book or calling the Community Chest office. However, it generally is not enough merely to know what or how many facilities exist. One needs to know more specific facts relating to their use or potential use, such as demographic data on the population served, its capacity, waiting lists, and eligibility requirements. It would also be useful to know the type of auspices, the funding source, cooperating organizations, and locus of decision-making (7).

SELECTING A SURVEY DESIGN

With a background of information provided by some of the above means, the researcher is better able to determine the specific information needs and select a survey research design. There are several designs from which to choose.

Cross-Sectional Survey

The cross-sectional survey involves the collection of data at one point in time from a sample of the population. (Sampling is discussed later in the chapter.) It may be used to describe a situation or to examine a relation between variables in a particular situation. The limitations of this approach are centered in the time boundaries of the data collection.

Longitudinal Survey

Longitudinal surveys permit the analysis of data over time. Data are collected at different intervals, thereby providing information on process or change. There are three major types of longitudinal design. The first is the *trend study,* in which a given characteristic of some population is monitored periodically. An example is the pattern of disability in a community—its changing extent and nature over a period of time—even though different samples of individuals would be studied each time. A second type is the *cohort study,* in which some specific group is studied over time, most typically a birth cohort, i.e., people born during the same period who then age together. The data may be collected from members of the group each time. For instance, one might study the occupational history of

---

6. See Porter, E. H.: *Community Wise* (The Woman's Press, New York, 1947). Although published more than 30 years ago, this pamphlet, which is in the form of a notebook, provides a method and forms for recording opinions and facts about a community. It is intended for use by professional workers and by board and committee members in social agencies as a means of keeping up to date on the community. It is not intended to be a survey of the community but, rather, a gathering of necessary information to which the worker adds his or her impressions.

those born before and after World War II. The participants might be followed over a period of years at given intervals.

A third type of longitudinal study is the *panel study*. Although trend and cohort studies permit the analysis of change over time in a way that is not possible in cross-sectional surveys, they fail to indicate which individuals are changing because the sample varies in each successive study. Panel studies, on the other hand, allow the collection of data through time from the same sample of respondents. The sample is referred to as a "panel." For instance, a researcher might interview a sample of respondents in a rehabilitation program at 1-month intervals for a period of a year. Such studies are most feasible when the phenomenon under study is relatively short in duration. Although panel studies remain among the most sophisticated designs and with the richest explanatory potential, they are not frequently used in survey research. There are several reasons: They are more time-consuming and expensive than other designs; there is a problem of attrition, i.e., the loss of respondents in successive waves of the study; and the analysis of panel data may be rather complicated.

Approximating the Longitudinal Survey

Despite the advantages of the cohort, trend, and panel studies, the cross-sectional survey is the most frequently used design. Because many of the questions a researcher wishes to answer involve some notion of change over time, a number of devices have been used in cross-sectional surveys for approximating the study of process or change. One technique is to have respondents provide data relevant to questions indicating change. They may be asked to provide information about a current situation as well as the state of the situation the previous year. There are two problems, however. First, the researcher must rely on the retrospective information provided by the respondents, which may not be accurate. The farther back in time for which information is requested, the less accurate it is likely to be. Second, the researcher must be cautious when interpreting the earlier time data as representative of a cross section of the population at that time, as the sample is, strictly speaking, limited to the present population.

Another means of approximating a longitudinal survey is to use age or cohort comparisons within a cross-sectional survey. Thus by comparing 40-year-olds with 50-year-olds, such cross-sectional data may be interpreted in longitudinal terms to suggest a process over time, but only with caution.

CONDUCTING THE SURVEY

There are three general considerations once a particular survey design has been selected: (a) defining and selecting the survey population; (b) choosing the methods for collecting the data; and (c) processing and analyzing the data.

Defining and Selecting the Survey Population

There is usually a wide variation in what or who is to be studied in order to gain the necessary information. These "units of analysis" may be individuals, groups, or formal organizations. Depending on the particular problem, the researcher designates a population that conforms to some set of specifications. That is, although survey research typically uses individuals as the units of analysis, certain categories of individuals rather than all individuals are used. For example, one might study men or women. These units are known as the *target population*. However, it is usually not feasible to study the entire population, e.g., all men or women in the community. As a result, a sample of the target population is selected for investigation, known as the *survey population* or *sample population*. The process by which the sample is chosen is called *sampling*.

If all members of a population were alike in all key respects, any sample selected would be appropriate. However, because there is usually variation or heterogeneity in the population under study, specific sampling techniques are required. There are two major sampling techniques: probability and nonprobability sampling.

Probability Sampling

If samples are to provide useful estimates of the population, they must be representative of the population from which they are drawn. Note that the sample need not be representative in all respects, only in those characteristics that are relevant to the issues of the study. Probability sampling provides a method for increasing the likelihood of obtaining a sample representative of the target population and for providing a method of establishing the degree to which it represents that population (see Note 7, below). Probability sampling is the most useful and respected method. There are several probability sampling designs.

Simple random sampling

The key to ensuring the representativeness of the sample is random selection. Random sampling allows each element in the population to have a known chance of being included in the sample. The basic random sampling design is simple random sampling (10).

Example: Suppose, for example, that one wants a simple random sample of two cases from a population of five cases. Let the five cases in the population be A, B, C, D,

---

7. Statisticians have calculated the relation between the size of the sample and the chance of making incorrect statements about the population. The larger the sample, the less chance there is of making incorrect statements (Cole, S.: *Sociological Method,* p. 42, Markham, Chicago, 1972). However, once a certain sample size is reached, e.g., 3,000, little accuracy is achieved by increasing the sample beyond that point.

and E. There are 10 possible pairs of cases in this population. AB, AC, AD, AE, BC, BD, BE, CD, CE, and DE. Write each combination on a disk, put the 10 disks in a hat, mix them thoroughly, and have a blindfolded person pick one. Each of the disks has the same chance of being selected. The two cases corresponding to the letters on the selected disk constitute the desired simple random sample.

This example illustrates, in simplest form, the method for selecting random samples from the population, but it is not a practical means for doing so. The same result may be obtained by selecting each case individually using a list of random numbers that can be found in most textbooks of statistics. They are sets of numbers that show no evidence of systematic order. Another, more recently developed method of selecting a random sample is by use of computer programming. In effect, the computer program numbers the elements in the population, generates its own series of random numbers, and prints out the selected sample list.

Systematic sampling

Simple random sampling is seldom used in practice. It is not the most efficient method; it may entail a laborious procedure; and it requires a list of the population. With such a list, researchers usually use a systematic sampling procedure, which involves the selection of every *n*th element in the total list for inclusion in the sample. For example, if a list contains 10,000 elements and the researcher desires a sample of 1,000, every tenth element is selected. To prevent human bias when using this method, the researcher selects the first element at random, and proceeds systematically down the list. The two procedures—simple random sampling and systematic sampling—are essentially the same in practice and in the results obtained.

Stratified sampling

Stratified sampling represents a modification of the above procedure. It allows a greater degree of representativeness. The population is divided into two or more strata based on a single criterion such as sex (i.e., men/women) or a combination of two or more criteria (e.g., age and sex: men under 65, women under 65; men 65 and over, women 65 and over). Stratification, then, organizes the population into homogeneous subgroups, and the appropriate number of elements are selected from each. This method allows the researcher to obtain a sample proportionate to that of the target population. For instance, if a community has a larger number of young than old people, the sample would reflect this difference.

Cluster sampling or multistage sampling

Large-scale surveys seldom use simple or stratified random sampling because of the difficulty or impossibility of listing all elements in the population. It is not a problem when dealing with small and spatially concentrated populations. Cluster sampling is often used when such a list is available. Instead of sampling individual elements, cluster sampling involves the initial sampling of groups of elements (i.e., clusters) on a simple or stratified random basis. Let us suppose that a researcher is interested in all individuals in a community who are receiving vocational rehabilitation services. Rather than compiling a list of all such individuals, a list of all vocational rehabilitation agencies is compiled instead. Using a cluster sample format, then, that list of agencies is sampled using simple or stratified sampling. Using lists of participants in each sampled agency, individuals are selected similarly. This process is called multistage cluster sampling because first the agencies are sampled and then the individuals within the sample of agencies. It might be possible to use all members within each sampled agency as a total sample if the numbers are small enough.

Nonprobability Sampling

Although probability sampling methods are generally superior to nonprobability methods, it is often more advantageous in terms of convenience and economy to use the latter. There are three major types of nonprobability samples.

1. *Accidental sampling*. With accidental sampling, one simply selects the most available cases until the sample reaches the desired size. For example, the researcher might select the first 100 persons on a street corner. Although this method is easy and inexpensive, it fails to provide a representative sample.

2. *Quota sampling*. Quota sampling, unlike accidental sampling, allows inclusion of specific elements in the sample in the proportion in which they are believed to occur in the population. The goal of quota sampling is selection of a sample that is a replica of the population to which one wants to generalize. For instance, rather than selecting the first 100 individuals who pass, the researcher would select a certain proportion of men and women.

3. *Purposive sampling*. Purposive sampling, also referred to as judgmental sampling, is based on the premise that one can hand-pick subjects to be included in the sample who are satisfactory in relation to one's needs. That is, individuals who are typical of the population in which one is interested are selected, e.g., community leaders.

Although the above-mentioned nonprobability methods are relatively easy and inexpensive to administer, they have serious shortcomings. First, information obtained from such samples cannot be generalized to a larger population. Second, the interviewer or field worker who selects the sample respondents may introduce his or her own bias into that selection, e.g., by selecting the most available or "approachable" individuals.

Collecting the Data

There are two basic approaches to collecting survey data: interviews and questionnaires. Interviewing involves members of a research team asking questions verbally of the respondents and recording these answers. It is typically done in a face-to-face situation, although telephone interviews are frequently used. The use of questionnaires involves having respondents read the questions and enter their own answers. The questionnaires may be delivered to the respondents by mail or in person, or a combination of the two. It may be delivered personally by a field worker, who gives instructions to the respondent and arranges to pick up the completed questionnaire at a later date or to have it mailed back. Alternatively, the questionnaire is mailed to the respondent and picked up in person by a field worker who is then able to check it for completeness.

Each of these techniques has advantages and disadvantages that must be weighed in terms of the nature of the specific study. It is not unusual for a study to use both techniques.

Some Advantages of Self-Administered Questionnaires

1. Questionnaires require less skill to administer, as they are often mailed to respondents or handed to them with a minimum of explanation.
2. Questionnaires can be administered to a large number of individuals simultaneously.
3. They ensure greater uniformity in terms of standardized wording and ordering of questions, as well as instructions for recording responses.
4. Respondents are more often at ease with the anonymity provided by a questionnaire, especially when dealing with sensitive issues.
5. Respondents are under less pressure to respond immediately; they may take time to think about each question.

Some Advantages of Interviews

1. Generally, interviews achieve a higher response rate, estimated at 80 to 85%, compared with 10 to 50% for mailed questionnaires.
2. More complete information may be provided by the respondent in the presence of an interviewer. The interviewer may clarify a question or probe for additional information if the intitial response seems inadequate or inappropriate.
3. Respondents may be more willing and able to cooperate when all they have to do is talk.
4. Interviews are more appropriate for certain segments of the population. Although

questionnaires are useful for those with a certain amount of education, there is a substantial proportion of the population who are illiterate.

5. Interviewers may observe characteristics of the respondents, such as manner of dress, speech, etc., as well as obtain responses to the questions.

Designing the Survey Instrument

Given the two basic ways of eliciting information, questionnaires and interviews, there are several general guidelines regardless of the technique used. Decisions must be made about question content, format, and wording.

Content

When formulating the research problem, the researcher may be interested in obtaining a variety of data about the study population. A survey may examine factual knowledge, attitudes or opinions, and reported behavior.

The first stage in designing a questionnaire or interview involves identifying and defining the variables of interest, e.g., health, and further specifying the associated dimensions or values. For example, health may be described as excellent, good, fair, or poor. Next, each variable must be defined in operational, or measurement-oriented, terms. Again, consider the variable health, which is defined in the dictionary as "the condition of being sound in body, mind, or spirit" (9). For purposes of survey research, this "nominal" definition is not adequate. We must define the variable health as something that can be measured. Some variables, e.g., age or weight, are clear-cut and can be measured easily. Others are more difficult. Rather than observing the variable directly, as with a person's weight, we must rely on indicators of the variable, i.e., evidence of its presence or absence. For instance, one indicator of health is a subjective measure, the person's perceived health status. Another more objective indicator is utilization of health services, e.g., the number of physician visits. There exists a probabilistic relation between the variable and the indicator; if the indicator exists, the variable exists. There is the risk of error, however. The indicator may exist in the absence of the variable; the variable may exist in the absence of the indicator. To minimize such error, it is best to rely on more than one indicator. There are a number of indicators for any given variable. None is absolutely correct or incorrect, only more or less useful.

The next process involves formulating specific questions, which when combined and analyzed are measures of the study variables. In other words, variables are operationalized by asking people questions as a way of gathering data.

It is advisable, before constructing questions, to examine questions that have been used by others. The mores of social science in general, and survey research in particular, not only permit but encourage the repeated use of the same questions in questionnaire studies by different researchers. This method eliminates the need for extensive pretesting and provides a comparative set of data. Under most circumstances, no permission from the originator of the questions is necessary, unless copyrighted (13).

Format

The form of interviews and questionnaires may vary in terms of the degree to which they are standardized and structured. In the standardized interview or questionnaire, questions are presented with exactly the same wording and in the same order to all respondents. This technique ensures uniformity in that all respondents are replying to the same thing. When interviews follow a fixed format, that format is referred to as an *interview schedule;* when such personal contact is replaced by a set of written questions, that set of questions is called a *questionnaire.* The use of a standardized instrument appears to be most appropriate when the respondents have similar personal and background characteristics, and when the subject matter allows the respondent to feel comfortable with relatively simple, unequivocal answers. Complex and subtle problems are more difficult but not impossible to objectify into effective questionnaire items so that interviews are more suitable.

Nonstandardized interviews allow a more flexible approach to obtaining information that is not possible with a questionnaire. With a nonstandardized procedure, neither the exact questions nor the order in which they are asked is predetermined. Such interviews take various forms and have been referred to as the focused interview (6), the in-depth interview, the clinical interview, and the nonstandardized interview. These approaches are more appropriate when the respondents are heterogeneous in their background and personal characteristics and when the study deals with sensitive issues. They allow more intensive examination of perceptions, attitudes, and motives than do the more standardized approaches. They do entail greater skill and training on the part of the interviewer. In addition, analysis of the information becomes more difficult and time-consuming, as the responses are not necessarily uniform or comparable.

Interviews and questionnaires may vary also in the degree to which the questions are structured. There are two basic types of question: closed-ended (or fixed alternative) or open-ended. Closed-ended questions are structured in that the respondent must select his answer from a list of alternatives provided on the questionnaire by the interviewer. These alternatives may be a simple "yes" or "no," or they may provide a Likert-type scale, indicating various degrees of agreement: like or dislike, etc. To illustrate, a respondent may be asked

"Do you like your job?"

    Yes ☐

    No ☐

Open-ended questions, however, allow respondents a free response. A respondent provides his own answer to the question, not being limited to a list of stated alternatives. For example, in this case, the respondent might be asked, "What do you like most about your job?" The respondent is provided with a space to write in the answer or is asked to report it verbally to the interviewer. If the answer does not seem sufficient or to the point, the interviewer may probe for additional information by saying, "Could you tell me a little more about that?" or "In what way?" Such probing, of course, cannot be done with a questionnaire, but the same effect may be achieved by asking a series of specific open-ended questions. Closed-ended questions are most appropriate for securing factual information or information on relatively clear-cut issues. Open-ended questions are used when the issue is more complex or when relevant dimensions are not known.

Each type of question has advantages and disadvantages. Closed-ended questions are standardizable, simple to administer, quick, and relatively easy to analyze. They ensure answers that are relevant to the researcher's frame of reference (e.g., time, quantity, degree) of a particular variable. Most of these advantages have disadvantages, however. The respondent is forced to answer in categories that may not include the desired response. The inclusion of a "don't know," "not applicable," or "other (please specify)" answer category helps eliminate this problem.

Wording

The wording of questions must be precise. Seemingly small changes in wording may cause large differences in response. Questions must be:

1. Clear and specific, with language appropriate for the population under study. Technical terms and jargon are not used except with special populations, e.g., physicians.
2. Short. A series of short, simple questions are more readily understood than one long, complex one.
3. Single-dimensional. The use of "double-barreled" questions is avoided. For example, "Do you like to travel on trains or buses?" does not allow the respondent to choose one and not the other.
4. Unambiguous. Words and phrases such as "generally" or "on the whole" are misleading.
5. Nondirective. Leading or biased wording such as "Don't you agree?" may lead the respondent in the direction of a certain answer.
6. Mutually exclusive and exhaustive. For example, in age categories the ranges must not overlap; use "18–25" and "26–33," not "18–25" and "25–33." Also, all possibilities must be considered. For example, when asking about community size the response categories are "under 100,000" and "100,000 or more," not "under 100,000" and "over 100,000."

Other Issues in Instrument Design

Introduction and instructions

Questionnaires and interviews should include introductory comments, clearly written general instructions, and, where indicated, specific instructions.

Overall appearance

The layout of questions is particularly important, both for the respondent in the case of self-administered questionnaires, and for the interviewer who records a respondent's answers. Two issues are accuracy and completeness. Generally, the instrument should be spread out and uncluttered, with a maximum of "white space," despite the concern that a questionnaire or guide appears too long.

Recording answers

A variety of methods are available for recording answers. Boxes, brackets, or parentheses, adequately spaced, are most effective, as illustrated below:

☐ yes	[ ] yes	( ) yes
☐ no	[ ] no	( ) no
☐ not sure	[ ] not sure	( ) not sure

Note that responses are listed vertically, rather than horizontally, again despite the interest in conserving space. A common pitfall is the following response format.

_____yes   _____no   _____not sure

A respondent or interviewer may inadvertently place an *X* or check on the line before *no,* when he really meant his answer to be "yes."

Precoding/direct punch

When laying the format for questionnaires and interviews, the researcher must anticipate the method of data processing to be used. Numbers may be assigned to response categories, as follows.

Yes	[ ] 1
No	[ ] 2
Not sure	[ ] 3

Such numbers should be written as inconspicuously as possible and should be mentioned in an introductory note: "The numbers shown next to answer categories are to assist in processing your answers."

Order of questions

It is always important to carefully consider the order in which questions are asked, as it can affect responses. There are also differences between self-administered questionnaires and interviews. With self-administered questionnaires, it is generally best to begin with questions that are interesting and so encourage cooperation. More sensitive or potentially threatening issues (e.g., age, income) are placed later in the questionnaire. In contrast, the interview guide must enable the interviewer to establish rapport by asking questions that are more easily answered, e.g., demographic data.

Pilot studies and pretests

Before actually beginning to collect data from the survey population, the research instruments are tested. Two types of such testing are pretests and pilot studies. A *pretest* refers to the initial testing of one or more aspects of the study, including the sample design, the study design, and a computer program, as well as the research instruments. *Pilot study* refers to a walk-through of the entire study design, though on a considerably smaller scale.

Processing the Data

Data may begin to be processed as the forms are returned from the field. Questionnaires and interviews are examined for completeness, legibility, comprehensibility, consistency, uniformity, and appropriateness of response. This process serves as a check to determine if interviewers or respondents have understood the instructions, are recording data in sufficient detail, etc. In addition, it helps avoid problems in later stages of processing, particularly during coding. Generally, data processing is concerned with converting the data collected into a form appropriate for analysis. Before data may be analyzed, however, the information must be tabulated. Tabulation may be done by hand or computer. Although manual tabulation is generally less expensive and time-consuming when there are only small or moderate numbers of cases, it becomes increasingly more efficient and economical to use computers as the number of cases increases. The process by which the questionnaire or interview responses are converted for tabulation is called *coding*. Raw data are transformed into symbols, usually numbers.

When planning the research instrument, each question is usually assigned one or more columns. In the case of closed-ended questions, the coding scheme is usually built into the questionnaire or interview. The categories provided to the respondent can be assigned numbers within each column and punched accordingly. The respondent or interviewer merely checks the box corresponding to the appropriate response. For example, a question might appear as follows:

Q. 10. "What is your marital status?"	*Column 5*
Single, never married	[ ] 1
Married	[ ] 2
Widowed, divorced, or separated	[ ] 3

Thus the data are collected and coded at the same time.

Open-ended questions, however, are somewhat more difficult. Often it cannot be predicted how respondents will answer a particular question. Although answers may vary considerably, they tend to fall into patterns or categories. A first step in establishing such response categories is to actually take a sample of questionnaires or interviews to determine the types of response. If there are 100 forms, the researcher may select every tenth one and list verbatim every response that comes up to a particular question. The list is reviewed and categories set up. This process may be illustrated as follows.

A question might be, "What do you like most about your job?" The sample of 10 forms might reveal the following answers: "I like the hours." "The people are friendly." "I like working the night shift." "It's close to my house." "I don't have to be there until 9:30." "I don't travel far." "The work is easy." "I get along well with my co-workers." "I get to use my hands." "The hours are convenient." After reviewing these responses, it is apparent that these categories emerge: likes the people, likes the location, likes the nature of the work, and likes the hours. The next step is to assign each category a number, assuming that a field (or column) had been assigned earlier. The code might look like this:

Q. 13.   "What do you like most about your job?"

Response	*Column 7*
Likes the people	[ ] 1
Likes the location	[ ] 2
Likes the nature of the work	[ ] 3
Likes the hours	[ ] 4
Don't know/no answer	[ ] 8
Not applicable	[ ] 9

As in the construction of fixed-choice questions, codes are constructed so that the items are exclusive and exhaustive. Often a response falls into more than one category. Decisions then must be made, for example, to take the first response or the most extreme response. Usually, however, a sufficient number of columns and punches can be assigned to each question to allow a wide range of codes. Two columns may initially be assigned to a question to allow for multiple responses. In addition, it is often not possible to anticipate all responses that will come up, even if a sample of the forms are reviewed. Typically, coders are instructed to keep a list of "other" responses, and at a later stage, if a pattern emerges, additional categories can be established and coded.

The process described for open-ended questions may be applied on a broader scale to interviews that are in-depth and may be audio-recorded. In this case they are transcribed and codes are developed. Coders, especially if there are many working on a particular job, must be carefully trained to make sure they fully understand the codes (collected in a codebook), and that they are consistent in their own work, as well as with the other coders. It is wise to have all coding that is done early in the process checked for reliability (consistency); later, it is wise to have a sample of the work checked similarly.

Analyzing the Data

Data may be analyzed in two ways: qualitatively or quantitatively. The difference between research that lends itself to one or the other type of analysis has to do generally with the number of units involved and the kind of data collected. If the units under investigation are relatively few in number and data are not easily confined to a close-ended answer, they are analyzed qualitatively. In contrast, if these units amount to a sizable number, they are analyzed quantitatively. Survey research usually involves large numbers of units, typically individuals. Thus questionnaires and interview schedules used to collect the data lend themselves to quantification. However, qualitative and quantitative analyses may be used in combination.

The key goals of the analysis of survey data are description and explanation. Univariate analysis, the examination of a single variable (usually a single questionnaire item) permits the description of the survey population. The basic format for presenting univariate data is the reporting of all individual responses in one of several ways. Assume that we are reporting the ages of the respondents. One procedure is to report all the individual responses separately, e.g., 18, 21, 30, and so on. This method presents the data in the greatest detail, but with large numbers of cases it is cumbersome for the reader. A more manageable presentation, without losing detail, is the frequency distribution.

Age	Frequency
18	3
19	5
20	9
.	.
.	.
.	.
80	2

A more manageable presentation is a frequency distribution of grouped data. This method, however, does not enable the reader to reconstruct the original data, that is, to know how many individuals are a specific age. It would appear as follows:

Age	No.
Under 20	17
20–29	40
.	.
.	.
.	.
80 or over	2

Such presentation of data, either individually or in frequency distributions, is referred to by the term "marginals," i.e., the number of cases falling within each category. Marginals may be presented in *raw numbers,* as above, or as *percentages.*

Another way of presenting data is in the form of a summary response, such as the central tendency. The statistics of central tendency include the mode (or the most frequently reported answer), the arithmetic mean (average), or the median (the middle response). Using the example of age, the most frequently reported age (mode) might be 40, the mean age 42, and the median age 39. The advantage of the measures of central tendency is that data are presented in the most manageable form, a single number. However, much detail is lost from the original data. To eliminate some loss of refinement, the range of response might be presented along with the average response, e.g., an age range of 18 to 80.

Survey research explains as well as describes, examining two or more variables simultaneously to determine the relation between them (bivariate or multivariate analysis). An example of bivariate analysis is the effect of age on a respondent's satisfaction with work.

This type of analysis depends on the logic of *dependent* and *independent variables*. The researcher attempts to explain the dependent variable on the basis of the independent variable. In other words, the independent variable is assumed to determine a dependent variable. There are two ways to decide which is a dependent and which is an independent variable. When there is a clear time order relating to the two variables, the earlier one is always the independent variable. In the above example, the relation between age and satisfaction with work, age is the independent variable. Age may determine if one is satisfied with work. If the two variables occur simultaneously in time, a decision must be made on a logical basis. Note that any given variable might be treated as an independent variable in one part of the analysis and as a dependent variable in another part.

The logic of bivariate and multivariate analysis can best be seen through the use of simple tables, called *contingency tables* or *cross-tabulations*. Much survey research data is presented as tabular analysis. Such tables present the relation between two or more variables in the form of percentage distributions (see Note 8, below).

To illustrate, let us expand the example above, using age as a single variable to construct a hypothetical table relating age and satisfaction with work. Age is the independent variable, satisfaction with work the dependent variable. Table 1 reveals that individuals aged 50 and over are satisfied with their work more often than those under 50, i.e., 65% compared with 45%, respectively (see Note 9).

---

8. Cross-tabulation presents a problem to the analyst. That is, in which direction when setting up a table, should the percent figures be computed—horizontally or vertically? The general rule for solving this problem, according to Hans Zeisel in *Say It With Figures* (Harper & Row, New York, 1968), is: "In a cross-tabulation, whenever one factor can be considered the cause (independent variable) and the other (or others) the effect (dependent variable), then the percents should be computed in the direction of the causal factor, provided the sample is representative in that direction." See Zeisel, pp. 29–36, for clarification of this guide and exceptions to it.

9. For greater detail on the presentation and analysis of data in tabular form, see Zeisel, H.: *Say It With Figures* (Harper & Row, New York, 1957). Tabular analysis is only one approach to presenting and analyzing data. For discussion of other approaches, see, for example, Senter, R. J.: *Analysis of Data: Introductory Statistics for the Behavioral Sciences* (Scott, Foresman, Atlanta, 1969), who discusses statistical analysis; see Babbie (1986) for discussion of regression analysis, path analysis, factor analysis, and smallest space analysis.

TABLE 1. *Age and satisfaction with work*

	Age < 50 (n = 400)	Age 50 and over (n = 400)
Satisfied (%)	45	65
Not satisfied (%)	55	35

Suppose, however, that we were interested in examining the additional influence of health status on satisfaction with work. Thus we are adding an additional independent variable to the above analysis (Table 2).

Table 2 may be presented more efficiently to enable easier analysis. Because the dependent variable, satisfaction with work, is dichotomous, knowing one value permits the reader to construct the other. Thus if we know that 75% of those under 50 who are in good health are satisfied with their work, we also know that 25% are not satisfied. Therefore reporting the percentage who are not satisfied is unnecessary. An alternative presentation of the above data is seen in Table 3.

Table 3 reveals that, regardless of age, those in good health are likely to be satisfied with their work more often than those in poor health. Seventy-five percent of those under age 50 who are in good health, compared with 60% who are in poor health, are satisfied with their work. Among those age 50 and over there is a similar relation. Eighty-five percent of those in good health, compared with 65% of those in poor health, are satisfied with their work. The impact of health on work satisfaction appears to be stronger for those age 50 and older, indicated by differences of 20% for those age 50 and over and 15% for those under age 50. The impact of age on work satisfaction is greater for those in good health, with a difference of 10% for those in good health and 5% for those in poor health. Finally, it appears that health has a greater impact on satisfaction with work than does age. Looking at the average differences, the impact of health is more than twice that of age: 17% compared with 7%.

Whether presenting univariate, bivariate, or multivariate data, there are two essential goals: to provide the reader with the fullest degree of data and to present it in the most manageable form. Often these goals contradict one another, and compromise is required (1).

TABLE 2. *Satisfaction with work by age and health status*

	Age < 50		Age 50 and over	
	Good health (n = 300)	Poor health (n = 100)	Good health (n = 250)	Poor health (n = 150)
Satisfied (%)	75	60	85	65
Not satisfied (%)	25	40	15	35

TABLE 3. *Satisfaction with work by age and health status*

Health status	Satisfied with work (%)	
	Age < 50	Age 50 and over
Good	75 ($n = 300$)	85 ($n = 250$)
Poor	60 ($n = 100$)	65 ($n = 150$)

Thus far we have examined examples of data based on a survey sample. We have looked at the relation between age and satisfaction with work and that between age, satisfaction with work, and health status. These relations have been expressed in terms of percent differences. Whether a percent difference of any size is meaningful depends on the size of the sample base. In general, the larger the base, the more significant is any percent difference. For example, in surveys dealing with samples of 3,000 cases or fewer, differences of 10 percentage points or less are seldom significant. On the other hand, when the samples or populations are unusually large, e.g., the United States labor force, even fractional percentage differences may be significant.

Although the researcher is interested in determining the relation between the variables in a sample of the population studied, it is often desirable to make assertions about the large population from which the sample was selected. That is, the researcher frequently wishes to interpret sample findings as the basis for inferences about the target population. The use of statistics enables one to examine the conditions under which, and the extent to which, it is reasonable to infer relations between two or more variables in the target population. As we already know, the procedure of random sampling makes it possible to generalize from a sample to a specific population. Even with the most effective random sampling procedures, however, there is always a difference between a sample and its population. This difference—which is inherent in the very nature of taking a sample—is called *sampling error*. It is due to chance and does not result from mistake or carelessness on the part of the researcher.

Thus the issue becomes, "In the face of inevitable sampling error, how is it possible to determine the probability that a relation found in a sample might be a product of chance or sampling error?" In other words, "If the research were repeated 100 times (i.e., 100 random samples drawn from the same population), how many times would the relation occur by chance—given no relation in the population?" In the social sciences, if a sample relation could occur by chance, or sampling error, five times or fewer in 100 ($p = 0.05$), it is generally regarded as being statistically significant or representative of a relation in the population. Other levels of significance that are frequently used are 0.01 and 0.001, i.e., that the chances of obtaining the measured association as a result of sampling error are 1 in 100 or 1 in 1,000.

There are numerous tests of significance, each with its own set of assumptions for appropriate usage. Statistical procedures can range from simple, straightforward techniques to highly complex conceptual and computational models (see Note 10, below). Selection of an appropriate statistic and its interpretation are not tasks for the unsophisticated. Even the simplest method, when misapplied, can lead to gross distortions of the results. Rather, it is best to obtain the services of someone who is knowledgeable in the areas of statistics and investigation.

Ethical Issues in Survey Research

Concern with the ethics of survey research has focused on three issues: the right to privacy, informed consent, and confidentiality. Related to the ethical issues in survey research, in general, are some pertaining more specifically to studying an aged population (8). Older populations are more likely to have problems with vision, hearing, and mentation, which may influence the extent to which they are able to participate. In addition, special efforts may be necessary for obtaining informed consent. For example, older populations have been identified as being more fearful. Furthermore, physical or mental problems may affect the degree to which explanations of research participation are understood.

We cannot treat this issue here in the full detail it deserves except to reinforce the fundamental clinical norm that applies to all science: There is never a justification for shortcuts that mislead or for any deliberate avoidance of those steps that are required for the protection of respondents' basic human rights.

SUMMARY

This chapter is intended to provide an overview of the issues involved in planning and executing a social survey, with special reference to elderly populations. We described the stages of the survey process: review of existing information, selection and definition of the survey population, choice of data collection methods, data processing and analysis. Note that the various stages are not necessarily mutually exclusive; that is, they are often carried out simultaneously. The activities of the later stages must be realized early in the planning of a survey. We have sought to make the reader aware of survey research in order to facilitate an understanding of such research conducted by others as reported in the literature, as well as to suggest it as a possibility for one's own research needs. Although we have outlined the fundamental steps, the chapter is not primarily a how-to-do-it guide for conducting a community survey. Rather, it is intended as an overview of the factors

---

10. The reader can find a discussion of these and other statistical tests in any textbook on statistics. See, for example, Blalock, H., Jr.: *Social Statistics* (McGraw-Hill, New York, 1960); or Senter, R. J.: *Analysis of Data: Introductory Statistics for the Behavioral Sciences* (Scott, Foresman, New York, 1969).

involved in such research to assist the reader in determining if it is an appropriate technique for a particular problem.

REFERENCES

1. Babbie, E. R. (1973): *Survey Research Methods.* Wadsworth, Belmont, CA.
2. Durkheim, E. (1951, 1897): *Suicide: A Study in Sociology.* Free Press, Glencoe, IL.
3. Graunt, J. (1939): *National and Political Observations Made Up on the Bills of Mortality,* edited by W. F. Wilcox. Johns Hopkins Press, Baltimore.
4. Jones, J. H. (1981): *Bad Blood: The Tuskegee Syphilis Experiment.* Free Press, New York.
5. Lazarsfeld, P., Berelson, B., and Gaudet, H. (1944): *The People's Choice: How the Voter Makes Up His Mind in a Presidential Campaign.* Duell, Sloan & Pearce, New York.
6. Merton, R. K., and Kendall, P. L. (1955): The focused interview. In: *The Language of Social Research,* edited by P. F. Lazarsfeld and M. Rosenberg. Free Press, New York.
7. Murphy, M. J. (1970): The utilization of community resources. In: *Community Organization: Planning and Resources and the Older Poor,* edited by S. K. Match. National Council of the Aging for the Office of Economic Opportunity, Washington, DC.
8. National Institute on Aging (1982): *Toward an Independent Old Age: A National Plan for Research on Aging.* Report of the National Research on Aging Planning Panel. NIH Publ. 82–2453. National Institutes of Health, Bethesda.
9. Random House (1975): *The Random House College Dictionary,* revised edition. Random House, New York.
10. Selltiz, C., Wrightsman, L. S., and Cook, S. W. (1967): *Research Methods in Social Relations,* revised edition. Holt, Rinehart & Winston, New York.
11. Selvin, H. C. (1968): Survey analysis. In: *Encyclopedia of Social Sciences,* edited by D. Sills. Macmillan, New York.
12. Stouffer, S. A., Guttman, L., Suchman, E. A., Lazarsfeld, P. F., Star, S. A., and Clausen, J. A. (1950): *Studies in Social Psychology in World War II,* Vol. 4. Princeton University Press, Princeton, NJ.
13. Sudman, S., and Bradburn, N. (1982): *Asking Questions: A Practical Guide to Questionnaire Design.* Jossey-Bass, San Francisco.

SELECTED READING

Babbie, E. R. (1973): *Survey Research Methods.* Wadsworth, Belmont, CA.

Babbie, E. R. (1986): *The Practice of Social Research.* Wadsworth, California.

Berg, R. C., editor (1973): *Health Status Indexes.* Hospital Research and Educational Trust, Chicago.

Cole, S., and Jonathan, C. G. (1972): *Sociological Method.* Markham, Chicago.

Fenalson, A. (1962): *Essentials in Interviewing,* revised edition. Harper & Row, New York.

Ferman, G. S., and Levin, J. (1975): *Social Science Research: A Handbook for Students.* Wiley, New York.

Kornhauser, A., and Sheatsley, P. B. (1967): Questionnaire construction and interview procedure. In: *Research Methods in Social Relations,* revised edition, edited by C. Selltiz, L. S. Wrightsman, and S. W. Cook, appendix C. Holt, Rinehart & Winston, New York.

Miller, D. C. (1983): *The Handbook of Research Design and Social Measurement.* Longman, White Plains, NY.

National Opinion Research Center (NORC) (Annual): *The NORC General Social Survey.* University of Chicago, Chicago.

Reeder, L. G., Ramacher, L. G., and Gorelnik, S. (1976): *Handbook of Scales and Indices of Health Behavior.* Goodyear, Pacific Palisades, CA.

Richardson, S. A., Dohrenwend, B. S., and Klein, D. (1965): *Interviewing: Its Forms and Functions.* Basic Books, New York.

Sudman, S., and Bradburn, N. (1982): *Asking Questions: A Practical Guide to Questionnaire Design.* Jossey-Bass, San Francisco.

Surveys, Polls, Census, and Forecast Directory: A Guide to Sources of Studies in the Areas of Business, Social Science, Education, Science and Technology (1982): Gale Research Company, Detroit, MI. Issue 1, October; Issue 2, December.

U.S. Department of Health and Human Services (1979): *Basic Data from Wave I of the National Survey of Personal Health Practices and Consequences.* Series 15, No. 1, HHS, Bethesda.

Human Aging Research: Concepts and Techniques,
edited by B. Kent and R. N. Butler.
Raven Press, Ltd., New York © 1988.

Clinical Trials

Thomas C. Chalmers

Harvard School of Public Health, Boston, Massachusetts 02115

Lives there a geriatrician or practitioner of adult medicine who would not agree that there is room for improvement in the methods by which we treat aging patients? So many areas of the body complain. Failure of the heart or lungs is not dissimilar from the same diseases in young people, and in general the problems are manageable in the same way. The answers lie in the results of randomized control trials (RCTs).

It is important to emphasize early in this chapter that many of the best RCTs have survival as their endpoint of primary interest, and clearly the geriatrician should be more interested in studies with the quality of life as the major endpoint. Relief must be directed toward relief of suffering rather than its prolongation. Like the drunk searching under the streetlight for his car keys when he lost them across the street in the dark, clinical investigators tend to rely on survival rather than quality of life because determination of the endpoint is much easier.

It is paradoxical that most of the RCTs in the field of heart disease, as in most other fields, have an age cutoff of 65 or 70, occasionally 80, and therefore it is uncertain if the results apply to the truly geriatric patient. The reason for this age cutoff is understandable: Those studying survival would like the frequency of death from causes other than the disease under study to be minimal; and those studying symptoms would like the endpoint not to be confused by multiple system complaints, as might be encountered in the aging patient. The result is that application of the results of many clinical trials to the aged patient must be done with caution because of the many differences in pharmacologic handling of agents and response to various factors. For example, there is ample evidence that the liver does not handle drugs and other agents requiring metabolism with the same alacrity as in younger people (7; see Popper, *this volume*).

It is ironic that diseases which occur most commonly and are most troublesome in the aged are least studied in that group for reasons of convenience; there is thus much room for RCTs specifically directed at the aging patient. Degenerative diseases of the bones, joints, and skin may be specific for older patients and require randomized control trials to determine the best therapy. The gastrointestinal tract has specific malfunctions of old age that are in general badly managed if discomfort of the patient is a criterion; randomized control trials are required to learn how best to improve therapy. Constipation and diarrhea are common at all ages; they are thoroughly trivial disorders in the young but can cause extremely distressing symptoms in older persons. They also seem to be more frequent in the aged. Urinary tract symptoms—obstruction, infection, incontinence—are troublesome and can be alleviated if the relative advantages of one treatment over another are better understood.

There seems to be no shortage of disorders, serious or trivial but annoying, which in therapy could be improved if physicians knew the comparative benefits of various available and yet to be discovered maneuvers. Side effects of new and old therapies can be more serious in the aged, and the benefit/risk ratio therefore requires more accurate data than one usually obtains from the observational practice of medicine. It is time physicians stop trying various methods of therapy on a trial-and-error basis and begin to think in terms of gathering data on relative efficacy and toxicity. It is a more ethical way to practice medicine.

RANDOMIZED CONTROL TRIALS

Given the tremendous need for RCTs of new and old therapies, there are three types in which the practicing physician can participate.

Large-Scale Cooperative Trial

The large-scale cooperative trial is necessary when the differences anticipated from a specific therapy are small and the variability in response large, such that large numbers of patients are necessary to obtain the useful positive or negative answer. These attempts require cooperative studies of many institutions and are best organized under the aegis of government or specific organizations such as pharmaceutical houses that have the funds to see that the studies are done properly. Large-scale cooperative studies are the least fun for the practicing physician because, although protocols must be adhered to no more rigidly than in a smaller study, the results of the efforts are slower to come by, and there is less individual participation in the construction of the protocol and decisions about indicated modifications as the study goes on. However, for those disorders that do have serious endpoints that one would like to evaluate properly, the cooperative trial may be the only way to go. The special attributes of cooperative trials are described elsewhere (2,4). It is likely that large-scale cooperative trials are less applicable to the aged patient because they are more often concerned with small reductions in the death rate, and studies oriented toward prolonging life, as indicated above, are less important in the geriatric patient.

One aspect of the large-scale cooperative trial needs to be emphasized. As with all trials, it is better to control bias related to admission and withdrawal of patients by keeping the ongoing results of the trial secret from the participating physicians and patients. In the case of cooperative trials it is easiest done by having a data-monitoring committee consisting of physicians with expertise in the area of study, epidemiologists or biostatisticians (or both), and a lay representative. The committee receives the data from the coordinating center and after examining it makes recommendations about modifications of the protocol or when the study should be stopped. In the really large studies, the data monitoring committee reports to policy advisory boards, which are directly responsible to the sponsors of the study as well as to the participating physicians and patients.

Intermediate Size Trial

The second type of RCT is the intermediate size trial that can be carried out in one or two local institutions. Here the need is not so great for large numbers, and the endpoints are often symptomatic ones in which larger differences between experimental and control groups can be expected. In the case of trials carried out in a few local institutions, the data monitoring committee may be small, occasionally just one person, but it is still important that the physicians entering and caring for the patients not know the details of the ongoing results, recognizing that it is less easy to keep them blinded when they are taking care of all the patients locally.

In the intermediate size study carried out at a single institution, it is just as important as in the cooperative trial to have a biostatistics office involved in the study. Randomization must be blinded (1), which is best accomplished by having the clinician telephone an office for a treatment assignment or employ identical medicines prepared in random order beforehand by the pharmacy. Double blinding of therapies is especially important when the physician knows the patient well, as in the uni-institutional study. When a decision must be made about whether to let a patient withdraw from the study it is important to have a second expert involved who is not biased with regard to the care of the patient or (because minor breaks do sometimes occur in the blinding) is not knowledgeable about which treatment group the patient belongs in.

Double Blinding

A word about double blinding is in order here. Sometimes randomized control trials are not performed because it is impossible to double blind them. Obviously it is better to have an answer that is biased by knowledge of which treatment the patient receives than to have no answer at all. There are ways in which the blinding can be partially performed by asking a neutral and blinded physician or other observer to observe or quiz the patient in a structured attempt to draw conclusions without the bias that would come from knowing which treatment the patient is receiving. This person would also be useful for talking with the patient about withdrawal before an endpoint has been achieved. Finally, data can be blinded before being shown to an objective observer for interpretation.

Soft Versus Hard Endpoints

There is an aspect of randomized control trials in the aged person that deserves some elaboration: the frequent need to employ what are called soft, or symptomatic, endpoints. Does a medication simply lessen or eliminate a specific symptom, or does it also make the patient feel generally better? Does it improve performance? Does it, in essence, improve the quality of life? This area of RCTs has been neglected because of the attraction of specific "hard" endpoints such as death or avoidance of surgery. Increasing attention must be paid to "soft" endpoints as the need for developing better symptomatic therapy for the aged becomes more and more apparent. A book has been written on the subject that is oriented toward cardiovascular disease (6), but many of the principles are applicable generally. The devising of relatively reproducible measures of such soft endpoints is a challenging research project in itself for geriatricians.

The physician developing forms to be filled out in a trial must spend time quizzing patients about their complaints and carry out dry runs of the reproducibility of the endpoint. It is important to appreciate that observer variability is a strong determinant of decisions about outcome, and that whenever observer variability is large in percentage terms there is an increasing opportunity for observer bias to distort results. In this case blinding the observer for the determination of an endpoint has two purposes: (a) it measures observer variability, which often cannot be reduced or eliminated but can be measured accurately by having two or three observers record the same observations; and (b) it reduces observer bias.

Another aspect of soft endpoints that require some discussion is the tendency to employ multiple observations in a search for a statistically significant therapeutic effect. Here it must be remembered that, by the rules of statistical error, if 20 observations are made on the average there is one that is significant at the 5% level. This factor must be taken into account when determining the alpha level at which one declares a study to be positive.

Of equal importance in determining the alpha level is the frequency with which the ongoing data are observed either by the data monitoring committee or the statistical center. If the possibility exists that a study will be called off when a significant difference between two groups has been detected, one cannot operate at the usual 5% level because under those circumstances type 1 error will occur more often than 1 in 20 times. There are various formulas for handling the problem; sequential design is one. Determination of the exact level of alpha can best be left to the biostatistical collaborator.

Beta, or the type two error, also has to be well understood by the clinician participating in randomized control trials among the aged as well as all age groups.

Far too often clinical investigators conclude that no difference exists between two treatments because no difference was demonstrated with the patients studied; they do not consider the possibility that a difference is missed by a given study because there are too few patients in the study (3). Beta, the inverse of power, should be calculated before all studies; to make this calculation one needs to know the rate at which the endpoint can be expected to occur among the control or standard therapy patients, as well as the change in that rate that is of clinical significance and worth discovering. Some textbooks and articles state that if this number is not achievable the study should not be undertaken, but the author believes this attitude to be wrong because the science of meta-analysis is developing to a stage where multiple small studies, if well done, can be combined to give the same answer as a large multi-institutional cooperative study.

Single-Patient Study

The third kind of randomized control trial in which geriatricians and primary care physicians should indulge much more often is the trial that has only one patient. Such trials may be replicated in a number of patients. This type of study is usually of a crossover design; in the past it has been called a diagnosis by therapy trial.

Whenever a patient has a symptom complex for which no known specific cure exists, it is worthwhile trying symptomatic or possibly specific therapy to determine if the patient benefits. However, many patients respond to suggestive therapy, and many diseases spontaneously remit at the time a new therapy is being evaluated, so both patient and physician may be misled by a response. For example, the last ointment put on poison ivy lesions is always considered the one that works. Continuing a potentially toxic drug that is not needed at all can be avoided by a randomized control trial. Physicians have been neglectful in not recognizing this phenomenon and in not designing therapeutic trials in individual patients so they can learn from that patient if the therapy is indicated in future recurrences or in the case of a continuing disease. No institutional review board need be involved when the trial is designed solely for the benefit of the individual patient unless said boards review all of medical practice.

This kind of research is a classic example of the application of the scientific method to the compassionate practice of medicine. The patient volunteering for such a regimen has everything to gain from proper interpretation of the efficacy of the therapy. Physicians must realize that they are undertaking a research project every time they prescribe a medicine for a patient, and that many times it is important to be able to draw proper conclusions from the response of the patient.

It is not easy, however, to practice medicine in the proper way. Placebos for common drugs are extremely difficult to come by, and it takes an extra effort to find someone who can design a double-blind trial such that the practicing physician and the patient can properly conduct the experiment. Many people are not interested in spending the time and effort, even though a number of instances can be demonstrated in which it is well worth it (5).

When placebos are not available, it is often possible to detect an effect in a blinded manner by having the patient meticulously record symptoms in such a way that the data can be presented to the observer who does not know when the medication was taken. For instance, in an older patient with adult-onset diabetes and moderate diarrhea, the question may arise as to whether the diarrhea is due to autonomic nervous involvement in the diabetic state or to acquisition of an infectious agent such as *giardia*. Therapy with metronidazole (Flagyl) is thoroughly specific for the parasitic infection and a mildly effective treatment for bacterial overgrowth. It also causes peripheral neuritis, however, which may already be bothersome to the diabetic patient. Therefore it is extremely important to determine if the drug is having a specific or a nonspecific antibacterial effect on a disease that may fluctuate in severity spontaneously, as well as to determine if the side effects are worsening an already annoying tingling in the hands and feet. Information of great use to the physician can be obtained by having the patient meticulously describe, in a well-designed chart, the frequency and consistency of bowel movements and the degree of tingling of hands and feet in such a way that the dates of administration of the medication can be obscured with differential photocopying. A decision can then be made, looking at the data, about whether the therapy is effective, toxic, or both. Obviously in this case the patient is biased throughout, but by being less informed than the physician the bias is not as important as that of the observing physician. The patient's bias can be controlled by making the effort to obtain a suitable placebo, although it is not easy to find a placebo for a drug long on the market.

The general purpose of this part of the discussion of RCTs in older people is to emphasize that they can be done in the ordinary practice of medicine by the untrained physician without much extra effort, and the payoff can be enormous. All one must do is attempt to blind medications when possible or to blind observation when not possible, and then to randomize the order in which medications are given or the time at which they are started and stopped. Such decisions are often a compromise between the usual therapeutic regimen and the observation time necessary to make critical decisions.

SUMMARY

Randomized control trials in the aged are unique because the endpoints of interest are "soft" and concerned with improving the quality of life rather than prolonging it. Much of the data in RCTs carried out so far are not applicable to aged people because they have been excluded from many trials by reason of their age. Much work remains to be done if geriatric patients are to be cared for in a rational manner.

REFERENCES

1. Chalmers, T. C., Celano, P., Sacks, H. S., and Smith, H., Jr. (1983): Bias in treatment assignment in controlled clinical trials. *N. Engl. J. Med.,* 309:1358–1361.
2. Friedman, L., Furberg, C. D., and DeMets, D. L. (1981): *Fundamentals of Clinical Trials,* pp. 211–222. John Wright, Boston.
3. Freiman, J. A., Chalmers, T. C., Smith, H., Jr., and Kuebler, R. R. (1978): The importance of beta, the type II error and sample size in the design and interpretation of the randomized control trial: survey of 71 "negative" trials. *N. Engl. J. Med.,* 299:690–694.
4. Meinert, C. L. (1986): *Clinical Trials. Design, Conduct and Analysis.* Oxford University Press, New York.
5. Taylor, D. W., and McLeod, R. S. (1985): Single-subject designs. *Controlled Clin. Trials,* 6:225.
6. Wenger, N. K., Mattson, M. E., Furberg, C. D., and Elinson, J. (1985): *Assessment of Quality of Life in Clinical Trials of Cardiovascular Therapies.* Le Jacq, New York.
7. Zamcheck, N., Chalmers, T. C., White, F. W., and Davidson, C. S. (1950): The Bromsulphalein test in the early diagnosis of liver disease in gross upper gastrointestinal hemorrhage. *Gastroenterology,* 14:343–361.

Human Aging Research: Concepts and Techniques,
edited by B. Kent and R. N. Butler.
Raven Press, Ltd., New York © 1988.

Ethics as an Enabler of Human Aging Research

Christine K. Cassel

The University of Chicago, Pritzker School of Medicine, Department of Medicine, Section of General Internal Medicine, Chicago, Illinois 60637

Using human subjects in biomedical experimentation is one of the major issues responsible for the birth of the field of bioethics. It starkly presents the ethical confrontation of means and ends. The principle attributed to Immanuel Kant requires that humans are valued only for themselves and never as objects to be manipulated for some larger goal, however laudable that goal may be (6). It challenges our notions of almost all of our relationships with other humans to consider that we use them to further our own knowledge. Yet progress in medical science and social science has been held to be important in improving the quality of life of our society, and therefore we want research to go forward. Such progress is a humanitarian and positive value. Thus we must walk a thin line between using people simply as means to an end and totally giving up our progress in research.

Rather than neglecting important research because of the ethical risks it entails, a more positive and productive alternative is suggested, i.e., researchers with greater competence in ethics. If investigators understand enough of the basic content of bioethics, better and more ethical research can be accomplished. The structures of informed consent and the process of institutional review would be better understood, and studies would be designed with more attention to these more formal issues. Investigators who are sensitive to ethical questions can design better studies and develop more creative approaches to protection of human subjects and promotion of the autonomy of the subjects. A basic part of this education is the recent history of biomedical research.

Professional and public attention was drawn forcefully to the ethical problems of human experimentation during the 1960s by the disclosure of unethical research within the medical community (1,8). The problems that were raised were so complex and so urgently in need of resolution that a federal commission was appointed to deal with them. It was the National Commission for the Protection of Human Subjects of Biomedical and Behavioral Research, which held meetings from 1974 through 1978. They examined many of the most problematic aspects of research with human subjects and came up with recommendations, of which many were accepted and made into regulations by the Department of Health, Education, and Welfare (later Health and Human Services). The one with which most people are probably familiar is the establishment of an institutional review board, or human subjects committee, at any institution that requires and receives federal funds for research. The purpose of this committee is to review the ethical soundness of the research endeavor and to affirm that the research going on in that institution is indeed done ethically.

The Commission published the Belmont Report, which reviewed the basic principles that institutional review boards should consider in their work (12). This report has become widely referred to as the basic statement of ethical research. In it the Commission described three basic principles that must be considered: (a) beneficence, (b) respect for persons, and (c) justice. If we review these principles, it becomes clear that most of the major questions that come up in research with the elderly can fit in one or more of these categories.

When the National Commission issued its report in 1978, they did not specifically consider the elderly as a separate group. They did, however, publish a report on research with those institutionalized as mentally infirm in which they included nursing home patients. The ethics of research indeed should not be different with normal elderly persons who are competent adults and who do not need special protection. The issue of institutionalization is a complicated one, however, affecting freedom and autonomy, even for those who are not mentally infirm. Because of the high prevalence of mental impairment in the institutionalized elderly, and because they are so vulnerable to exploitation, special cautions were urged that affected all elderly people who were institutionalized. The National Commission recommended much stricter guidelines for the participation of these groups—basically that they should participate only in experimentation of low risk that had a high probability of helping them directly.

BENEFICENCE

Every health care professional has a responsibility to his or her patient: to act on behalf of that patient in what he or she believes to be the patient's best interest and to protect the patient from harm. This principle of "beneficence" is one of the most basic principles to the health care professions. In medicine it stems from the early hippocratic writings. In those early writings, little or nothing was ever said about informed consent or the autonomy of patients. The emphasis was rather on doing what the physician thought was best for the patient: to do good, to do no harm.

This principle, in obvious ways, raises many questions when we conduct research with subjects of any age. First, if the research is "nontherapeutic," the case for doing no harm strongly takes precedence. For example, if one simply wanted to conduct a descriptive study of certain laboratory values in normal elderly people, they would be asked to submit to venipuncture for a study that did not stand to benefit them directly. Venipuncture may not be such an invasive procedure in our view, but many elderly people see it that way (10). Still, we probably would believe that it would not hurt them physically to participate in this project. The conduct of research, however, must always take into account the psychological and social effects as well. In a purely optional, "nontherapeutic" study, it is much more difficult to justify even the smallest amount of risk or discomfort. The only potential benefits are intangible ones, such as participation in a social good, altruistic feelings derived from a contribution to society, increasing medical knowledge that might help others, etc. These benefits are seen as purely optional; i.e., we cannot ask people to do it because we know it is good for them. Altruistic feelings may be good for some and not for others. Thus we cannot justify any participation in nontherapeutic research except that of minimal risk—and that with the most complete and explicit consent.

If, however, the research is investigating a new treatment for a disease the patient has, it becomes somewhat easier to justify interventions in the name of the combined benefits of therapy and research. To evaluate beneficence essentially means the risk/benefit assessment. If the patient has a serious disease the experimental treatment has a good chance of helping, perhaps it is worth the risk of participating in the project, especially if the proposed treatment does not have serious detrimental side effects.

Of course, the risks and benefits of any given experimental therapy are subject to personal value judgments. Thus what the physician may believe to be a reasonable risk may be viewed differently by a lay person, particularly an elderly lay person, who might not hold it to be a reasonable risk. The idea of beneficence in many ways calls up the image of paternalism, an attitude that has become discredited among many ethicists and health care providers, particularly those dealing with elderly people, where rights and respect may be as important values as any others. It has been thought that we have been too paternalistic and protective of elderly people, and we need to change our attitude to one of promoting greater autonomy for them. This area is one that needs more research.

When selecting a value preference for "autonomy" or for "paternalism" in dealings with persons of advanced age, we select an ideological stance that does not necessarily reflect the diversity of that group and their unique individuality. For some, the security of a protective environment and protective caregivers may be the greatest good, whereas for others independence is the highest value, even at significant personal risk. Does a choice by an older person to accept greater risks (11) mean that we should honor that choice, even in research situations where the person does not stand to gain personally? This area is the most difficult aspect of the risk/benefit assessment, and it is not an unusual situation. Thus the specific challenge related to beneficence in geriatric and gerontologic research is that of avoiding undue paternalism, either with too much or too little protection. In "doing good" lies significant risk of impairing the independence of the subject. Thus the "do no harm" injunction must be seen here as referring not only to physical harm but to interpersonal and intergenerational harm. To refrain from participation in research is no guarantee of no harm done.

One of the most difficult jobs of the investigator and the institutional review board is the risk/benefit assessment. It must take into account the scientific merit of the study being done because, if valid new knowledge does not emerge from the study, subjecting patients to any risk at all is not ethical. Any use of a human for research entails the "objectification" of that person, and it can be justified only in a study where some value to self or others is likely to be gained.

To take the injunction "do no harm" seriously in an institutional long-term care setting still means that we must be careful not to devalue the people who are the objects of the research. The statutory and institutional restrictions are meant to prevent this devaluing. However, we may devalue persons also by excluding them from research. One of the problems with the general restrictions on research with institutionalized populations is that we disqualify people from participation in the human enterprise of altruism. For many people, participating in a research project can give meaning to life. A sense of purpose could certainly benefit many people who are in nursing homes. The limitations of life in an institutional setting added to the limitations of advanced age and chronic disability may in fact obscure the meaning of life and lead to depression and a feeling of isolation. The philosopher Hawerwas maintained that the challenge of suffering that cannot be cured is to invest it with meaning, to include the victim in a meaningful human context (5). To participate in a research project that might bring understanding of the cause of disability and suffering in future generations could be a great benefit to the person.

Some philosophers (7) extend the "privilege" of participating in research to being a "duty." They believe that because elderly people, particularly those with chronic illness, are the recipients of the progress of medical science due to past generations, they owe society their participation to help further that medical science for future generations. It seems, however, that the burden of the argument is on those who insist that the elderly participate in research because, in fact, their great vulnerability reinforces our duty to support them to be as autonomous as possible.

RESPECT FOR PERSONS

Respect for persons is a principle supporting the notion that individuals should be treated as autonomous agents and, as a corollary, that persons with diminished autonomy are entitled to special protections. This principle mirrors the premise of self-determination and individualism on which the United States Constitution and most of our legal traditions are based. The application of respect for persons in the conduct of research comes primarily in the procedures involved with informed consent. The need for standards of informed consent culminated in the Code of Helsinki (4) in response to the atrocities perpetrated by Nazi physicians. The Code established that the fundamental principle of ethical experimentation is that the subject be fully informed and that he consent freely to participation. The criteria for valid informed consent, derived from codes, the law, and the principle of respect for persons, are that (a) full information be given, (b) the subject be competent to consent, and (c) the subject be free and not coerced into consenting.

Full information seems to be the most straightforward of these criteria, but it is remarkable how many people feel uncomfortable relaying the full risks of any intervention to elderly people. One of the problems with communication associated particularly with frail elderly people, who may be hard of hearing or who have visual impairment, is especially highlighted in the consent interview for participation in research.

The question of competence is of course a major question, particularly when doing research with patients who have cognitive impairment. Alzheimer's disease and the other dementing diseases of old age are a great scourge, and research is therefore badly needed to ameliorate the suffering of future patients. It is difficult, however, to justify the intrusiveness of any research procedure with a person who cannot understand enough to give full consent. The National Institute on Aging and the National Institute of Mental Health have been working in these areas for several years (9). They continue to struggle with achieving the optimal balance between protection of individuals' rights and respect for their independent decisions.

Freedom and noncoercion are issues of special importance in the long-term care setting. In their examination of the research that had been done with prisoners, the National Commission decided that the institutionalized status of those persons meant that their consent could never be truly free and, in particular, could be unduly swayed by small amounts of money, cigarettes, or other inducements. Therefore the main thing that distinguished institutionalized populations from other people, in their minds, is that they are not free; this condition is something that prisoners have in common with residents of nursing homes. Obviously, people in nursing homes are not restrained by law, but the fact of their institutionalization creates a situation whereby their consent may be influenced by institutional pressures or peer pressures (2).

With community-dwelling elderly people, the issue of freedom again hinges primarily on the problem of conflict of interest. As many scholars have pointed out, the trust of patient in physician is often such as to preclude truly free consent in these situations. In addition to the patient's desire to please the physician, we also find that the physician's attitude toward the research project strongly influences a patient's decision. Although this situation may be a geriatric stereotype, it is, in this generation, common that elderly people are extremely trusting of and dependent on health care providers. In general, they may turn informed consent decisions about clinical matters back to the nurse, physician, or investigator. "I don't know, doctor, what do you think I should do?" This pattern, however, may be a cohort effect that will change as people who are familiar with the concepts of patients' rights and personal autonomy in health care grow into old age.

An area where beneficence and respect for persons come into play is in the question of conflict of interest. The inherent conflict of interest between the roles of physician or caregiver and investigator has been described in depth by philosophers, social scientists, and clinical researchers. It is that attitude of a caregiver, acting on behalf of his or her patient, with only the particular patient's well-being in mind, that may not be sustained by a physician or caregiver whose goals include completion of a successful research project. For example, the patient may feel pressured to consent, however subconsciously, by a fear of "disappointing" the caregiver and perhaps spoiling the relationship. The investigator may be influenced to make decisions in the interest of the research project, rather than the interest of the patient. For these reasons, some writers recommend that the two functions of primary care and research never be joined in the same person, thereby avoiding the risk of conflict of interest.

Avoiding this situation requires a third party, one who either obtained the consent or conducted the research. The National Institutes of Health (NIH) has examined the role of a "group consent auditor" for this purpose (3). This group consists of three persons who are not directly involved with the care of the patient or the research and who can thus objectively monitor the consent process. This strategy has been criticized as unduly cumbersome and expensive. (Someone must pay the consent auditors. NIH? The home institution?) In geriatrics it can be especially problematic, as many regard the intrusion of a "stranger" in the form of a researcher as more potentially damaging to the world view of the patient.

Another approach is to depend on the procedural safeguards of the institutional review board. An emphasis on teaching ethics to clinical researchers in order to ensure the moral integrity of the research enterprise is yet another consideration.

JUSTICE

The original and basic issues of justice considered by the National Commission were related to the fair distribution of the burdens of being a research subject. The principle of justice suggests that there ought to be an equitable distribution of these burdens. To use elderly persons in a research project that is studying some aspect of aging is good study design. To use nursing home residents to study something related in general to aging, or even unrelated to aging, is not necessary and therefore not equitable. In the latter case the nursing home is chosen as a site simply because it is more convenient for the investigator to find all the subjects in one place, and the burden of being a research subject is unfairly placed with people who have too many burdens in life already, e.g., chronic illness, disability, and isolation. Persons in institutions also are less likely to have family and friends who can function as advocates in the consent process.

More consideration also is needed not only in regard to the burdens but also to the benefits of participation in good research. Potential benefits include socialization, human interaction, and an enhanced sense of meaningful participation in the human community. As mentioned, the burdens of overly zealous protection must be considered. The concern to protect this vulnerable population may lead to procedures and attitudes that are infantilizing and unduly paternalistic, and that themselves limit the autonomy and freedom of the subjects. Here too is a ripe area for research.

Equity raises other questions too. Fairness must be considered in relation to present versus future benefit. Justification for some research can be made on the basis of a high probability of great benefit to future sufferers of the disorder. Previously, it was considered wrong to place concern for future persons in the ethical equation for risk and benefit. However, if there is only minimal risk involved, perhaps constraint should be loosened to include the sense of people contributing to the human community, both present and future. Another aspect of the tension between benefit to present and future generations appears in the choices of research to support. Simply stated, research about the clinical treatment of the disorders or disabilities of old age is more likely to help more people sooner. Research into systems of health care delivery and the provision of long-term care services likewise, if successful, will reveal ways to improve the quality of care for persons who need it right now. On the other hand, basic research into the cellular mechanisms of aging and the pathogenesis of diseases that afflict the elderly may provide a much greater benefit to more people if prevention or eradication of disability can be attained. That benefit, however, would go to future persons, not to those who are currently afflicted. This question is a straightforward utilitarian one that is difficult, partly because we are gambling with outcomes that cannot be definitively predicted. The choice between present and future benefit will always present a challenge to humanism and to ethical analysis.

In the specific area of long-term care, inequities of great magnitude are long-standing. The efforts of the ''teaching nursing home'' and the broad field of gerontologic research and education are responses to needs that are quite clear. This statement raises the question of whether (a) the resources of the teaching nursing home should be allocated to only the highest quality nursing homes, where residents are more likely to be treated with respect and consent is more likely to be fully valid for that reason, or (b) the resources should be applied to institutions that need upgrading, where residents are likely to benefit to a much greater degree from the improved quality of care and level of tension. We must ask if research studies from the middle-range institutions, which we believe to be more typical, would provide more useful knowledge overall because they apply to the more common situation. Serious concern for justice requires us to take the resources of the teaching nursing home as social goods and to carefully weigh these different and sometimes competing benefits when we decide how to allocate research funds.

ETHICS RESEARCH: ENABLING A RESOLUTION

There are questions about research that themselves are susceptible to further research. Many of the ethical dilemmas we face would be less difficult if we had better data. Advanced methodologies in social science and psychology can help to design studies about value choices. Combined with philosophical expertise in ethics that elucidates which values to study and the meaning of the data that results, these methods can ascertain the practical correlates of values such as autonomy and justice. In addition, attitudes about participation in research can be investigated and described to get a better idea of the risks and benefits. While biomedical, social, or psychological research is being done, it is possible through observational and interactional techniques to elicit and anticipate the ethical problems that arise and develop more realistic structures for dealing with them. This situation is an agenda for "ethics research." The following is a list of some of the important research areas that need to be addressed in order to further understand ethical research in geriatrics.

1. What are the attitudes of elderly people about participation in research? Are there differences between independent persons and those in nursing homes?
2. What is the efficacy of the consent process? How can it be improved?
3. What are the structures that effectively support free and informed consent in geriatrics? Should there be a more definitive process that occurs over time?
4. What is the appropriate interpretation of risk in this population?
5. What institutional structure can help with fostering ethical research? Do ethics committees work?
6. Are there cultural or religious views of research that can aid in the development of general guidelines for certain groups of people or certain kinds of institutions?

These and other questions like them need to be answered to enable progress in ethical research in geriatrics. Open discussion of the issues and study of them will help foster a more sophisticated understanding of the ethical issues by investigators and institutional review boards. In the final analysis, elderly persons of our society will benefit.

ACKNOWLEDGMENT

Dr. Cassel is a Henry J. Kaiser Family Foundation Faculty Scholar in General Internal Medicine.

REFERENCES

1. Beecher, H. K. (1966): Ethics and clinical research. *N. Engl. J. Med.*, 274:1354–1360.
2. Cassel, C. K. (1985): Research in nursing homes: ethical issues. *J. Am. Geriatr. Soc.*, 33:795–799.
3. Cassel, C. K., Dubler, N. N., Tablowski, P., and Zimmer, A. W. (1987): Informed consent in geriatric research. *J. Am. Geriatr. Soc.* 35:542–544.
4. Declaration of Helsinki (1977): In: *Ethics in Medicine,* edited by S. J. Reiser, A. J. Dyck, and W. J. Curran, pp. 328–329. MIT Press, Boston.
5. Hawerwas, S. (1979): Reflections on suffering, death and medicine. *Ethics Sci. Med.,* 6:229–237.
6. Kant, I. (1959): *The Foundations of a Metaphysics of Morals.* Bobbs-Merrill, Indianapolis.
7. Kaplan, A. (1984): Is there a duty to serve as a subject in biomedical research? *IRB: A Review of Human Subject Research,* 6:1–5.

8. Katz, J. (1973): *Experimentation with Human Beings.* Russell Sage Foundation, New York.
9. Melnick, V., and Dubler, N., editors (1985): *Alzheimer's Dementia.* Humana Press, Clifton, NJ.
10. Ratzan, R. (1980): Being old makes you different. *Hastings Cent. Rep.,* 10(5):32–80.
11. Stanley, B., Guido, J., Stanley, M., and Shortell, D. (1984): The elderly patient and informed consent. *JAMA,* 252:1302–1306.
12. *The Belmont Report* (1979): FR document 79–12065. National Commission for the Protection of Human Subjects of Biomedical and Behavioral Research, Washington, DC.

Human Aging Research: Concepts and Techniques,
edited by B. Kent and R. N. Butler.
Raven Press, Ltd., New York © 1988.

Research in the Nursing Home: Obstacles and Opportunities

Leslie S. Libow and Richard R. Neufeld

*The Jewish Home and Hospital for Aged, Mount Sinai School of Medicine,
New York, NY 10025*

There is no geriatric medicine without the nursing home (12). Nursing beds already outnumber acute hospital beds in the United States, and the ratio is increasing as hospital beds are eliminated. Among the fastest-growing segment of our population, those over 85 years of age, 20 to 25% require nursing home care (3,13). Thus research in geriatric medicine must include hypotheses and issues relevant to the nursing home, and it will increasingly involve the nursing home as the most practical and fruitful site for such research.

As recognized by Rowe, there are pitfalls to avoid when initiating research in the nursing home setting (19). Unique challenges are presented by the historically nonmedical origin and orientation of the nursing home, economic and administrative realities, and the special social and medical circumstances of the frail elderly. The rewards for meeting these challenges are great, however, with potential for both research excellence and improvement in patient care.

Since 1982 we have been involved in a nursing home medical school partnership of broad nature. We have brought together two autonomous institutions and selectively integrated their geriatric–gerontologic programs and staff. The success of the program is much in evidence at The Jewish Home and Hospital for Aged (JHHA) in New York City and the Department of Geriatrics and Adult Development at the Mount Sinai School of Medicine. We draw from our experience at JHHA for much of the material in this chapter.

OBSTACLES

Distrust of the Medical Establishment

The precursor of the nursing home was not a medical institution. The Social Security Act (SSA) of 1935 coupled its income security for the elderly with an incentive for the aged to live at home (13). To accomplish this goal, the SSA barred funds from those residing in poorhouses and other public institutions. The effect was to displace tens of thousands of elderly persons from public institutions to new, privately owned, profit-making boarding homes. As the boarders became older and their health deteriorated, nurses were added to the staff, and the nursing home was born. With the advent of Medicare and Medicaid, nursing homes changed from usually small, family enterprises into big business. The involvement of the medical profession remained sparse.

Understandably, the administrative and clinical leadership of nursing homes is uncomfortable, with the medical establishment centered at hospitals and medical schools. Although they have criticized physicians and institutions for lack of involvement, nursing home administrators do not wish to duplicate the rhythm, style, technology, or goals of acute care medicine. Indeed, it would guarantee incompatibility and rejection for medical people to directly transplant the aggressive, sometimes exploitative acute hospital approaches to the nursing home. It is necessary to develop a humanistic geriatric medicine approach based on realistic and attainable goals appropriate to the elderly that includes nursing home staff in the decision-making process. Equally serious but often less overtly expressed apprehensions— such as the fear that budgetary control will be lost and expenses will be greatly increased—must be addressed.

History of Abuse of the Elderly as Research Subjects

The impetus for the entire "informed consent" movement in the United States was the discovery that during the 1950s clinical scientists experimented by injecting live tumor cells into fragile, uninformed, elderly residents of a nursing home/chronic disease hospital (7). In more recent years congressional committees have questioned the informed consent approach of numerous research efforts at nursing homes.

With the frail patients at JHHA, more than one-half of whom have dementia and whose average age is 85 years, there are special challenges to scientists and administrators to obtain both legal and meaningful consent before accepting a patient as a research participant. Some of the barriers to standard consent procedures are as follows (8).

1. Vision and hearing disturbances that may compromise the patient's ability to understand an explanation of the research procedure or to read a consent form
2. Language barriers between patient and researcher, as well as poor vocabulary, limited education, dysphasias, and aphasias that may hamper attempts to assess competence
3. Fluctuations in mental status dependent on the medical condition, medications, and environment
4. Fear of signing documents, even when verbal consent is offered
5. Dependence on the institutional caregivers possibly resulting in subtle coercion to participate, particularly when patients no longer maintain a relationship with a primary physician outside the nursing home

6. The exaggerated importance of peer pressure, inactivity, and loneliness as incentives to research participation in this population

The social situation of most nursing home residents also makes it difficult to launch appropriate and ethical research with proper informed consent. In addition to individual circumstances, it must be remembered that most nursing home patients are widowed or never married, and their families are composed of elderly adults, children in their late fifties or sixties who are overwhelmed by the emotional, social, and economic threats that nursing home placement and residence brings to them.

However, it is clear to most families and residents that much research needs to be done in order to enhance the quality of these later years and to prevent some of the illnesses that diminish both the quality and quantity of late life.

Lack of Exposure to Academic Medicine Among Nursing Home Staff

Most administrative and nursing staffs working in nursing homes have had little if any exposure to academic medical centers. Most nursing homes do not have experienced research or human protection committees to evaluate research proposals, and they approach with great caution research that might be approved more expeditiously in a hospital setting. Scientists from the medical centers often misinterpret the nursing home's cautious response as rejecting, inconsiderate, and thoughtless. Physicians and scientists who have spent little time in nursing homes may also meet rejection because they lack familiarity with the research questions of central importance as well as an awareness of the special situations of the nursing home patients, their families, and the institution's staff.

Short-term or small pilot projects are valuable in overcoming these obstacles (19). Collaborative experience alleviates concern by administrative and nursing staffs that patient care will be compromised. Just as importantly, researchers who have not worked in an extended care facility have an opportunity to adjust their protocols to the realities of the nursing home, including overworked staff, frail patients, and less available data in patient charts.

In our experience, one finds that the first year or two of research proceeds relatively slowly. However, after a degree of trust is established and experience reveals the benefits of these approaches, the speed with which things are started is quite remarkable compared to that in a hospital or medical school environment.

News Media, Sensationalism, and the Nursing Home

With the news media's record of focusing only on negative conditions in nursing homes, there is concern over the potential for the television camera or newspaper article to sensationalize events related to research. Administrators and medical directors understandably fear that research efforts in a nursing home might be inappropriately portrayed in the media and presented in a negative fashion.

Concerns About Cost of Research

Research is expensive, and the overhead cost is significant. Nursing home leadership understandably fears lack of compensation for the overhead expenses, as their budgets are at least as tight as that of any hospital, and there is little flexibility with regard to increased overhead expense. Financial concerns require the scientist to work closely with the administration to minimize and plan reimbursement for overhead expenses.

Absence of Scientists and Clinicians Based at the Nursing Home

Too often research at the nursing home is engendered by scientists from other institutions, in particular the acute care hospital and medical school. The nursing home needs its own medical and scientific representatives in order to provide a balanced approach to the research endeavors. Naturally, the essential institutional review boards help maintain this balanced approach.

OPPORTUNITIES FOR RESEARCH IN THE NURSING HOME

The nursing home and its frail elderly population provide a spectrum of research challenges that include the study of health care delivery, diseases and clinical problems, cost-effectiveness, and human effectiveness (1,2,5,6,8,11,14,21). As seen in Table 1, even a selected listing of areas for research is remarkable in its breadth. The nursing home is a microcosm of the universe of health care issues relevant to the elderly and often applicable to the young.

There are highly prevalent problems encountered at the nursing home which, if understood, would provide insight for the care of patients within and outside the institution. For example, we need to study at the nursing home problems such as urinary incontinence, dementia, insomnia, falls, effect of environment on symptoms, efficacy of psychotropic medications on Alzheimer patients' symptoms, ethics of informed consent, excessive surgery, transfer to hospitals, and multiplicity of medications.

Interdisciplinary, Longitudinal Control Studies

Without the formalized departmental structure and territorial divisions found in hospitals, nursing homes are ideal for interdisciplinary investigations. The opportu-

TABLE 1. *Selected areas of research in the nursing home and with the frail elderly*

Longitudinal studies
Cross-sectional studies
Psychosocial studies
   Alzheimer's disease
   Influence of environment on behavior
   Benign memory loss
   Efficacy of psychotropic medication
   Cost-effectiveness vs. human effectiveness
Ethical issues
   Informed consent and appropriateness of "proxy"
   "Do not resuscitate" orders
   Enteral feeding
   Transfer to hospital
Clinical issues
   Clinical evaluation in the absence of adequate historical information
   Transmitting and storage of medical information
   The team
   Rehabilitation techniques
   Functional assessment
   Urinary and fecal incontinence
   Preventive care
      Vaccination
      Nursing approaches
      Falls and fractures
      Polypharmacy
      Pressure sores
   Pharmacology
   Postmortem studies

nity for longitudinal control studies in a nursing home is evident. How many health professionals have the chance to follow their patients for the rest of their lives? At JHHA, which is the largest nonprofit long-term facility for care of the aged in the United States, residents ordinarily are followed for the rest of their lives after admission. Although autopsies at nursing homes are a rarity, JHHA has been conducting autopsies for 40 years. Illnesses such as Alzheimer's disease, pulmonary embolus, coronary artery disease, and a variety of eye diseases have yielded important insights when the natural history is obtained via comprehensive clinical follow-up until death and postmortem examination (16,18).

One early investigation at JHHA illustrates the fruitful efforts of long-term, rigorous clinical investigation by a subspecialist. In 1952 Kornzweig and associates undertook a survey of the ocular status of old-age persons to determine the prevalence of visual handicap and to document the causes of such disability (10). Complete eye examinations were performed on admission and annually. This study was among the first to include all ocular disabilities in a single, large group of individuals and to correlate the frequency of occurrence of cataracts, glaucoma, and macular disease with age, sex, and pathological findings.

The results provided insights into the process of natural aging of the human eye and challenged common assumptions and treatment practices for ocular disease. Whereas earlier statistical studies had shown that cataracts could be expected in almost 100% of individuals if they lived long enough, this survey documented that only a relatively few older people are sufficiently handicapped visually by cataract to require surgery. Sixty-one percent of the entire group (1,300) had some degree of cataracts, but in only 9% of the eyes were the cataracts considered operable and mature. Of the total number of eyes evaluated (2,136), only 95 (4.4%) were operated for cataracts. The study helped redefine surgical guidelines for cataract surgery. Patients with one strong eye and those who represented a high surgical risk were excluded. Patients whose advanced age would have previously constituted a sufficient contraindication were offered surgery. Visual function greatly enhances the quality of life at any age; therefore 67% of the surgical candidates at the JHHA were 80 years of age or more.

With regard to glaucoma, previous surveys had documented an increase in intraocular pressure with age, and the JHHA survey confirmed that glaucoma was present in 5.3% of all residents and that the chance of glaucoma onset increased with age between 50 and 70 years. However, because Kornzweig's subjects included those in extreme old age, he was able to document that the onset of glaucoma in the nursing home population is less common after age 70, and the prevalence of glaucoma is lower in persons over 80 years of age than in those under 80.

By contrast, macular disease, present in 29% of the total eyes studied, was far more common in persons over 80 (38%) than in those under 80 (24%). Of the patients with macular degeneration, 30% had bilateral involvement resulting in visual impairment. The insights obtained in this study of the aged eye have produced advances in health care relevant to individuals in the community and those in midlife as well as those who live in the nursing home.

Cross-Sectional Studies of the Very Old

A cross-sectional study means information is taken at one period in time, in contrast to a longitudinal study where data are collected in the same subjects over several intervals of time.

In the area of blood chemistries, one cross-sectional investigation correlated blood lipid profiles with risk for stroke and cardiac disease in an elderly nursing home population (17). Cardiovascular disease is the greatest cause of mortality in the aged. About 15 to 25% of JHHA patients have suffered stroke, and many will develop strokes during their stay. Among younger age groups, abnormal serum lipid levels are a significant risk factor for coronary artery disease. It is also known that total cholesterol, low density lipoprotein (LDL) cholesterol, and triglycerides increase with age until approximately age 55 to 65 years, but few data were available for persons over age 65.

A randomly chosen cross-section of the female population at JHHA, ranging in age from 67 to 104 years, had blood lipids evaluated in an on-site laboratory.

Results indicated a significant decrease in total and LDL cholesterol with advancing age, with a slight decrease in triglycerides and high-density lipoprotein (HDL) cholesterol. No significant difference in lipid profiles distinguished those elderly women with a history of coronary heart disease or cerebrovascular disease from those without these diseases.

As a result, in the clinical follow-up we acknowledged that lipid values were not a useful predictor of coronary heart disease in this patient group. However, a correlation was found between prior history of cerebrovascular disease and coronary heart disease. This finding is consistent with earlier studies, which reported that the leading cause of death among those with transient ischemic attacks is acute myocardial infarction.

The nonspecific diagnosis of senile dementia is carried by more than 50% of the occupants of the United States' 1.5 million nursing home beds. The nursing home is thus one of the best sites at which scientists and clinicians can focus on this difficult and consuming illness. In addition, the remaining 50% of the patients vary in terms of their cognitive adequacy and age. The fact that many individuals of varying cognitive status will be residing in the nursing home for the remainder of their lives, an average of 3 to 5 years, provides the opportunity for in-depth research on a minilongitudinal basis.

Urinary Incontinence: Study of Classification and Treatment

Specific diagnostic evaluation has often been neglected for common problems that severely impact on quality of life for the aged and that may lead to nursing home placement. Urinary incontinence, which is estimated to occur in about half of elderly individuals in long-term care facilities and at least 10% of those living in the community, is pursued by specific diagnostic evaluation in fewer than 5% of cases. Although studies of incontinence have generally remained confined to the realm of the urologist and gynecologist, clinicians have commonly accepted mental impairment as the untreatable cause of most incontinence. To undertake the complex task of determining the etiology of urinary incontinence in the elderly, a urinary incontinence consultation service has been established at JHHA and fully equipped with an on-site urodynamic laboratory. The prevalence of incontinence in this nursing home has been established (20). More than 100 individuals have been evaluated with urodynamic studies, which are revealing unsuspected causes of incontinence.

Pharmacology and Pharmacy Studies at the Nursing Home

Too much pharmacologic research is based on the body's handling of a medication in the absence of any other medication in the system. This situation is unrealistic for the nursing home, where the opportunity exists to study the pharmacology of one medication in the setting of many others. The epidemiology of medications in the nursing home is another area for fruitful investigation.

Digoxin has been a medication of great concern to physicians at JHHA and one for which careful research resulted in changes in clinical practice (9). It is one of the most frequently prescribed drugs in the elderly, and its use is often initiated when the diagnosis of heart failure is unsubstantiated. Furthermore, once the order is written, it is seldom discontinued, despite the possibility of digoxin toxicity.

The research design was a double-blind discontinuation of maintenance digitalis in patients who met strict criteria that cast doubt on the need for continued therapy. The criteria, satisfied by 22 of 98 residents who were receiving maintenance digoxin, were (a) no documentation of congestive heart failure before or after admission, (b) no evidence of supraventricular tachycardia within the last 6 months, (c) a current electrocardiogram (ECG) showing regular sinus rhythm, and (d) a history of digoxin therapy lasting 6 months or more prior to the study.

During the first 3 months of the study, half of the patients remained on digoxin while the other subgroup was switched to placebo. Patients were closely monitored throughout the study by physicians blinded to their treatment group. During this time no existing treatment or other medications were altered. During the second phase of the study, lasting 6 months, both subgroups received placebo capsules.

Only 5 of 22 patients had recurring heart failure or arrhythmias that required reinstitution of digoxin. The detection of patients who do not need digoxin maintenance therapy is valuable, especially in the aged in whom there is an increased incidence and severity of digitalis toxicity.

The diagnosis of digitalis toxicity is difficult in the nursing home population. Its clinical symptoms—nausea, vomiting, diarrhea, confusion, headache, fatigue, malaise, and apathy—are similar to nonspecific manifestations often found in elderly patients with organic brain syndrome. Moreover, the high incidence of arrhythmias and conduction disturbances that occur in the elderly are often identical to those cause by digitalis.

Guided by this research, a closely monitored trial off digoxin is now considered for carefully selected JHHA patients who have no evidence of congestive heart failure and in whom the indications for initiation of digoxin appear inappropriate or of a transitory nature.

Ethical Issues in Care of the Nursing Home Patient

Treatment decisions in the nursing home may have as much to do with psychosocial factors, whether acknowledged or unacknowledged, as with traditional medical standards of care. Much research is needed into the obvious ethical issues, including issues of informed consent, "do not resuscitate" orders, use of nasogastric feedings, decisions by patients not to accept treatment, and the effect of malpractice on nursing home treatment decisions.

Much biomedical research within the nursing home will remain incomplete if it does not incorporate psychosocial and ethical factors in its data. For example, a study on fever in nursing home patients included in its analysis factors associated with the decision by caregivers not to treat the fevers (4). It was revealed that, rather than dementia and aphasia being prominent factors resulting in nontreatment decisions, social factors such as "no close relatives" correlated highly with patients not being given antibiotics for fever.

Vaccination and treatment of asymptomatic bacteriuria are other common areas in which scrutiny of factors related to the day-to-day decision-making process would be valuable.

Research Concerning Events Within the Nursing Home

As a setting designed specifically for the frail elderly, nursing homes can benefit directly from research on health and safety within the institution. For example, falls are a frequent, worrisome, and sometimes dramatic health event within the nursing home. Early research in this area by an attending physician and cardiologist at JHHA significantly advanced our understanding and preventive efforts (15).

Evaluating a series of 147 consecutive accidents that occurred over a 6-month period among 96 nursing home residents, fewer than half of the accidents occurred in individuals in good health. About 30% occurred in close conjunction with the onset of acute diseases, and another 30% occurred in persons who had one or more chronic disease conditions predisposing to accidents. Many of these disease-associated accidents occurred despite close supervision. Of the 147 accidents in the nursing home, there were only two major injuries, 67 minor injuries, and 78 accidents without any overt injury.

When analyzing the circumstances in which the accidents occurred, it was found that most falls were associated with transferring to and from beds, chairs, wheelchairs, or toilets. Although the staff/patients ratio is highest during the daytime, the maximum frequency of accidents was found between 6:00 A.M. and 12:00 noon, corresponding to arising, dressing, and the greatest general activity of the residents. Because of this study, improvements were made in the continuous program of accident prevention at JHHA, including changes in instructions to staff and visitors and alterations in the height of beds and railings.

Investigation of the Relation Between Nursing Home and Hospital

Gaps in communication between nursing home and hospital have a detrimental effect on patient care. It is well known that after a major clinical and financial effort in the hospital a patient is often transferred to the nursing home with only a five or six-sentence transfer note, theoretically summarizing the major effort that has just occurred. This inadequacy of information then leads to diminished patient care and repetition of expense and effort. Similarly, when patients go from nursing home to hospital, there is often an inappropriate note of exchange between the institutions. Remedies for this problem need to be studied; correctional measures include portable medical records, use of computers, and the institution of staff who work as a bridge between the two institutions.

Nursing home patients are evident in the acute care wards of hospitals, but they are rarely considered its primary patients (11). Not only do they often come with inadequate information and an inability to give a lengthy history, but they often experience a change of physicians with the move. New approaches, e.g., nursing home nurses making periodic rounds with hospital colleagues and the institution of geriatric consultation services, appear to have value that could be documented and refined with appropriate collaborative research.

SUMMARY

It is obvious that the nursing home presents remarkable opportunities for research. The results from these efforts will not only enhance the quality of life of the nursing home patient, they will almost certainly contribute to better knowledge of health changes in the aged who live in the community and provide insights into illnesses in younger persons as well.

REFERENCES

1. Aronson, M. K. (1984): Implementing a teaching nursing home: lessons for research and practice. *Gerontologist,* 24:451–454.
2. Beard, W. J., Kalau, E. I., and Noback, R. K. (1983): Geriatric education in a nursing home. *Gerontologist,* 23:132–135.
3. Brody, J. A., and Foley, F. J. (1985): Epidemiological considerations. In: *The Teaching Nursing Home: A New Approach to Geriatric Research, Education, and Clinical Care,* edited by E. J. Schneider, pp. 9–25. Raven Press, New York.
4. Brown, N. K., and Thompson, D. J. (1979): Nontreatment of fever in extended-care facilities. *N. Engl. J. Med.,* 300:1246–1250.
5. Butler, R. N. (1981): The teaching nursing home. *JAMA,* 245:1435–1437.
6. Duthie, E. H., Priefer, B., and Gambert, S. R. (1982): The teaching nursing home: one approach. *JAMA,* 247:2787–2788.
7. Guttentag, O. E. (1964): Human experimentation. *Science,* 145:768.
8. Hoffman, P. B., and Libow, L. S. (1985): The need for alternatives to informed consent by older patients: psychological and physical aspects of the institutionalized elderly. In: *Alzheimer's Dementia: Dilemmas in Clinical Research,* edited by V. L. Melnick and N. N. Dubler, pp. 141–148. Humana Press, Clifton, NJ.
9. Kirsten, E., Rodstein, M., and Iuster, Z. (1973): Digoxin in the aged. *Geriatrics,* 28:95–101.
10. Kornzweig, A. L., Feldstein, M., and Schneider, J. (1957): The eye in old age: ocular survey of over 1,000 aged persons with special reference to normal and disturbed visual functions. *Am. J. Opthalmol.,* 44:29–37.
11. Leaf, A. (1977): Medicine and the aged. *N. Engl. J. Med.,* 297:887–890.
12. Libow, L. S. (1982): Geriatric medicine and the nursing home: a mechanism for mutual excellence (The Donald P. Kent Memorial Lecture—1981). *Gerontologist,* 22:134–141.

13. Libow, L. S. (1984): The teaching nursing home: present and future. *J. Am. Geriatr. Soc.,* 32:600–602.
14. Pawlson, L. G. (1982): Education in the nursing home: practical considerations. *J. Am. Geriatr. Soc.,* 32:600–602.
15. Rodstein, M. (1964): Accidents among the aged: incidence, causes and prevention. *J. Chronic Dis.,* 17:515–526.
16. Rodstein, M. (1980): Research in geriatric medicine at the Jewish Home and Hospital for Aged, New York—1944–1980. *Mt. Sinai J. Med.,* 47:96–98.
17. Rodstein, M., Neufeld, R. R., and Nadelman, J. (1984): Correlation of serum lipid levels with cardiac and cerebrovascular disease in the aged. *N.Y. State J. Med.,* 84:387–389.
18. Rossman, I., Rodstein, M., and Bornstein, A. (1974): Undiagnosed diseases in the aged population: pulmonary embolism and bronchopneumonia. *Arch. Intern. Med.,* 133:366–369.
19. Rowe, J. W. (1985): Factors facilitating and impeding research in the teaching nursing home setting. In: *The Teaching Nursing Home: A New Approach to Geriatric Research, Education, and Clinical Care,* edited by E. J. Schneider, pp. 287–292. Raven Press, New York.
20. Starer, P., and Libow, L. S. (1985): Obscuring urinary incontinence: diapering of the elderly. *J. Am. Geriatr. Soc.,* 33:842–846.
21. Wieland, D., Rubenstein, L. Z., Ouslander, J. G., and Martin, S. E. (1986): Organizing an academic nursing home: impacts on institutionalized elderly. *JAMA,* 255:2622–2627.

Human Aging Research: Concepts and Techniques,
edited by B. Kent and R. N. Butler.
Raven Press, Ltd., New York © 1988.

Library Research and Information Retrieval in Gerontology and Geriatrics

Dorothy R. Hill

*Gustave L. and Janet W. Levy Library, Mount Sinai School of Medicine,
New York, New York 10029*

When designing a research project or writing a grant application, a comprehensive knowledge of the work that has already been done and that is currently being done is essential for formulating pertinent, nonambiguous questions to be answered by the proposed research. The justification for asking such questions is based on what has gone before, and the significance of those questions relies on the current state of knowledge. Searching the gerontology and geriatrics literature is an integral component of research in human aging. To search effectively it is necessary to determine what that literature encompasses and to develop a strategy for accessing it as comprehensively and efficiently as possible, both currently and retrospectively.

Because aging is a complex process having physical, psychological, and societal ramifications, the range of knowledge required to understand this phenomenon is vast. Gerontology as a recognized field of scientific endeavor is relatively young, but it cuts across a number of established fields of study and draws most of its knowledge base from medicine, biological sciences, psychology, anthropology, and sociology, thereby resulting in an extensive literature. Retrieving much of this literature through traditional print indexing sources can be difficult because the age aspect has not always been taken into consideration. Only a relatively small amount of the literature on aging and the aged is neatly packaged in journals and books devoted specifically to gerontology and geriatrics, and most of these publications have appeared only within the last 10 to 15 years.

All too often literature searching is viewed as one of the nuisance adjuncts of "real" research and is approached in a haphazard manner. The interrelation of scientific communication and scientific research, be it clinical, experimental, or field, is obvious though frequently overlooked. The literature of a scientific discipline serves archival as well as current awareness functions; the researcher must be equally concerned with both aspects. Retrospective literature transmits to the present generation the skills, methodologies, discoveries, and misconceptions of previous generations, thereby providing a springboard for present-day original research. Science is progressive and cumulative only because information can be and has been retrieved and preserved from generation to generation. Observation and experimentation yield the raw data of scientific information. The data are recorded, analyzed, sorted, correlated, and synthesized into a body of organized, integrated knowledge. This retrievable body of scientific knowledge serves as a basis for new experiments and observations that in turn produce further growth of information by injecting more new data into the communication cycle.

In our ahistorical, technologically oriented scientific community, the archival function of its literature is being bypassed more and more. In fact, in this electronic era, the body of scientific knowledge will very likely be skewed toward that information that can be retrieved by computer. It is important to realize that the existing body of biomedical knowledge accumulated during the first two-thirds of this century and all preceding centuries cannot be accessed electronically, and searching the literature manually is fast becoming a lost art.

Because of the rapidly changing developments in the biosciences, the current awareness function of scientific literature is much more obvious, for it is essential that one be aware of the ongoing work of his or her peers. However, even this function is being underutilized because often research workers today do not exhaustively search even the current and contemporary literature before undertaking new research projects. There is a tendency to overlook non-English-language sources in general, but especially those published in Russia, the Eastern Block countries, and Japan. Time limitations, lack of staff, competition, irrelevance, and the massive amounts of literature being produced are given as reasons for such underutilization.

As a result of not searching the scientific literature comprehensively in a structured manner, many dollars are likely to be wasted by repeating old investigations. Worthless repetitions and unnecessary verifications are published in the disguise of new works. The unreliability of claims to priority—reporting a "first"—is well recognized by many medical journals (34). Rediscovery in the library is much less expensive and far less embarrassing than it is in the laboratory or in print.

Research in the biomedical library, if done properly, is motivating, rewarding, and exciting. Because there are detailed discourses of how to use a medical library (2,14) that information is not repeated in its entirety here. Instead, general attitudes and concepts are addressed, and then the topic of retrieving information relating to gerontology and geriatrics is dealt with in depth.

Even though the journal article is unquestionably the basic unit so far as scientific information is concerned, darting off blindly to the *Index Medicus* is not necessarily the best way to initiate a comprehensive search of the literature of aging and the aged; actually, this topic is difficult to search in the *Index Medicus*. When starting library research, the traditional premise of "I need journal articles" should be replaced with a more realistic one, "I need information." Next, the question is asked, "What do I know about the subject I intend to investigate?" If the answer is, "Not much," then perhaps books or review articles, if such exist, would save a considerable amount of time, effort, and frustration in establishing a base on which to build subject expertise. Neither a biomedical book nor a review article is intended to transmit the most up-to-date information; that is the purpose of the journal article. Instead, books and review articles correlate information from many primary sources and present the subject in context, and for this reason they are extraordinary time-savers. A well-documented monograph with a comprehensive bibliography or an authoritative review article with its list of references also give access to relevant journal literature. After having approached an unfamiliar subject in this manner, one can subsequently relate to the primary literature with a sense of understanding and proficiency. Establishing this kind of knowledge base by searching the original journal literature could take weeks or months.

Another time-saver is the subject bibliography, a frequently neglected resource in the typical biomedical library. Many of these bibliographies are retrospective because online data bases are now supplanting them, but when available, they can be important work-savers for accessing the literature for the years they cover. They are likely to include older material that cannot be retrieved via computer, as this capability goes back only about two decades or less. When using a subject bibliography one should always determine whether it is selective or comprehensive. Some of these bibliographies are landmark works themselves; there are two of this caliber on gerontology and geriatrics, *A Classified Bibliography of Gerontology and Geriatrics* and *Gerontology: A Cross-National Core List of Significant Works,* which are discussed later.

In most cases locating existing information to support a research project entails an intensive review of the literature of the subject under investigation, not merely a search for a few current references. The literature review for the research project should be carefully planned before the project itself is undertaken and should continue to its completion. Time spent developing a comprehensive literature search strategy often helps conceptualize the problem to be studied and puts the researcher truly in control of *all* aspects of his or her project. This part of the research process often can be made more proficient by consulting with resource persons such as librarians or information specialists early on in the formulation of the literature search. By so doing, one becomes acquainted with the wide range of available information sources and services that exist and learns how to use them to the greatest advantage.

INDEXING METHODOLOGIES

Fundamental to all literature searching, either print or electronic, is an understanding of the concept of bibliographic control through indexing. Theoretically, an index can be defined in the information transfer process as an orderly guide to the intellectual content and physical location of knowledge records; in other words, indexes are guides for locating journal articles, abstracts, books, chapters in books, and a host of other items. Indexes are necessary because items of information are dispersed in time, in space, and among languages; many are unknown to the potential user, and others are remembered imperfectly. The medium of indexes can be in the form of print (e.g., library card catalogs, periodical indexes, book indexes, and back-of-the-book indexes), or it can be electronic (e.g., information retrieval system indexes and automated library catalogs). Indexing can be done for whole works or for contents of works. Of all indexes, author and subject are the most familiar. Author indexes have as their primary function guidance to specific works. In addition, in indexing and abstracting tools, they indicate what authors are doing, how active they are, and if they have changed their areas of interest. Author indexes are usually self-explanatory and easy to use.

A comparable situation is not necessarily true for subject indexes, which are the most important in the information retrieval process. There are myriad subject indexing techniques that exist, but just knowing a little about the two fundamental differences in the methodology of subject indexing can greatly enhance one's skills in literature searching, either manually or electronically. In view of the current trend in the biomedical community toward user-friendly retrieval systems and independent or end-user searching (12,13,15), this knowledge becomes especially important even for quick searches. Although it is possible to retrieve information from such systems with little or no knowledge of indexing or searching techniques, the result is not necessarily an efficient, cost-effective, comprehensive literature search needed to support a research project. Online systems that are user-friendly to vendors may not be particularly *friendly* so far as users are concerned.

Subject indexing is done by means of either controlled or natural language. Controlled language is sometimes referred to as controlled vocabulary, assigned term, or conceptual indexing; a subject is *always* represented by the *same* designated or assigned term, sometimes chosen from among a group of synonyms, e.g., either "physician" or "doctor," "diazepam" or "Valium," but not both terms for the same concept. Subject terms or subject headings are frequently referred to as descriptors, especially in online systems. Many controlled language vocabularies have subheadings that define the main subjects more precisely than does the subject heading alone and group together important aspects of the subject headings, e.g., "Diazepam—adverse effects" or "Diazepam—therapeutic use." Subheadings are extremely useful when searching subject headings that have a massive number of references such as "Myocardial infarction," "Liver," or "Lung neoplasms." Another aspect of controlled vocabulary indexing that is often overlooked is the principle of specificity. Information is indexed only under the most specific subject term or terms available in the vocabulary. An article on hepatitis in elderly alcoholics indexed under the subject heading "Hepatitis, alcoholic" would not also be assigned more general terms such as "Hepatitis" or "Liver diseases." The principle of specificity holds true for both manual and automated literature searching. In a controlled vocabulary that is made up of an alphabetical list of subject headings, it is in some cases difficult to be certain of the most specific term for a given concept because related terms are scattered throughout the list without being drawn together. However, if the controlled vocabulary is structured as a thesaurus that relates broader and narrower terms to each other, the most specific term can be determined quickly. The subject indexing vocabulary of *Index Medicus* is a thesaurus. If there is no designated term for a specific subject, it is usually indexed under the next broader term that is in the vocabulary. In *Index Medicus* an article on the sinoatrial block would be indexed under "Heart block" because the controlled vocabulary has no specific term for this particular type of heart block.

Controlled indexing vocabularies, in order to be effective, must be kept dynamic with the introduction of new subject headings along with the elimination of existing outdated subject headings. The intellectual part of controlled vocabulary indexing is still done by humans; the mechanics are controlled by computer. Indexing skills and interpretations vary from one indexer to the next, which accounts for inconsistencies that do occur. If there is a possibility of a research topic being interpreted in more than one way, the use of multiple search terms may be necessary when comprehensive retrieval is mandatory; obviously, multiple-term searching is much easier to do online than manually.

The second method of subject indexing is natural language, also referred to as free-text, keyword, or derived-term indexing. The indexing terms are derived directly from the text of the document, i.e., the exact words of the authors. Both "physician" and "doctor" or "diazepam" and "Valium" along with any other synonyms would have to be searched in a natural language index; concepts are not drawn together in one place as with controlled vocabulary indexing. In print indexes natural language terms are usually derived from the titles, and in automated systems having abstracts both the title and abstract are free-text indexed. Full-text data bases can also be searched by natural language. At present titles and abstracts are the two main sources of free-text retrieval, although the number of full-text medical journals and books that are available online is rapidly increasing. The potential usefulness for health care professionals to have direct online access to the full text of medical journals and books by user-friendly terminals in patient care areas, laboratories, or offices is being recognized (5). Natural language subject indexes are computer-produced, and their print versions have less than conventional appearances; *Science Citation Index* has a free-text subject index consisting of pairs of words from journal article and chapter titles. Most automated retrieval systems whose print format is searchable only by means of a controlled vocabulary can be searched online by both controlled and natural languages. Searching by natural language generally requires more time and effort than searching by a controlled vocabulary system. It necessitates a great deal more pondering to retrieve all relevant documents, simply because all possible synonyms and related terms that authors might have used must be searched; and with semantic imprecision and a constantly changing vocabulary, this aspect can be a significant undertaking. In general, natural language indexes can be searched more effectively by computers than by people, but it is also true for many controlled vocabulary indexes. Retrieval from natural language indexes tends to produce more irrelevancy than from controlled vocabulary indexes. However, natural language indexes are usually more current and less expensive to produce. They are also invaluable for locating new subject concepts for which subject headings have not been established and for finding articles when only catchwords or catchphrases are recalled. Before using any print indexing or abstracting tool, one must always be sure to read the introductory material to find out how it is structured and intended to be used. This approach also holds true for online databases; the user must be familiar with the database vendor's command sequences and protocols as well as the characteristics of the specific database being searched.

To begin a comprehensive search of the literature on topics relating to age, aging, or the aged, machine-readable databases are the most efficient sources. The database most widely used and best known for accessing the journal literature of biomedicine is MEDLINE, one of the databases of MEDLARS (Medical Literature Analysis and Retrieval System), the computerized information system consisting of more than 20 databases developed by and established at the National Library of Medicine (NLM) in Bethesda. Since 1879 NLM and its predecessors have led the world in the field of biomedical indexing beginning with John Shaw Billings (7,16). The print counterparts of MEDLINE are *Index Medicus, International Nursing Index,* and *Index to Dental Literature.*

MEDICAL SUBJECT HEADINGS

In order to use MEDLARS databases and print indexes efficiently, it is necessary to have at least an overview of *Medical Subject Headings (MeSH)*, the vocabulary of the retrieval system, which is a highly sophisticated controlled language thesaurus consisting of nearly 14,000 subject headings and 10,000 cross references. The familiar "black-and-white" *MeSH,* so called because of its cover, appears annually as Part 2 of the January issue of *Index Medicus* and is intended for use with the print index. It consists of an alphabetical listing of subject headings with various types of cross references to related and synonymous terms (Fig. 1, top). After the alphabetical list, the subject terms are displayed in a hierarchical arrangement (tree structures) in which broader and narrower terms are related to each other within 15 broad subject categories (Fig. 1, bottom). Some terms appear in more than one category; for example, "Alzheimer's disease" appears in both the neurologic diseases (C10) and the behavioral and mental disorders (F3) tree structures. Whenever an appropriate term is located in the alphabetical list, the alphanumeric string(s) of characters just below the subject heading, the tree number(s), should always be checked in the tree structures to determine relations with other relevant subject headings. Any tree number ending in a "+" indicates that the subject concept has more specific headings. *MeSH* subject heading terms range from natural language to highly technical usage.

The information in the "black-and-white" *MeSH* may not be adequate for carrying out many MEDLINE searches. Instead, the three-part annotated *MeSH,* available from the National Technical Information Service, should be used; it is made up of (a) *Medical Subject Headings, Annotated Alphabetic List,* (b) *Tree Structures,* and (c) *Permuted Medical Subject Headings.* Even user-friendly online systems recommend that the annotated *MeSH* be available. Obviously, subject heading changes cannot be retrospectively corrected in the print indexes produced from MEDLINE, but that is not necessarily true for the database itself. For example,

→ **AGED**
M1.471.116.100+
66; was see under GERIATRICS 1963-65
see related
    HEALTH INSURANCE FOR AGED AND DISABLED, TITLE 18
    HEALTH SERVICES FOR THE AGED
    HOMES FOR THE AGED
    LONGEVITY
    PENSIONS
    RETIREMENT
XR GERIATRICS

AGED ABUSE see ELDER ABUSE

NAMED GROUPS BY AGE (NON MESH)	**M1.471**
ADOLESCENCE	**M1.471.80**
ADOLESCENT, HOSPITALIZED	**M1.471.80.280**
ADOLESCENT, INSTITUTIONALIZED	**M1.471.80.305**
ADULT	**M1.471.116**
AGED	→ **M1.471.116.100**
AGED, 80 AND OVER	**M1.471.116.100.80**
MIDDLE AGE	**M1.471.116.630**

FIG. 1. *Top.* Section from alphabetical list of *MeSH* (Black and White, 1987) showing subject heading Aged and its tree number. *Bottom.* Section from tree structures of *MeSH* showing subject heading Aged in its hierarchical arrangement with a correlation of the tree number from the alphabetical list. The tree numbers for Aged are indicated by arrows.

the subject heading "Alzheimer's disease" can be searched from 1975 to date online even though it can be searched only back to 1984 in the print indexes. This kind of information appears in the annotated *MeSH* but not in the "black and white" version. In the list of permuted headings, each significant word that appears in the *MeSH* terms is listed with all subject headings containing that word indented under it. Such an arrangement makes it possible to locate a multiple-term heading by any significant word; "Health services for the aged" can be found by looking up "Health," "Services," or "Aged." It also brings together in one place all subject headings of the vocabulary that contain a specific word; in the *Permuted Medical Subject Headings, 1987,* there are five subject headings and two cross-references that contain the word "Aged" (Fig. 2). Note that the permuted terms are not available in the "black-and-white" *MeSH*. The tree structures and permuted subject heading list are good sources for locating elusive subject headings.

Specificity must be kept in mind when using *MeSH*. If the research topic is Alzheimer's disease, such broad headings as "Brain diseases" or "Psychotic disor-

AGED
    AGED
    AGED ABUSE see ELDER ABUSE
    AGED, 80 AND OVER
    HEALTH INSURANCE FOR AGED AND DISABLED, TITLE 18
    HEALTH SERVICES FOR THE AGED
    HOMES FOR THE AGED
    INSURANCE, HEALTH, FOR AGED AND DISABLED see HEALTH
        INSURANCE FOR AGED AND DISABLED, TITLE 18

FIG. 2. The word Aged as it appears in the *Permuted MeSH*. Below Aged are listed all *MeSH* subject headings and cross references that contain the word.

ders'' used as search terms yield poor retrieval because the specific term ''Alzheimer's disease'' appears in the *MeSH* vocabulary. Using too-broad terms is a common error. However, ''Alzheimer's disease'' has been a *MeSH* heading only since 1984. From 1967 to 1983 articles on Alzeheimer's disease appeared in the print indexes under ''Dementia, presenile,'' and before that under ''Psychoses, presenile.'' *MeSH* is a dynamic vocabulary, and subject headings may change frequently. A list of subject heading changes appears at the beginning of each annual update of *MeSH,* and it must be consulted routinely. If the specific subject cannot be located in the *MeSH* vocabulary, synonyms should be checked along with the possibility of inverted subject headings; for example, presenile dementia is indexed as ''Dementia, presenile.'' Although many cross references do appear in *MeSH,* cross references do not appear for *all* synonyms and inversions.

When using *MeSH* subject headings in print or online, a number of points must be kept in mind.

1. The subject heading ''Aging'' is interpreted as the physiological and psychological aging process anywhere between birth and old age and is not restricted to elderly people. Many articles indexed under ''Aging'' involve experimental animals.

2. The *MeSH* term ''Aged'' refers to age 65 and over and is used as a subject heading when the aged person or persons are the dominant focus of the article as social, sociological, psychological, or cultural beings. Prior to age 65, the term ''Middle age'' is used.

3. The *MeSH* term ''Age factors'' is used to index articles on specific diseases, physiological processes, and social, cultural, psychological, and demographic concepts when the emphasis of such an article is on the age and other factors with statistical implications. ''Age factors'' is not generally used as a print *Index Medicus* heading except when age is both the sole factor and the point of the article.

4. Physiological processes, organs, and diseases in various age groups are indexed under the specific process, organ, or disease, not under the age group, which makes these topics difficult to search in the *Index Medicus* from an age perspective.

5. The *MeSH* subject heading ''Geriatrics'' covers both gerontology and geriatrics even though the terms are not exactly synonymous. Generally only articles on gerontology and geriatrics as disciplines or on the geriatrician and gerontologist are indexed under this term. Articles on diseases of the aged or the aging patient should not be indexed under ''Geriatrics,'' but this subject heading is sometimes used for general articles on geriatric diseases.

6. The most specific *MeSH* subject heading is used unless the article discusses *both* the specific and the general topic; it should then appear under both specific and general terms.

7. Drugs are indexed under common or generic names, not under proprietary or trade names.

8. Neoplasms are indexed under the site as an organ neoplasm heading as well as by histologic type.

9. Animal research on a subject is indexed under the subject of the research, not under the *MeSH* term "Laboratory animals."

10. Research methods pertaining to diseases, substances, etc., are indexed under the specific disease, substance, etc., not under the research method.

11. Pathological processes of various organs are indexed under the organs with the subheading "Pathology," not under the various pathological processes.

12. Negative findings are indexed along with positive findings under the appropriate subjects.

13. A subject for which there is no exactly equivalent *MeSH* term is indexed under the most closely related available term, generally a broader term.

These points are but a few of which to be aware when using the *MeSH* vocabulary. The *MEDLARS Indexing Manual* (4) is the source of all indexing rules for MEDLINE and *Index Medicus,* but it is highly detailed and not always available for use; moreover, it is geared to the indexer and librarian, not to the end-user.

MEDLINE DATABASE

For searching the journal literature of gerontology and geriatrics from 1966 to date, MEDLINE is definitely the preferred source. In MEDLARS indexing, age is one of the concepts routinely checked for all human subjects of an article regardless of whether it is the major focus of the study. In the *MeSH* vocabulary there are eight age group check tags, with three of them being of special interest to geriatricians and gerontologists:

Adult	19–44 years
Middle age	45–64 years
Aged	65 years and over

Age designation applies to humans, not to animals.

As previously mentioned, MEDLINE contains references not only in *Index Medicus* but also in the *International Nursing Index* and the *Index to Dental Literature* as well, so that articles on dentistry and nursing involving the elderly can be retrieved, even if age is not the major point of the articles. MEDLINE provides multiple access points, with an average of eight to ten *MeSH* subject headings per article representing both major points of the article and other points of discussion worthy of retrieval. In addition, there are check tags—descriptors designating such elements as age, sex, human, animal, case report, etc.—that are routinely applied to every article that is indexed. There is also free-text access to the titles and abstracts of articles. All *MeSH* terms can be searched in MEDLINE. English-language author abstracts accompany about 60% of the articles indexed since 1975; up to 250 words of an abstract appear in MEDLINE; if the article is more than 10 pages long, up to 400 words appear. MEDLINE contains more than 5 million references to journal articles. There are more than 3,200 biomedical journals from the United States and other countries indexed from 1966 to the present. MEDLINE is usually about 1 month more current than *Index Medicus* and is available directly from NLM or from user-friendly systems such as BRS Colleague, BRS/After Dark, MEDIS, and EasyNet. GRATEFUL MED, a software package produced by the National Library of Medicine, is designed to make accessing MEDLINE and CATLINE by personal computer simpler for the novice user (32). CATLINE contains 600,000 records for books and serials in the NLM collection. Anyone planning to search MEDLINE for information on aging and the aged should first read an enlightening article titled ''Searching the MEDLARS File for Information on the Elderly'' (11). Because the oral health of the elderly is an integral part of their health problems, the literature of geriatric dentistry and strategies for accessing that literature via MEDLINE should be kept in mind (10). A MEDLINE manual published by the National Library of Medicine especially for the health professional to learn to search the system is also helpful (20).

An online database is much more than a mere computer version of its print counterpart(s). The benefits are not just speed and convenience; often the quality of the output is superior to that of a manual search because of multiple-concept searching and so many access points.

INDEX MEDICUS

Index Medicus, a print index derived from MEDLINE, is not an especially efficient source for locating information on aging and the aged. Unless an article has as its major focus some aspect of aging or the aged for which there is a *MeSH* print heading, it is not likely to be retrieved because age check tags cannot be accessed in *Index Medicus.* This point is especially true when searching for diseases, organs, or specific processes in various age groups, as those articles are indexed under the topics, not under the age groups. Some subject headings relevant to geriatrics and gerontology appearing in *Index Medicus* are the following.

Aged	Health services for the aged
Aged, 80 and over	Home care services
Chronic disease	Homes for the aged
Elder abuse	Hospices
Geriatric dentistry	Longevity
Geriatric psychiatry	Middle age
Geriatrics	Public assistance
Health insurance for the aged and dis-	Retirement
abled, Title 18	Terminal care

References are found in *Index Medicus* only under *MeSH* terms that are in large type (print headings) in the alphabetical listing. On the average, articles appear under three or four subject headings in the print index, which represent only major points of the articles, not in-depth subject analysis.

The current version of *Index Medicus* began in 1960, six years before online access to MEDLINE. However, its predecessors with varying titles (*Index Medicus, 1879–1927; Quarterly Cumulative Index to Current Medical Literature, 1916–1926; Quarterly Cumulative Index Medicus, 1927–1956; Current List of Medical Literature, 1941–1959*) supply contemporary indexing of the world's biomedical literature back to 1879.

HEALTH PLANNING AND ADMINISTRATION DATABASE

Health Planning and Administration is another of the MEDLARS databases that is especially pertinent to the researcher in gerontology and geriatrics, as the medical and social problems of the aged are tightly interwoven with the administrative, economic, and political aspects of health care delivery. This database, consisting of more than 280,000 records covering 1974 to date, focuses on the nonclinical aspects of health care delivery including such topics as hospital administration, health insurance, quality assurance, financial management, regulation, and related subjects. It is searched in a manner comparable to MEDLINE using the same controlled vocabulary, *MeSH*. Age check tags can be searched, which is important because there is a great deal of material relating to the elderly in articles that do not have the elderly as the major focus and are indexed under other subjects in the print counterpart of the database, *Hospital Literature Index,* which began publication in 1945, nearly 30 years before inception of the database.

AGELINE

AgeLine is a database produced by the American Association of Retired Persons (AARP) that became available in August 1985. It contains information on middle age through old age. Although middle and old age are dealt with predominantly from a psychosocial aspect, the economic, political, and health-related perspectives are also covered. The database references include journal articles, books, chapters of books, reports, government documents, conference papers, and dissertations published since 1978, with a selected coverage of earlier works. It also contains the SCAN (Service Center for Aging Information) documents funded by the Administration on Aging. In addition to document citations, AgeLine provides more than 2,000 descriptions of federally funded research projects on aging, which are indexed by subject. Journal coverage includes gerontology, social sciences, health, business, and current event periodicals including both scholarly journals and popular magazines.

AgeLine provides access to citations and abstracts and can be subject searched by both natural and controlled languages. The *Thesaurus of Aging Terminology* (1), the controlled indexing vocabulary of AgeLine, is available from the AARP. By no means does AgeLine usurp MEDLINE as the database for searching biomedical topics on middle and old age, but it does complement it. Although some health-related material is included, the strengths of AgeLine lie in furnishing access to nonmedical data, such as psychosocial needs, political activity, family relationships, community involvement, legal services, demographic characteristics, occupational mobility, advocacy, intergenerational programs, and information and referral services. AgeLine, which has no print counterpart, is available through two user-friendly search systems: BRS/After Dark, and BRS Colleague.

EXCERPTA MEDICA

The most convenient print source for locating journal literature on aging and the aged is *Excerpta Medica*—Section 20: *Gerontology and Geriatrics. Excerpta Medica,* consisting of 44 abstracting journals each devoted to a specific specialty or discipline, is the most comprehensive and only English-language abstracting service committed exclusively to medicine and related disciplines. The section on gerontology and geriatrics began in 1958 and covers basic sciences, body systems, psychology and psychiatry, nutrition, rehabilitation, hospitalization, demography and statistics, and social welfare as they relate to aging and the aged. Articles are abstracted from journals in all fields of medicine and ancillary disciplines, not just from gerontology and geriatrics journals.

All abstracts are in English, regardless of the language of the original article. The abstracts are arranged according to the gerontology and geriatrics subfile (outlined in the table of contents) of EMCLAS, the polyhierarchical *Excerpta Medica* classification system. Subcategories are assigned specific numbers based on a five-level hierarchy; for example, articles on hypertension in Section 20 are always assigned the EMCLAS number 5.5.3.

In addition to the classified arrangement, subject access is also available through controlled vocabulary indexing based on MALIMET (Master List of Medical Terms) consisting of 220,000 controlled terms and 255,000 synonyms. In MALIMET, terms are not inverted as they often are in *MeSH,* and they tend to follow common rather than technical usage. This vocabulary is not the trim, concise vocabulary of MEDLARS; it is available only on microform and is cumbersome to use. Instead, one should consult the *Guide to the Classification and Indexing System* (9). This publication includes an alphabetical listing of the most frequently used terms from MALIMET, the major concepts in the EMCLAS system, and the descriptive tags (EMTAGS). It also indicates the section(s) of *Excerpta Medica* in which the subject heading or concept appears.

Each subject indexing entry appearing in print format is composed of several terms, preferred terms from MALIMET and secondary terms, either free text or EMTAGS, which add more information about the article. The multiterm indexing entry gives an overview of the scope of the article and tends to serve as a mini abstract. Each of the preferred terms is systematically rotated to its alphabetical place in the index, which provides the user with multiple subject access points.

Although the arrangement of *Excerpta Medica* makes it an ideal source for browsing and current awareness, the lag time between the publication of an article and its appearance in the abstracting journal tends to be 9 months or more, much longer than for MEDLARS. *Excerpta Medica* has often been used to locate abstracts for foreign-language article references retrieved from sources such as *Index Medicus* (which has no abstracts) or MEDLINE (which provides abstracts only since 1975). Unfortunately, there is no annual index covering all sections of *Excerpta Medica,* which makes searching the print volumes tedious; each section has its own annual index. However, all articles relevant to gerontology and geriatrics should appear in Section 20, even if they also appear in other sections.

The *Excerpta Medica* database, EMBASE, can be searched online via user-friendly systems such as BRS Colleague, or EasyNet back to 1978 and can be accessed through DIALOG back to 1974. The database is purported to contain about 40% more information than the print abstracting journals and to have a lag time of several months less, with 65% of its records containing abstracts. Subject access to EMBASE is by either controlled vocabulary (MALIMET) or free-text, EMCLAS numbers, or EMTAGS. EMBASE is an especially good source for locating information on drugs and the elderly, as it is the database of two major drug indexes, *Drug Literature Index* and *Adverse Reaction Titles.* Drugs can be searched by trade names as well as generic names; 46% of EMBASE records cover the pharmaceutical literature. Free-text searching is important when using EMBASE because the most recent citations are entered into the database before assigned subject indexing is done.

A CLASSIFIED BIBLIOGRAPHY OF GERONTOLOGY AND GERIATRICS

The retrospective literature of geriatrics and gerontology is readily accessible through the landmark work of Shock, *A Classified Bibliography of Gerontology and Geriatrics,* which includes 18,036 references and covers the literature through 1948 (28). Two supplements were also issued: The first, containing 15,983 references, covers the literature published between 1949 and 1955 (29); and the second, having 18,121 references, spans the years 1956 through 1961 (30). From the time the bibliography first appeared in 1951, it was updated by supplementary lists published in the *Journal of Gerontology* through 1980 (27), when the work was discontinued because Shock thought that advanced computer technology would make the literature of gerontology and geriatrics easily accessible. Unfortunately, none of these lists has been cumulated since 1961, but they are well worth checking even in their inconvenient form, especially those that appeared during the 1960s.

This work is the standard bibliography on aging and includes journal articles, books, chapters of books, reports, and a variety of other publications in all languages covering subjects ranging from biochemistry and medicine to social science and social work as they concern aging and the aged. It is the first and only comprehensive bibliography that covers all aspects of gerontology.

When compiling the bibliography, Shock and his associates searched such sources as the first three series of the *Index–Catalogue of the Library of the Surgeon-General's Office*, *Index Medicus* and its predecessors, *Biological Abstracts, Psychological Abstracts, Social Science Abstracts, Population Index, Excerpta Medica—* Section 20: *Gerontology and Geriatrics, Current Contents*, bibliographies published after 1940, texts and reference books in gerontology and geriatrics, and lists of references appearing in clinical and scientific articles.

The bibliography is classified into a hierarchy of related topics in which every concept starts with broad topics and works down to the specific. Such a subject arrangement pulls together related topics in a logically presented visual hierarchy. The scheme of the classification used in the bibliography is indicated in the table of contents, which is the major subject access point. There are also author indexes and broad subject indexes. Note that the subject indexes refer to classification topics rather than to specific references. The major classification topics are (a) gerontology, general orientation; (b) biology of aging; (c) organ systems; (d) geriatrics; (e) psychological processes; (f) social and economic aspects; and (g) miscellaneous. The classification system remains for the most part stable throughout the supplements and the supplementary lists. References to historical items and to nonliving systems that originally appeared in the "Miscellaneous" category were incorporated into "Gerontology, general orientation" in the supplements, and the category was divided into a number of subcategories.

Points to be remembered when using *A Classified Bibliography on Gerontology and Geriatrics* are the following.

1. The table of contents should be checked carefully to identify all relevant subject categories.
2. The classification is based on organ systems, so references to many disease states appear under the subcategory "Pathology" of the organ involved.
3. The literature that is indexed deals with adult life and later maturity; the literature dealing with growth and development, which is also part of the study of aging, has been excluded.
4. Studies that contrast adult with prenatal or neonatal status have been included.
5. Studies showing adult status or change in some structure or function over time have been covered.
6. Papers reporting observations on young adults that could serve as background data for comparative observations on older individuals have been included.
7. Articles on hypertension, neoplasms, arteriosclerosis, gastric ulcers, etc. have been cited only when elderly persons have been the study subjects.
8. The "Geriatrics" category includes references on general medical care and

treatment of patients, but much information of interest to clinicians appears in the organ categories.

9. References that apply to two or more categories appear in all relevant categories (original bibliography) or in the primary classification category and as "See also" references in the other categories (supplements).
10. Citations for abstracts of articles are given when available.

GERONTOLOGY: A CROSS NATIONAL CORE LIST OF SIGNIFICANT WORKS

The second landmark bibliography in gerontology is titled *Gerontology: A Cross National Core List of Significant Works* (8). The information cited in this volume represents evaluative judgment on the part of the editors and 84 consultants from Canada, the United Kingdom, the United States, and other countries. In the foreword the statement is made that "this volume has been designed to facilitate access to the best gerontological knowledge appearing in print over the past half-century."

This bibliography is the result of the broadest cross-national bibliographic project ever undertaken in the field of gerontology. The primary focus is on work from Canada, the United Kingdom, and the United States, although works from other countries are included; emphasis is on social gerontology. The bibliography consists predominantly of books and special issues of journals dedicated to some aspect of gerontology. Journal articles have been limited in the subject bibliography because they can be accessed by other means.

The entire work consists of three parts: (a) historical perspectives, (b) reference works, and (c) subject sources. Each of these parts is further subdivided by country: Canada, the United Kingdom, and the United States. The historical overviews have been written by an eminent gerontologist from each of the three countries. The "reference works" section not only cites reference sources such as abstracts, indexes, directories, and handbooks but also includes a list of gerontology and geriatric journals as well as an extensive listing of bibliographies relating to aging and the aged. The broad categories under which the subject bibliography (part 3) is arranged are listed in the table of contents, which provides the subject access. There are alphabetical author and title indexes but no subject index. For anyone engaged in gerontology and geriatrics, this book should be a desk reference, not merely a library source.

"GERIATRICS: A SELECTED UP-TO-DATE BIBLIOGRAPHY"

Since 1983 "Geriatrics: A Selected Up-to-Date Bibliography," consisting of approximately 500 to 600 references, has been appearing annually in the *Journal of the American Geriatrics Society* (21–25). The original bibliography has been revised from year to year by adding new references and new topics, and deleting older references. Most of the references are contemporary, within the past 4 to 5 years, with preference being given to recent publications. In general, the articles cited deal specifically with the elderly patient population. References are divided into categories and then further subdivided. The bibliographies cover such topics as possible causes of aging, physiological decline accompanying aging, characteristics of illness among geriatric patients, nonphysician services for the elderly, and disease processes arranged by pertinent medical specialties. These bibliographies present excellent overviews of the contemporary journal literature of geriatrics and provide ideal sources for identifying articles to be used for citation searching.

SCIENCE CITATION INDEX AND SOCIAL SCIENCES CITATION INDEX

Citation indexing is based on the presumption that an individual interested in a particular article is also interested in others that cite it, and that the citing indicates subject relations. Therefore to use this kind of index effectively it is necessary to have knowledge of a relevant article(s) at the onset of a citation search. Actually it is a unique type of subject indexing in which the citation takes the place of a subject heading and serves as the surrogate of the indexing term. The concept has been employed in the legal profession for years, but it was not used to index scientific and technical documents until the mid-1960s with the inception of the *Science Citation Index*. Basically, a citation index is a list of articles with a sublist under each article of subsequently published papers that cite that particular article.

Citation indexing does not depend on the interpretation of indexing terms, critical judgment, or the ability of the indexer. Instead, it is the author who determines the subject by means of the document itself. Although it is assumed that references in a paper are relevant to the topic the author is addressing, it is not always the case; and sometimes references useful to one individual are not viewed as such by another. Articles that might not be found during a conventional subject search may be located by citation searching. Of course, significant articles are just as likely to be overlooked using the citation approach. Ideally, subject and citation searching complement each other in a thorough scholarly retrospective literature search. One of the most important aspects of citation searching is that scientific findings or ideas set forth in a paper can be assessed over time, as applications, corrections, modifications, updates, errors, and misconceptions can be detected by following subsequent articles that cite the original paper; this unique process cannot be accomplished by traditional subject searching.

Science Citation Index (*SCI*) and *Social Sciences Citation Index* (*SSCI*) are sources to be considered when searching the literature on aging and the aged, as they each cover the major gerontology and geriatrics journals; in addition, *SCI* indexes a large number of biomedical journals, and *SSCI* includes demography, social work, biomedical social sciences, and psychology. Both indexes are international in scope; they include author, corporate, and free-text subject indexes as well as citation indexes. The *Source* (author) *Index* lists all of the authors of journal articles or book chapters that have been indexed for the year shown on the spine of the volume, with full bibliographic references, and it is the only part of *SCI* or *SSCI* that has complete bibliographic references (Fig. 3A). The *Corporate Index* lists the senior authors' names under corporate affiliation with an abbreviated bibliographic entry; the *Source Index* must be consulted for the complete reference. The *Permuterm Subject Index* is a free-text subject index based on the titles of the articles or chapters included in the *Source Index;* each significant word in the title is paired with every other significant word as a keyword or primary heading and then again alphabetically under other significant words in the title as a secondary term (Fig. 3B). The author's name following each pair of terms must then be looked up in the *Source Index* for the full bibliographic reference. The *Citation Index* is compiled from references or bibliographies at the end of journal articles or chapters that are included in the *Source Index* (Fig. 3C). The cited articles or chapters are arranged alphabetically by the senior authors' names (cited authors) and then chronologically by publication date. Under each cited article is an alphabetical sublisting of the authors appearing in the *Source Index* who have cited that article. In order to use the *Citation Index,* it is necessary to have a reference to a pertinent article. The reference should be at least 2 years old to allow time for it to be cited in the literature. When the reference is located in the *Citation Index,* under the senior author's name, it is followed by a list of authors (from the *Source Index*) who have cited that particular article or chapter. Both of these indexes are available online, but only one, SOCIAL SCISEARCH, can be accessed by a "user-friendly" system. SCISEARCH, the online counterpart of *Science Citation Index,* is available through DIALOG back to 1974, and SOCIAL SCI-SEARCH, the online version of *Social Science Citation Index,* through DIALOG, BRS, and BRS Colleague from 1972 to date.

BIBLIOGRAPHIC SOURCES IN RELATED SCIENCES

Depending on the research topic and the comprehensiveness of the information that is required, it may be necessary to go beyond the indexes and databases that have been discussed here, as abstracting and indexing sources and databases in related sciences may well contain additional information that would be essential for a comprehensive search. Among these are *Biological Abstracts, Biological Abstracts/RRM, Chemical Abstracts, Psychological Abstracts,* and *Sociological Abstracts* (14). Online counterparts of these print abstracting sources are *BIOSIS, CA Search, PsycINFO,* and *Sociological Abstracts* databases. Obviously, there is a significant amount of overlap among indexing and abstracting services (14).

DEMOGRAPHIC DATA AND STATISTICS

Information on health, demographic, and socioeconomic characteristics of the aged is essential for the efficient provision, evaluation, and planning of health care services for this group. Because this information, like the literature of gerontol-

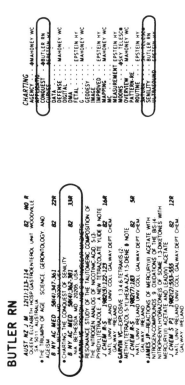

FIG. 3. **A:** Entry from 1982 *SCI Source Index* on which the reference to an article by R. N. Butler is circled. **B.** Entry from 1982 *SCI Permuterm Index* showing the first word of the title of Butler's article paired with other title words, which are circled. **C.** Entry from *SCI Citation Index* on which the citing by J. Busby in 1985 of Butler's 1982 article is circled. Reprinted with permission from the *Science Citation Index* 1985 annual. Copyright 1986 by the Institute for Scientific Information, Philadelphia, PA.

ogy and geriatrics, is scattered throughout various sources, it is frequently difficult and time-consuming to locate. Statistical data are often difficult or impossible to find in the exact format desired, and reliable statistics on a given topic might not even exist. There can be a time lag of several years between data gathering and publication, so in some instances the latest available statistics on a given topic may be 5 to 10 years old. Available data vary in quality, coverage, and completeness. When using statistical sources, it is important to read any introductory material on the methods used to collect and analyze the statistics, and the timeliness and sources of the data should also be noted. Contacting organizations and government agencies by telephone is often a time-saving approach when attempting to locate demographic and statistical information.

Statistical data relevant to the aged are available from: (a) national and international government agencies; (b) professional, special interest, and commercial organizations; and (c) original research projects. When searching for statistical information, it is easier to keep in mind organizations and government agencies as data sources instead of specific publications; exact titles can be identified through library catalogs, indexes, or other sources (31). In fact, a selected annotated bibliography on statistical sources on the aged has been published and is a convenient reference (35).

Generally, data provided by governments are considered to be the most important and up-to-date sources of information. In the United States most of the statistical information relating to the health, demographic, and socioeconomic characteristics is compiled by the National Center for Health Statistics, the Health Care Financing Administration, the Census Bureau, and the Social Security Administration.

The National Center for Health Statistics (NCHS) collects, analyzes, and disseminates vital statistics and statistics on health status, health needs, diseases, manpower, resource utilization, and health care facilities. Among its ongoing publications are *Vital Statistics of the United States,* the definitive and final tabulations of vital statistics; *Monthly Vital Statistics Report,* which contains provisional and current figures; *Vital and Health Statistics Series* (popularly known as the ''Rainbow Series''), data supplied by NCHS surveys and studies; and *Advance Data from Vital and Health Statistics,* a publication issued several times a year that provides early release of selected data that eventually is included in the *Vital and Health Statistics Series.* Statistics compiled by NCHS are grouped by age categories when appropriate. The NCHS can be contacted by telephone for information regarding services, access to microdata tapes, or specific statistical data (301–436–8500).

The HCFA is responsible for overseeing the Medicare and Medicaid programs, and it publishes much statistical data on these two programs and other aspects of long-term care. The HCFA accepts requests for specific data needs (301–594–6705), but its machine-readable data sets are not available for public use. The HCFA quarterly publication, *Health Care Financing Review,* is an especially fruitful source for statistics on demographics related to health care use by the aged.

The Bureau of the Census is the major source of demographic information for the United States, and many of those data are age-related. In addition to its decennial census of the population and housing, the Bureau publishes estimates and projections of the population and provides current data on population and housing characteristics. The Bureau can be contacted for specific statistical information, and machine-readable data tapes are available for purchase (301–763–4100).

The SSA publishes statistical data on socioeconomic factors affecting the aged, e.g., pensions, retirement, demographic and economic characteristics, and supplemental security income. The *Social Security Bulletin* and its annual statistical supplement contain a great deal of age-categorized data.

There are two federal agencies directly concerned with the aged that might serve as statistical sources. The National Institute on Aging (NIA) conducts and sponsors biomedical and behavioral research to enhance the knowledge of the aging process and associated physical, psychological, and social factors resulting from advanced age. The Administration on Aging (AOA) deals with the needs of the elderly from a service point of view and develops programs to promote their welfare. The NIA does not make its machine-readable data sets available for general use but does answer inquiries regarding data collection, analysis, or other aspects of its published statistics (301–496–9795). The AOA provides statistical information by telephone on the topics of aging and the aged. The AOA statistician attempts to keep track of what statistics on aging and the aged are being collected throughout the federal government (202–245–0641).

The Select Committee on Aging of the House of Representatives (202–226–3375) and the Special Committee on Aging of the Senate (202–224–5364) are two other sources to keep in mind when looking for up-to-date data on aging. The Gerontological Society of America has issued a report on the availability of federal data on the aged that includes a detailed guide compiled by the Senate Special Committee on Aging (33). Health-related and socioeconomic statistics collected by many state and local governments contain age-categorized data.

The *Statistical Handbook on Aging Americans* is a convenient print source of current information about the aging population (26). It contains more than 300 statistical tables and charts covering demographics, social characteristics, health aspects, employment conditions, economic status, and expenditures for the elderly. This book is based on data from more than 120 publications including the 1980 decennial census. Most of the information included is dated no earlier than 1980, but in a few cases late 1970 data are given because no more recent figures could be obtained.

The Oldest Americans: State Profiles for Data Based Planning (17) provides statistical data to define and profile the population groups 75 to 84 years of age and 85 years and over at a state level. Until the publication of this report, such data on the oldest Americans (age 85 years and over) were sparse and few were available in print form. This report is based on the 1980 Microdata Program of the Census Bureau, which produced a 5% sample of individual census records and made them available on computer tape. From this 1-in-20 sample file, it became possible to profile the oldest age group separately within individual states. There are four tables for each state covering demographic, socioeconomic, relational, and environmental characteristics for age groups 75 to 84, 85+, and 75+.

On a worldwide scope, the World Health Organization (WHO) publishes a vast amount of health-related statistical information based on data supplied by the governments of the participating countries. Much of it appears in the WHO ongoing publication *World Health Statistics Annual,* which contains vital statistics, life tables, and detailed information on causes of death by sex and age as well as age-sex-specified death rates. The annual publication is supplemented by the *World Health Statistics Quarterly*. These publications can be used effectively with the *Demographic Year Book* published by the United Nations.

Two of the most important organizations providing statistical data on aging and the aged are the American Association of Retired Persons (202–728–4883) and the National Council on the Aging (202–479–1200). Both of these organizations are geared predominantly to social gerontology but are able to supply statistical information on varied aspects of aging and the aged. They routinely accept requests for specific statistical data, and if the information is not held by the organization the requester is referred to other appropriate sources.

Geriatric Length of Stay by Diagnosis and Operation, published annually by the Commission on Professional and Hospital Activities (CPHA), is compiled from individual patient discharge records submitted by hospitals participating in the Professional Activity Study (PAS) of the CPHA (6). These statistics provide a wealth of information for physicians, administrators, utilization review authorities, and planners who are involved in the hospital care of the elderly. The length of stay information can be used to establish check points for continued stay review. These statistics are also available on machine-readable magnetic tape from the CPHA (313–769–6511).

Statistical data on the incidence of diseases are often found in the journal literature, but remember that such statistics are sometimes based on small samples. When searching for statistical information in indexes or databases that use *MeSH* as the indexing vocabulary, one should look first under the topic of interest; the statistical aspect is designated by subheadings such as "Occurrence," "Mortality," "Man-power," "Supply and distribution," and "Utilization." The subject heading "Statistics" is used primarily when indexing articles on statistical concepts, methods, or theories.

MACHINE-READABLE DATA FILES

Machine-readable data files contain actual raw or primary data that may or may not be available in print format. They differ from machine-readable bibliographic files that contain only bibliographic information (citations and abstracts) and not the data itself. Massive amounts of health care data are being collected in machine-readable format by public and private sector organizations. Many of these files can be identified from the *Inventory of U. S. Health Care Data Bases, 1976–1983* (18), which was scheduled to be revised in late 1987. Multiple access to machine-readable data files permits greater advantage to be taken of the substantial investments made in original data collections, which are frequently underutilized by principal investigators. Few investigators exhaust the full analytical potential of a data set, and data collection is an expensive part of any research project. In addition to providing statistical information gleaned by the primary investigators, machine-readable files can be reanalyzed for such purposes as replication, comparative studies, longitudinal studies, or secondary analysis. However, because of the great variability in documentation, it is often difficult for those unfamiliar with the original data collection to use the files efficiently.

It is the purpose of data archives to simplify access to data files. Data archives are depositories that systematically collect quantitative data stored in machine-readable format after the analysis for which the original data was collected has been completed. They preserve the data sets, often cleaning and organizing the data and improving the documentation to assist the secondary user in manipulating the data on magnetic tape.

There are two data archives in the United States that collect machine-readable files on aging and the aged. The National Archive of Computerized Data on Aging (NACDA) is sponsored by the National Institute on Aging and is conducted by the Inter-university Consortium for Political and Social Research (ICPSR) at the University of Michigan. Its data collections are available in readily usable formats free of charge to researchers who are affiliated with academic institutions that are members of the ICPRS or to other researchers at a modest charge based on the size of the data collection. Data sets cover such topics as the process of aging, health-related subjects, and attitudes and behavior of or toward the aged population; each data set is described in the NACDA catalog (19). Requests for data may be sent to: National Archive of Computerized Data on Aging, P. O. Box 1248, Ann Arbor, MI 48106 (313–763–5010).

The Data Archive for Aging and Adult Development (DAAAD) at Duke University provides research resources and support services to facilitate the study of aging and the life cycle from a social science perspective. Its major activity is to identify, process, and distribute social surveys of special relevance to investigators with interests in aging or the adult life cycle. For most of its data sets, DAAAD can supply tapes and relevant materials directly to users, but a few are restricted. The cost of data sets varies depending on the length of the file and other factors, but the charge is usually the cost of reproducing the material. Data sets are described in the DAAAD catalog (3). Inquiries for data sets may be sent to: Data Archive for Aging and Adult Development, Box 3003, Duke University Medical Center, Durham, NC 27710 (919–684–3204).

NATIONAL DATA BASE ON AGING

The National Data Base on Aging (NDBA) is an up-to-date information system dealing with statistics about the elderly and the services provided by the Network on Aging, which is composed of the Administration on Aging, State Units on Aging, and Area Agencies on Aging. Service programs, which operate in every county in the United States, include in-home care, nutrition, transportation, and other services that enhance independence for the elderly. The NDBA was established in 1981 and covers a wide range of data from numbers and characteristics of persons served to units and costs of services provided. In September 1981 baseline data were requested from all State Units and Area Agencies; annual updates involve the collection of data from all the State Units and a one-third sample of the Area Agencies (a different group of area agencies is selected each year). Data must be accessed through the NDBA staff (202–785–0707), who for a fee provide data retrieval, analyses, write-ups, charts and tables, and computer-generated graphics in response to requests for specific information.

CONCLUSION

When searching for information relating to age, aging, or the aged, there is no one ''best'' way that satisfies every situation. For comprehensive access, automated information retrieval is by far the method of choice because of the large amount of literature that can be searched in a relatively short time and because of the many available access points. However, in some instances manual searching must be done simply because the information cannot be accessed via computer. There are times when the telephone may prove to be a better information source than either print or electronic retrieval media, especially when one is attempting to locate demographic or statistical information. Despite the complex literature base of geriatrics and gerontology, the search process is not as formidable as it may first appear if the search strategy is carefully planned at the onset to meet the requirements of the research project and is systematically documented throughout its course.

REFERENCES

1. American Association of Retired Persons (1986): *Thesaurus of Aging Terminology,* 3rd ed. Association of Retired Persons, Washington, DC.
2. Beatty, W. K. (1981): Libraries and how to use them. In: *Coping With the Biomedical Literature: A Primer for the Scientist and the Clinician,* edited by K. S. Warren, pp. 199–225. Praeger, New York.
3. Burchett, B. M., and George, L. K. (1985): *Duke University Data Archive for Aging and Adult Development: Reference Guide.* Survey Data Laboratory, Center for the Study of Aging and Human Development, Duke University, Durham, NC.
4. Charen, T. (1976–1981): *MEDLARS Indexing Manual.* National Library of Medicine, Bethesda. Reproduced by National Technical Information Service, Springfield, VA, 2 volumes.
5. Collen, M. F., and Flagle, C. D. (1985): Full-text medical literature retrieval by computer: a pilot study. *JAMA,* 254:2768–2774.
6. Commission on Professional and Hospital Activities (1982–1987): *Geriatric Length of Stay by Diagnosis and Operation, United States.* Commission on Professional and Hospital Activities,

Ann Arbor, MI, 7 volumes. Published annually. (From 1977 to 1981 it was published as *Geriatric Length of Stay in PAS Hospitals, by Diagnosis and Operation, United States.*)

7. Cummings, M. M. (1981): The National Library of Medicine. In: *Coping With the Biomedical Literature: A Primer for the Scientist and the Clinician,* edited by K. S. Warren, pp. 161–181. Praeger, New York.

8. Edwards, W. M., and Flynn, F. (1982): *Gerontology: A Cross National Core List of Significant Works.* Institute of Gerontology, University of Michigan, Ann Arbor.

9. Excerpta Medica (1987): *Guide to the Classification and Indexing System.* 3rd ed. Excerpta Medica, Amsterdam (*in press*).

10. Glaser, J. (1986): Geriatric dentistry: the specialty and its literature. *Med. Ref. Serv. Q.,* 4:29–46.

11. Green, E. W. (1981): Searching the MEDLARS file for information on the elderly. *Bull. Med. Libr. Assoc.,* 69:359–367.

12. Haynes, R. B., McKibbon, A., Fitzgerald, D., Guyatt, G. H., Walker, C. J., and Sackett, D. L. (1986): How to keep up with the medical literature. V. Access by personal computer to the medical literature. *Ann. Intern. Med.,* 105:810–816.

13. Haynes, R. B., McKibbon, A., Walker, C. J., Mousseau, G., Baker, L. M., Fitzgerald, D., Guyatt, G., and Norman, G. R. (1985): Computer searching of the medical literature: an evaluation of MEDLINE searching systems. *Ann. Intern. Med.,* 103:812–816.

14. Huth, E. J. (1982): *How to Write and Publish Papers in the Medical Sciences,* pp. 11–35. ISI Press, Philadelphia.

15. Huth, E. J. (1985): Needed: an economics approach to systems for medical information. *Ann. Intern. Med.,* 103:617–619.

16. Kunz, J. (1979): Index Medicus: a century of medical citation. *JAMA,* 241:387–390.

17. Longino, C. F. (1986): *The Oldest Americans: State Profiles for Data Based Planning.* Center for Social Research in Aging, University of Miami, Coral Gables, FL.

18. Mullner, R. M., and Byre, C. S. (1985): *Inventory of U. S. Health Care Data Bases, 1976–1983.* DHHS Publ. (HRSA) HRS-P-OD 84–5. U. S. Dept. of Health and Human Services, Public Health Service, Health Resources and Services Administration, Bureau of Health Professions, Office of Data Analysis and Management, Bethesda.

19. National Archive of Computerized Data on Aging (1986): *Catalog of Data Collections: October 1986.* Inter-university Consortium for Political and Social Research, Ann Arbor, MI.

20. National Library of Medicine; MEDLARS Management Section (1985): *The Basics of Searching MEDLINE: A Guide for the Health Professional.* National Library of Medicine, Bethesda.

21. Rosenthal, M. (1983): Geriatrics: a selected up-to-date bibliography. *J. Am. Geriatr. Soc.,* 31:83–98.

22. Rosenthal, M. (1984): Geriatrics: a selected up-to-date bibliography. *J. Am. Geriatr. Soc.,* 32:64–79.

23. Rosenthal, M. (1985): Geriatrics: a selected up-to-date bibliography. *J. Am. Geriatr. Soc.,* 33:69–85.

24. Rosenthal, M. (1986): Geriatrics: a selected up-to-date bibliography. *J. Am. Geriatr. Soc.,* 34:148–171.

25. Rosenthal, M. (1987): Geriatrics: a selected up-to-date bibliography. *J. Am. Geriatr. Soc.,* 35:560–586.

26. Schick, F. L., editor (1986): *Statistical Handbook on Aging Americans.* Oryx Press, Phoenix.

27. Shock, N. W. (1950–1980): Index to current publications in gerontology and geriatrics. *J. Gerontol,* 5–35. (For volumes 5 to 15, 1950–1960, the title was Index to current periodical literature.)

28. Shock, N. W. (1951): *A Classified Bibliography of Gerontology and Geriatrics.* Stanford University Press, Stanford, CA.

29. Shock, N. W. (1957): *A Classified Bibliography of Gerontology and Geriatrics. Supplement One 1949–1955.* Stanford University Press, Stanford, CA.

30. Shock, N. W. (1983): *A Classified Bibliography of Gerontology and Geriatrics. Supplement Two 1956–1961.* Stanford University Press, Stanford, CA.

31. Singer, I. D., Meyerhoff, A. S., and Schiffman, S. B. (1985): *A Guide to Health Data Resources.* Center for Health Affairs, Project HOPE, Millwood, VA.

32. Snow, B., Corbett, A. L., and Brahmi, F. A. (1986): Grateful Med: NLM's front end software. *Database,* 9:94–99.

33. Storey, J. R. (1986): *Availability of Federal Data on the Aged: Recent Changes and Future Concerns. A Report of the Geronotological Society of America.* Gerontological Society of America, Washington, DC.
34. Vaisrub, S. (1979): To the best of our knowledge, which is limited at best. *JAMA,* 241:278.
35. Weise, F. O. (1983): Statistical sources on the aging: a selected bibliography. *Med. Ref. Serv. Q.,* 2:53–70.

Human Aging Research: Concepts and Techniques,
edited by B. Kent and R. N. Butler.
Raven Press, Ltd., New York © 1988.

Aging in Cultured Human Cells

Leonard Hayflick

*University of California, San Francisco, School of Medicine; VAMC, Cell Biology and
Aging Section (151E), 4150 Clement St., San Francisco, California 94121*

The fact that human and animal life-spans are finite is not only apparent from simple observation and actuarial data, it is now demonstrable at the most fundamental level, the cell itself.

This is a relatively new discovery. As recently as 25 years ago, it was believed that animal and human cells cultured in laboratory glassware were potentially immortal. In 1961 we reported that cell cultures derived from normal human tissues *do* have a limited capacity to divide and function. Normal cells, like the humans from which they come, are mortal. We proposed an intrinsic biological limit on life-span that is governed by intracellular events (16–23,26,28).

Whatever causes age changes and death in the whole organism undoubtedly does not produce identical changes, and at equivalent rates, in each cell composing that organism. If the rates of aging vary among organs, tissues, and their constituent cells, then the fundamental causes of aging may occur as a consequence of decrements in only a few cell types where the rate is fastest and the effects are greatest.

The limited proliferative capacity of cultured normal human and animal cells is called the "phase III phenomenon" (28). In recent years it has been found that as cultured normal human cells approach phase III they incur dozens of irreversible functional decrements that are expressed as the cells age. Many of these losses are identical to changes expressed in humans as they age. The results of these and other studies have profound implications for our understanding of human aging and for gerontological theory generally.

HISTORICAL PERSPECTIVE

An essential element in considering the role of the cell as the fundamental locus of age changes is whether or not those cells are normal. Because age changes do not occur in abnormal cancer cells, cultured cells must be determined to be normal if they are to yield valid information on the biology of aging.

The controversy that arose in efforts to address this issue actually began about 100 years ago, but even this fact has been brought to light only recently (32). In 1891 the great German biologist August Weismann speculated that the somatic cells of higher animals would be found to have a limited doubling potential. Although he provided no experimental evidence for his surmise, Weismann stated " . . . death takes place because a worn-out tissue cannot forever renew itself, and because a capacity for increase by means of cell division is not everlasting but finite" (55).

There are at least two ways in which the mortality or immortality of normal cells can be determined. First, vertebrate cells can be serially cultured in laboratory glassware. Second, similar cells, containing specific markers allowing them to be distinguished from host cells, can be serially transplanted in isogenic laboratory animals. The transplanted tissue is regrafted to a younger host when the previous host becomes old. The goal of both *in vitro* and *in vivo* studies has been to answer this fundamental question: Can normal vertebrate cells that function and replicate under ideal conditions escape from the inevitability of aging and death that is obligatory for the animal from which they were derived?

Immortal Heart Cells?

In respect to studies undertaken in cell culture before 1960, one investigation has stood out as the classic response to this question. In the early part of this century, Alexis Carrel, a noted cell culturist, surgeon, and Nobel Laureate, described experiments purporting to show that fibroblasts derived from chick heart tissue could be cultured serially indefinitely. The culture was voluntarily terminated after 34 years (44). This finding sparked intense interest worldwide not only in the scientific community but in the lay press as well.

Its importance to gerontologists was clear. If true, it strongly implied that cells released from *in vivo* control had the potential to divide and function normally for a period of time in excess of the life span of the species. Thus either the types of cells cultured play no role in the aging phenomenon, or aging results from changes in the intracellular matrix or from changes that occur at higher levels of cell organization. That is, aging results from physiological interactions between cells only when they are organized as tissues or organs. In any case Carrel's results and their interpretation were of vital concern to biogerontologists because both strongly suggested that aging is not the result of events occurring within individual cells.

In the years that followed Carrel's observations, support for his experimental results seemed to be forthcoming from many laboratories in which it was observed that several other cell populations also seemed to have the striking ability to replicate, apparently indefinitely.

Immortal cell populations derived from a variety of human and animal tissues were reported to occur spontaneously in dozens of laboratories in the 20-year period from the early 1940s to the early 1960s. These cell populations, numbering in the hundreds, are best known by the prototype cell lines HeLa (derived from a human cervical carcinoma in 1952) and L cells (derived from mouse mesenchyme in 1943). They continue to florish in cell culture laboratories throughout the world even to this day.

Immortal cell populations still occasionally arise spontaneously from normal cell cultures by a mysterious process. Today, however, they can be created purposely, albeit at low efficiency, by exposing them to radiation, chemical carcinogens, or certain oncogenic viruses. More recently this process of "immortalization," as it has come to be called, can be accomplished routinely by fusing mortal antibody-producing lymphocytes to immortal myeloma cells. The resulting hybrid, known as a hybridoma, continues to express specific antibody indefinitely (34). Use of this technique is one important cause of the current revolution in biotechnology.

Nevertheless, what seemed to be incontrovertible evidence for the existence of immortal cells soon fell to new insights and a preponderance of opposing information. Before further discussion, however, it is necessary to understand how cells are cultured.

AGING UNDER GLASS

Millions of cells can be released from virtually any piece of tissue and from almost any animal species, usually with a substance called "trypsin." (The name is misleading because it is actually an aqueous extract of porcine pancreas and therefore a mixture of many enzymes of which trypsin is only one.) The released cells are then placed in a culture vessel with growth medium, incubated at 37°C if they are derived from homoiotherms, and after a few days are observed to have replicated.

The Primary Culture

The first vessel(s) into which the original cells are placed is referred to as the primary culture. Once cells have divided in the primary culture to the point where the entire surface of the vessel floor is covered with cells, division stops. This condition is referred to as a "confluent culture." If additional cells are desired, it is necessary to provide them with additional surface. The procedure by which this is accomplished is called a "subcultivation" or, in laboratory jargon, a "split."

Subcultivations

A subcultivation is accomplished first by removing the spent growth medium. The cells remain attached to the vessel floor and can then be released by introduction of trypsin. The resulting cell suspension is then centrifuged, the trypsin discarded, and the cells resuspended in fresh growth medium. This suspension is then divided into two equal parts, placed into two new daughter culture vessels, and incubated again. After a few days the cells are once again found to have replicated to the point of confluency, necessitating further subcultivation. This process can be repeated until the normal cells ultimately stop dividing, age, and die. We called this last stage the phase III phenomenon (28).

Population Doublings

It is important to realize that the cell population has doubled at each subcultivation. Thus if one million cells are introduced into the primary culture, and if the vessel floor has room enough for only two million cells, the original cell population will double one time. If two daughter vessels are produced from each mother vessel at every subcultivation, the cell population will be found to increase exponentially as $2^{2 \cdots n}$ each time confluency is reached. For normal human fibroblasts derived from embryonic tissue the number of population doublings that will occur before phase III is reached is 50 ± 10 (28).

Finite Replicative Capacity of Cultured Normal Cells

When cells from human embryonic tissue were first cultivated, the dogma insisted that if cultured cells replicate successfully for a few doublings any ultimate death of the cells could be blamed only on errors in technique. The dogma further maintained that all cultured cells capable of division were intrinsically immortal. Indeed a number of authentic immortal populations were then known, and this lent support to the belief. There was, for example, the HeLa cell and the L cell, which are truly immortal cell populations. Nevertheless, we reported that cultures derived from human fetal tissue consistently failed to divide after about 50 population doublings (28). Identical culture conditions consistently permitted the luxurious growth of the same cells when they were at fewer than 50 population doublings.

We suggested that the reason our cultured cells consistently failed to replicate indefinitely was because they were normal cells and therefore were intrinsically incapable of replicating or functioning indefinitely. They are mortal. We further suggested that immortal cell populations such as HeLa and L cells were immortal because they are abnormal in one or more important properties (16,28).

Cell Strains, Cell Lines, and Transformation

We defined cell populations that have properties identical to the cells composing the tissue of origin as ''cell strains'' and immortal cell populations having abnormal properties as ''cell lines'' (28). The phenomenon by which a cell strain becomes a cell line we called an ''alteration'' (28). These terms are not now used by others to describe these conditions, and consequently references to the phenomena themselves have become hopelessly blurred in the scientific literature. The names of course are unimportant, but the phenomena and the conditions they describe are.

The phenomenon of alteration came to be known as "transformation," but in the last 20 years even this term has become so misused that, despite its original clear definition, few now agree on its meaning. The original meaning of transformation was defined by us as the acquisition by normal cells of abnormal properties frequently characteristic of cancer cells (16,28). The phenomenon is therefore fundamental to our understanding of aging and of how normal cells become cancer cells. Nevertheless, the term now is so misunderstood and misused that unless it is specifically defined by the user it is impossible to assume correctly what is meant.

Phase III Phenomenon

We showed that cultured human embryonic fibroblasts, which have the greatest capacity for replication *in vitro,* undergo 50 ± 10 population doublings in about 1 year before division ceases (28). We divided these events into three phases. Phase I represents the primary culture, phase II the active replication period, and phase III the period when cell replication slows, ceases, and ultimately ends with complete cell degeneration and death. We suggested that the phase III phenomenon represents aging at the cellular level (28). Research on this phenomenon conducted over the next 25 years has confirmed our results and has substantially supported the suggestion that the phenomenon represents aging at the cellular level (17,18,21–23,42). It has given rise to the new field of study that we named "cytogerontology" (18,20).

CYTOGERONTOLOGY

Central to the question of cell immortality as it relates to biogerontology is whether the cell populations studied *in vitro* are composed of normal or abnormal cells. Clearly the aging of animals occurs in normal cell populations. If we are to equate the behavior of normal cells *in vivo* with that of similar cells *in vitro,* then the latter must be shown to be normal as well.

Twenty-three years ago Moorhead and I postulated that all immortal cell populations are abnormal in at least one important property (28). As such they are not proper subjects for the study of aging and indeed are not proper subjects for the study of many other biological phenomena for which they are frequently wrongly used. All immortal cell lines vary in chromosome number, morphology, or banding pattern from the original animal or human cells from which they are derived. Most, but not all, produce tumors when inoculated into experimental animals. Most abnormal cell lines can grow in suspension culture, that is, unattached to a solid substrate. Normal cells can grow attached only to a solid substrate.

Aging Is Inevitable

Moorhead and I demonstrated that when normal human embryonic cells are grown under the most favorable conditions aging and death are the inevitable consequence after about 50 population doublings (28). We also showed that the death of cultured normal human cells was not due to some trivial cause involving medium components or culture conditions but was an inherent property of the cells themselves (16,28). This observation now has been confirmed in hundreds of laboratories where variations in medium components and cultural conditions have been as numerous as the laboratories themselves.

Since our observation and interpretation 25 years ago, no normal human or animal cell population has been shown to be immortal. Immortality is defined as continuous serial cultivation *in vitro* or *in vivo* in which at least 150 population doublings occur over a minimum of at least 2 years. Cultured or transplanted normal cells are defined as having properties identical to those of the normal cells that compose the tissue of origin.

All Immortal Cells Are Abnormal

The widespread use of immortal, abnormal cell populations for a variety of research purposes has created enormous problems in the interpretation of experiments in which these cells are used. It is virtually impossible to extrapolate results obtained with these abnormal cell populations to the behavior of normal cells *in vivo*. The failure to recognize this fundamental pitfall is the reason why much of the effort in modern cancer biology is seriously flawed. The current widespread use of such abnormal, immortal cell lines as C3H 10 T1/2, NIH 3T3, and BHK 21 in efforts to understand the conversion of normal cells to cancer cells is indefensible.

These cells are widely believed to be normal cells. They are used to determine if various treatments will convert them to cancer cells. There is little regard for the fact that these cells already are transformed and have been proved to produce tumors when inoculated into laboratory animals (2,3). Even if they did not, the fact that they are chromosomally abnormal and are immortal should be sufficient reason not to use them for studies in which the use of normal cells is mandated.

This fundamental flaw in the conduct of much research in modern cancer biology can be circumvented by appreciating the fact that entirely normal cell populations can be cultured *in vitro*. Such cultures are normal in every respect if they are derived from normal tissue, and of course they ultimately age and die just like the animal or human from which they came.

Conceptual Origins

Although there were many reports prior to ours that described the failure of most cultured cells to proliferate indefinitely, none characterized the cells as normal, ruled out artifacts as the cause, or suggested that the phenomenon might be associated with aging (45,51). In fact, the observation that cultured cells frequently failed to replicate indefinitely was probably made thousands of times from the genesis of cell culture techniques in the early 1900s to our report 60 years later.

Those prior failures went unreported because the existing dogma insisted that the failure of cells to proliferate indefinitely *in vitro* must be attributable to errors in the "art" required to keep cells dividing forever. That dogma was so well entrenched that our original manuscript (28) was rejected by *The Journal of Experimental Medicine* with the statement that "The largest fact to have come out from tissue culture in the last 50 years is that cells inherently capable of multiplying will do so indefinitely if supplied with the right milieu *in vitro*" (25).

That belief was tantamount to believing that, given the right milieu *in vivo*, human beings also will live forever. The search for the Fountain of Youth was alive and well, at least until 1960. In fact, believers in the Fountain of Youth still exist today. They steadfastly maintain that someday a growth medium will be found that will permit normal cells to divide and function indefinitely. That has not occurred in 25 years despite tens of thousands of attempts to do so. Even under the best possible "culture" conditions where the serial transplantation of normal tissue is made from animal to animal, immortality cannot be achieved.

Our finding that cultured normal cells have a finite capacity to replicate has had important implications in gerontological theory. Before these implications are considered, however, it will be necessary to discuss how Carrel was misled into believing that he had successfully cultured chick heart fibroblasts for 34 years.

ALEXIS CARREL AND THE MYTH OF IMMORTAL NORMAL CHICK CELLS

By the late 1960s it became apparent to me and others that Carrel's claim to have cultured chick fibroblast cells for 34 years was spurious (17,18). It had to be assumed that Carrel's chick cultures consisted of normal cells because no one (with one possible exception described below) has ever reported a spontaneously arising transformed chicken cell strain. Several reports of alleged immortal chick cell lines did begin to appear in the 1970s, but all were purposefully produced with oncogenic viruses, chemical carcinogens, or radiation (7,11). In 1984 Ogura et al. (43) reported their development of two immortal chick cell lines. One was produced by exposure of the cells to the carcinogen N-methyl-N'-nitro-N-nitroso-guanidine, and the other arose spontaneously. However, both the spontaneously transformed cell line and the chemically induced transformed cells were shown to be abnormal and to produce the avian leukosis retrovirus.

It has been 50 years since the voluntary termination of Carrel's alleged immortal chick fibroblasts, and no one other than Ogura's group has reported a spontaneous transformation of normal chick fibroblasts. Even their report is clouded by the finding that the population produces a retrovirus.

The rarity of this event can be appreciated when one considers that chick tissues have been one of the most frequently cultured tissues in the past 50 years. Thus the likelihood that Carrel had found such a population is remote, especially because all attempts to confirm his findings have failed except for the possibility noted above. Furthermore, even if Carrel's observation was legitimate, his "immortal" cells must have been abnormal, as there are no known exceptions to this rule. Thus Carrel's findings cannot be used as evidence that normal cells have escaped the inevitability of the phase III phenomenon.

I have proposed one explanation for Carrel's findings in which the method of preparation of chick embryo extract, used as a source of nutrients for his cells, permitted the introduction of new, viable fibroblasts into the so-called immortal culture at each feeding (18). Although I believe that Carrel was unaware of this artifact, Witkowski, in a lengthy study of Carrel's immortal cells, suggests otherwise (56–58).

INVERSE RELATION BETWEEN DONOR AGE AND CELL POPULATION DOUBLINGS

In the decade that followed our first report (28), further evidence appeared that provided important new insights into cellular aging or "cytogerontology."

In 1965 we reported that cultured fibroblasts derived from older humans replicated fewer times than those derived from embryos (16). Because the technique for determining population doublings at that time was crude, we were unable to establish a direct relation between donor age and population doubling potential. Subsequently, studies done by others not only confirmed the principle that we had observed but extended it significantly.

Martin and his colleagues derived cultures from human donors ranging from the fetus to adults 90 years of age (38). Although the data revealed considerable scatter, Martin et al. observed a regression coefficient, from the first to the ninth decade, of -0.2 population doublings per year of life with a standard deviation of 0.05 and a correlation coefficient of -0.50. The scatter found is not unlike that reported to occur with virtually any age-related change that is measured cross-sectionally and not longitudinally. Nevertheless, at least nine more studies have confirmed the finding that the number of population doublings of cultured human cells is inversely proportional to donor age.

This inverse relation has now been shown to occur in normal human cells derived from such diverse tissue as lung (16), skin (13,38,48,53), liver (36), arterial smooth muscle (1), lens (52), and T-lymphocytes (8,54).

DIRECT RELATION BETWEEN MAXIMUM SPECIES LIFE SPAN AND POPULATION DOUBLINGS OF THEIR CULTURED CELLS

Several years ago we suggested that the population doubling potential of cultured fibroblasts from several animal species revealed a surprisingly good direct correlation with maximum species life span (19). In the years that followed several other reports have appeared that have added substantially to this idea, especially the work of Rohme (47). One report in which several marsupial species were studied did not support this finding; however, the authors did not determine population doublings by conventional means nor are the maximum life-spans of the species they studied known (50). We have suggested that there may be a direct proportionality between the maximum life-spans of 10 different vertebrate species and the population doubling potential of their cultured fibroblasts (26). These species range in diversity from mouse to humans to the Galapagos tortoise.

If this relation can be extended and confirmed, it suggests the presence of a chronometer or pacemaker within normal cells that is characteristic for each species and that dictates maximum cell doublings or functional capacity. The postulated chronometer may or may not be the same one that we suggest might control the inverse relation between donor age and population doubling potential.

PROGERIA AND WERNER'S SYNDROME

Progeria (Hutchinson-Guilford syndrome) is a human condition leading to a severe deceleration of growth in patients as young as 9 years of age (46). A very rare disease, it is thought by many to represent a model for precocious aging in which individuals at the end of the first decade of life manifest the physical signs of aging typical of their normal counterparts at the seventh decade of life.

Werner's syndrome is similar to progeria in many ways, although its salient manifestations occur in later years. The full clinical picture shows early graying and loss of hair, short stature, juvenile cataracts, proneness to diabetes, atherosclerosis and calcification of the blood vessels, osteoporosis, and a high incidence of malignancy (9).

If Werner's syndrome and progeria are examples of accelerated aging, when does aging occur in cultured fibroblasts taken from these donors? From 2 to 18 doublings were found to occur, whereas normal values would be between 20 and 40 (12). Others have reported decreased mitotic activity, DNA synthesis, and cloning efficiency of cultured progeria cells (5,40).

MEMORY OF CULTURED NORMAL HUMAN CELLS

When we first established human diploid cell strains 28 years ago, it became apparent that their finite lifetime imposed a serious limit on the capacity to work with any single strain. We found that a strain derived from fetal tissue underwent 50 ± 10 population doublings over a period of about 1 year and was then lost (16,28). In order to circumvent this important limitation we succeeded in freezing viable normal human cells at subzero temperatures (28). In this way it was possible to fully characterize a single human diploid cell strain and have it available for study for long periods of time. The potential yield of cells from a population capable of 50 population doubling is about 20 million metric tons (16).

In 1962 we developed and placed into liquid nitrogen storage several hundred ampules of our normal human diploid cell strain WI-38, which subsequently became the most completely characterized normal human cell population in the world. It is today the archetype normal human fibroblast and is used worldwide for applications in biological research, virus isolation and identification, and the production of several human virus vaccines.

WI-38 has been in cryogenic storage for 26 years, which represents the longest period of time that a viable normal human cell population has ever been stored. The ability to preserve normal cell strains has permitted experimentation directed toward answering a fundamental question in cytogerontology: If cells are frozen at various population doubling levels up to phase III, how many population doublings will the cells undergo when they are thawed or reconstituted? Do they have a "clock" that is arrested in the cold at the population doubling level at which they were frozen? If so, then the total cumulative number of doublings both before and after freezing would be about 50 in the case of a fetal strain. Or does freezing reset the "clock" to zero or to some random number?

In the 26 years since 1962 we have shown that WI-38 and other human cell strains have an extraordinary memory. Even after 26 years WI-38 cells remember at which population doubling level they were frozen and, upon reconstitution, undergo the number of population doublings that remain from the time they were frozen to 50. More than 130 ampules have been reconstituted by us in the past 26 years, and the memory of the cells is as accurate today as it was in 1962.

FUNCTIONAL FAILURE AS CULTURED NORMAL HUMAN CELLS REACH PHASE III

The probability that animals age because one or more cell types loses its ability to proliferate is unlikely. It is more likely that decrements in physiological functions that appear before cells lose their capacity to replicate are the true causes of age changes. In 1971 we reported the first functional decrement in a normal human cell population before its loss of proliferative capacity (31). We found that WI-38 cells lost much of their ability to synthesize collagen and to induce collagenolytic activity after almost 40 population doublings.

In the next decade almost 200 functional changes have been found to occur in cultured normal human cells prior to their loss of replicative capacity. A full tabulation is presented in a review of this field (22). The changes reported to occur cover virtually all aspects of cell biochemistry, morphology, and behavior. They include changes in lipids, carbohydrates, amino acids, proteins, RNA, DNA, enzymes, cell cycle dynamics, cell size and morphology, synthesis, incorporation, and stimulation.

Mitotic Failure Does Not Cause Aging

It is more likely that these changes, which herald the approaching loss of division capacity, play the central role in the expression of aging and result in the death of the individual animal or human well before its cells fail to divide.

Of great importance is the realization that many of the same changes that have been reported to occur in cultured normal human cells as they age *in vitro* are identical to changes that are known to occur in cells *in vivo* as humans age (22). This finding adds considerable weight to our contention that the phase III phenomenon is indeed an expression of aging at the cellular level.

Nevertheless, there are several classes of cells that are incapable of division in mature animals, and it is just as likely, if not even more likely, that these cells play a greater role in the expression of age changes than those cells that are capable of dividing. Examples of nondividing cells are neurons and muscle cells. It is important to emphasize that the cessation of mitotic activity is only one functional decrement whose genetic basis may be similar to those functional decrements known to occur in aging nondividing cells.

We have proposed, therefore, that the same genetic basis may underlie the loss of division capacity in normal fibroblasts and the loss of function in aging nondividing normal cells. It is not our belief that age changes result necessarily from loss of the function to divide but simply in the loss of any function characteristic of an aging cell. The genetic basis for loss of any of these functions is thought to be the common denominator.

If these conclusions are accurate, an understanding of the mechanism by which normal cells lose their capacity to replicate could provide insights into the causes of decrements in other functional properties such as those that occur in aging neurons or muscle cells.

FINITE LIFETIME OF NORMAL CELLS *IN VIVO*

As indicated at the outset of this discussion, there are two ways in which a determination of cell immortality can be made. The first method is to grow normal cells in culture. That has been discussed, and the conclusion is that under these conditions normal cells do have a finite capacity to replicate and function. The second way in which this question can be answered is to determine if normal cells can proliferate indefinitely *in vivo*.

If all cell types were continually renewed without loss of function or capacity for self-renewal, organs composed of such cells would be expected to function normally indefinitely. Their host would live forever. Regrettably, renewal cell populations do not occur in most tissues; and when they do, cell proliferation is not indefinite.

Is it possible, then, to circumvent the death of normal animal cells that results from the death of the "host" by transferring marked cells to younger animals seriatim? Such experiments would provide an *in vivo* counterpart to the *in vitro* experiments described above. If the analogy is accurate, we would predict that normal cells transplanted serially to proper inbred hosts would, like their *in vitro* counterparts, age. Such experiments would largely rule out objections to *in vitro* studies that are based on the artificiality of the *in vitro* environment. The question could be answered by serial orthotopic transplantation of normal somatic tissue to new, young, inbred hosts each time the recipient approaches old age.

Data reported from many laboratories in which rodent mammary tissue (6), skin (35), and hematopoietic cells (4,10,14,15,29,49) were employed demonstrated that normal cells serially transplanted to inbred hosts do not proliferate or survive indefinitely. Studies done with hematopoietic cells to investigate this point actually number in the dozens (24).

The trauma of transplantation does not appear to influence the results, and in heterochronic transplants survival time is related to the age of the grafted tissue (35). Cancer cells, on the other hand, frequently can be transplanted indefinitely. Thus the immortality of cancer cells *in vitro* is also expressed *in vivo*.

Many grafts transplanted *in vivo* have been found to survive much longer than the life-span of the host or donor species before aging and dying. This fact has been erroneously interpreted by some to mean that normal cells can replicate continuously for periods of time in excess of the species' known life-span. However, grafted tissue behaves quite differently from cultured cells. The latter are usually kept in a state of continuous proliferation. The cells in grafted tissue are not dividing continuously, nor are the number of cells in the dividing pool as great as that in cell cultures.

If fibroblasts in grafted tissue replicated to the extent that comparable cells do *in vitro*, the graft would quickly weigh more than its host. Thus it is important to appreciate that long survival time is not equivalent to proliferation time or rounds of division. Cells in grafts have a very low reproductive turnover rate. This is analogous to holding normal cell cultures at room temperature, which extends calendar time for cell survival but does not result in increased population doublings.

CURRENT STATUS OF RESEARCH IN CYTOGERONTOLOGY

The phase III phenomenon has been established with certainty to be an intrinsic property of normal cells and clearly associated with biological aging. Consequently, cytogerontology, like the evolution of most developed fields in biology, is emerging from a period of descriptive findings to the mature stage of theory testing. The theories that are being tested in cytogerontology are the same that form the underpinning for all of biogerontology. These theories can be reduced to six or eight nonmutually exclusive hypotheses, most of which are based on changes in the expression of information-containing molecules (27).

Theories that are dependent on the role of the genome in aging can be divided into two general categories. The first category considers aging as a programmed genetic event caused by (a) the active expression of specific ''aging genes,'' (b) the active expression of ''longevity genes,'' or (c) the passive exhaustion of accurate genetic information. Within this group of theories the fundamental cause of cellular senescence would involve mostly nuclear rather than cytoplasmic events.

The second category of theories considers senescence to be the result of progressive damage to organelles or errors in molecules not associated with the genetic apparatus. Thus decrements that occur mostly in the cytoplasm are encompassed by these theories.

In recent years our laboratory studies have been directed toward understanding how normal cells keep time and how they know how old they are. Our approach to answering these fundamental questions centers on elucidating events in the cell genome. We are attempting to (a) identify the chromosome(s) or gene loci associated with cellular senescence in the cultured normal human fibroblast strain WI-38 and (b) determine if these same loci are also implicated in the transformed state (immortality) of cell lines. This approach follows from previous work that led us to conclude that the clock(s) governing the occurrence of phase III are located in the cell nucleus.

CELL HYBRIDIZATION AND LOCATION OF THE CHRONOMETER

Littlefield (37) was the first to probe cellular aging in normal human diploid fibroblasts by the use of cell hybridization techniques. He fused pairs of young and old human fibroblasts and pairs of old human fibroblasts hoping to observe complementation and prolongation of *in vitro* life-span. He did not observe this and concluded that the senescent phenotype behaved as if it were dominant in all combinations of the hybrid colonies that he examined. Later Hoehn et al. (30) fused young human fibroblasts from different sources and with slightly different total population doubling potentials. They concluded that senescence behaved codominantly. Hybrids displayed growth potentials intermediate between the parental cells.

Norwood and co-workers (41,42) reached essentially the same conclusion using heterokaryons composed of senescent and young human diploid fibroblasts. It should be noted, however, that one of the four cell strains that Norwood et al. (41) examined was karyotypically 47, XXY and therefore not normal diploid. Rather than measuring the *in vitro* life-span, they examined ^{3}H-thymidine incorporation in di- and polykaryons. Again, the senescent phenotype was observed to be dominant. Hybrids consisting of young and old cells behaved as if they were senescent and failed to incorporate ^{3}H-thymidine. In all of these studies, the results are consistent with both groups of theories described above.

Wright and Hayflick (59,60) and Muggleton-Harris and Hayflick (39) were the first to provide an answer to the question of the cytoplasmic or nuclear location of the initiating events of the phase III phenomenon. Proof of the location of the initial events would serve to distinguish between the two main categories of theories of cellular aging. We found that fusion of cytochalasin B-induced anucleate cells (cytoplasts) obtained from young or old human diploid fibroblasts with young or old whole cells failed to alter the time of expected occurrence of phase III in the whole cells.

Our second study (39) employed reconstructed cells composed of cytoplasts and karyoplasts from young and old cells. These studies confirmed the dominance of the senescent nucleus. However, cytoplasts derived from senescent cells in this study contained factors that affected the doubling potential of young nuclei. Thus *in vitro* aging of human diploid fibroblasts may involve a combination of several processes.

The ability of immortal cell lines to rescue mortal, normal human diploid fibroblasts from cellular senescence has been the subject of many investigations (42). Most have shown that mortality is dominant over immortality.

Our current goals are twofold: First, we are attempting to determine which gene loci in human cells are responsible for governing cellular senescence (phase III). Second, we are attempting to determine which gene loci are associated with the ability of transformed cells to replicate indefinitely. The chromosomes in normal human cells that suppress or reduce tumorigenicity in heteroploid human or rodent cell hybrids have been identified (33).

Our ultimate goal is to determine the location and molecular basis of operation of the putative clock(s) that limits the replication of normal human cells and that, by inference, imparts immortality on transformed cells.

REFERENCES

1. Bierman, E. L. (1977): The effect of donor age on the in vitro lifespan of cultured human arterial smooth-muscle cells. *In Vitro,* 14:951–955.
2. Boone, C. W. (1975): Malignant hemangioendotheliomas produced by subcutaneous inoculation of Balb/3T3 cells attached to glass beads. *Science,* 188:68–70.
3. Boone, C. W., Takeichi, N., and Paranjpe, M. (1976): Vasoformative sarcomas arising from Balb/3T3 cells attached to solid substrates. *Cancer Res.,* 36:1626–1633.
4. Cudkowicz, G., Upton, A. C., Shearer, G. M., and Hughes, W. L. (1964): Lymphocyte content and proliferative capacity of serially transplanted mouse bone marrow. *Nature,* 201:165–167.
5. Danes, B. S. (1971): Progeria: a cell culture study on aging. *J. Clin. Invest.,* 50:2000–2003.
6. Daniel, C. W., deOme, K. B., Young, J. T., Blair, P. B., and Faulkin, L. J., Jr. (1968): The in vivo lifespan of normal and preneoplastic mouse mammary glands: a serial transplantation study. *Proc. Natl. Acad. Sci. USA,* 61:53–60.
7. Dinowitz, M. (1977): A continuous line of Rous sarcoma virus-transformed chick embryo cells. *J. Natl. Cancer Inst.,* 58:307–312.
8. Effros, R. B., and Walford, R. L. (1984): T cell cultures and the Hayflick limit. *Hum. Immunol.,* 9:49–65.
9. Epstein, C. J., Martin, G. M., Schultz, A. L., and Motulsky, A. G. (1966): Werner's syndrome: a review of its symptomatology, natural history, pathologic features, genetics and relationship to the natural aging process. *Medicine (Baltimore),* 45:177–221.
10. Ford, C. E., Micklem, H. S., and Gray, S. M. (1959): Evidence of selective proliferation of reticular cell-clones in heavily irradiated mice. *Br. J. Radiol.,* 32:280.

11. Geder, L., Vaczi, L., and Boldogh, I. (1973): Development of cell lines after exposure of chicken embryonic fibroblasts to herpes simplex virus type 2 at supraoptimal temperature. *Acta Microbiol. Acad. Sci. Hung.*, 20:119–125.
12. Goldstein, S. (1969): Lifespan of cultured cells in progeria. *Lancet*, 1:424.
13. Goldstein, S., Moerman, E. J., Soeldner, J. S., Gleason, R. E., and Barnett, D. M. (1978): Chronologic and physiological age effect replicative lifespan of fibroblasts from diabetics, prediabetics, and normal donors. *Science*, 199:781–782.
14. Harrison, D. E. (1973): Normal production of erythrocytes by mouse marrow continuous for 73 months. *Proc. Natl. Acad. Sci. USA*, 70:3184–3188.
15. Harrison, D. E. (1975): Normal function of transplanted marrow cell lines from aged mice. *J. Gerontol.*, 30:279–285.
16. Hayflick, L. (1965): The limited in vitro lifetime of human diploid cell strains. *Exp. Cell Res.*, 37:614–636.
17. Hayflick, L. (1970): Aging under glass. *Exp. Gerontol.*, 5:291–303.
18. Hayflick, L. (1972): Cell senescence and cell differentiation in vitro. In: *Aging and Development.* Academy of Science and Literature, Mainz, Germany; F. K. Schattauer Verlag, Stuttgart.
19. Hayflick, L. (1973): The biology of human aging. *Am. J. Med. Sci.*, 265:433–445.
20. Hayflick, L. (1974): Cytogerontology. In: *Theoretical Aspects of Aging*, edited by M. Rockstein. Academic Press, New York.
21. Hayflick, L. (1977) The cellular basis for biological aging. In: *Handbook of the Biology of Aging*, edited by C. Finch and L. Hayflick, pp. 159–186. Van Nostrand Reinhold, New York.
22. Hayflick, L. (1980): Cell aging. In: *Annual Review of Gerontology and Geriatrics*, edited by C. Eisdorfer. Springer, New York.
23. Hayflick, L. (1980). The cell biology of human aging. *Sci. Am.*, 242:58–66.
24. Hayflick, L. (1984): Immortality. *Science*, 225:268.
25. Hayflick, L. (1984): The coming of age of WI-38. In: *Advances in Cell Culture*, Vol. 3, edited by K. Maramorosch, pp. 303–316. Academic Press, New York.
26. Hayflick, L. (1985): The cell biology of aging. In: *Clinics in Geriatric Medicine.* The Aging Process, Vol. 1, No. 1, pp. 15–27. W. B. Saunders, Philadelphia.
27. Hayflick, L. (1985): Theories of biological aging. *Exp. Gerontol.*, 20:145–159.
28. Hayflick, L., and Moorhead, P. S. (1961): The serial cultivation of human diploid cell strains. *Exp. Cell. Res.*, 25:585–621.
29. Hellman, S., Botnick, L. E., Hannon, E. C., and Vigneulle, R. M. (1978): Proliferative capacity of murine hematopoietic stem cells. *Proc. Natl. Acad. Sci. USA*, 75:490–494.
30. Hoehn, H., Bryant, E. M., and Martin, G. M. (1978): The replicative lifespans of euploid hybrids derived from short-lived and long-lived human skin fibroblast cultures. *Cytogenet. Cell Genet.*, 21:282–295.
31. Houck, J. C., Sharma, V. K., and Hayflick, L. (1971): Functional failures of cultured human diploid fibroblasts after continued population doublings. *Proc. Soc. Exp. Biol. Med.*, 137:331–333.
32. Kirkwood, T. B. L., and Cremer, T. (1982): Cytogerontology since 1881: a reappraisal of August Weismann and a review of modern progress. *Hum. Genet.*, 60:101–121.
33. Klinger, H. P., Baim, A. S., Eun, C. K., Shows, T. B., and Ruddle, F. H. (1978): Human chromosomes which affect tumorigenicity in hybrids of diploid human with heteroploid human or rodent cells. *Cytogenet. Cell Genet.*, 22:245–249.
34. Kohler, G., and Milstein, C. (1975): Continuous cultures of fused cells secreting antibody of predefined specificity. *Nature*, 256:495–497.
35. Krohn, P. L. (1962): Review lectures on senescence. II. Heterochronic transplantation in the study of aging. *Proc. R. Soc. Lond. [Biol.]*, 157:128–147.
36. LeGuilly, Y., Simon, M., Lenoir, P., and Bourel, M. (1973): Long-term culture of human adult liver cells: morphological changes related to in vitro senescence and effect of donor's age on growth potential. *Gerontologia*, 19:303–313.
37. Littlefield, J. W. (1973): Attempted hybridizations with senescent human fibroblasts. *J. Cell. Physiol.*, 82:129–132.
38. Martin, G. M., Sprague, C. A., and Epstein, C. J. (1970): Replicative lifespan of cultivated human cells: effect of donor's age, tissue, and genotype. *Lab. Invest.*, 23:86–92.
39. Muggleton-Harris, A. L., and Hayflick, L. (1976): Cellular aging studied by the reconstruction of replicating cells from nuclei and cytoplasms isolated from normal human diploid cells. *Exp. Cell Res.*, 103:321–330.

40. Nienhaus, A. J., DeJong, B., and Tenkate, L. P. (1971): Fibroblast culture in Werner's syndrome. *Humangenetik,* 13:244–246.
41. Norwood, T. H., Pendergrass, W. R., Sprague, C. A., and Martin, G. M. (1974): Dominance of the senescent phenotype in heterokaryons between replicative and post-replicative human fibroblast-like cells. *Proc. Natl. Acad. Sci. USA,* 71:2231–2235.
42. Norwood, T. H., and Smith, R. (1985): The cultured fibroblast-like cell as a model for the study of aging. In: *Handbook of the Biology of Aging,* edited by C. E. Finch and E. L. Schneider, pp. 291–321. Van Nostrand Reinhold, New York.
43. Ogura, H., Fujiwara, T., and Namba, M. (1984): Establishment of two chick embryo fibroblastic cell lines. *Gann,* 75:410–414.
44. Parker, R. C. (1961): *Methods of Tissue Culture.* Harper & Row, New York.
45. Puck, T. T., Cieciura, S. J., and Robinson, A. (1958): Genetics of somatic mammalian cells. III. Long-term cultivation of euploid cells from human and animal subjects. *J. Exp. Med.,* 108:945–956.
46. Reichel, W., Garcia-Bunuel, R., and Dilallo, J. (1971): Progeria and Werner's syndrome as models for the study of normal human aging. *J. Am. Geriatr. Soc.,* 19:369–375.
47. Rohme, D. (1981): Evidence for a relationship between longevity of mammalian species and life spans of normal fibroblasts in vitro and erythrocytes in vivo. *Proc. Natl. Acad. Sci. USA,* 78:5009–5013.
48. Schneider, E. L., and Mitsui, Y. (1976): The relationship between in vitro cellular aging and in vivo human aging. *Proc. Natl. Acad. Sci. USA,* 73:3584–3588.
49. Siminovitch, L., Till, J. E., and McCulloch, E. A. (1964): Decline in colony-forming ability of marrow cells subjected to serial transplantation into irradiated mice. *J. Cell Comp. Physiol.,* 64:23–31.
50. Stanley, J. F., Pye, D., and MacGregor, A. (1975): Comparison of doubling numbers attained by cultured animal cells with the life span of species. *Nature,* 255:158–159.
51. Swim, H. E., and Parker, R. F. (1957): Culture characteristics of human fibroblasts propagated serially. *Am. J. Hyg.,* 66:235–243.
52. Tassin, J., Malaise, E., and Courtois, Y. (1979): Human lens cells have an in vitro proliferative capacity inversely proportional to the donor age. *Exp. Cell Res.,* 123:388–392.
53. Vracko, R., and McFarland, B. M. (1980): Lifespan of diabetic and non-diabetic fibroblasts in vitro. *Exp. Cell Res.,* 129:345–350.
54. Walford, R. L., Jawaid, S. Q., and Naeim, F. (1981): Evidence for in vitro senescence of T-lymphocytes cultured from normal human peripheral blood. *Age,* 4:67–70.
55. Weismann, A. (1891): *Essays Upon Heredity and Kindred Biological Problems,* 2nd ed. Clarendon Press, Oxford.
56. Witkowski, J. A. (1979): Alexis Carrel and the mysticism of tissue culture. *Med. Hist.,* 23:279–296.
57. Witkowski, J. A. (1980): Dr. Carrel's immortal cells. *Med. Hist.,* 24:129–142.
58. Witkowski, J. A. (1985): The myth of cell immortality. *Trends Biochem. Sci.,* 10:258–260.
59. Wright, W. E., and Hayflick, L. (1975): Nuclear control of cellular aging demonstrated by hybridization of anucleate and whole cultured normal human fibroblasts. *Exp. Cell Res.,* 96:113–121.
60. Wright, W. E., and Hayflick, L. (1975): Contributions of cytoplasmic factors to in vitro cellular senescence. *Fed. Proc.,* 34:76–79.

Human Aging Research: Concepts and Techniques,
edited by B. Kent and R. N. Butler.
Raven Press, Ltd., New York © 1988.

Animal Models for Human Aging Research

Barbara Kent

*Geriatrics and Adult Development, Department of Physiology and Biophysics, Mount Sinai
Medical Center, New York, New York 10029*

Historically, progress of biomedical research depended heavily on the use of animal models. Current research targeted to understand underlying biological concepts in order to improve medical treatment relies on the use of animals, whether vertebrate, invertebrate, whole animal, tissue culture, or cells (11,12,14,17). Likewise, the answers to gerontological questions concerning the biology, physiology, and pathophysiology of human aging are being sought through experiments utilizing animals.

Often animal models are chosen for aging research because of unique characteristics such as life-span, genetic definition, or cellular simplicity; these characteristics can be exploited to answer specific questions about the aging process. Other times animals that are phylogenetically close to humans are used in experiments that could not practically be done on human subjects. These studies are usually designed to answer questions about interventions in biological aging, e.g., testing the effects of a new synthetic compound thought to alter aging, manipulating the environment by diet or exercise, or examining the neuroendocrine control of aging by experiments requiring surgical alteration or hormonal supplements or deficiencies. Quite clearly, many such experiments, important for insights into human aging, could not be done without the use of animals.

This chapter discusses why particular animal models are chosen for research in human aging and how these animals have become valuable and unique tools to the gerontological biomedical researcher. Additionally, the availability of animal models for aging research and the conditions necessary for maintaining aged research animals are addressed.

Biomedical research can be thought of as progressing through three interlinked phases: the descriptive phase, the mechanistic phase, and the therapeutic phase. Animal models provide an invaluable resource in all three. The descriptive phase observes the natural history of a phenomenon and delineates its role in the biological hierarchy or homeostasis of the individual. A well-known example of an early use of animal models to describe a system is Harvey's observation more than 300 years ago of the circulation of blood in the heart and lungs of deer. His careful dissections provided the first valid description of the path of blood flow and thereby formed the basis for cardiovascular physiology. Most of what we know about the heart and blood vessels, ranging from the specific configuration of proteins responsible for opening and closing cell membrane channels, which elaborate signals such as those on the electrocardiogram (ECG), to the minute workings of the microcirculation and lymphatics, was learned from experiments on living animals and their tissues.

Likewise, the descriptive phase of neurology was built on research in animal models. By stimulation and ablation of the central nervous system (CNS) using cats (cats have a uniform head size amenable to stereotaxic analysis), the first maps of cerebral function were constructed. More recent studies of refined neural pathways exploited the primate model because of its similarity to man. Phylogenetic proximity, however, is not a prerequisite for relevant observations from animal models. Clever selection of two species of saltwater fish, one possessing kidneys with glomeruli and the other with aglomerular kidneys, allowed formulation of the concepts of filtration and clearance, basic tenants of nephrology. Models may be close to or distant from man phylogenetically, but because of evolutionarily preserved homologies information relevant to humans is present.

The descriptive phase of gerontology benefits from the use of animal models. The diversity of genetic background and life styles in the human population often blurs pure aging effects. Rodent models such as genetically inbred mice are as similar in genome as identical twins, and the environment of an animal colony can be precisely controlled. Genetically and environmentally well-defined rodent models are used extensively to describe time-related changes in biological structure and function (1,6,13,18). Rodent models manifest most of the same aging changes as human beings but in a faster time frame. The rate of accumulation of information about the aging process can be accelerated by the use of species with relatively short life-spans (3 years for the rodent as opposed to 85 years for man). Because of these and many other advantages, the descriptive phase of aging research relies heavily on animal models.

The mechanistic phase—research aimed at determining how systems interrelate— is equally dependent on animal models. Claude Bernard utilized the visible blood vessels in the ear of the rabbit to demonstrate underlying principles of neural and hormonal control of blood flow. The bioassay continues to be an important tool for uncovering mechanisms of action of a variety of compounds. An appropriate animal model, chosen from the array of living organisms because of specific traits, can be pivotal in answering specific biological questions. For instance, the mechanisms of action of the atrial natriuretic factor (ANF) are being unraveled by studying the effects of the hormone on physiological functions in animals as diverse as sharks and sheep. Sharks have a unique salt-secreting gland for testing mechanisms of action of ANF on membrane transport processes related to kidney function, and sheep have large accessible blood vessels and lymphatics for testing systemic hemodynamic effects.

The mechanistic phase of human aging research profits from the proper selection of animal models as well. The animal kingdom has produced life-span diversity of hundreds of years between species. Basically it means that the quantity and quality of genetic material across species, randomized and selected in nature, produces vastly different aging rates. Comparisons between long-lived and short-lived species are used to explore basic mechanisms of aging. Positive correlations have been found between cultured fibroblast cell doublings and life-span of the species or individual. Whether aging depends on it is not known, but probing the mechanism that determines cell doubling from animals with different life-spans is a promising path in human aging research. Again, using life-span differences, an inverse proportionality has been described between specific metabolic rate in mammalian species and longevity. This observation gave rise to the theory that free radicals, particularly the oxygen-initiated free radicals, may be intimately involved in the aging process. Experiments testing the free radical hypothesis of aging make use of mammalian species of differing longevities to compare evidence of the time-accumulated free radical damage as well as quantitating differences in cellular defenses against free radicals (20).

The mechanistic phase includes other paradigms that necessitate the use of animal models. Are human aging and eventual death the result of time-dependent damage accumulation in a particular vital organ or system? An obvious experiment to test this hypothesis is to transplant organs from elderly individuals into the young and to assess the effect on the life-span of the recipient. Conversely, do vital organs transplanted from a young donor prolong life in the elderly? Not only do ethical constraints preclude the sort of testing needed to answer the question in human subjects, but the length of the human life makes this study impractical. The inbred mouse is the model of choice to answer this question. Because of genetic homogeneity transplant rejection is not a problem; and with the 3-year life-span of mice, conclusions can be reached in a reasonable period of time (18).

The third phase of biomedical research, the therapeutic phase, engages the experimental approach of utilizing interventions to prevent, delay, or reverse processes deleterious to human well-being and health. Animals have been used to enormous advantage in this phase of research. When testing new therapeutic agents, for instance, extensive animal experimentation to ensure safety and benefit is a required step in development before testing in humans. Determining the causes as well as the cures of infectious diseases has relied on research in animals that could first be tested for their reaction to disease vectors and then used in studies of cures.

Many of the inherited diseases common in man are also found in animals, primarily mammals. Genetic models of diabetes, thalassemia, muscular dystrophy, hypertension, and hundreds of other conditions of genetic origin are available in mice (1). With the use of selective breeding techniques, animal models of human inherited conditions can be developed. The development of the rat models of hypertension is an example of this advantage of animal use.

The therapeutic phase of gerontological research is geared to deter or correct the debilitating physical changes that are often a part of aging and to find strategies or life styles that maximize robust good health for the duration of the human life-span. Questions concerning dietary supplements with antioxidants or broadly acting substances such as dehydroepiandosterone (DHEA) are being tested on animals, primarily rodents, to assess the effect on biological aging changes and life-spans. The posited ameliorating effect of exercise on physical well-being can be rigorously tested in animals where confounding factors can be kept to a minimum. Studies of interventions or cures of the diseases accompanying aging utilize animals. For example, in the study of Alzheimer's disease, elegant techniques have been devised using rats to demonstrate neural lesions that mimic brain cell loss in Alzheimer's disease with subsequent repopulation of the lesioned area using brain cells from neonatal rats (4). These studies, impossible to perform without animal use, have the potential of alleviating one of the most debilitating diseases of old age. Animal models are indispensable in human aging research. These models give us the biological material and the flexibility for unraveling the mystery of aging. Gerontology and an understanding of the human aging process will progress through appropriately designed experiments utilizing the wealth of biological material nature has provided.

ANIMAL MODELS USEFUL IN AGING RESEARCH

Invertebrates

It may surprise clinicians, who are accustomed to thinking of aging as a complex of interrelated physiological events complicated by disease and psychosocial problems, to learn that time-related changes leading to a finite life-span, i.e., aging, occurs in simple, one-cell organisms. *Paramecium* and *Tetrahymena* are two examples of unicellular organisms that show aging changes and have a defined life-span. Aging in these single-cell creatures is accompanied by such universal characteristics as an increase in age pigment, abnormal mitochondria and lysosomal activity, and a decrease in longevity in progeny from older parent cells (3). There is an increase in micronuclear damage with age in older cells that may reflect accumulating damaging events from the environment, a loss in DNA repair capacity, or both. The similarity with human cell aging is striking. If there is an underlying biological aging process, events in the life of the unicellular organism, free of tissue, hormonal, or other interactions, may provide the most direct evidence.

A commonly quoted witticism in answer to the question of what one should do to achieve a long life is "select long-lived parents." The basis for this answer, of course, is the compelling evidence of a genetic basis for longevity. Genome-specific life-spans of animal species and the phenomenon of hybrid vigor support a genetic basis for aging. Which specific genes affect life-span and how is a subject of controversy and investigation. The best characterized animal model for the study of genetics is the fruit fly, *Drosophila melanogaster*. It has four large, easily observable chromosomes, each of which has been mapped in exquisite detail. There are more than 5,000 known mutations, and large numbers of offspring (more than 1,000) can be generated in 20 to 25 days (3). The life-span of 1 to 2 months at 25°C is variable, depending on experimental conditions, e.g., temperature, lighting, population density, and activity. *Drosophila* show the Lansing effect in that parental age effects (longevity, number of abdominal bristles, wing size, DNA and RNA content, etc.) are a linear function of parental age. The flies develop tumors, and their cells accumulate lipofuscin at a rate inversely proportional to life-span. Answers concerning the genetic control of human aging will undoubtedly arise from use of this model.

During all phases of the human life cycle from embryogenesis to development and through adulthood to senescence, cells and tissues proliferate or are deleted in an orderly, seemingly programmed fashion. Programmed events such as thymic involution are thought to play a role in normal aging. An animal model for studying time-related sequencing of cellular events is the nematode *Caenorhabditis elegans*. This tractable little worm has only two chromosomes for which elaborate gene maps have been constructed (3). Its adult body is composed of fewer than 1,000 somatic cells, and every somatic cell developmental linkage has been mapped. During development 159 cells die. The life-span is usually less than a month, and the following time-related changes have been documented: decreased rate of movement, greater osmotic fragility, accumulation of altered enzymes, increase in intracellular lipofuscin accumulation, and a decrease in protein turnover. The worm normally grazes on carpets of *Escherichia coli* in petri dishes (3). As in rodents, its life-span can be extended by food restriction. Using analogies provided by this well-programmed simple animal model, genetic and biochemical processes fundamental to aging are being explored.

Vertebrates

Nonmammalian Vertebrates

Some vertebrate species exhibit exceptional characteristics that are useful for studying aging. The events at the end of life of the salmon, for instance, show that nature uses programmed control of certain hormones to effect senescence and longevity. The story of the adult salmon returning to its place of birth to spawn is well known. The rapid decrease in function and death of the animal shortly after ejection of eggs is triggered by a massive outpouring of adrenal steroids. Understanding the neural and endocrine interactions at the end of life of this semelparous creature may give a clue to how hormonal control is programmed.

Some species of sharks and reptiles are of interest in aging research because they are thought not to age. They form the ultimate "control" group, as it were. These animals simply grow larger with passing time, but age-related changes are not found. According to our present knowledge, the life-span in these creatures is not a consequence of aging but is limited by either accident or disease. It could be enlightening to discover what basic differences account for the protection from aging in these animals.

In terms of the dictums of mammalian aging, birds are also exceptional. They live much longer than would be expected from body size and metabolic rate. The life-span of 70 to 80 years achieved by some parrots is ten times that expected from a similarly sized mammal. Here again, understanding the reasons for the slower aging rate might prove helpful in determining mechanisms of human aging.

Mammalian Vertebrates

For the most directly clinically applied aging research, mammals are the models of choice. The reasons are obvious. The ultimate target of aging research, man, is a mammal, so observations on mammalian systems often are directly analogous to human biology. Following this line of thought, the value and applicability of research on nonhuman primates is clear. At some point, however, it is necessary to weigh other factors, e.g., availability of the species, ease of maintenance, life-span (if studies are to be longitudinal or necessitate aging the animal), and expense, when choosing the appropriate animal model. If a question on human aging could as easily be answered using mice in a 3-year study as opposed to using chimpanzees, which would increase the time of the experiment by a factor of 15 and the expense enormously, economics and time dictate the choice of the former. The importance of mammalian models at all levels of human aging research cannot be overestimated. For an excellent review of available models the reader is referred to *Mammalian Models for Aging Research* (13). This volume gives comprehensive coverage to all mammalian groups used in aging research and includes a section on the major diseases accompanying human aging and the established animal models for these diseases.

Rodents

Rodents have been and continue to be used extensively in aging research. The reasons are many. Of the class Mammalia, mice and rats are relatively close to man phylogenetically, so most of the physiological and biochemical age-related changes in these animals are directly translatable to humans. The maximum life-span of the rodent is 3 to 4 years, so these animals age at a rate 30 times faster than man. The relatively short life-span facilitates longitudinal studies in which a given parameter can be followed in individuals from birth to death. Implicit here also is that treatment or perturbations of the aging process can be assessed in a relatively short period of time.

Two important variables that are difficult to control in human aging studies are heredity and life style. The racial, ethnic, and socioeconomic groupings made in human studies attempt to control for these major confounding factors; but, except for identical twin studies, there is a great deal of heterogeneity in any grouping of people. Mice and rats have been inbred (brother–sister mated for more than 40 generations) so that a member of a particular strain is as genetically similar to the other animals in that strain as identical twins are to each other. The use of inbred mice or rats in aging studies obviates the confounding factor of genetic diversity.

Mutations, which can be faithfully propagated to offspring in rodents, have been developed, sometimes spontaneously and other times by design. Within the available strains of mice and rats are genetic models of obesity, diabetes, hypertension, autoimmune diseases of all sorts, many kinds of spontaneously developing tumors, etc. Life-span itself is a phenotype and specific for each strain. For instance, in a particular colony, BALB/c mice may live to be 700 days old whereas C57B1/6 live to be 1,000 days.

In studies of aging in rodents in which life-span is used as an endpoint, care must be taken to ensure homogeneity in environment. The environment of an animal colony can be controlled to make the "life-style" variables of each occupant as similar as possible. Dark–light cycles, temperature, humidity, and noise level can be precisely regulated. Diet and to some degree exercise can be patterned similarly for all animals. Because immune function decreases with age, older animals are more susceptible to disease and environmental pathogens. It is clear that diseases accompanying aging in people are often responsible for spurious results in human gerontological research, and the same holds true for animals. The design of human aging studies, in which healthy young people were compared cross-sectionally with unscreened elderly populations, led to some questionable conclusions about the aging process. Many of those studies are being repeated using stringent screening techniques to rule out pathology in the study populations, and conclusions concerning normal changes with age are being revised. It is equally important to use healthy, high-quality older animals for studies of aging.

A high degree of protection from outside pathogens can be achieved in contained animal colonies. Careful environmental control ensures the same quality of health in older animals as in younger ones. In first-rate aging animal colonies, air is pumped into the room through a filter that removes particles down to 0.03 μm. Because the inside air is under positive pressure, ambient air is prevented from entering. All cages, bedding, bottles, water, and food (a special commercially available autoclavable diet) are autoclaved before entry into the colony. Colonies are generally started from cesarean-derived stock to prevent contamination at the outset. In barrier colonies, the number of people allowed to enter is kept to a minimum, and those who do must don sterile caps, gowns, masks, gloves, and booties. Strict environmental control minimizes the possibility of infection and disease in the older animals as well as the young. Rodents with well-defined genetics, from barrier-controlled environments, are excellent reagents for research in the biology of aging. Changes with age in behavior, physiology, immunology, anatomy, histology—virtually every area of biomedical investigation—have been studied, but the surface has barely been scratched.

Although rodents are the best characterized of the mammalian models of aging, one glaring deficiency exists: the pathology and histopathology of the animals at the end of life. Life-span is predictable for inbred strains, and many strains were developed to model human pathology (AKR, leukemia; C3H, mammary tumor) (6). The cause of death in these strains is built into the model; but in many of the long-lived strains causes of death have not been precisely defined, and they seem to be multifactorial, as in humans. These important data would be of benefit to the interpretation of rodent aging studies, particularly those in which life-span is altered.

A population of a particular strain of rat or mouse in a given environment, over time, produces a characteristic survival curve. The reproducibility of this curve has been exploited by gerontologists to test treatments that might alter the aging process. For instance, if aging is an accumulation of damage caused by free radicals (ultraviolet light or superoxide anions), increasing the free radical scavenging ability of the individual might be expected to increase the life-span. To test this hypothesis, Harman put a group of C3H mice on a lifelong diet supplemented with vitamin E and compared the survival of these animals with a group not on the vitamin supplement (7). He found that the supplemented group's mean life-span increased significantly, but the maximum life-span was the same as that of the control. Vitamin E protected the mice in some way (as seat belts protect U.S. citizens and will undoubtedly correlate with increased mean life-span for the population), but because maximum life-span was not affected the contention that free radical scavengers slow the aging process was not proved by this experiment. Indeed, the only treatment that reliably increases life-span in rodents is food restriction. Food-restricting most strains of mice from weaning to maintain body weight at 70% of ad libitum fed controls shifts the entire survival curve to the right and increases the maximum life-span by 20 to 30% (18). The mechanisms responsible for this phenomenon, called the "McCay effect" after the scientist who first observed it, are the subject of intense investigation. The slower rate of aging in food-restricted rodents is reflected in attenuated aging decreases of many of the biomarkers of aging, including the immune system. Food restriction is a powerful tool for gerontologists; discovery of the mechanisms involved should begin to unlock the secrets of aging. Skeptics, however, point out that rodent life-span in the wild is rarely more than 6 months, and ad libitum feeding of laboratory chow may itself have deleterious effects.

Because of the importance of the rodent as a model in aging research, the National Institute on Aging (NIA) currently has available specific-pathogen-free mice and rats from barrier colonies, ranging in age from 3 to 36 months. Small numbers of rodents for pilot experiments or for graduate student projects can be obtained by application to Dr. DeWitt G. Hazzard, Building 31, Room 5C19, NIA, National Institutes of Health, Bethesda, Maryland 20892 (19). The 10 to 20 cents per diem for maintaining rodents in animal facilities of most research insitutions makes the aging of animals a costly endeavor. The NIA recognizes this fact and subsidizes its aging animal program to make animals more affordable ($30 for a 30-month-old mouse and $75 for a 30-month-old rat). Additionally, the NIA is in the process of constructing a large aging rodent resource that will contain four genotypes of mice and three of rats, and each strain will be available as either food-restricted or ad-libitum-fed (19). These genetically pure animals, raised under identical state-of-the-art environmental control, will be available to investigators throughout the United States for research on biomarkers of aging. A biomarker is any biological system demonstrating age-related change in a predictable fashion. This large investment by the NIA, in a resource to supply defined animal models to gerontologists, will enhance the contribution of animal models to human aging research.

Rabbits

Use of the laboratory rabbit in research in the United States has increased dramatically over the past 15 years. It can be attributed mostly to the rabbit's popularity as a producer of antibodies for study paradigms requiring identification of particular biological proteins. Immunological response can be produced with ease using standard injection technique, and blood can be obtained conveniently and repeatedly for antibody harvesting via the large ear veins of the rabbit. The rabbit does not require much space for housing (1.5 sq ft for rabbits under 2 kg), yet tissues and organs are of adequate size to provide material for assays and *in vitro* experiments.

Life-span data on disease-free rabbits is not available, but an 8- to 13-year life is generally expected. Age-related changes that have been studied include a decreased affinity of hemoglobin for oxygen, increased cholesterol and beta-lipoprotein levels, an increase in antidiuretic hormone levels and sensitivity to angiotensin administration, a decrease in cardiac function, and an increase in atherosclerosis (13). The rabbit is the model of choice for many studies of atherosclerosis. It was the first animal model developed for this type of research. Young rabbits spontaneously develop mediomineralization in the aortic arch and thoracic aorta on a normal laboratory diet, and on a high cholesterol diet they develop fatty deposits rapidly (5). Older rabbits (more than 2.5 years old) are useful models for some of the other pathological changes that accompany human aging, including emphysema, osteoarthritis, glaucoma, and cataract development.

Cats

Of the close to 50 million cats in the United States, more than two-thirds are companion animals living in homes where they are well fed, protected from the environment, and given careful veterinary care. Under these conditions, life expectancy has reached 16 to 20 years (5). Because cats undergo many of the same aging changes as humans, it has been suggested that pet cats, for which the age is known, might be a good population for noninvasive studies of aging. As a different sort of experimental tool, cats have been used in nursing homes as companions for residents in an attempt to enhance the quality of life.

One of the most feared aspects of human aging is the threat of memory loss.

The "split-brain" cat is an invaluable model for psychologists studying how learned information is processed. When the two hemispheres of the brain are surgically separated from each other, each functions independently and can be perturbed and studied separately (5). Many of the anatomical changes with age in humans in the CNS are also found in cats, but neurofibrillary tangles (a hallmark of human Alzheimer's disease) have not been reported.

A drawback to the use of the cat or any of the longer-lived mammals in aging research is, of course, the expense of maintaining an animal to old age and the length of the time commitment to complete the experiment.

Dogs

The use of both dogs and cats has dropped sharply during the last few years. It can be traced to the increased cost of procurement and maintenance, increased public sentiment against the use of companion animals in research, and the availability of other, more appropriate, large animal models. Anecdotal data suggest a 15 to 20-year life-span for dog breeds not disposed to early death by a specific disease. Studies of longevity in laboratory beagles revealed a mean life-span around 13 years with a maximum of 19 years (13).

Canine renal, cardiovascular, CNS, and musculoskeletal systems age similarly to those in humans. Bone loss with age is a feature of the dog's skeleton as it is in humans. Female dogs lose bone at a faster rate than male dogs (13). Amyloid deposits in the canine kidney as it ages are similar to those found in aging humans. The CNS cell loss and information-processing speed are features of aging in both dog and man. As with the cat, however, one of the most promising research uses of the dog in human aging may be as a companion to the elderly to enhance their quality of life.

Nonhuman primates

The value of nonhuman primates in biomedical research is obvious. With 98% homology to the human genome, these animals are almost identical to man physiologically. Difficulty of procurement, expense of maintenance, lack of birth records, and a long life-span have limited the usefulness of this model in aging research. Presently, as primate centers and primate supply houses mature and thrive, the supply, quality, and available data on primates are improving.

REGULATIONS GOVERNING THE USE OF ANIMALS IN RESEARCH

Aging research is dependent on animal studies to answer a variety of biological questions about aging because the characteristics of the life of the individual animal are similar to those in the human in terms of development, maturation, and senescence. As we are in awe of the delicate mechanisms of cell division in simple one-celled animals, so must we respect not only the physiological functioning but also the needs, feelings, and comfort of the sentient animals that are so much a part of aging research (9,10). The special facilities for aging mammals discussed earlier highlight the fragility of this model. The counterpart of the aging rodent model in nature does not exist. Disease, predators, climate, etc. limit life-span in the wild to about one-third of the animal's potential. In the care of research animals, then, the goal is usually not to emulate natural conditions but to maximize the physical well-being of the animals so as to increase accuracy in research.

The first federal law addressing animal care was passed in 1873. The so-called "24 hour law" regulated shipment of farm animals so that 24 hours was the maximum length of time an animal could be transported before receiving food and water (8). The first law protecting nonfarm animals, however, was not passed until 1966. This Public Law 89-544 is commonly called the "Animal Welfare Act," and it specifically regulates the use of animals in research (15). It is meant to protect owners of pet animals from theft and to prevent the sale or use of stolen animals. It ensures humane care and treatment for research animals and provides guidelines for transportation, sale, housing, care, handling, and treatment of animals. The Act mandates adequate veterinary care and requires the appropriate use of anesthetics, analgesics, and tranquilizing drugs for animals in research. The 1966 Act and subsequent additions, revisions, and amendments include language protecting the freedom of biomedical researchers in designing and performing their experiments.

Enforcement of animal welfare laws governing the use of animals in research is under the auspices of the U.S. Department of Agriculture (USDA). Veterinarians employed by the USDA Animal, Plant Health Inspection Service inspect research facilities on a regular basis (at least yearly) to see that they comply with the Animal Welfare Act and its amendments. The *Guide for the Care and Use of Laboratory Animals* (last revised in 1985 at this writing) outlines the basics for research animal programs and facilities (2). The guide details proper caging and housing systems, veterinary care, anesthesia and analgesia, animal procurement, surgery, postsurgical care, and physical plant characteristics, among others. On the subject of euthanasia, the best reference is to the Panel on Euthanasia, the latest of which was promulgated by the American Veterinary Medicine Association in 1986. The chairman of the Panel on Euthanasia is A. W. Smith, D.V.M., Ph.D., College of Veterinary Medicine, Oregon State University, Corvallis, OR 97331. Here the rationale and requirements for humane euthanasia methods are outlined in detail.

In addition to federal laws, the research use of animals is governed by state and local regulations. Laws such as the one regulating the use of pound animals for research vary from state to state. State inspections ensure compliance with state and local regulations.

The U.S. Department of Health and Human Services exerts influence over the care and use of laboratory animals via the Public Health Service (PHS) and its component National Institutes of Health (NIH). The NIH is a major funding source for biomedical research involving animal use and so can exert regulatory control simply by withdrawing financial support. In the 1986 document "Public Health

Service Policy on Humane Care and Use of Laboratory Animals by Awardee Institutions'' biomedical research centers using PHS funds for animal research are made much more accountable for the laboratory practices utilizing animals (16)

Before the PHS funds research projects involving animals, two criteria must be met. First, the awardee institution must have an assurance, an acceptable statement of its animal welfare program, on file with the NIH Office of Protection from Research Risks; and second, the animal protocol portion of the grant must be approved concerning animal welfare issues by an institutional animal care and use committee. The committee must have at least five members with each of the following represented: (a) a biomedical scientist working with animals, (b) a veterinarian involved with the program, (c) a person who is not affiliated with the institution, and (d) a person whose interests are in nonscientific areas. The committee works with investigators in designing the animal use section of the grant application to ensure that the selection of animal model and numbers needed is optimal, that distress and discomfort are minimized through proper use of anesthetics and analgesics, that animals are obtained from USDA-certified sources, and that the investigator and other personnel involved in use of the animals are properly educated in the animal handling techniques to be used.

A private accrediting organization, The American Association for Accreditation of Laboratory Animal Care (AAALAC), is a group of experts in laboratory animal science who inspect research facilities and animal welfare programs. Most research institutions using animals subscribe to AAALAC for accreditation. AAALAC inspections are also based on the PSH *Guide*.

There are many layers of inspections and regulations governing animal research in the United states. Good practices, of course, start with the individual investigator, and the most effective monitoring takes place at the local level. The quality of aging research using animals is only as good as the quality of the animal itself. For ethical, practical, and legal reasons, then, it is imperative that research animals, particularly aging ones, have the best of care.

REFERENCES

1. Altman, P. L., and Katz, D. O., editors (1979): *Inbred and Genetically Defined Strains of Laboratory Animals*. FASEB, Bethesda.
2. Committee on Care and Use of Laboratory Animals (1985): *Guide for the Care and Use of Laboratory Animals*. DHEW Publ. (NIH)78-23. Government Printing Office, Washington, DC.
3. Finch, C. E., and Schneider, E. L., editors (1985): *Handbook of the Biology of Aging*. Van Nostrand Reinhold, New York.
4. Gash, D. M., Collier, T. J., and Sladek, J. R. (1985): Neural transplantation: a review of recent developments and potential applications to the aged brain. *Neurobiol. Aging,* 6:131–150.
5. Gay, W. I., editor (1985): *Health Benefits of Animal Research*. Foundation for Biomedical Research and American Physiological Society, Bethesda.
6. Gibson, D. C., editor (1972): *Development of the Rodent as a Model System of Aging*. DHEW Publ. (NIH) 72–121. U.S. Department of Health, Education and Welfare, Washington, DC.
7. Harman, D. (1981): The aging process. *Proc. Natl. Acad. Sci. USA,* 11:7124–7128.

8. Inglehart, J. K. (1985): Health policy report: the use of animals in research. *N. Engl. J. Med.,* 6:395–400.
9. Kitchell, R. L., and Erickson, H. H., editors (1983): *Animal Pain: Perception and Alleviation.* American Physiological Society, Bethesda.
10. Moberg, G. P., editor (1985): *Animal Stress.* American Physiological Society, Bethesda.
11. National Academy of Sciences (1975): *Animals for Research.* Institute of Laboratory Animal Resources, National Research Council, Washington, DC.
12. National Academy of Sciences (1977): *The Future of Animals, Cells, Models, and Systems in Research, Development, Education, and Testing.* Institute of Laboratory Animal Resources, Washington, DC.
13. National Academy of Sciences (1981): *Mammalian Models for Reserach on Aging.* Institute of Laboratory Animal Resources, National Academy Press, Washington, DC.
14. National Research Council (1985): *Models for Biomedical Research: A New Perspective.* National Academy Press, Washington, DC.
15. National Society for Medical Research (1976): *Animal Welfare Act.* Public Law 89–544 (Amended by 91–579 and 94–279), Washington, DC.
16. NIH (1986): *Public Health Service Policy on Humane Care and Use of Laboratory Animals.* OPRR, Bethesda.
17. NIH, OPRR (1984): *National Symposium on Imperatives in Research Animal Use: Scientific Needs and Animal Welfare.* NIH Publ. 85–2746, Bethesda.
18. Reff, M. E., and Schneider E. L., editors (1982): *Biological Markers of Aging.* NIH-PHS Publ. 82–2221. U.S. Department of Health and Human Services, Washington, DC.
19. Sprott, R. (1986): Animal resources available from the National Institute on Aging. *Fed. Proc.,* 45:42.
20. Woodhead, A. D., Blackett, A. D., and Hollander, A., editors (1985): *Molecular Biology of Aging.* Plenum Press, New York.

Human Aging Research: Concepts and Techniques,
edited by B. Kent and R. N. Butler.
Raven Press, Ltd., New York © 1988.

Human Genetic Models for Aging Research

W. Ted Brown

*New York State Office of Mental Retardation and Developmental Disabilities, Institute for
Basic Research in Developmental Disabilities, Staten Island, New York 10314*

Aging appears to be encoded in our genes, reflected by the wide range of maximal life-span potential (MLP) that animal species possess. The MLP in different animal species varies over a 50,000-fold range, from about 1 day in the may fly (*Ephemera* sp., imago form) to more than 150 years in the Galapagos tortoise (*Tedudo summeri*) (47). Among mammals, a 100-fold range exists from about 1 year in the smokey shrew (*Sorex furneus*) (37) to 118 years in man (53). This 100- to 50,000-fold variation reflects the fact that there are underlying differences in the genetic constitution of species that control the rate of aging.

It appears likely that the genetic basis of aging involves two types of species-specific difference. The first difference is in rates of maturation and programmed timings of developmental stages. The second type relates to biochemical systems involving self-maintenance. Evidence suggests that the most common type of evolutionary genetic change is due to changes in the regulated levels of expression of genes rather than changes in the specific activity of enzymes (3). Regulatory changes in gene expression may have major influences on morphological development, increased brain size, and increased longevity.

Some key enzymatic systems show species-specific levels of expression that are genetically determined. They include DNA repair processes and systems involved in protection from internal and external insults to the genetic machinery. The regulation of expression of these systems appears to have evolved coordinately with increased MLP. Specific examples include an ultraviolet repair system that allows for increased ability to repair DNA (39), an aryl hydrocarbon hydroxylase system that produces reactive intermediates that could lead to carcinogenic mutations (72), and increased levels of certain antioxidant enzymes, e.g., superoxide dismutase (78), that protect against the damaging effects of an oxidizing environment. Other enzymes and factors may also have evolved species-specific levels of expression designed to protect longer-lived species against an oxidizing environment and free radical intermediates including α-tocophorol, β-carotene, glutathione, ascorbic acid (38), and uric acid (1). Changes in gene regulation and expressed levels of self-protective enzyme systems are examples of the types of defined evolutionary genetic change that appear to encode the process of aging.

Although more than 3,000 specific human genetic conditions are known (52), no single mutation appears to lead to a significantly longer maximal life-span (3). This fact suggests the evolution of increased longevity may be the result of the modification of a number of genes. To attempt to bracket the number of genes that may underlie the evolution of human longevity, Cutler (15–18) and Sacher and Staffeldt (66–69) analyzed the genetic complexity of this process. Based on the apparent rapid increase in human brain size and corresponding life-span over the period 200,000 to 100,000 years before the present, and assuming known rates of amino acid substitution, they estimated that from 70 to 240 genes may have received one adaptive substitution. Because most amino acid substitutions have a minimal effect on enzyme activity, it seems likely that only a small percent of these substitutions, perhaps 10%, might have had a significant bearing on increasing life-span and brain size. Thus aging and the determination of species longevity may be the result of the action of a few major genes, perhaps 7 to 24.

If life-span had a simple genetic basis, one might predict that parental and offspring life-span would be strongly correlated. Based on multiple longitudinal studies, it appears that it is only a weak correlation at best (58). Although there is an almost uniform familial component to length of life, expressed as a number, it adds only about 1 year of expected life to the offspring for every 10 extra years of parental life-span beyond the expected mean. This increase is as likely to be due to social or environmental factors as to genetic factors. Familial patterns of exercise, smoking, and drinking appear to be of greater importance than parental longevity when determining average life expectancy.

A long-term study comparing life-spans of identical and fraternal twins has shown that identical twins generally have had a smaller difference in their life-spans (41). However, this difference was statistically significant ($p < 0.05$) only for female monozygotic twins. When one female twin died in the age range 60 to 69 years, there was a mean difference of 6 years 9 months of life-span for monozygotes compared to a mean difference of 14 years 5 months for dizygotes. The differences were found to be not significant for female twins at other ages or for male twins. The simplest interpretation of this study is that single gene differences may tend to shorten life-span because of detrimental effects rather than lengthen it because of beneficial effects. People are apt to show increasing homogeneity in their physical characteristics as they approach the upper limits of their natural life-span potential, as they have been selected for superior health and any detrimental genes have been eliminated. Therefore the basis for the inheritance of longevity seems unlikely to be simple from a genetic point of view but, rather, to reflect the interaction of number of genes and to be multifactorial in its origin.

There are rare autosomal dominant genetic conditions of serum lipids (hypo-beta-lipoproteinemia and hyper-alpha-lipoproteinemia) that decrease susceptibility to atherosclerosis and resultant coronary disease (26). However, they appear to increase the average life expectancy without affecting the expected maximal life-span. It seems likely that the human maximal life-span is approximately 118 years (53). In the absence of acceptable documentation, reports of extreme longevity must be viewed with skepticism. As summarized by Medvedev (54), the supposed longevity of individuals in the Russian Caucasus seems unfounded and without scientific basis.

Although no specific genes have been identified that appear specifically to increase the maximal life-span, there are many life-shortening diseases that may involve specific genes. About 20% of the population suffer from diseases that have a genetic component and lead to a reduced life expectancy. These diseases include diabetes, arthritis, HLA-associated life-shortening disease, hyperlipidemia, α_1-antitrypsin deficiency, and cystic fibrosis. Furthermore, it is estimated that about 40% of infant mortality is a result of genetically determined conditions. In some families cancer proneness may have a genetic component, as with familial colon cancer.

McKusick's catalog of recognized human genetic conditions inherited in a mendelian fashion lists more than 3,000 autosomal dominant, recessive, and X-linked conditions (52). Martin (51) reviewed the 1975 edition of the catalog of some 2,400 genetic conditions along with the three common chromosomal conditions, Down's syndrome (trisomy 21), Turner's syndrome (XO), and Klinefelter's syndrome (XYY), to select those with the highest number of phenotypic features he judged to be associated with senescence. The features he included were intrinsic mutagenesis, chromosomal abnormalities, associated neoplasms, defective stem cells, premature loss of or gray hair, senility, slow virus susceptibility, amyloid deposition, lipofusion deposition, diabetes mellitus, disturbed lipid metabolism, hypogonadism, autoimmunity, hypertension, degenerative vascular disease, osteoporosis, cataracts, mitochondrial abnormalities, fibrosis, abnormal fat distribution, and a single group of other associated features of aging. Ten genetic diseases were identified that had the highest number of these senescent features. They were ranked in the following order: Down's syndrome, Werner's syndrome, Cockayne syndrome, progeria (Hutchinson-Gilford syndrome), ataxia telangectasia, Seip's syndrome, cervical lipodysplasia, Klinefelter's syndrome, Turner's syndrome, and myotonic dystrophy. It is noteworthy that selected for inclusion in this list of genetic syndromes with the highest number of premature aging features were the three chromosomal syndromes. It suggests that regulatory abnormalities such as those reflected in the quantitative type of gene dosage differences seen in chromosomal syndromes play an important role in producing the senescent phenotype.

In the following analysis the clinical features and a summary of research being done on the four human genetic models with the highest number of features of premature aging are reviewed.

DOWN'S SYNDROME

Down's syndrome (DS) may have the greatest number of features associated with the senescent phenotype and may be the highest ranking candidate as "segmental progeroid syndrome" according to Martin's analysis. Patients with DS show premature graying of hair and hair loss, increased tissue lipofuscin, increased neoplasms and leukemia, variations in the distribution of adipose tissue, amyloidosis, increased autoimmunity, hypogonadism, degenerative vascular disease, and cataracts. The life expectancy of patients with DS is markedly reduced (74). Most neuropathological studies have reported findings indistinguishable from those of senile dementia of Alzheimer type (SDAT) in many DS patients over age 40 (12,85). Progressive neurological and psychiatric abnormalities in older DS patients have have been reported indicating that the neuropathological changes are reflected as precocious aging and dementia (84). The features for and against DS as a model of aging are summarized in Table 1.

A specific qualitative gene defect is not present in DS. Rather, the syndrome is most commonly due to an extra chromosome 21 (trisomy 21), which leads to disturbances in gene dosage and quantitative differences in expression of genes located on chromosome 21. However, it is also possible that the extra genetic material may cause effects on the expression of genes on other chromosomes as well.

Although most cases of DS are due to the presence of an extra chromosome 21, about 4% are due to mosaicism, where the individual is composed of a mixture of both normal diploid and abnormal trisomic cells. Another 4% of cases are due to translocations, mostly of the robertsonian type, with nearly the whole of chromosome 21 translocated to another chromosome. In addition, a small number of cases of partial trisomy 21 have been reported with translocations of part of 21 to other chromosomes (42).

The specific pathogenesis of DS and other aneuploidies is unknown. Current research efforts are under way to apply to the powerful methods of DNA recombinant

TABLE 1. *Down's syndrome as a model of aging*

Pathological changes related to aging
   Premature graying and hair loss
   Increased tissue lipofuscin
   Increased incidence of leukemia
   Amyloid deposition
   Increased autoimmunity
   Hypogonadism
   Adipose tissue redistribution
   Degenerative vascular changes
   Cataracts
   Senile dementia of Alzheimer type
   Calcification in the basal ganglia
   Chromosome abnormalities
   Possible DNA repair defects

Pathological changes unrelated to aging
   Generalized developmental delays
   Mental retardation
   Developmental reduction in neuronal population and synaptic arborizations
   Cardiac and other organ malformation

technology to understand just what genes are involved in DS. We have isolated and identified a series of unique gene segments that we located by *in situ* hybridization to be only on chromosome 21 (7). Studies of gene segments such as these, employing the recombinant DNA technological approaches, promise to yield insights into how abnormalities in gene dosage can produce the features of accelerated aging as well as developmental disabilities.

WERNER'S SYNDROME

Werner's syndrome (WS), called progeria of the adult (4,11,20,70), has a number of features that resemble premature aging and some features that do not (Table 2). WS patients, as illustrated in Fig. 1, generally appear normal during childhood but cease growth during their early teenage years. Premature graying and whitening of hair occurs. Striking features include early cataract formation, skin that appears aged with a sclerodermatous appearance, a high-pitched voice, peripheral musculature atrophy, poor wound healing, chronic leg and ankle ulcers, hypogonadism, widespread atherosclerosis, soft tissue calcification, osteoporosis, and a high prevalence of diabetes mellitus. About 10% of patients develop a neoplasm with a particularly high frequency of sarcomas and meningiomas. The diagnosis of WS is usually made during the third decade. Patients commonly die of complications of atherosclerosis during the fourth decade. There are fewer than six known living WS patients in the United States. In Japan, where there is a higher consanguinity rate, a large number of cases have been reported (34–36,56,57).

Werner's syndrome is clearly inherited in an autosomal recessive mode. By analogy with other recessive diseases in which the basic defect is known, it could be due to the absence of a single specific enzyme. However, a basic enzymatic

TABLE 2. *Werner's syndrome as a model of aging*

Pathological changes related to aging
  Generalized atherosclerosis
  Graying and loss of hair
  Aged and pigmented skin changes
  Osteoporosis
  Hypogonadism
  Frequent diabetes
  Cataracts
  Cortical atrophy without senile dementia or accelerated plaque and tangle formation
  Frequent neoplasms

Pathological changes unrelated to aging
  Unusual calcifications in skin
  Ankle ulcerations
  Chromosomal translocation mosaicism
  Elevated urinary hyaluronic acid

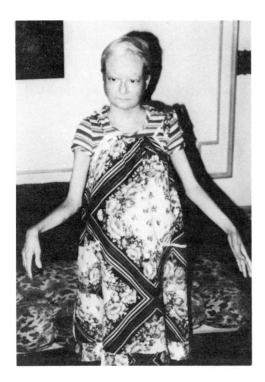

FIG. 1. A 37-year-old woman with Werner's syndrome. She had a history of white hair since age 12, bilateral cataracts requiring surgery, insulin-dependent diabetes, and nonhealing leg ulcers. She had required bilateral femoral popliteal bypass surgery and a left leg below-the-knee amputation for vascular insufficiency.

or metabolic abnormality has not yet been established for WS. Several investigations have provided tantalizing clues as to the nature of the underlying defect.

Cultured fibroblasts from WS patients uniformly show a greatly reduced *in vitro* life-span potential. Whereas some 40 to 80 generations *in vitro* are typical for normal cells, WS fibroblasts show a life-span of only 5 to 20 generations (50,70). Thus WS cells show rapid aging in culture, a trait that appears to mimic the apparent rapid aging of WS patients. WS fibroblasts and lymphocytes have been found to have chromosome abnormalities. Examination of chromosomes in cultured fibroblasts have shown that a wide variety of translocations occur spontaneously (70).

People normally excrete a small amount of glycosaminoglycans (GAGs) in the urine. Patients with metabolic storage diseases, e.g., mucopolysaccharidoses, may excrete large amounts of GAGs. Normally, less than 1% of the GAGs are in the form of hyaluronic acid (HA). WS patients appear to have elevated levels of urinary HA but normal total GAG levels. HA levels of 10 to 20% of GAGs are usually seen (35,44,48,56,70). This elevation of HA is distinctly abnormal, and with the exception of progeria (discussed below) it has not been recognized for any other genetic disease. Thus an elevated urinary level of HA appears to be a metabolic marker for WS. We have suggested that the elevated HA may play a role as an inhibitory growth factor of angiogenesis (9,11). Whether it relates to the abnormalities of cell growth and chromosomes seen in WS has yet to be determined. However by inhibiting angiogenesis it may explain the premature aging phenotype.

COCKAYNE SYNDROME

Cockayne syndrome (CS) is a rare recessive disease associated with the appearance of premature senescence. It is usually also associated with mental retardation (14). Patients generally have a normal appearance during infancy. They develop growth retardation with a variable age of onset. The eyes are sunken, and microcephaly is usually present. The skin frequently shows marked photosensitivity. They lose subcutaneous fat. The ears are usually prominent. Patients have long limbs and large hands and usually develop progressive joint deformities. Hypogonadism develops, but people may develop secondary sexual characteristics. They are usually not bald, but optic atrophy, deafness, and progressive ataxia develop. A striking feature is progressive intracranial calcification, which can be detected by computed tomography (CT) scan or skull x-ray film. Although the degree of neurological deterioration can be variable, death usually is a result of progressive neurodegeneration during late childhood or early adolescence.

Cockayne syndrome fibroblast cultures exhibit increased sensitivity to ultraviolet (UV) irradiation (71). Growth of cells, as assayed by colony-forming ability following UV irradiation, is much reduced compared to normal. This abnormal sensitivity to UV radiation has been used for prenatal diagnosis of the syndrome (75). No known defect in excision or DNA repair has yet been defined. It has been suggested that UV irradiation produces a chromatin alteration that inhibits replicon initiation (13). Three complementation groups have been defined based on RNA synthesis following somatic fusion and UV irradiation (46), which suggests that heterogeneity is present in the syndrome. This disease illustrates that abnormal sensitivity to irradiation can be associated with a premature aging phenotype.

PROGERIA (HUTCHINSON-GILFORD PROGERIA SYNDROME)

Progeria, as illustrated in Fig. 2, is a rare genetic disease with striking clinical features that resemble those of premature aging (11,19). Patients with this condition generally appear normal at birth, but by about 1 year of age severe growth retardation is usually seen. Balding occurs, and loss of eyebrows and eyelashes is common during the first few years of life. Widespread loss of subcutaneous tissue occurs, and as a result the veins over the scalp become particularly prominent. The skin appears aged, and pigmented age spots develop. The patients are short, averaging about 40 inches in height, and usually weigh no more than 25 or 30 pounds even as teenagers. Their weight/height ratio is thus low. The voice is thin and high-pitched. Sexual maturation usually does not occur. They have a characteristic

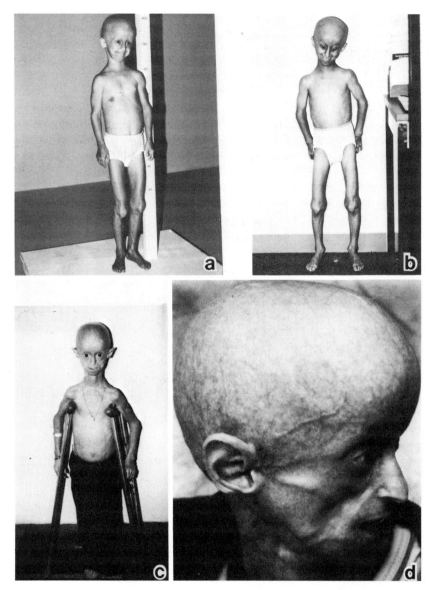

FIG. 2. Progeria patients. **a:** An 8-year-old girl (B.S.). At age 13 she underwent coronary bypass surgery. **b:** This 14-year-old boy (F.M.) died 1 year later of congestive heart failure. **c:** This 10-year-old girl (T.S.) suffered bilateral hip dislocations. **d:** The same subject at age 13. She died at age 14 of congestive heart failure.

facial appearance with prominent eyes, a beaked nose, a "plucked bird" facial appearance, and facial disproportion, with a small jaw and a large cranium. The large, balding head and small face gives them an extremely aged appearance. The bones show distinctive changes with frequent resorption of the collar bones and replacement by fibrous tissue. Resorption of the terminal finger bones, stiffening of finger joints, and a peculiar horse-riding stance are seen. Aseptic necrosis of the head of the femur and hip dislocation are common.

Progeria subjects have a normal to above-average intelligence. The median age of death is 12 years. More than 80% of deaths are due to heart attacks or congestive heart failure. Widespread atherosclerosis, with interstitial fibrosis of the heart, is usually seen at postmortem examination (2). Occasionally marked enlargement of the thymus gland is noted. However, some features often associated with normal aging such as tumors, cataracts, diabetes, and hyperlipidemia, although occasionally reported (45,65,80), are not usually present. Progeria represents a model disease for studies of aging as summarized in Table 3.

We have had the opportunity to examine 24 cases of progeria. Information on these cases is summarized in Table 4. We have established an International Progeria Registry. As of 1987 the Registry included 20 living patients: 15 living in the United States, 3 in Canada, 1 in Holland, and 1 in South Africa. We have had correspondence regarding three other cases from Russia, China, and Iran, but confirmation that they have true progeria is lacking. We have helped to organize an annual progeria family conference. Beginning in the summer of 1981, all interested progeria families have been brought together for 1 week. At each meeting there have been 8 to 14 progeria children and their families present. It has allowed the children and families to meet each other and to share common experiences. Several interested physicians have been present, and counseling has been given to the families regarding this rare condition.

A consideration of the mode of inheritance in progeria is important for genetic counseling purposes and may help to define the nature of the underlying mutation. Recessive diseases often appear to be due to enzymatic deficiencies that lead to metabolic abnormalities, whereas dominant diseases often involve structural proteins. However, dominant diseases also may be due to partial deficiencies of rate-limiting enzymes (i.e., porphyria) or cell-surface receptors (i.e., familial hypercho-

TABLE 3. *Progeria as a model of aging: pathological changes related to aging*

Generalized atherosclerosis
Balding
Hypogonadism
Osteoporosis
Loss of subcutaneous fat
Pigmented skin changes
Variable elevated tissue lipofusin

TABLE 4. *Summary of 24 cases of progeria*

Pt.	Sex	Age at exam.	Birth date	Died	Mother	Father	Diff.	Sibs
					Age (year.month)			
M.C.	F	27	10/01/55	05/25/85	40.0	45.8	5.8	6
R.M.	F	15	08/06/66	04/24/83	27	27	0	1
F.M.	M	13	1966	1981	28	25	−3	2
K.C.	M	10	1968	—	24	24	0	2
T.S.	F	10	02/01/68	09/11/82	25.8	26	0.8	3
A.F.	F	12	09/12/69	—	37.4	45.6	8.2	3
A.G.	F	13	02/20/70	04/01/85	24.5	49.11	25.6	6
B.S.	F	10	1970	—	26	38	12	2
M.H.	M	11	06/30/72	—	19	26	8	1
F.G.	M	11	12/31/72	—	21.0	27.0	6	1
D.P.	M	12	1973	—	38	44	6	13
R.P.	M	9	11/26/73	06/20/73	20.0	27.4	7.4	1
J.E.	M	9	08/16/74	—	17	17	0	1
S.K.	F	2	06/09/76	—	33	47	14	1
P.S.	M	6	05/10/77	—	24.0	23.9	−0.3	2
A.K.	F	5	06/28/78	—	29.11	34.10	4.11	1
A.B.	F	6	09/10/78	—	16.11	16.9	−0.2	1
L.C.	M	4	08/20/79	—	33.0	41.4	8.4	3
A.F.	F	3	04/18/80	—	23.0	23.0	0	1
B.S.	M	3	07/26/80	—	28.8	28.8	0	1
C./C.R.[a]	M/M	2	01/26/81	—	25.6	26.2	0.8	1
M.B.	M	2	05/02/82	—	31.8	39.1	7.5	1
K.S.	F	1	06/22/82	—	26.4	28.3	1.11	1
M.S.	F	1	07/11/82	—	28.6	25.3	−3.3	1
Total (average)					27.0	31.6	4.6	55

[a] Twins.

lesterolemia) where half the normal level of the gene product can lead to a disease.

Several genetic considerations suggest that progeria is most likely a sporadic dominant mutation. First, high rates of consanguinity, i.e., first cousin marriages, are expected for rare recessive diseases, but high consanguinity rates are not seen with progeria. Debusk (19) noted that consanguinity was present in only 3 of 19 families in which it was specifically discussed. Some of these patients had come from areas of the world with high background population levels of consanguinity. In addition, it was not reported in 41 other families. Thus 3 of 60 (5%) was the reported frequency as of 1972. A family history of consanguinity was not present in any of the 24 progeria cases we examined. We estimate the frequency of progeria patients born to consanguineous marriages to be less than 3 in 84 (3.6%). For rare recessive diseases, an estimate of expected frequency of consanguinity can be derived using the Dahlberg formula (20). Assumption of a birth incidence of progeria of 1 per 8 million and a background population consanguinity frequency of 1% leads to an estimate of expected consanguinity of 64% in progeria families. The less than 3.6% observed consanguinity frequency in progeria is much lower than the high level that would be expected for such a rare recessive disease.

Although the reported incidence of progeria in the United States is about 1 in

8 million births (19), the true population incidence may be somewhat higher, as not all cases are reported. Based on our experience, we estimate that about 50% of all cases in the United States do get reported, which leads to an estimate of 1 in 4 million births. Even if progeria were to have an incidence of 1 in 1 million, it would still lead to a much higher expected consanguinity frequency, 45%, than the low frequency that is seen in progeria families. This lack of consanguinity suggests that progeria is unlikely to be a rare recessive.

Second, a paternal age effect is seen with progeria that is also observed in some sporadic dominant-type mutations. Jones et al. (43) reported that among 18 progeria cases the fathers were older than expected by an average of 2.56 years when controlled for maternal age, a difference that was highly significant ($p <$ 0.005). In addition to progeria, Jones et al. reported a paternal age effect with seven other disorders (basal cell nevus syndrome, Waardenburg's syndrome, Crouzon's syndrome, cleidocranial dysostosis, oculo-dental-digital syndrome, Treacher Collins syndrome, and multiple exostoses) involving new mutations for which autosomal dominant inheritance had been clearly established and in four disorders (achondroplasia, Apert's syndrome, fibrodysplasia ossicans progressiva, and Marfan's syndrome) in which older paternal age in the setting of new mutation had been previously shown.

We have also observed a paternal age effect in the 24 cases of progeria we examined, as indicated in Table 4. The fathers were older than the mothers by an average of 4.6 years, which is higher than the expected control value of 2.8 years (43). The paternal age effect observed in these 24 cases confirms the previously reported paternal age effect in the 18 earlier cases by Jones et al. (43) and suggests dominant inheritance. The paternal age effect appears to be due to an excess of a few older fathers, which produces a secondary age peak. A similar secondary paternal age peak has been reported in new cases of neurofibromatosis, another dominant disease (63).

Third, for a recessive condition, the proportion of affected siblings is expected to be 25%. With progeria it is clearly much less than 25%. Most cases are sporadic. A case of identical progeria twins with 14 normal siblings was reported (79). Here, three or four affected siblings would be expected if it was a recessive disease. It is recognzied that for new dominant mutations occasionally the mutation can occur in a germ line leading to somatic mosaicism within the ovary or testes (52). Several cases could then occur within one family. Probable cases of familial progeria have been reported in only a few instances among more than 100 families, and some of them may have been misidentified (24,25,55,61). Among the 24 patients we examined (Table 4), no family had more than one affected child; and there were 55 unaffected siblings. One would expect there to be 14 or 15 of the 55 siblings affected (25%) if a recessive mode of inheritance were to apply to these 24 progeria families.

In general, the lack of consanguinity, the paternal age effect, and the lack of affected siblings argue that progeria is not a rare recessive but probably is a sporadic dominant mutation. Progeria was formerly considered to be a recessive disease and was so classified in early editions of McKusick's catalog of mendelian inheritance in man. Because of a lack of consanguinity, a lack of affected siblings, and a paternal age effect, we suggested that progeria be classified as a sporadic autosomal dominant mutation (5). Subsequently, it was moved from the recessive to the dominant section of the catalog (52). The possibility of genetic heterogeneity in progeria, in which some cases have a similar clinical presentation but with a recessive mode of inheritance seems possible but, because of the rarity of the condition, quite unlikely. Most cases appear to represent isolated sporadic dominant mutations, although a few may be the result of a germ line mutation. For genetic counseling of families with a progeria child, the recurrence risk can be stated to be low but may be on the order of 1 in 500 with each pregnancy.

Laboratory investigations of progeria have involved a search for a genetic marker in an attempt to help define the underlying defect. The cultured life-span of progeric fibroblasts was initially reported to be reduced (27). Subsequent studies have shown that although difficulties sometimes occur in the initial establishment of a culture, once established, a normal or only a modest reduction in life-span is seen (28,50). We have examined the *in vitro* life-spans of 11 progeria cell cultures: 4 WS cultures, 4 parents of progeria subjects, and 3 control cultures. The WS cell lines showed extremely rapid senescence with a range of 9 to 15 maximal population doubling levels. The progeria cell lines had a range of about 20 to 60 population doubling levels. It was reduced by about one-third compared to the parent lines and the normal controls. The WS line population doubling levels were greatly reduced. Thus a markedly reduced *in vitro* life-span of progeria cells such as was seen in WS was not present. The modest and variable reduction in life-span in culture is unlikely to represent a useful marker for the disease.

Goldstein and Moerman (28) reported finding an increased fraction of abnormally thermolabile enzymes, including glucose-6-phosphate dehydrogenase (G6PD), 6-phosphogluconate dehydrogenase (6PGD), and hypoxanthine phosphoribosyltransferase (HPRT) in progeria fibroblasts. Based in part on the Orgel error–catastrophe hypothesis of aging (59), it was suggested that diseases resembling premature aging may be the result of widespread errors in protein synthesis (32). Abnormally high thermolabile enzyme levels in circulating erythrocytes from one progeria patient with intermediate levels in the parents was also reported (30,31). It was suggested that this finding supports autosomal recessive inheritance. Our studies of three progeria patients and their families did not confirm these elevations, as no increased erythrocyte thermolabile enzyme elevations were seen (5). In our opinion, this lack of confirmation indicates that a defect in protein synthetic fidelity is unlikely to be the basic defect in progeria and does not support the suggestion of autosomal recessive inheritance. Subsequent work by Wojtyk and Goldstein (86) on cell-free protein synthesis using progeria fibroblast extracts also found no decreased translation ability, which also argues against a generalized defect in progeria protein synthesis.

Abnormal immune function has been postulated as a defect in progeria. Walford suggested that progeria could reflect an abnormality of immune function because of the similarity to experimental graft-versus-host reaction and to runting disease (81). In support of this concept, Singal and Goldstein (73) reported that HLA expression on two cultured progeria fibroblast strains was absent. They later reported that there was not an absence but a greatly reduced concentration of HLA cell-surface molecules (32,33). In studies of ten progeria fibroblast strains, we were unable to confirm this reported abnormality. We found no evidence for either qualitative or quantitative abnormalities of HLA expression, and no association with HLA type was detected (6). Thymic hormone levels have been reported as age-appropriate (40). Thus no immune abnormalities have been established for progeria.

An abnormality of x-ray DNA-repair capacity in progeria fibroblasts was suggested by Epstein et al. (21,22), who detected decreased single-strand rejoining of gamma-irradiated DNA using alkaline sucrose gradients. The presence of altered DNA-repair capability was not found in another study. Using a somewhat modified method for assay of single-strand rejoining, no differences between one progeric strain and two atypical progeric strains were seen compared to normals (62).

Brown et al. (8,10) showed that co-cultivation of two progeric cell strains with normal strains or with each other reversed the single-strand DNA-rejoining defect and suggested that complementation groups for DNA repair might exist in progeria. Weichselbaum et al. (82) assayed the x-ray sensitivity of various types of human fibroblasts by measuring their ability to form colonies following irradiation. They found two progeric strains with increased sensitivity and three strains with normal sensitivity. These studies suggested some increase in radiosensitivity but left open the possibility that damage to cellular components other than DNA might be responsible.

Rainbow and Howes (60), using a sensitive host-cell-reactivation (HCR) assay of x-irradiated adenovirus, reported that two progeric strains showed a deficiency of DNA-repair capacity. Brown et al. (6) studied HCR in two other strains and found one strain to show decreased HCR whereas another showed normal HCR under a variety of cell growth conditions. These results suggested that heterogeneity of DNA-repair capacity exists among progeria fibroblasts. Defective DNA-repair capacity therefore does not appear to be a consistent marker for progeria, and it seems unlikely to represent a basic genetic defect.

A few other isolated reports have suggested abnormalities in progeria. Elevated levels of fibroblast tissue factor were reported in both progeria and WS cells (32). It could reflect variations in culture conditions or the growth state of cells unrelated to genotype, such as has been reported for other cell types (49). A normal insulin-binding receptor response but decreased binding of insulin to nonspecific receptors in progeria cells has been reported (64). The significance of nonspecific receptor binding is unclear.

HYALURONIC ACID URINARY LEVELS WITH PROGERIA AND WS

A potentially unique marker for both progeria and Werner's syndrome appears to be urinary HA excretion. HA excretion has been found to be elevated in these two syndromes and has not been reported to be elevated for any other genetic disease. HA levels in controls are normally considered to represent less than 1% of total GAGs. Elevated HA levels have been reported to vary from 2 to 22% in a series of Japanesse WS subjects (48,56,57,76). With progeria, urinary HA as a percent of total GAGs present was also reported to be elevated to 4.4% in one Japanese subject compared to controls of 0.2 and 0.3% (77).

We determined the total urinary excretion of GAGs and HA in one WS patient, three progeria patients, one patient with an atypical progeroid syndrome, and a control subject using standard methods for GAG analysis including CPC precipitation, pronase digestion, trichloroacetic acid (TCA) treatment, ethanol precipitation, and uronic acid determination before and after hyaluronidase digestion (11,44). The results showed a significant elevation of HA in these subjects compared to controls. This method is tedious, and to examine normal controls more thoroughly we developed a high-performance liquid chromatography (HPLC)-based method for quantitation of HA. Using this method we found a modest increase in HA excretion per creatinine with age. Eleven progeria urine samples were examined using this method, and we found an average 16-fold increase in HA excretion compared to age-matched controls (11,87). The results are illustrated in Fig. 3.

To determine if the elevated HA excretion seen in progeria was also reflected in cell culture, we analyzed HA and GAG production in normal, progeria, and WS fibroblasts (11). HA and GAG production by progeria, WS, and control cells was assayed by measuring both total glucosamine and sulfate incorporation into cells and media. HA production was found to be elevated in progeria and WS compared to normal cultures at all cell densities measured. A pronounced difference in total GAG production was also observed when normal fibroblasts were compared with WS and progeria fibroblasts as a function of cell density. A similar difference in GAG and HA excretion into the media was seen when comparing WS and progeria to normals as a function of cell density. Non-HA-containing GAGs, assayed by sulfur incorporation, were also found to decrease as a function of cell density and were found to be produced in excess in WS and progeria fibroblasts.

In order to determine whether the overproduction of GAGs in general and HA in particular was related to increased synthesis or to faulty degradation, cultures from normal, WS, and progeria lines were labeled for 4, 8, and 24 hours and then assayed. There was little comparative difference in either total tritiated GAGs or HA produced, unlike the marked difference that was seen at 72 hours of cultivation. This finding suggested that a degradative pathway abnormality is apparently present, as the initial synthesis was relatively unimparied.

Hyaluronic acid and GAG production during embryogenesis is believed to play an important role in morphogenesis. In chick embryos a striking correlation between hyaluronate synthesis and cell movement and proliferation is observed, as well as between HA degradation and differentiation. HA also appears to act as an antiangiogenesis factor. During development tissue regions that have high HA concentrations are invariably avascular zones. HA-containing implants were shown to cause avascularity when implanted into normal vascular wing mesoderm (23). West et al. (83), found degradation products of HA (sacaroids 4–24 units long)

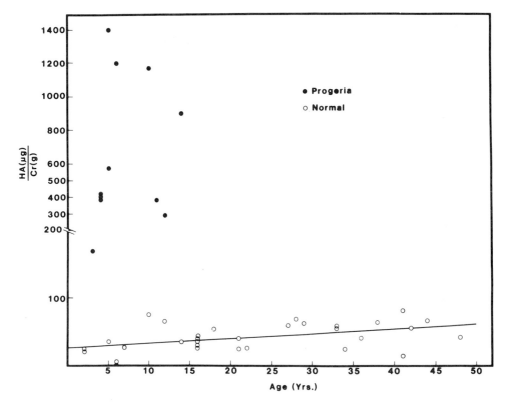

FIG. 3. Elevation of urinary hyaluronic acid in progeria. An average 16-fold elevation for 11 subjects was seen. A modest age-related increase was also observed with normals. Samples were analyzed by HPLC as described by Zebrower et al. (87).

to have the opposite effect and to stimulate angiogenesis. HA thus appears to be crucial in the morphogenesis of blood vessels in the embryo and may be expected to play an equally important role controlling angiogenesis maturation and aging. Our results with progeria and WS suggest that abnormalities of HA excretion on degradation may provide a consistent marker. Mutations of HA metabolism may underlie these diseases and relate to major genes affecting accelerated aging.

SUMMARY

A consideration of the evolution of longevity suggests that a few genes, perhaps 10 to 20, play a key role in determining the rate of aging and the species-specific maximal life-span potential. Current information suggests that these genes encode enzymatic systems that play a self-protective role in maintaining the integrity of the genetic material itself and in regulating the timing of development. Twin and parent–child longevity correlation studies suggest that single genes do not increase longevity. Rather, longevity is likely to be multifactorial and due to the action of a number of genes. Some human genetic diseases shorten the life-span. Several of these diseases, e.g., Down's syndrome, Werner's syndrome, Cockayne syndrome, and progeria, produce a picture of apparent accelerated aging. They are considered model diseases for the study of genetic aspects of the aging process. Understanding the basic defects involved in these diseases may lead to insights into how specific genes control the aging process.

REFERENCES

1. Ames, B. N., Cathcart, R., Schwiers, E., and Hochstein, P. (1981): Uric acid provides an antioxidant defense in humans againt oxidant- and radical-caused aging and cancer: a hypothesis. *Proc. Natl. Acad. Sci., USA,* 78:6858–6862.
2. Baker, P. B., Baba, N., and Boesel, C. P. (1981): Cardiovascular abnormalities in progeria. *Arch. Pathol. Lab. Med.,* 105:384.
3. Brown, W. T. (1979): Human mutations affecting aging—a review. *Mech. Aging Dev.,* 9:325–336.
4. Brown, W. T. (1983): Werner's syndrome. In: *Chromosome Mutation and Neoplasia,* pp. 85–93. Alan R. Liss, New York.
5. Brown, W. T., and Darlington G. J. (1980): Thermolabile enzymes in progeria and Werner syndrome: evidence contrary to the protein error hypothesis. *Am. J. Hum. Genet.,* 32:614–619.
6. Brown, W. T., Darlington, G. J., Fotino, M., and Arnold A. (1980): Detection of HLA antigens on cultured progeria fibroblasts. *Clin. Genet.,* 17:213–219.
7. Brown, W. T., Devine, E. A., Nolin, S. L., Houck, G. E., Jr., and Jenkins, E. C. (1985): Localization of chromosome 21 probes by in situ hybridization. *Ann. N.Y. Acad. Sci.,* 450:69–83.
8. Brown, W. T., Epstein, J., and Little, J. B. (1976): Progeria cells are stimulated to repair DNA by co-cultivation with normal cells. *Exp. Cell. Res.,* 97:291.
9. Brown, W. T., Kieras, F. J., Houck, G. E., Dutkowski, R., and Jenkins, E. C. (1985): A comparison of adult and childhood progerias: Werner syndrome and Hutchinson-Gilford progeria syndrome, In: *Werner's Syndrome and Human Aging,* pp. 229–244. Plenum Press, New York.
10. Brown, W. T., Little, J. B., Epstein, J., and Williams, J. R. (1977): DNA repair defect in progeria cells In: *Genetic Effects on Aging,* edited by D. Bergsma and D. E. Harrison, p. 417. Alan R. Liss, New York.
11. Brown, W. T., Zebrower, M., and Kieras, F. J. (1985): Progeria, a model disease for the sutdy of accelerated aging. In: *Molecular Biology of Aging,* ediited by A. D. Woodhead, A. D. Blackett, and A. Hollaender, pp. 375–396. Plenum Press, New York.
12. Burger, P. C., and Vogel S. (1973): The development of the pathologic changes of Alzheimer's disease and senile dementia in patients with Down's syndrome. *Am. J. Pathol,* 73:457–468.
13. Cleaver, J. E. (1982): Normal reconstruction of DNA supercoiling and chromatin structure in Cockayne syndrome cells during repair of damage from ultraviolet light. *Am. J. Hum. Genet.,* 34:566–575.
14. Cockayne, E. A. (1936): Dwarfism with retinal atrophy and deafness. *Arch. Dis. Child.,* 11:1–5.
15. Cutler, R. G. (1975): Evolution of human longevity and the genetic complexity governing aging rate. *Proc. Natl. Acad. Sci. USA,* 72:4664–4668.
16. Cutler, R. G. (1976): Nature of aging and life maintenance processes. *Interdiscip. Top. Gerontol.,* 9:83–133.
17. Cutler, R. G. (1980): Evolution of human longevity. *Adv. Pathol.,* 7:43–49.
18. Cutler, R. G. (1985): Antioxidants and longevity of mammalian species. In: *Molecular Biology of Aging,* edited by A. D. Woodhead, A. D. Blackett, and A. Hollaender, Vol. 35, pp. 15–17, Plenum, New York.
19. DeBusk, F. L. (1972): The Hutchinson-Gilford progeria syndrome. *J. Pediatr.,* 80:697–724.

20. Epstein, C. J., Martin G. M., Schultz, A. L., and Motulsky, A. G. (1966): Werner's syndrome: a review of its symptomatology, natural history, pathologic features, genetics and relationship to the natural aging process. *Medicine* (Baltimore), 45:177–221.
21. Epstein, J., Williams, J. R., and Little, J. B. (1974): Rate of DNA repair in human progeroid cells. *Proc. Natl. Acad. Sci. USA*, 70:977.
22. Epstein, J., Williams, J. R., and Little, J. B. (1974): Rate of DNA repair in progeria and normal fibroblasts. *Biochem. Biophys. Res. Commun.*, 59:850.
23. Feinberg, R. N., and Beebe, D. C. (1983): Hyaluronate in vasculogenesis. *Science*, 220:1177–1179.
24. Franklin, P. P. (1976): Progeria in siblings. *Clin. Radiol.*, 27:327.
25. Gabr, M., Hashem, N., Hashem, M., Fahni, A., and Satouh, M. (1960): Progeria, a pathologic study. *J. Pediatr.*, 57:70.
26. Glueck, C. J., Gartside, P., Fallat, R. W., Sieski, J., and Steiner, P. M. (1976): Longevity syndromes: familial hypobeta and familial hyper-alpha lipoproteinemia. *J. Lab. Clin. Med.*, 88:941–957.
27. Goldstein, S. (1969): Lifespan of cultured cells in progeria. *Lancet*, 1:424.
28. Goldstein, S., and Moerman, E. (1975): Heat-labile enzymes in skin fibroblasts from subjects with progeria. *N. Engl. J. Med.*, 292:1305.
29. Goldstein, S., and Moerman, E. (1976): Defective protein in normal and abnormal fibroblasts during aging in vitro. *Interdiscip. Top. Gerontol.*, 10:24.
30. Goldstein, S., and Moerman, E. J. (1978): Heat-labile enzymes in circulating erythrocytes of a progeria family. *Am. J. Hum. Genet.*, 30:167.
31. Goldstein, S., and Moerman, E. J. (1978): Unstable enzymes in erythrocytes of a family with the Hutchinson-Gilford progeria syndrome. In: *The Red Cell,* edited by C. J. Brewer, p. 217. Alan R. Liss, New York.
32. Goldstein, S., and Niewiarowski, S. (1976): Increased procoagulant activity in cultured fibroblasts from progeria and Werner's syndromes of premature aging. *Nature*, 260:711.
33. Goldstein, S., Niewiarowski, S., and Sinegal, D. P. (1975): Pathological implications of cell aging in vitro. *Fed. Proc.*, 34:55.
34. Goto, M., Horiuchi, Y., Tanimoto, K., Ishii, T., and Nakashima, H. (1978): Werner's syndrome: analysis of 15 cases with a review of the Japanese literature. *J. Am. Geriatr. Soc.*, 26:341–347.
35. Goto, M., and Murata, K. (1978): Urinary excretion of macromolecular acidic glycosaminoglycans in Werner's syndrome. *Clin. Chim. Acta*, 85:101–106.
36. Goto, M., Tanimoto, K., Horuichi, Y., and Sasazuji, T. (1981): Family analysis of Werner's syndrome: a survey of 42 Japanese families with a review of the literature. *Clin. Genet.*, 19:8–15.
37. Hamilton, W. J. (1940): The biology of the smokey shrew (Sorex fumeus fumeus Miller.) *Zoologica*, 23:473.
38. Harman, D. (1981): The aging process. *Proc. Natl. Acad. Sci. USA*, 78:7124–7128.
39. Hart, R. W., and Setlow, R. B. (1974): Correlation between deoxyribonucleic acid excision repair and life span in a number of mammalian species. *Proc. Natl. Acad. Sci. USA*, 71:2169–2173.
40. Iwata, T., Incefy, G. S., Cunningham-Rundles, S., Smithwick, E., Geller, N., O'Reilly, R., and Good, R. A. (1981): Circulating thymic hormone activity in patients with primary and secondary immunodeficiency diseases. *Am. J. Med.*, 71:385.
41. Jarvik, L. F., Falek, A., Kallman, F. J., and Lorge, I., (1960): Survival trends in a senescent twin population. *Am. J. Hum. Genet.*, 12:170–179.
42. Jenkins, E. C., Duncan, C. J., Wright, C. E., Giordano, F. M., Wilbur, L., Wisniewski, K. W., Sklower, S. L., French, J. H., Jones, C., and Brown, W. T. (1983): Atypical Down syndrome and partial trisomy 21. *Clin. Genet.*, 24:97–102.
43. Jones, K., Smith, P., Harvey, M., Hall, B., and Quan, L. (1975): Older paternal age and fresh gene mutation: data on additional disorders. *J. Pediatr.*, 86:84.
44. Kieras, F. J., Brown, W. T., Houck, G. E., and Zebrower, M., (1986): Elevation of urinary hyaluronic acid in Werner syndrome and progeria. *Biochem. Med. Metab. Biol.*, 36:276–282.
45. King, C. R., Lemmer, J., Campbell, J. R., and Atkins, A. R. (1978): Osteosarcoma in a patient with Hutchinson-Gilford progeria, *J. Med. Genet.*, 15:481.
46. Lehmann, A. R. (1982): Three complementation groups in Cockayne syndrome. *Mutat. Res.*, 106:347–356.

47. Lints, F. A. (1978): Genetics and ageing. *Interdiscip. Top. Gerontol.* 14:1–31.
48. Maekawa, Y., and Hayashibar, T. (1981): Determination of hyaluronic acid in the urine of a patient with Werner's syndrome. *J. Dermatol.*, 8:467.
49. Magniord, J. R., Dreyer, B. E., Stemerman, M. B., and Pitlick, F. A. (1977): Tissue factor coagulant activity of cultured human endothelial and smooth muscle cells and fibroblasts. *Blood*, 50:387.
50. Martin, G. M., Sprague, C. A., and Epstein, C. J. (1970): Replicative life-span of cultivated human cells: effects of donor's age, tissue and genotype. *Lab. Invest.*, 23:86–92.
51. Martin, G. M. (1977): Genetic syndromes in man with potential relevance to the pathobiology of aging. *Birth Defects*, 14:5–39.
52. McKusick, V. A. (1986): Mendelian inheritance in man. In: *Catalogues of Autosomal Dominant, Autosomal Recessive and X-linked Phenotypes*, 7th ed. John Hopkins University Press, Baltimore.
53. McWhirter, N. (1987): *Guinness Book of World Records*, pp. 15–19. Bantam Books, New York.
54. Medvedev, Z. A. (1974): Causasus and Altay Longevity: a biological or social problem? *Gerontologist*, 14:381–387.
55. Mostafa, A. H., and Gabr, M. (1954): Hereditary progeria with follow-up of two affected sisters. *Arch. Pediatr.*, 71:163.
56. Murata, K. (1982): Urinary acidic glycosaminoglycans in Werner's syndrome. *Experientia*, 38:313–314.
57. Murata, K., and Nakashima, H. (1982): Werner's syndrome: twenty-four cases with a review of the Japanese medical literature. *J. Am. Geriatr. Soc.*, 30:303–308.
58. Murphy, E. A. (1978): Genetics of longevity in man. In: *The Genetics of Ageing*, edited by E. L. Schneider, pp. 261–302. Plenum Press, New York.
59. Orgel, L. E. (1963): The maintenance of the accuracy of protein synthesis and its relevance to aging. *Proc. Natl. Acad. Sci. USA*, 49:517.
60. Rainbow, A., and Howes, M. (1977): Deceased repair of gamma ray damaged DNA in progeria. *Biochem. Biophys. Res. Commun.*, 74:714.
61. Rautenstrauch, T., Snigula, F., Kreig, T., Gay, S., and Muller, P. K. (1977): Progeria: a cell culture study and clinical report of familial incidence. *Eur. J. Pediatr.*, 124:101.
62. Regan, J. D., and Setlow, R. B. (1974): DNA repair in human progeroid cells. *Biochem. Biophys. Res. Commun.*, 59:858.
63. Riccardi, V. M. (1983): Neurofibromatosis. In: *Principles and Practice of Medical Genetics*, edited by A. Emery and D. Rimoin, p. 314. Churchill Livingstone, New York.
64. Rosenbloom, A. L., and Goldstein, S. (1976): Insulin binding to cultured human fibroblasts increases with normal and precocious aging. *Science*, 19:412.
65. Rosenbloom, A. L., Kappy, M. S., DeBusk, F. L., Francis, G. L., Philpot, T. J., and Maclaren, M. K. (1983): Progeria: insulin resistance and hyperglycemia. *J. Pediatr.*, 102:400.
66. Sacher, G. A. (1975): Maturation and longevity and relation to the cranial capacity in huminid evolution. In: *Antecedents of Man and After. I. Primates: Functional Morphology and Evolution*, edited by R. Tuttle, pp. 417–441. Montox, The Hague.
67. Sacher, G. A. (1976): Evaluation of the ectrophy and information terms governing mammalian longevity. *Interdiscip. Top. Gerontol.*, 9:69–82.
68. Sacher, G. A. (1980): Mammalian life histories: their evolution and molecular-genetic mechanism. *Adv. Pathobiol.*, 7:21–42.
69. Sacher, G. A., and Staffeldt, E. F. (1974): Relationship of gestation time to brain weight for placental mammals: implications for the theory of vertebrate growth. *Am. Natural*, 108:593–615.
70. Salk, D. (1982): Werner syndrome: a review of recent research with an analysis of connective tissue metabolism, growth control of cultured cells, and chromosomal aberrations. *Hum. Genet.* 62:1–20.
71. Schmickel, R. D., Chu, E. H. Y., Trosko, J. E., and Chang, C. C., (1977): Cockayne syndrome: a cellular sensitivity to ultraviolet light. *Pediatrics*, 60:135–139.
72. Schwartz, A. G., and Moore, C. J. (1977): Inverse correlation between species life-span and capacity of cultured fibroblasts to bind 7,12-dimethylbenz(a)anthracene to DNA. *Exp. Cell Res.*, 94:109–448.
73. Singal, D. P., and Goldstein, S. (1973): Absence of detectable HL-A antigens on cultured fibroblasts in progeria. *J. Clin. Invest.*, 52:2259.
74. Smith, G. F., and Berg, J. M. (1976): *Down's Anomaly*, pp. 239–245. Churchill Livingstone, New York.

75. Sugita, T., Ikenaga, M., Suehara, N., Kozuka, T., Furuyama, J., and Yabuchi, H. (1982): Prenatal diagnosis of Cockayne syndrome using assay colony-forming ability in ultraviolet light irradiated cells. *Clin. Genet.,* 22:137–142.

76. Tokunaga, M., Futami, T., Wakamatsu, E., Endo M., and Yosizawa, Z. (1975): Werner's syndrome as "hyaluronuria." *Clin. Chim. Acta,* 62:89–96.

77. Tokunaga, M., Wakamatsu, E., Sato, K., Satake, S., Aoyama, K., Saito, K., Sugawara, M., and Yosizawa, Z. (1978): Hyaluronuria in a case of progeria (Hutchinson-Gilford syndrome). *J. Am. Geriatr. Soc.,* 26:296–302.

78. Tolmasoff, J. M., Ono, T., and Cutler, R. G. (1980): Superoxide dismutase: correlation with lifespan and specific metabolic rates in primate species. *Proc. Natl, Acad. Sci. USA,* 77:2777–2781.

79. Viegus, J., Souza, P. L. R., and Salzanio, F. M. (1974): Progeria in twins. *J. Med. Genet.,* 11:384.

80. Villee, D. B., and Powers, M. L. (1978): Progeria: a model for the study of aging, In: *Senile Dementia: A Biomedical Approach,* edited by K. Nandy, p. 259. Elsevier, New York.

81. Walford, R. L. (1970): Antibody diversity, histocompatibility systems, disease states and aging. *Lancet,* 2:1226.

82. Weichselbaum, R. R., Nove, J., and Little, J. B. (1980): X-ray sensitivity of fifty-three human fibroblast cell strains from patients with characterized genetic disorders. *Cancer Res.,* 40:920.

83. West, D. C., Hampson, I. N., Arnold, F., and Kumar, S. (1985): Angiogenesis induced by degradation products of hyaluronic acid. *Science,* 228:1324–1326.

84. Wisniewski, K., Howe, J., Williams, D. G., and Wisniewski, H. M. (1978): Precocious aging and dementia in patients with Down's syndrome. *Biol. Psychiatry,* 13:619–627.

85. Wisniewski, K., Wisniewski, H. M., and Wen, G. Y., (1984): Occurrence of Alzheimer's neuropathy and dementia in Down syndrome. *Ann. Neurol.,* 17:278–282.

86. Wojtyk, R., and Goldstein, S. (1980): Fidelity of protein synthesis does not decline during aging of cultured human fibroblasts. *J. Cell. Physiol.,* 103:299.

87. Zebrower, M., Kieras, F. J., and Brown, W. T. (1986): Hylauronic acid elevation in progeria. *Mech. Ageing Dev.,* 35:39–46.

Human Aging Research: Concepts and Techniques,
edited by B. Kent and R. N. Butler.
Raven Press, Ltd., New York © 1988.

Endocrinology and Aging

Jeffrey B. Halter

Division of Geriatric Medicine, Department of Internal Medicine, University of Michigan Medical School and Veterans Administration Medical Center, Ann Arbor, Michigan 48109

The field of endocrinology is concerned primarily with understanding the mechanisms by which hormones or chemical messengers help to regulate internal homeostasis and the diseases of internal homeostasis that result from pathologic changes in the endocrine system. The concept of internal homeostasis, as an essential function to allow free interaction with the environment, was first developed more than a century ago by the French physiologist Claude Bernard. Loss of internal homeostatic mechanisms in the elderly can be a cause of functional impairments that markedly restrict their freedom, as external supports need to be employed to counterbalance the loss of internal adaptation.

Endocrine research in the elderly has included study of age-related changes in the physiology of endocrine systems, description of the epidemiology of age-related diseases, and definition of clinical endocrine syndromes that are particularly present in the elderly. This chapter presents selected examples of the research approaches used, some of the problems encountered, and insights that have been provided about age-related changes in endocrine system function in humans.

EPIDEMIOLOGY OF ENDOCRINE DISEASE IN THE ELDERLY

Several factors contribute to methodologic problems in understanding the epidemiology of endocrine diseases in the elderly. Although clinical features of endocrine diseases have been well described, diagnoses of these diseases are based almost entirely on laboratory measurements of circulating hormone or substrate levels. In fact, diagnoses are increasingly based on laboratory abnormalities prior to the onset of clinical findings. For example, the diagnosis of hypothyroidism is often made because of an elevated serum thyroid-stimulating hormone (TSH, thyrotropin) level in the absence of clear symptoms of hypothyroidism.

Because values for most of the measured hormones and substrates are normally distributed in the population, the distinction between normal and abnormal values may become arbitrary and based on statistical considerations. Thus the diagnosis of hypercholesterolemia is based on having a serum cholesterol level greater than that of a certain percentage of the population. Age-related changes in hormone or substrate levels must then be considered as diagnostic criteria are established. Under such circumstances, the distinction between a normal aging phenomenon and the diagnosis of an endocrine or metabolic disease may become the subject of discussion and controversy.

A striking example of this phenomenon is in the field of carbohydrate metabolism. The age-related deterioration of glucose tolerance in humans has been carefully documented (8,9). Based on studies of a large population of healthy people of varying age at the Gerontology Research Center in Baltimore, Andres (1) developed a nomogram relating age, 2-hour post glucose ingestion blood glucose level, and percentile rank, as illustrated in Fig. 1. Because less than 1% of healthy 20-year-olds have a 2-hour glucose value of 160 mg/dl or more, this value clearly defines abnormal glucose metabolism for that age group. However, more than 35% of people age 75 have a 2-hour glucose value of 160 mg/dl or more. Do all of these 75-year-old people have diabetes mellitus? Or does this finding reflect an age-related decrease of glucose tolerance that is not a marker of the disease diabetes mellitus?

In part to help resolve this difficulty the National Institutes of Health (NIH) convened the National Diabetes Data Group during the late 1970s to develop new diagnostic criteria for diabetes mellitus. This group reviewed prospective longitudinal studies of patients who met criteria for imparied glucose tolerance. As a result, they determined that the risk of developing overt diabetes or diabetes-related complications was not great enough to justify a diagnosis of diabetes mellitus in these individuals (22). Thus for the moment the issue has been resolved. The age-related change of glucose tolerance is not an acceptable marker for diabetes mellitus. Only overt fasting hyperglycemia or grossly abnormal glucose tolerance for a person of any age establishes a diagnosis of diabetes mellitus. The key point here is that the availability of carefully collected prospective epidemiologic data was crucial to allow the development of rational criteria based on laboratory measurements for the diagnosis of a common metabolic disease.

The finding of a high incidence of elevated TSH levels in elderly populations (27,28) raised similar questions. Do elderly people with mild TSH elevations have subclinical thyroid failure? At what level of TSH should a diagnosis of hypothyroidism be made and treatment instituted? Because these patients may not have any clinical findings of hypothyroidism, assessment of therapeutic response is not helpful. Unfortunately, only limited prospective epidemiologic data are available at present. The likelihood that someone with a TSH level of 12.5 μU/ml will develop more clear-cut evidence of thyroid failure in the future cannot be predicted accurately. Some preliminary data suggest that if mild TSH elevation is associated with the presence of anti-thyroid antibodies, the likelihood of progression to overt thyroid failure is high (28).

Thus epidemiologic data regarding endocrine/metabolic diseases in the elderly must be scrutinized carefully. Disease incidence and prevalence rates depend on

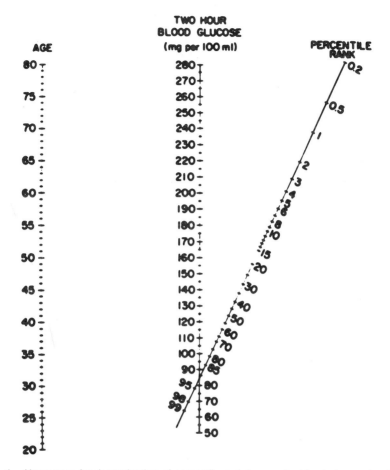

FIG. 1. Nomogram for determination of percentile rank by age for blood glucose level 2 hr after oral glucose ingestion. Place a ruler connecting age and the 2-hr blood glucose level. Read percentile rank from the scale at the right. (From Andres, ref. 1.)

the use of well-defined criteria. Because such criteria for endocrine and metabolic diseases are generally based on laboratory measurements, the subjectivity involved in establishing clinically based criteria is not a major problem. On the other hand, interlaboratory assay standardization and assay reproducibility can become limiting factors. In general, good research in this area includes active participation of a laboratory in which the key hormones being measured are the subject of active investigation in that laboratory. Although clinical laboratories can provide useful hormone data for disease diagnosis in individuals, the main purpose of such clinical laboratories is not to provide data that form the basis for future research needs.

HORMONE SECRETION IN THE ELDERLY

Indirect Measurements

A variety of approaches of varying degrees of sophistication have been used to assess regulation of hormone secretion in human aging. When direct hormone measurements are difficult to make or are not available, indirect methods have been used to estimate hormone status. Rate of growth continues to be used as an indirect measure of adequacy of growth hormone secretion in young people, although it cannot distinguish between diminished growth hormone secretion (e.g., pituitary dwarfism) and impaired growth hormone action (Laron-type dwarfism). Heart rate and blood pressure are sometimes used to assess sympathoadrenal catecholamine release. However, simple interpretation of heart rate and blood pressure is not possible because these parameters are under complex neuroendocrine control. Thus a heart rate increase may reflect diminished parasympathetic nervous system input to the heart as well as increased sympathetic nervous system stimulation.

Prior to the availability of direct measurements of thyroid hormones, the basal metabolic rate (BMR) was used as an index of thyroid function because thyroid hormone is an important determinant of the BMR. Early studies demonstrating an age-related fall of BMR suggested that thyroid function decreased in the elderly. However, the fall of BMR with age is directly related to the age-related decrease in lean body mass (17). Because fat tissue is less metabolically active than muscle tissue, BMR decreases as the ratio of lean body mass to total body weight falls.

More recently, pulsatile secretion of pituitary hormones has been used to indirectly estimate the frequency and magnitude of hypothalamic secretion of important peptides that regulate the pituitary. These peptide hormones are secreted in small amounts into the hypothalamic–pituitary portal circulation and do not reach the systemic circulation in sufficient quantities to be easily measurable. Studies using this approach have suggested a relation between hypothalamic peptide hormone secretion and postmenopausal flushing (6). It is likely that similar studies in the future will help to define alterations with age in the regulation of gonadotropin secretion in men and provide insight into age-related changes of other hypothalamic regulatory peptides as well.

Circulating Hormones

The simple, direct approach to studies of the endocrine system is to measure circulating levels of the hormone in question. The wide availability of sensitive hormone assays at modest cost has allowed widespread, sometimes indiscriminate, application to aging human populations. Interpretation of such data must consider several important aspects of endocrine research in the elderly.

Subject Selection

As in any field of human aging research, selection of the study population may be critical to the interpretation of circulating hormone levels. Several factors to be considered when selecting an appropriate study population are summarized in Table 1.

Because a change in the circulating level of a number of hormones occurs normally during acute, stressful situations, selection of an ill elderly population can lead to difficulty in interpretation of results. An example of this problem is provided by studies of thyroid hormone levels. Some studies of plasma triiodothyronine (T_3) levels have reported an age-related decrease. Because T_3 is the most active thyroid hormone, this finding suggested that some elderly people are, in fact, somewhat hypothyroid. However, in a more comprehensive study of various elderly populations, the explanation for the apparent age-related decrease in T_3 became evident. Olsen el al. found low T_3 levels in elderly residents of a long-term care facility (23), but T_3 levels of healthy active elderly people were not different from those of young controls. Because stressful illness causes a reduction in deiodinization of thyroxine (T_4) to T_3, the previous reports of a decrease in T_3 with age most likely represent an effect of coexisting illness rather than aging.

The presence of specific coexisting disease in an elderly individual may also influence interpretation of a measured hormone level. For example, a patient with congestive heart failure may have an elevated plasma level of arginine vasopressin (representing an appropriate neuroendocrine response to decreased effective blood volume). Thus careful screening for evidence of heart failure would be important for any study of age-related alterations in regulation of arginine vasopressin secretion. Nutritional factors may also affect interpretation of hormone levels. For example, it is essential to document the vitamin D status of individuals involved in studies of parathyroid hormone secretion in the elderly, as the hypocalcemia associated with vitamin D deficiency results in a compensatory secondary hyperparathyroidism.

The role of adiposity in interpretation of metabolic rate has been referred to

TABLE 1. *Some important factors in human subject selection for studies of endocrine aspects of aging*

Overall health status
Specific coexisting disease
Nutritional status
Degree of adiposity
Medication use
Physical activity level

previously. Adiposity is also an important factor in interpretation of studies of pancreatic islet hormone secretion. Because of the insulin resistance associated with obesity, hyperinsulinemia develops in obese individuals, as illustrated in Fig. 2 (2). Thus interpretation of pancreatic B-cell function requires that comparisons be made among groups in which adiposity is controlled for. Medication use can also affect circulating hormone levels. Table 2 is a list of some of the drugs that may affect circulating levels of norepinephrine. Specific effects of other drugs must be carefully evaluated in any studies of hormone secretion in the elderly. Finally, the degree of physical fitness and training of study populations need to be considered, although assessment of physical fitness may be beyond the scope of many studies. The degree of physical fitness can clearly affect glucose tolerance (3) and may potentially influence a number of other neuroendocrine systems as well.

Fluctuations of Hormone Levels

Studies of circulating hormones must take into account the fact that most hormones do not circulate at constant levels but fluctuate considerably. The most widely recognized type of fluctuation is related to the circadian cycle. Although it is well recognized that hormones such as cortisol have considerable circadian variation, circadian variation of other hormones also occurs and may affect the interpretation of results. For example, there has been considerable controversy about whether circulating testosterone levels decrease in elderly men. Most of these studies have relied on single measurements made during the day. However, as illustrated in Fig. 3, there is a diurnal rhythm of serum testosterone (4). The largest age-related difference occurs at night when testosterone levels are highest in the young. It is apparent that measurements made during midday are most likely to miss the age-related fall in testosterone levels. Similarly, growth hormone levels are considerably lower in the elderly than in the young, but this difference cannot be detected if measurements are made only during the day. In young adults growth hormone secretion occurs at night in association with deep slow-wave sleep. It is this aspect of growth hormone secretion that is specifically lost in the elderly (24).

In addition to the diurnal swings of hormone levels that must be taken into account when interpreting aging studies, there are shorter-term fluctuations in hormone levels that can interfere with interpretation of results. It is clear that gonadotropins are secreted in a pulsatile manner (6), reflecting responses to pulsatile secretion of hypothalamic peptides. As a result, interpretation of a single measurement of luteinizing hormone (LH), for example, is difficult. Characterization of the frequency and magnitude of pulsatile LH secretion is essential for adequate assessment of the integrity of this system. Pulsatile secretion of other hormones including pancreatic islet hormones and catecholamines has also been recognized.

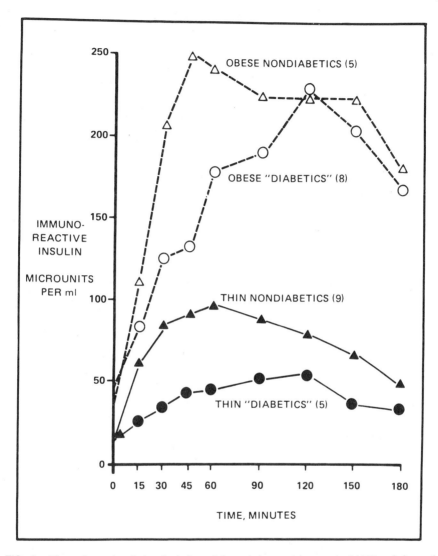

FIG. 2. Mean plasma insulin levels during a 3-hr oral glucose tolerance test (100 g of glucose) in thin and obese subjects (number in each group in parentheses). The "diabetics" are people meeting current criteria for impaired glucose tolerance but not overt diabetes mellitus. Note that both obese groups have much higher insulin levels than the thin groups, reflecting an appropriate response to insulin resistance. The "diabetic" groups have lower insulin responses than the appropriately weight-matched "nondiabetics" despite their high glucose levels during the test. (From Bagdade et al., ref. 2).

TABLE 2. *Some drugs affecting plasma catecholamine levels*

Diuretics	Phenothiazines
Antihypertensives	Antidepressant drugs
↓ Catecholamine release	Tricyclics
α-Methyldopa	Monoamine oxidase inhibitors
Reserpine	Tranquilizers/anesthetics
Guanethidine	Barbiturates
Clonidine	Benzodiazepines
↑ Catecholamine release	Opiates
α-Adrenergic blockers	Halothane
Prazosin	Others
Phentolamine	L-DOPA
Phenoxybenzamine	Caffeine
Vasodilators	Theophylline
Dipyridamole	Cigarettes (nicotine)
Nitroprusside	Marijuana
↓ Catecholamine clearance	Salicylates
β-Adrenergic blockers	Fenfluramine
	Bromocriptine
	Insulin

Circulating Hormone Kinetics

Measurement of the concentration of a hormone in the circulation often provides a direct index of the rate of hormone secretion, which is the primary parameter of interest. However, the circulating hormone level is a function of a dynamic equilibrium between rates of hormone secretion and hormone metabolism. Thus a change in hormone level can reflect not only a change in the rate of hormone secretion but also a change in the rate at which the hormone is metabolized. A more sophisticated approach to the study of circulating hormones involves a kinetic assessment of both secretion and removal rates. Estimates of removal rates can be made by infusing the hormone of interest and measuring the level of hormone achieved, allowing estimation of the hormone clearance rate:

Clearance = infusion rate ÷ (hormone level achieved − basal hormone level)

Because infusion of a hormone may cause physiological effects that may influence the hormone's clearance rate, a better approach is to infuse tracer amounts of radiolabeled hormone. One example of a change in hormone kinetics in the elderly is the observation from several laboratories that the clearance rate of insulin is diminished in healthy elderly subjects (13,19,25). Thus plasma insulin levels in the elderly tend to be an overestimate of actual insulin secretion. The clearance rate of norepinephrine from the circulation also tends to be diminished in the elderly, but tracer kinetic studies have indicated that the age-related increase in plasma norepinephrine is primarily due to an increased rate of norepinephrine spillover into the circulation (29). Sophisticated mathematic approaches are now available that allow extensive kinetic evaluation of circulating hormone or substrate

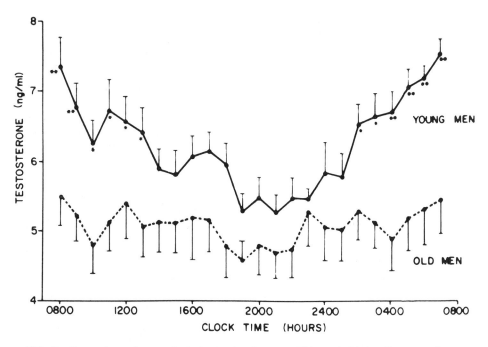

FIG. 3. Comparison of serum testosterone levels over a 24-hr period in healthy young (*n* = 17) and old (*n* = 12) men. Note the diurnal rhythm of serum testosterone that is apparent in the young but blunted in the elderly. Thus there are significant age differences at night and in the morning (asterisks) but little age difference at midday. (From Bremner et al., ref. 4.)

levels, thereby providing considerable information about production and removal mechanisms. It is likely that future studies on aging of the endocrine system will be enhanced by the use of such technology.

Feedback Control Mechanisms

The study of endocrine system regulation requires assessment of factors that stimulate and inhibit hormone secretion. Such studies may define abnormalities in hormone regulation that are not apparent from measurement of resting hormone levels. In addition, when abnormalities of hormone levels are observed, systematic study of various stimulating or inhibiting factors may help to pinpoint the mechanism underlying the alteration of hormone secretion. Thus the finding of higher norepinephrine levels in the elderly under a variety of conditions associated with sympathetic nervous system activation including upright posture, mental stress, and exercise (see ref. 16 for review) has helped to establish the validity of the findings in the basal state. The lack of an age-related increase of epinephrine levels in the resting state or following the stimuli of hypoglycemia (18) or mental stress (16) has helped to establish that the adrenal medullary system may not participate in the sympathetic neural activation accompanying human aging.

The glucose intolerance of aging is defined by an abnormal serum glucose response to the challenge of oral glucose ingestion. Some studies have suggested that the insulin secretory response of the elderly is increased because during oral glucose tolerance testing they may have higher insulin levels than younger subjects. However, such interpretation does not take into account the importance of the glucose–insulin feedback system. The high glucose levels in elderly people with glucose intolerance should lead to greater insulin levels because of the greater stimulus present. An important advance in the study of endocrine feedback control systems has been to try to break the feedback loop by controlling carefully for the stimulus. For example, the glucose clamp technique has been developed (9) to allow the circulating glucose level to be maintained constant by varying the rate of exogenous glucose administration, thereby preventing changes of insulin secretion and insulin action from altering the level of the glucose stimulus. Using the hyperglycemic glucose clamp technique, DeFronzo (9) demonstrated that in the elderly insulin responses to an intravenous glucose challenge are similar to or slightly lower than those in young subjects, as illustrated in Fig. 4. The key

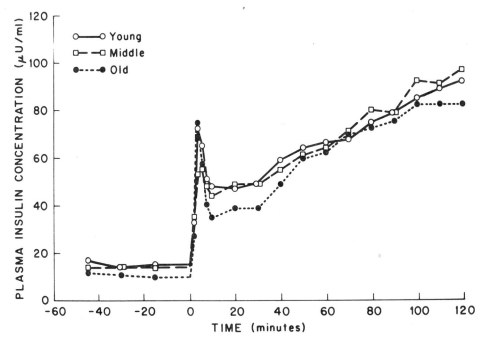

FIG. 4. Mean plasma insulin levels in groups of young (*n* = 20), middle-aged (*n* = 15), and old (*n* = 13) subjects during a hyperglycemic glucose clamp study. The plasma glucose level was raised by 125 mg/dl above the basal glucose level and maintained from 0 to 120 min by a variable-rate glucose infusion. Note that insulin levels are similar in the old group, despite their insulin resistance. (From DeFronzo, ref. 9.)

point here is that the stimulatory glucose level was kept identical in the two subject groups.

Of further importance to understanding regulation of endocrine systems is the interaction between hormone secretion and hormone action. Resistance to hormone action may lead to a compensatory increase in secretion of the hormone, mediated by the feedback control mechanism for that hormone's secretion. For example, the insulin resistance of obesity is associated with the development of hyperinsulinemia (Fig. 2). Although the feedback mediator of this hyperinsulinemia has not been clearly defined, it is likely to be secondary to slight increases of circulating glucose levels in response to insulin resistance. Although, as shown in Fig. 4, insulin secretion in the elderly tends to be similar to that of young subjects in the presence of a constant glucose stimulus, this finding does not take into account the fact that these elderly individuals have evidence of insulin resistance (see Discussion, below). Thus these relatively normal-appearing insulin secretory responses may represent a subnormal response if insulin resistance is taken into account. Work controlling for differences in insulin resistance in the elderly supports this hypothesis (7,20).

The detailed assessment of feedback control of endocrine hormones has been performed thus far in only a limited way in the elderly. Further insight into subtle alterations of a number of endocrine systems may be provided by future studies in which such feedback control systems are evaluated.

HORMONE ACTION

Altered responsiveness to hormone action may contribute to a number of age-related changes in physiological regulation. Hormone action at the cellular level initially involves interaction with a specific hormone receptor. As a result of this interaction, a signal(s) is generated that activates mechanisms ultimately leading to the cellular response. In the case of peptide hormones and the catecholamines, which do not readily penetrate cell membranes, the receptor is located on the cell surface. The hormone–receptor interaction results in activation of one or more intracellular protein kinases that phosphorylate enzymes that initiate a cascade of events resulting in the cellular response. In the case of steroid hormones, which penetrate cell membranes readily, the receptors are located intracellularly and mediate transfer of the steroid hormone to the nucleus of the cell where the hormone acts to regulate cellular protein synthesis by affecting the translation of DNA. Thus it is apparent that alterations of hormone action in the elderly may involve any of these complex processes. Because hormone binding to specific receptors can be measured readily, many studies of human aging have involved such measurements. However, as more is being learned about the mediators resulting from the hormone–receptor interaction, more work has focused on this aspect of hormone action.

In Vivo Studies

In vivo studies of hormone action have provided the basis for subsequent work at the cellular level to attempt to define mechanisms for alterations in hormone responsiveness. Diminished cardiac beta-adrenergic receptor function has been suggested by studies that demonstrate decreased heart rate responses to beta-adrenergic agonist stimulation in the elderly (15). A number of elegant studies using the hyperinsulinemic glucose clamp technique have demonstrated impaired insulin-mediated glucose disposal in the elderly (9,11,26). This resistance to insulin action may not be generalized to all tissues, however, as some studies have suggested that sensitivity of the liver to the inhibitory effects of insulin on glucose production is not diminished in the elderly (9). As illustrated in Fig. 5, there is a rightward shift in the dose–response curve for the effect of insulin to enhance glucose disposal in the elderly, compatible with diminished sensitivity to insulin. However, at maximal stimulatory insulin concentrations, this defect is overcome.

In Vitro Studies

In general, measurements of hormone binding to specific receptors have not shown consistent defects in the elderly. Human studies are obviously limited in terms of tissues available for assessment of receptor function. Receptors on cellular elements of the blood have tended to be utilized for this purpose, although some studies have also involved measurements of hormone receptors in fat tissue biopsies, muscle biopsies, and fibroblasts from skin biopsies. For example, beta-2-adrenergic receptors are clearly present on circulating mononuclear leukocytes. Furthermore, there is evidence of a close relation between the density of beta-2-adrenergic receptors on membranes from mononuclear leukocytes and from heart tissue (5), thus tending to validate the use of receptor measurements on circulating cells as an index of tissue responsiveness. However, beta-adrenergic receptor number is not altered in the elderly (15). Similarly, mononuclear leukocytes have insulin receptors that may provide a good marker of insulin receptors on other tissues. Again, the age-related change in sensitivity to insulin is not accompanied by an alteration of insulin receptor number (11,26). Thus defects in hormone action distal to the receptor appear to be the more likely explanation for the observed in vivo changes in hormone sensitivity in the elderly.

An important adjunct to measurement of hormone receptors in vitro is assessment of the cellular response to the hormone. An example is the assessment of hormone-mediated activation of the enzyme adenylate cyclase by measuring the production of cyclic AMP by the cell. The adenylate cyclase system functions in circulating mononuclear leukocytes and again can serve as a marker of hormone action at the cellular level. An age-related impairment of production of cyclic AMP in response to beta-adrenergic stimulation has been demonstrated in several human studies using mononuclear leukocytes (see ref. 15 for review). Some work has

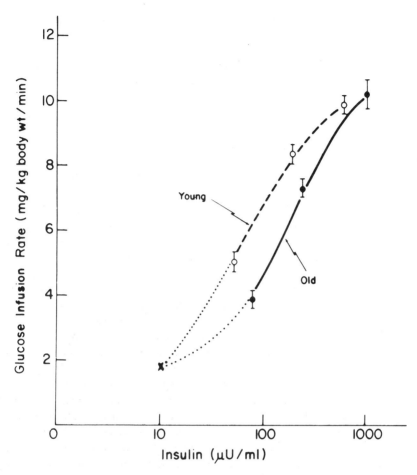

FIG. 5. Comparison of the glucose infusion rates needed to maintain euglycemia in young (*n* = 17) and old (*n* = 10) men during infusion of insulin to achieve plasma insulin levels ranging from 50 to 1,000 μU/ml (hyperinsulinemic glucose clamps). The observed experimental data have been extrapolated to known values for basal glucose utilization at basal insulin levels. During the hyperinsulinemic clamp, the glucose infusion rate is a measure of insulin-mediated glucose disposal. The lower values for the old group during the two lower insulin levels achieved provide evidence for resistance to the effect of insulin to enhance glucose disposal. (From Rowe et al., ref. 26.)

suggested that this abnormality is part of a generalized defect in the catalytic unit of the adenylate cyclase enzyme system, whereas others have reported that the catalytic unit function is normal. The latter studies imply that the defect in the elderly is in the process of coupling of the hormone–receptor complex to the adenylate cyclase enzyme.

Studies of insulin action have proceeded along analogous lines. An impairment of insulin stimulation of glucose transport has been demonstrated in fat cells from humans (12), and more recent work suggests that the age-related defect in insulin action is due to impaired ability of insulin to increase the number of glucose transport units in the cell membrane (14). However, this event is distal to the insulin–insulin receptor interaction. Because the details by which insulin binding to its receptor results in activation of processes such as glucose transport have not yet been worked out, precise localization of the aging defect requires further investigation.

The relation between altered cellular responsiveness to hormones and the circulating hormone level also needs to be considered. An elevation of circulating levels of the hormone could represent an appropriate response to resistance to the action of the hormone. Alternatively, if there is a primary mechanism resulting in increased circulating hormone levels, changes in receptor function may occur that are secondary. A number of studies have indicated that exposure to increased agonist levels results in down-regulation of hormone responsiveness. In some cases a decrease in cell membrane receptor number occurs. Perhaps of more physiological significance is a change in coupling of the hormone–receptor complex to the cellular mechanism for activation.

Again, the beta-adrenergic receptor has been a model system for definition of this phenomenon, as the initial events in hormone action have been clearly worked out. Both *in vitro* and *in vivo* exposures to increased concentrations of agonist (catecholamines) lead to uncoupling of the hormone–receptor complex from the catalytic unit of adenylate cyclase, thereby down-regulating the cellular generation of cyclic AMP in response to a given concentration of agonist (21). This situation can occur with no change in the number of receptors for catecholamines. It is of interest that this agonist-mediated desensitization leads to the identical uncoupling process that has been observed in some studies of beta-adrenergic receptor function in the elderly (10). Because circulating norepinephrine levels are elevated in the elderly, it may be that the altered beta-adrenergic receptor sensitivity that has been observed is secondary to the elevation of the agonist. This situation may contrast with the alteration in insulin action in the elderly, as in this case concentration of the agonist (insulin) does not tend to be elevated.

Thus as more is learned about the precise mechanisms by which hormones result in cellular events, there will be more opportunities to investigate potential age-related changes in hormone action. As such observations are made, it will be important to try to understand whether such changes in hormone action are a primary event in the elderly or represent a phenomenon that is secondary to changes in the level of hormone to which the cells are exposed. It is essential to perform dynamic studies in which hormone–receptor interactions are studied not only in the basal state but also after manipulations of the hormone level in order to define potential changes in agonist-mediated regulation.

REFERENCES

1. Andres, R. (1971): Aging and diabetes. *Med. Clin. North Am.*, 55:835–845.
2. Bagdade, J. D., Bierman, E. L., and Porte, D., Jr. (1967): The significance of basal insulin

levels in the evaluation of the insulin response to glucose in diabetic and nondiabetic subjects. *J. Clin. Invest.*, 46:1549–1557.

3. Bjorntorp, P., Berchtold, P., Grimby, G., Lindholm, B., Sanne, H., Tibblin, G., and Wilhelmsen, L. (1972): Effects of physical training on glucose tolerance, plasma insulin and lipids and body composition in men after myocardial infarction. *Acta. Med. Scand.*, 192:439–443.

4. Bremner, W. J., Vitiello, M. V., and Prinz, P. N. (1983): Loss of circadian rhythmicity in blood testosterone levels with aging in normal men. *J. Clin. Endocrinol. Metab.*, 56:1278–1281.

5. Brodde, O., Kretsch, R., Ikezono, K., Zerkowski, H., and Reidemeister, J. C. (1986): Human beta-adrenoceptors: relation of myocardial and lymphocyte beta-adrenoceptor density. *Science*, 231:1584–1585.

6. Casper, R. F., Yen, S. S. C., and Wilkes, M. M. (1979): Menopausal flushes: a neuroendocrine link with pulsatile luteinizing hormone secretion. *Science*, 205:823–825.

7. Chen, M., Bergman, R. N., Pacini, G., and Porte, D., Jr. (1985): Pathogenesis of age-related glucose intolerance in man: insulin resistance and decreased beta-cell function. *J. Clin. Endocrinol. Metab.*, 60:13–20.

8. Davidson, M. B. (1979): The effect of aging on carbohydrate metabolism: a review of the English literature and a practical approach to the diagnosis of diabetes mellitus in the elderly. *Metabolism*, 28:688–705.

9. DeFronzo, R. (1981): Glucose intolerance and aging. *Diabetes Care*, 4:493–501.

10. Feldman, R. D., Limbird, L. E., Nadeau, J., Robertson, D., and Wood, A. J. J. (1984): Alterations in leukocyte β-receptor affinity with aging. *N. Engl. J. Med.* 310:815–819.

11. Fink, R., Kolterman, O., Griffin, J., and Olefsky, J. M. (1983): Mechanism of insulin resistance in aging. *J. Clin. Invest.*, 71:1523–1535.

12. Fink, R. I., Kolterman, O. G., Kao, M., and Olefsky, J. M. (1984): The role of the glucose transport system in the postreceptor defect in insulin action associated with human aging. *J. Clin. Endocrinol. Metab.*, 58:721–725.

13. Fink, R. I., Revers, R. R., Kolterman, O. G., and Olefsky, J. M. (1985): The metabolic clearance of insulin and the feedback inhibition of insulin secretion are altered with aging. *Diabetes*, 34:275–280.

14. Fink, R. I., Wallace, P., and Olefsky, J. M. (1986): Effects of aging on glucose-mediated glucose disposal and glucose transport. *J. Clin. Invest.*, 77:2034–2041.

15. Heinsimer, J. A., and Lefkowitz, R. J. (1985): The impact of aging on adrenergic receptors: clinical and biochemical aspects. *J. Am. Geriatr. Soc.*, 33:184–188.

16. Linares, O. A., and Halter, J. B. (1987): Sympathochromaffin system activity in the elderly. *J. Am. Geriatr. Soc.*, 35:448–453.

17. Masoro, E. J. (1985): Metabolism. In: *Handbook of the Biology of Aging*, edited by C. E. Finch and E. L. Schneider, pp. 540–563. Van Nostrand Reinhold, New York.

18. Meneilly, G. S., Minaker, K. L., Young, J. B., Landsberg, L., and Rowe, J. W. (1985): Counter-regulatory responses to insulin-induced glucose reduction in the elderly. *J. Clin. Endocrinol. Metab.*, 61:178–182.

19. Minaker, K. L., Rowe, J. W., Tonino, R., and Pallotta, J. A. (1982): Influence of age on clearance of insulin in man. *Diabetes*, 31:851–855.

20. Morrow, L., Rosen, S., Linares, O., Bergman, R., Sanfield, J., Supiano, M., and Halter, J. (1986): Impaired B-cell adaptation to insulin resistance in the elderly is specific for a glucose stimulus. *Diabetes*, 35(Suppl. 1):15A.

21. Motulsky, H. J., and Insel, P. A. (1982): Adrenergic receptors in man: direct identification, physiologic regulation, and clinical alterations. *N. Engl. J. Med.*, 307:18–29.

22. National Diabetes Data Group (1979): Classification and diagnosis of diabetes mellitus and other categories of glucose intolerance. *Diabetes*, 28:1038–1057.

23. Olsen, T., Laurberg, P., and Weeke, J. (1978): Low serum triiodothyronine and high serum reverse triiodothyronine in old age: an effect of disease not age. *J. Clin. Endocrinol. Metab.*, 47:1111–1115.

24. Prinz, P. N., Weitzman, E. D., Cunningham, G. R., and Karacan, I. (1983): Plasma growth hormone during sleep in young and aged men. *J. Gerontol.*, 38:519–524.

25. Reaven, G. M., Greenfield, M. S., Mondon, C. E., Rosenthal, M., Wright, D., and Reaven, E. P. (1982): Does insulin removal rate from plasma decline with age? *Diabetes*, 31:670–673.

26. Rowe, J. W., Minaker, K. L., Pallotta, J. A., and Flier, J. S. (1983): Characterization of the insulin resistance of aging. *J. Clin. Invest.*, 71:1582–1587.

27. Sawin, C. T., Chopra, D., Azizi, F., Mannix, J. E., and Bacharach, P. (1979): The aging

thyroid: increased prevalence of elevated serum thyrotrophin levels in the elderly. *JAMA*, 242:247–250.

28. Tunbridge, W. M. G. (1982): Screening for thyroid disease in the community. *Thyroid Today*, 5:1–5.

29. Veith, R. C., Featherstone, J. A., Linares, O. A., and Halter, J. B. (1986): Age differences in plasma norepinephrine kinetics in humans. *J. Gerontol.*, 41:319–324.

Human Aging Research: Concepts and Techniques,
edited by B. Kent and R. N. Butler.
Raven Press, Ltd., New York © 1988.

Cardiovascular System Aging

Edward G. Lakatta

Laboratory of Cardiovascular Sciences, Gerontology Research Center, National Institute on Aging, National Institutes of Health, Baltimore, Maryland 21224

An empirical approach to defining aging of a given organ, e.g., the cardiovascular system, is to determine how function of that organ system varies with age. This strategy compares measurements obtained from young and old subjects or tissues (cross-sectional approach) or serial measurements made over long periods of time in the same individual (longitudinal approach). A review of the literature that describes measured functional decreases in various organ systems indicates that the rate of decrease varies dramatically among organs within an individual subject, and that for a given organ system there is substantial variation among subjects. It implies that some other factor(s) are potent modulators of a "biological clock" or of genetic mechanisms that determine how we age. Thus neither differences among age groups that are observed in cross-sectional studies nor changes with time in a given individual in observed longitudinal studies can necessarily be interpreted as manifestations of an "aging process."

One factor that modulates the aging process is the occurrence of specific processes that we have traditionally referred to as "diseases" (Fig. 1). We might wonder if we should also classify the aging process as a disease because, like specific disease states, it too may cause functional decreases in vital organ systems and eventually death. Disease and aging must be specifically delineated in order to identify and characterize the latter. It is not difficult to do when clinical signs or symptoms of a disease are present. However, occult disease, which can cause marked functional impairments, can be easily overlooked. This consideration is especially pertinent to investigation of the effect of age on cardiovascular function in man because the prevalence of coronary atherosclerosis increases exponentially with age. It is present in an occult form in a larger number of elderly persons than the overt form of the disease (see below).

In addition to diseases, changes in life style occur concomitantly with advancing age (Fig. 1). These changes include an individual's "habits" of physical activity, eating, drinking, smoking, thinking, etc. Although our understanding is far from complete, over the last few decades we have become aware of the impact of smoking, eating, behavioral, and possibly physical activity habits on the clinical manifestations of coronary artery disease. On the other hand, the impact of life

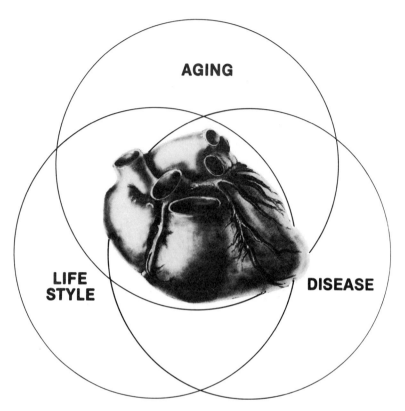

FIG. 1. Changes in life style and diseases occur with advancing age. It is interactions among these factors and aging that make it difficult to identify or characterize the presence of an aging process in the heart. (From ref. 16.)

style variables on an aging process is presently less well defined. It is likely that many changes in cardiovascular function that have been attributed to an aging process are in part due to the sedentary life style or the presence of occult coronary disease that accompanies aging.

With advancing age, because the prevalence of disease increases sharply and major changes in life style occur, the effects of aging, disease, and life style on the cardiovascular system are intertwined (Fig. 1). Above and beyond the confusion imparted by the presence of either of the other two factors on description of the third factor in Fig. 1, interactions among these factors can alter the nature of each. Thus elucidation of the presence and nature of an aging process is a formidable task.

RECOGNIZED IMPACTS OF LIFE STYLE, DISEASE, AND AGE ON CARDIOVASCULAR FUNCTION

Coronary Artery Atherosclerosis

Measurements of myocardial function are necessary to describe how the heart changes with age. Coronary artery atherosclerosis can modify myocardial function by reducing myocardial blood flow. Although coronary atherosclerosis is usually perceived as a problem of advanced age, this perception is somewhat incorrect. This vascular disease begins at a young age, its severity increases progressively over the entire adult age span, and when threshold severity is reached symptoms or signs of its presence become evident.

Over a period of 5 years (1960–1965) the International Atherosclerosis Project collected a large number of coronary artery specimens from autopsy material. The specimens were graded for various manifestations of pathology within the vascular intima, including fibrous plaques (areas of scarring due to the atherosclerotic process), deposition of calcium, and the extent of narrowing (stenosis) of the vessel. Figure 2 illustrates the prevalence of fibrous plaques, calcific lesions, and stenosis in coronary arteries in a subset of the sample (New Orleans Caucasian population). A major point of interest here is that between the ages of 15 and 24 years the early manifestations of this disease, i.e., fibrous plaques, are present in 30% of

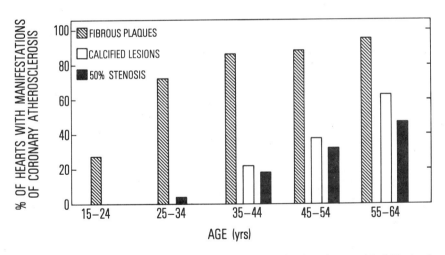

FIG. 2. Manifestations of atherosclerosis in coronary arteries from hearts of individuals of a New Orleans Caucasian population. The data for fibrosis and calcific lesions were derived from those individuals who died from accidents, infections, and miscellaneous causes other than heart disease. Data for stenotic lesions were derived from individuals of this population who died from any cause. (Redrawn from ref. 26.)

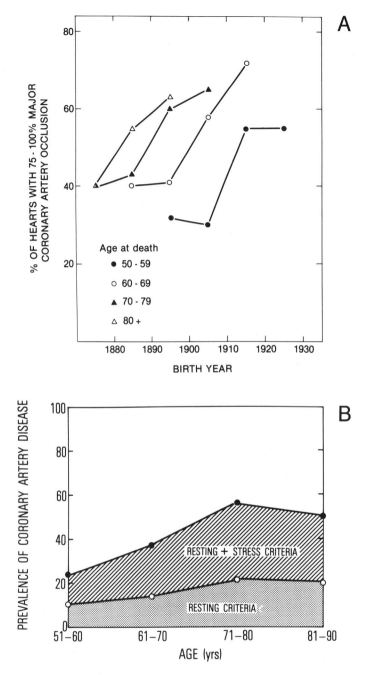

FIG. 3. A: The percentage frequence of 75% of complete occlusion of either the right or left anterior descending or the left circumflex coronary artery by age at death as a function of birth cohort. Note the high prevalence of this disease in these elderly subjects. (Redrawn from ref. 6.) **B:** Estimate of the prevalence of coronary artery disease in men aged 51 to 90. Subjects were participants of the Baltimore Longitudinal Study of Aging. Resting criteria were a history of angina pectoris or myocardial infarction, or an abnormal ECG at rest. Stress

hearts. By age 35 to 44, coronary arteries from more than 85% of hearts demonstrated this finding. Calcification also increased with age: By age 55 to 64, more than 60% of hearts exhibited vascular endothelial calcification.

The most important vascular abnormality to consider regarding myocardial function is not the presence of fibrous or calcific lesions but, rather, vessel narrowing or stenosis. Figure 2 illustrates that the prevalence of vessel narrowing also increases with age, so that by age 55 to 64 half of all hearts studied have 50% or more occlusion of at least one of the three major coronary arteries. An extensive autopsy study in Rochester, Minnesota, found that 40 to 60% of subjects in this age range or older who died from all causes had a 75 to 100% occlusion (Fig. 3A) of at least one major coronary artery (6).

A case might be made for defining the vascular changes in Figs. 2 and 3A as aging rather than denoting them as a disease called atherosclerosis. However, in most instances, although death caused by myocardial infarction is due to a lack of blood supply to the heart, the intrinsic myocardial function is preserved to a substantial degree (16). That the vessels supplying an organ should age out of phase with the organ they supply seems teleologically unsound. Thus it seems to make more sense to consider the process demonstrated by the data in Figs. 2 and 3 as a disease rather than as aging per se.

Although a high percentage of elderly individuals have stenosis at autopsy, a much lower percentage has symptoms while living. In other words, coronary artery disease is present in an occult stage during life in a large number of individuals. It is imperative to detect the occult form of this disease in order to determine if interventions, e.g., a change in life style variables, can have an impact on its progression or in order to develop pharmacological means to retard its progression. Because heart function, particularly during stress, is highly dependent on coronary blood flow it is critical to detect the presence of occult coronary disease when investigating the impact of an aging process on function of the myocardium.

Technological advances have been made in radionuclide imaging of the myocardium, i.e., obtaining a picture of the heart after it has taken up a radioactive substance. This technique, coupled with electrocardiographic (ECG) monitoring during an exercise stress on the cardiovascular system, has helped identify the prevalence of occult coronary disease prior to death (10). In a person who has coronary artery stenosis that is not so severe as to limit blood supply at rest when the heart is working minimally, the heart image and ECG are normal. During exercise, if increased demand for blood flow in a area of the myocardium supplied by a stenotic vessel exceeds the blood supply, that area appears as a "cold spot" relative to other areas on the image of the heart in which blood supply has increased normally. The ECG may exhibit "ischemic changes." The potential effectiveness of these two relatively noninvasive techniques, ECG and thallium imaging, during

⊲───────────────────────────────────

criteria were the presence of an abnormal ECG (J point depression of at least 1 mm and flat ST segment for at least 0.04 sec), a thallium scan perfusion defect during exercise, or both. (Redrawn from ref. 10.)

exercise when screening for occult coronary disease is demonstrated in Fig. 3B. The lower shaded area indicates the prevalence of coronary disease as estimated by the usual epidemiological or clinical techniques, i.e., history of myocardial infarction or angina pectoris or an abnormal resting ECG. The addition of stress criteria, i.e., ECG or thallium scan abnormalities during exercise, doubles the estimate of the prevalence of coronary disease in these men of middle and advanced age (hatched area). The estimated prevalence of the disease utilizing both stress and resting criteria approaches that observed in postmortem studies (Fig. 3A).

The ability of the heart to function as a pump is often assessed by determining the proportion of end-diastolic volume that is ejected during each stroke, i.e., the ejection fraction. Studies utilizing the gated blood pool scan technique (20,22) to measure the ejection fraction have indicated that in subjects with coronary artery disease the ejection fraction during exercise decreases or fails to increase from the resting level. It has been suggested (20) that such a reduction in ejection fraction from rest to exercise could also be attributed to aging per se (Fig. 4A). In this study subjects were not rigorously screened as in the study of Fig. 3B. An insufficient blood supply to an area of the heart causes the contraction in that area to be weak resulting in wall motion abnormalities on the gated blood pool scan. The presence of occult coronary artery disease in some subjects in Fig. 4A was at least in part a cause for the results obtained as suggested by the documentation of wall motion abnormalities in roughly 30% of individuals over age 60. Figure 4B shows that, in a population rigorously screened for study, as in Fig. 3B,

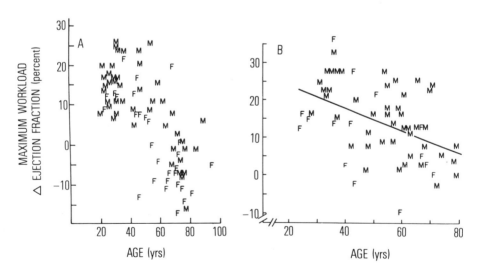

FIG. 4. A: Effect of age on change in the left ventricular ejection fraction from resting level to that at maximum voluntary exercise in apparently healthy subjects. (Redrawn from ref. 20.) **B:** Effect of age on change in the left ventricular ejection fraction from resting level to that at maximum voluntary exercise in subjects from the Baltimore Longitudinal Study of Aging. *M =* men. *F =* women. (Redrawn from ref. 22.)

even though the ejection fraction during exercise did not increase to the same extent in the elderly as it did in younger subjects, a reduction in ejection fraction during exercise from that at the basal level was rarely observed (22). The difference in the results in Figs. 4A and 4B is a vivid example of different perspectives obtained when different populations are screened for study by different criteria.

Arterial Stiffness and Pressure

The increased stiffness of blood vessels that accompanies advancing age apparently results from alterations that occur in the vascular media. Unlike the vascular intimal changes that cause atherosclerosis, the changes that occur within the vascular media do not usually produce severe vascular narrowing or clinical disease. They do affect cardiac function, however, in that they may alter the resistance to blood flow from the heart. With each heartbeat the large vessels expand somewhat to accommodate the blood. When an equivalent volume of blood is pumped into stiff arteries, the resulting pressure is higher than in normal arteries. The heart must do more work to pump its blood into a higher-pressure system, which may cause the heart wall to thicken. The vascular medial changes that increase vascular stiffness appear to be a cause of the modest increase in heart mass that occurs with aging (11).

Arterial stiffening manifests as an increase in pulse wave velocity (Fig. 5). It increases with age and is considered to be a major factor for the age-related increase in systolic pressure within the normal arterial pressure range. Is this increase in vascular stiffness a manifestation of normal aging? Such a conclusion can be seriously challenged by cross-cultural studies, as in Fig. 5, for example, which show that populations differing in life style also differ in the magnitude of the increase in arterial stiffness with age. Specifically, in Fig. 5 in the Beijing population, which, on the average, excretes three times the amount of sodium as the rural southern population (Guanzhou), the vascular stiffening and arterial pressure increases with age are accelerated (1).

The risk of cardiovascular morbidity and mortality associated with systolic blood pressure forms a continuum, albeit a nonlinear one, that encompass the clinically designated normal range (19). The decisive impact of both systolic and diastolic arterial pressures as risk factors for cardiovascular disease is clearly evident in Fig. 6, which depicts the interaction of arterial pressure and age on the risk of developing the first evidence of either myocardial infarction, sudden death due to coronary disease, angina pectoris, cerebrovascular accident, or intermittent claudication. For these pooled data collected from 8,000 individuals in eight outcome studies (19), at any given age the chance of experiencing a cardiovascular event within the next 5 years increases with the pressure level even when it is within the clinically normal range. The risk associated with systolic hypertension is substantial and in fact carries at least as much risk as elevations in diastolic pressure (13). There is some evidence to indicate that the risk of systolic hypertension is

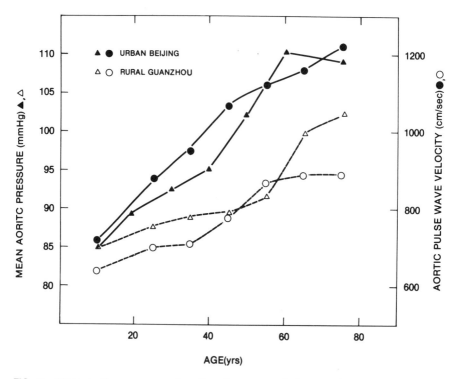

FIG. 5. Mean aortic pressure and aortic pulse wave velocity as a function of age in two Chinese populations. (Redrawn from ref. 1.)

not due to the associated arterial stiffening but, rather, to the elevated pressure per se (13). The risk of arterial pressure is not linear but exponential, as indicated in Fig. 5 by the unequal vertical separation of the points at a given age. For any quintile of arterial pressure the curve slopes upward with advancing age in an exponential fashion. The relative risk of an event for arterial pressure in the lowest quintile at age 60 is the same as that of the upper quintile at age 40. Thus age (or time) itself is as potent a predictor of a cardiovascular endpoint as is arterial pressure. Also, note in Fig. 6 that pressure and age account for only a fraction of the total variance. In other words, knowledge of the pressure or age, or both, cannot predict the risk of an event in a given individual with acceptable accuracy.

Life-style Variables

The *raison d'etre* of the cardiovascular system is to (a) deliver nutrients and other substances in the blood to body organs, (b) circulate blood cells, and (c) to remove CO_2 and maintain a constant temperature for cellular function. With stress such as exercise, the cardiac, respiratory, and tissue metabolic systems acutely

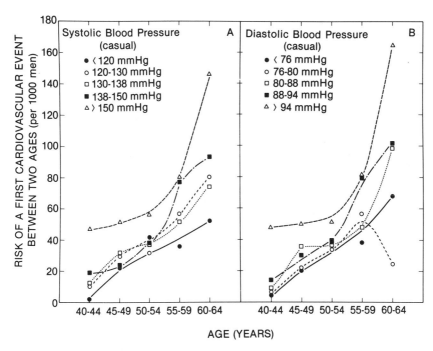

FIG. 6. Risk of a first cardiovascular event as a function of age and blood pressure [systolic (**A**) and diastolic (**B**)]. (Redrawn from ref. 19.)

increase above basal levels. These systems also chronically adapt their level of function (23). This point is illustrated in Fig. 7, which depicts the effects of bed rest and subsequent mild exercise conditioning on maximum cardiac output in different individuals. Note that among the differing activity states depicted in Fig. 7 there is a 50 to 70% difference in the cardiac output at peak exercise. Chronic exercise changes not only the function of the heart but also the heart size. Because the magnitude of the conditioning effect can be so great, studies that attempt to investigate to what extent a disease or an aging process alters cardiovascular function (particularly reserve function) must control for the physical activity status or at least consider it when interpreting the results. It has been well established that the average daily physical activity level decreases progressively with age in unselected populations (17). The magnitude of this age effect is undoubtedly greater in chronically institutionalized subjects than in independent community dwellers, which might seriously hamper the interpretation of studies seeking to define an age effect on cardiovascular function in institutionalized populations.

The example in Fig. 7 depicts the effect of drastic changes in exercise status, i.e., from bed rest to a regular mild exercise program. However, less dramatic changes in exercise status may be of great importance as well. Documentation of the effects of the interaction of aging and mild exercise on myocardial function

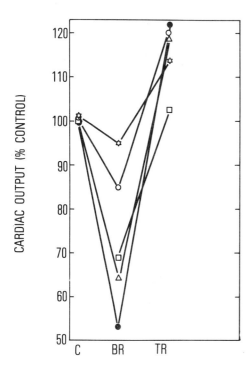

FIG. 7. Effect of a 21-day bed rest period followed by a 60-day period of moderate physical training on maximum cardiac output in five healthy young volunteer subjects. *C* = control prior to bed rest (*BR*). *TR* = physical training. (Redrawn from ref. 23.)

has been provided in aging animal models. In one study it was noted that treadmill exercise performed at a rate equivalent to a "brisk walk" was insufficient to change body weight or heart weight in young adult or aged animals (Fig. 8). Cardiac muscle performance measured as contraction duration in cardiac muscle isolated from the heart of young animals was likewise unaffected. However, the duration of cardiac muscle contraction, which is prolonged in sedentary rats of advanced age relative to younger adult ones (as it is in other species including man) was markedly reduced in the older rats that had exercised (24).

Maximum Work Capacity and Cardiovascular Reserve with Aging

It might be expected that age-related changes in the cardiovascular system may initially manifest or be most pronounced in response to stress because cardiovascular function must increase (as much as four- to fivefold) above the basal level. In normal subjects the increased pumping function of the heart during exercise stress is mediated by an increase in contractile performance of the myocardium and an increased ability of blood to flow through the circulation. The latter is due to a two- to threefold diminution in systemic resistance and is reflected as a decrease in the circulation time. A shift of blood from the venous system into the central circulation also occurs, such that the central circulatory volume increases twofold

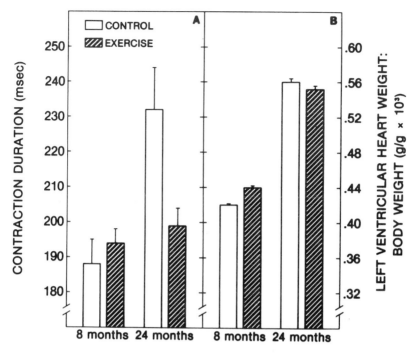

FIG. 8. Effect of chronic (4 months) daily wheel exercise on **(A)** contraction duration (time to peak force plus time from peak to 50% force decay) in isometric muscles stimulated L_{max} at 29°C at 24 min^{-1} in $[Ca^{2+}]$ of 2.5 mM and **(B)** relative heart mass in adult (8 month) and senescent (24 month) rats. (Redrawn from ref. 24.)

(18). The internationally accepted standard of the level of cardiorespiratory fitness, i.e., the maximum oxygen consumption rate (Vo_{2max}) achieved during stress, however, can increase more than ninefold over the basal level. This increase cannot be achieved by the four- to fivefold increase in cardiac output alone. In addition to an increase in cardiac output, an increase in oxygen extraction by working tissues occurs that causes an increase on the arteriovenous oxygen difference (up to twofold) during strenuous exercise. It results in part from an increase (up to 15-fold) in the relative proportion of cardiac output delivered to working muscles (4). Thus

$$Vo_{2max} = \text{cardiac output} \times (A\text{-}V)O_2$$

The arterial oxygen content at a given flow is determined by hemoglobin concentration and oxygen uptake in the lungs. The arteriovenous oxygen difference, which is determined by oxygen utilization in various organs, depends on the blood flow and oxygen extraction by the working muscles.

There has been a persistent debate among exercise physiologists as to which of these factors limits Vo_{2max} in individuals of a given age. Similarly, whether the same factors are limiting in subjects of different ages is not known with certainty (21).

Muscle mass can decrease substantially (10–12%) and can occur even in individuals in whom total body mass is maintained (2). Thus normalization of Vo_{2max} for total body size does not precisely account for differences in the lean body (muscle) mass. A decrease peak Vo_2 with age cannot be considered to be due to an age-related decrease in central circulatory performance if an age difference in muscle mass or in the ability to shunt blood to exercising muscles cannot be excluded with certainty. This issue is not a trivial one given that a more than 10-fold increase in blood flow and oxygen utilization by muscle occurs during exercise. Whereas total muscle mass is difficult to quantitate directly, 24-hour creatinine excretion is among the most reliable, easily measured indices of it (27). The impact of normalization of peak Vo_2 for creatinine excretion is shown in Fig. 9. Note that although peak Vo_2 normalized for total body mass in the study population decreases with age (Fig. 9A), normalization for lean body mass markedly reduces (and in fact in this preliminary study statistically eliminates) the apparent age effect (2).

Some additional factors need to be considered in the interpretation of literature on this subject. The extent of the decrease in the maximum work capacity and Vo_{2max} with advancing adult age varies with the life style, e.g., physical conditioning status, and with the presence of disease (occult or clinical) (26). There is increasing prevalence of occult coronary artery disease and generalized atherosclerotic vascular

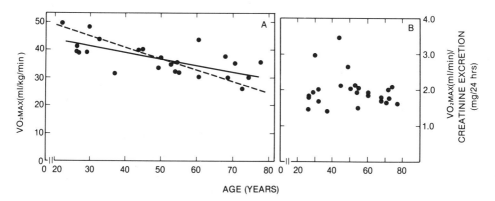

FIG. 9. A: Effect of age on peak Vo_2 (Vo_{2max}) during treadmill exercise in healthy human male subjects of the Baltimore Longitudinal Study of Aging (BLSA). Solid line is the best least-squares linear fit of the individual data points: Vo_{2max} (ml/kg/min) = 47.5 − 0.22 [age], $r = 0.65$, $p < 0.001$. Heart rate at maximum exercise (not shown) also decreased with age: heart rate (beats/min) = 203.5 − 0.66 [age], $r = -0.79$, $p < 0.0001$. The dotted line is the average age regression of pooled data from 17 individual cross-sectional studies in the literature. (Data from refs. 5 and 19.) **B:** Peak Vo_2 in subjects in **A** normalized to lean body mass as indexed by 24-hr creatinine excretion. The 24-hr creatinine excretion (Cr ex) decreased with age: Cr ex/mg = 2,032 − 10.36 [age], $r = -0.54$, $p < 0.01$. Vo_2/24 hr Cr ex/min is not age-related: 2.17 − 0.0002 [age], $r = 0.14$, $p < 0.41$. (Redrawn from ref. 8.)

changes occur with advancing age. Changes in life style are such that elderly subjects become less physically conditioned than their younger adult counterparts. The motivation to continue to exercise may decrease in sedentary elderly subjects. Orthopedic function may limit maximum work capacity in some subjects. Although Vo_{2max} is, by definition, a plateau in Vo_2 at two successive work loads, most studies that have investigated the effect of aging on Vo_{2max} have not demonstrated this plateau in Vo_2. The presence of any of the above limitations prevents interpretation of the peak measured Vo_2 as the true Vo_{2max}. Given these formidable obstacles to the interpretation of measurements of peak Vo_2 in elderly subjects, the extent to which Vo_{2max} decreases owing to age per se and the mechanisms of this decrease need to be reassessed.

There is some evidence to suggest that the central circulatory function may not limit the peak Vo_2 achieved during exercise in advanced age. Studies to date have failed to demonstrate a plateau in cardiac output across the two highest external work loads achieved (Fig. 10) and have been interpreted to indicate that the cardiac response for the Vo_2 achieved in elderly subjects during exercise is as adequate as that in younger subjects (12,25). These studies provided no evidence that cardiac function in elderly subjects was maximally stressed or, alternatively stated, that these subjects stopped exercising for cardiovascular reasons. Thus the results cannot be interpreted that the adequacy of central circulatory function decreases with age even though the cardiac output achieved at peak exercise was less in the elderly than in younger subjects (because the work performed and thus the demand on the heart was less in elderly than in younger individuals).

Although measurements of cardiac output during exercise fail to directly substantiate the notion that cardiac output limits peak Vo_2 or work capacity in elderly subjects, this notion continues to be popularized, based on estimates of cardiac output from measurements of peak Vo_2 and heart rate and extrapolated estimates of stroke volume and $(A-V)O_2$ (3). Such extrapolation requires a prior assumption that the relation between peak Vo_2 and cardiac output is unique to all individuals. It specifically ignores age-related changes that have been noted to occur in the peak arteriovenous Vo_2 difference (12) and variations in some individuals with aging that occur in the pattern of the stroke volume increase during exercise (22).

ADAPTATIONS THAT OCCUR WITH AGING TO MAINTAIN CARDIOVASCULAR PERFORMANCE IN THE ABSENCE OF DISEASE

Successful adaptation in some aspects of the variables that determine cardiovascular function may overcome deficits in others. There are clear examples of it in the basal state. For example, if myocardial hypertrophy did not occur with increasing age (11), the volume of the heart at end-diastole and end-systole in older persons would be larger than in younger ones because of the increases in arterial stiffness and pressure. Thus the moderate myocardial hypertrophy with aging is a successful adaptation that maintains heart volume and normal pump function in the presence of increased arterial pressure.

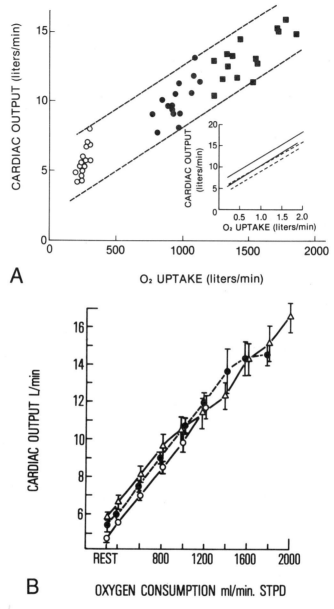

FIG. 10. **A:** Cardiac output at rest (*open circles*) and during progressive exercise work load (*solid circles* and *squares*) in the recumbent position in relation to Vo₂ in men 61 to 83 years old. **Inset:** Mean regression lines for cardiac output on Vo₂ in elderly men and 25 young men (average age 23 years) in recumbent (*solid lines*) and sitting (*broken lines*) positions. Note that at a given Vo₂, although the cardiac output was lower in either position in elderly versus younger subjects, no plateau in cardiac output in elderly subjects is observed. (Redrawn from ref. 25.) **B:** Cardiac output in 35 men and 19 women, apparently healthy, aged 18 to 34 years (△), 35 to 49 (●), and 50 to 69 years of age (○) as a function of Vo₂ in the upright position at rest and increasing bicycle work loads. With increasing work loads, some subjects in each group dropped out, and the last recorded work load is that in which at least six subjects in each age group participated. Note that no plateau in cardiac output was observed in the older subjects. (Redrawn from ref. 12.)

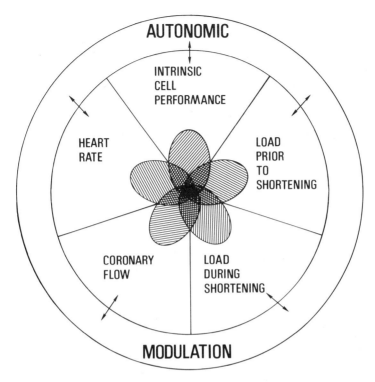

FIG. 11. Factors that govern cardiac output. The overlap depicted in the center of the figure indicates the interdependence of these determinants of function. The bidirectional arrows indicate that each function not only is modulated by autonomic tone but that there is negative feedback on this modulation. (From ref. 14.)

The rate of left ventricular filling with blood during early diastole is markedly (50%) reduced with aging between 20 and 80 years (11); yet the left ventricular volume at the end of diastole does not decrease with age (22). Thus enhanced filling later in diastole in elderly subjects is an adaptive mechanism to maintain an adequate filling volume. In part it may result from an enhanced atrial contribution to ventricular filling.

During exercise cardiovascular function is determined by a complex interaction of many variables (Fig. 11). The level of effectiveness of each of these variables is determined by basic cellular and extracellular biophysical mechanisms, many of which are subject to autonomic modulation. Alterations in cardiovascular function during exercise due to aging (or disease) can be attributed to an effect of age on the basic (intrinsic) cellular mechanisms that determine the performance of the variables in Fig. 11 or on the autonomic modulation of these mechanisms. During exercise a given overall level of cardiovascular performance, i.e., cardiac output, can be achieved with differential performance of each variable. An example is depicted in Fig. 12 in which two individuals who achieve a similar cardiac output during exercise exhibit striking differences in heart rate and cardiac volumes.

The increase in heart rate during vigorous exercise is often less in elderly than in younger subjects, but in many elderly subjects stroke volume can increase to compensate for a heart rate deficit (Fig. 13). Thus some elderly subjects use Starling's law of the heart as an adaptive mechanism to preserve cardiac output during exercise in the presence of a reduced heart rate. The hemodynamic profile in Fig. 13 is strikingly similar to that in younger subjects who exercise in the presence of β-adrenergic blockade (15). These findings have led to the hypothesis that perhaps the most marked changes in cardiovascular response to stress that

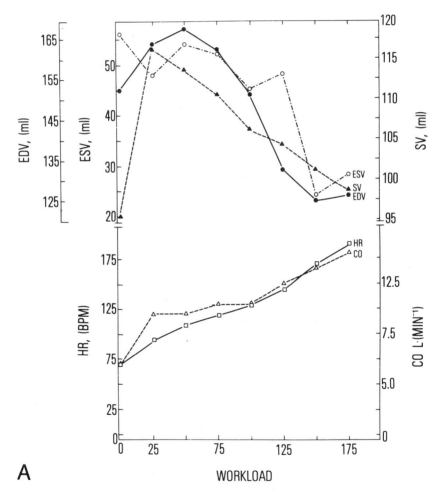

FIG. 12. Hemodynamic response to graded upright bicycle exercise in two subjects. Note that the same high cardiac output (*CO*) is obtained by different patterns in **A** and **B**. **A:** Heart rate (*HR*) increased substantially more than in **B**. **B:** End-diastolic (*EDV*) and stroke (*EVS,SV*) volumes increased more than in **A**. *BPM* = beats per minute. (From ref. 16.)

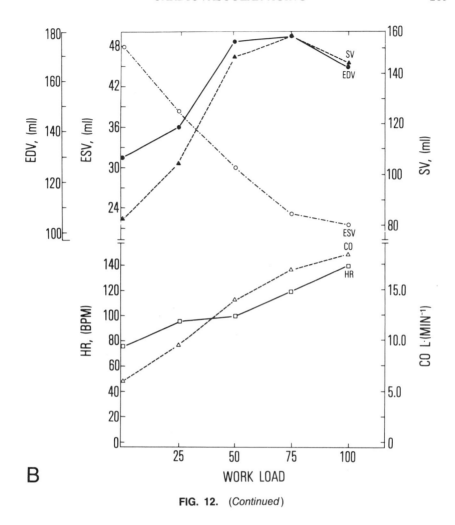

FIG. 12. (*Continued*)

occur with aging in the absence of disease are due to a reduction of the β-adrenergic modulation of cardiovascular function (7,15). There is abundant evidence to suggest that this deficit, in part at least, is due to an ineffectiveness of catecholamines to act in cardiovascular target cells, i.e., atrial pacemaker cells, vascular smooth muscle cells, and cardiac myocytes (15). Given the negative feedback of autonomic modulation of cardiovascular function (Fig. 11), an adaptation to this diminished efficacy of neurotransmitters or hormones at the target site might result in the greater elaboration of these neurotransmitters in elderly than in younger subjects during stress. This situation indeed has been found to be the case (Fig. 14). Thus elaboration of catecholamines by the neuroendocrine system in elderly subjects during exercise is intact. The β-adrenergic deficit must then be a postreceptor event (15) (Fig. 14).

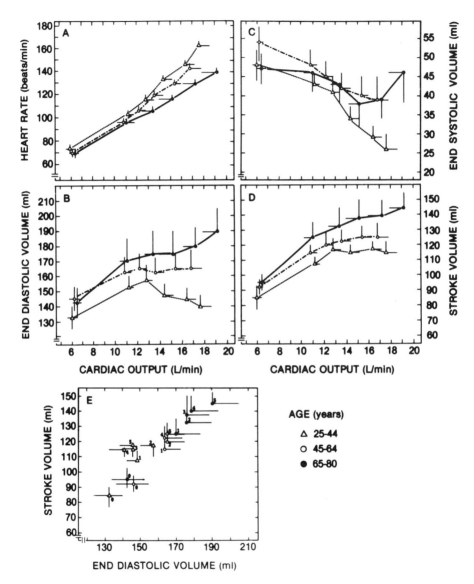

FIG. 13. Relation of heart rate (**A**), end-diastolic volume (**B**), end-systolic volume (**C**), and stroke volume (**D**) to cardiac output at rest and during graded upright bicycle exercise in healthy subjects screened prior to study by the method described in Fig. 3B. The major point of the figure is that a *unique* mechanism for augmentation of cardiac output during exercise does not exist in all subjects: To achieve the same high output as in younger subjects, older subjects increase the heart rate (**A**) to a lesser extent but increase stroke volume (**D**) to a greater extent than the younger subjects; this situation is not accomplished by a greater reduction in end-systolic volume (**C**) but, rather, by an increase (as much as 30%) in end-diastolic volume (**B**) compared to resting values. **E:** Relation between stroke and end-diastolic volume. 0 = rest. 1–5 = progressive increments in work load. This hemodynamic profile is an example of Starling's law of the heart. (Redrawn from ref. 22.)

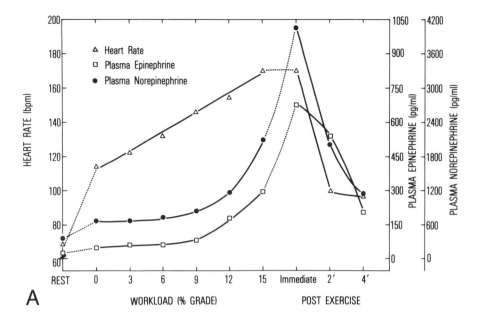

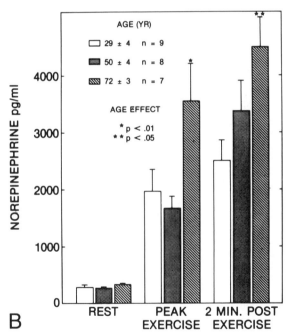

FIG. 14. A: The increases in heart rate, plasma epinephrine, and norepinephrine as functions of graded treadmill exercise in a representative subject. **B,C:** Effect of age on plasma norepinephrine (**B**) and epinephrine (**C**) levels at rest, during maximum treadmill exercise, and shortly after exercise. Subjects were participants of the BLSA who were judged free from occult coronary artery disease by a thorough examination that included prior stress testing with ECG monitoring. (**A–C:** from ref. 9.)

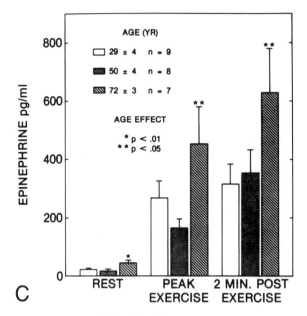

FIG. 14. (*Continued*)

REFERENCES

1. Avolio, A. P., Fa-Quan, D., We-Qiang, L., Yao-Fei, L., Zhen-Dong, H., Lian-Fen, X., and O'Rourke, M. F. (1985): Effects of aging on arterial distensibility in populations with high and low prevalence of hypertension: comparison between urban and rural communities in China. *Circulation,* 71:202–210.
2. Borkan, G. A., Hults, D. E., Gerzof, A. F., Robbins, A. H., and Silbert, C. K. (1983): Age changes in body composition revealed by computed tomography. *J. Gerontol.,* 38:673–677.
3. Bruce, R. A. (1984): Functional aerobic capacity, exercise, and aging. In: *Principles of Geriatric Medicine,* edited by A. Andres, E. L. Bierman, and W. R. Hazzard, pp. 87–103. Academic Press, New York.
4. Clausen, J. P. (1969): Effects of physical conditioning: a hypothesis concerning circulatory adjustment to exercise. *Scand. J. Clin. Lab. Invest.,* 24:305–311.
5. Dehn, M. M., and Bruce, R. A. (1972): Longitudinal variation in maximal oxygen intake with age and activity. *J. Appl. Physiol.,* 33:805–807.
6. Elveback, L., and Lie, J. T. (1984): Combined high incidence of coronary artery disease at autopsy in Olmstead County, Minnesota, 1950–1979. *Circulation,* 70:345–349.
7. Filburn, C. R., and Lakatta, E. G. (1984): Aging alterations in β-adrenergic modulation of cardiac cell function. In: *Aging and Cell Function,* Vol. 2., edited by J. Johnson, Jr., pp. 211–246. Plenum Press, New York.
8. Fleg, J. L., and Lakatta, E. G. (1985): Loss of muscle mass is a major determinant of the age-related decline in maximal aerobic capacity. *Circulation,* 72:III–464.
9. Fleg, J. L., Tzankopf, S. P., and Lakatta, E. G. (1985): Age-related augmentation of plasma catecholamines during dynamic exercise in healthy males. *J. Appl. Physiol.,* 59:1033–1039.

10. Gerstenblith, G., Fleg, J. L., Vantosh, A., Becker, L., Kallman, C., Andres, R., Weisfeldt, M., and Lakatta, E. G. (1980): Stress testing redefines the prevalence of coronary artery disease in epidemiologic studies. *Circulation,* 62:111–308.
11. Gerstenblith, G., Frederiksen, J., Yin, F. C. P., Fortunin, J. J., Lakatta, E. G., and Weisfeldt, M. L. (1977): Echocardiographic assessment of a normal adult aging population. *Circulation,* 56:273–278.
12. Julius, S., Antoon, A., Whitlock, L. S., and Conway, J. (1967): Influence of age on the hemodynamic response to exercise. *Circulation,* 36:222–230.
13. Kannel, W. B., Wolf, P. A., McGee, D. L., et al. (1981): Systolic blood pressure, arterial rigidity, and risk of stroke: the Framingham Study. *JAMA,* 245:1225–1229.
14. Lakatta, E. G. (1983): Determinants of cardiovascular performance: modification due to aging. *J. Chronic Dis.,* 36:15–30.
15. Lakatta, E. G. (1985): Altered autonomic modulation of cardiovascular function with adult aging: perspectives from studies ranging from man to cell. In: *Pathobiology of Cardiovascular Injury,* edited by H. L. Stone and W. B. Weglickil, pp. 441–460. Martinus Nijhoff, Boston.
16. Lakatta, E. G. (1985): Health, disease and cardiovascular aging. In: *Health in an Older Society,* pp. 73–104. National Academy Press, Washington, DC.
17. McGandy, R. B., Barrows, C. H., Jr., Spanias, A., Meredity, A., Stone, J. L., and Norris, A. H. (1966): Nutrient intakes and energy expenditure in men of different ages. *J. Gerontol.,* 21:581–587.
18. Mitchell, J. H., Sproule, B. J., and Chapman, C. B. (1958): The physiological meaning of the maximal oxygen intake tests. *J. Clin. Invest.,* 37:538–547.
19. Pooling Project Research Group (1978): Relationship of blood pressure, serum cholesterol, smoking, relative weight and ECG normalities to incidence of major coronary events: final report of the Pooling Project. *J. Chronic Dis.,* 31:201–306.
20. Port, E., Cobb, F. R., Coleman, R. E., and Jones, R. H. (1980): Effect of age on the response of the left ventricular ejection fraction to exercise. *N. Engl. J. Med.,* 303:1133–1137.
21. Raven, P. B., and Mitchell, J. (1980): The effect of aging on the cardiovascular response to dynamic and static exercise. *Aging,* 12:269–296.
22. Rodeheffer, R. J., Gerstenblith, G., Becker, L. C., Fleg, J. L., Weisfeldt, M. L., and Lakatta, E. G. (1984): Exercise cardiac output is maintained with advancing age in healthy human subjects: cardiac dilation and increased stroke volume compensate for a diminished heart rate. *Circulation,* 69:203–213.
23. Saltin, B., Blomquist, G., Mitchell, J. H., Johnson, R. L., Jr., Wildenthal, K., and Chapman, C. B. (1968): Response to exercise after bed rest and after training: a longitudinal study of adaptive changes in oxygen transport and body composition. *Circulation,* 38(Suppl. 7):VII-1–78.
24. Spurgeon, H. A., Steinbach, M. F., and Lakatta, E. G. (1983): Chronic exercise prevents characteristic age-related changes in rat cardiac contraction. *Am. J. Physiol.,* 244:H513–H518.
25. Strandell, T. (1964): Circulatory studies on healthy old men: with special reference to the limitation of the maximal physical working capacity. *Acta Med. Scand. [Suppl. 414],* 175:2–44.
26. Tejada, C., Strong, J. P., Montenegro, M. R., Restrepo, C., and Solberg, L. A. (1968): Distribution of coronary and aortic atherosclerosis by geographic location, race, and sex. *Lab. Invest.,* 18:49–66.
27. Tzankoff, S. P., and Norris, H. A. (1977): Effect of muscle mass decrease on age-related BMR changes. *J. Appl. Physiol.,* 43:1001–1006.

Human Aging Research: Concepts and Techniques,
edited by B. Kent and R. N. Butler.
Raven Press, Ltd., New York © 1988.

Skeletal Aging

Diane E. Meier

*Department of Geriatrics and Adult Development, Mount Sinai Medical Center,
New York, New York 10029*

The distinction between normal aging processes and disease is particularly important in the study of bone disorders. Loss of skeletal calcium is a nearly universal concomitant of aging regardless of gender, race, or body size. This process becomes pathological when it significantly increases vulnerability to fracture, the endpoint associated with adverse consequences such as pain, immobility, and death. Defining the time at which a normal aging process becomes a problem requiring prevention or treatment presents a major challenge to clinicians and researchers alike, as it does with many other chronic illnesses associated with aging.

Metabolic bone disease is a major cause of morbidity and mortality in older adults, yet its diagnosis and treatment remain perplexing and controversial. Reasons for this difficulty include the fact that there is a long latent period of bone loss prior to the onset of clinically apparent disease, that diagnostic procedures are as yet unable to clearly separate those at risk of fracture from those not at risk, and finally that currently recommended treatment modalities are based largely on short-term studies of a disease that requires decades of therapy of uncertain ultimate benefit and side effects. Research efforts in these spheres have increased dramatically as a result of demographic changes leading to a large aging female population at high risk for osteoporosis and because of rapidly improving technologies in the measurement of bone mineral content.

DEFINITION OF TERMS

Osteoporosis is characterized by a gradual, universal, and continuous decrease in bone mass leading to loss of skeletal mechanical strength such that even minor trauma may lead to fracture. Histomorphometrically, osteoporosis is defined as a loss of total bone volume resulting in a normal ratio of uncalcified osteoid protein matrix to calcified bone. Osteomalacia, in contrast, is characterized by a normal bone volume with an increased proportion of uncalcified osteoid protein matrix to calcified bone usually due to calcium or vitamin D deficiency. It is often difficult to distinguish these two processes clinically, and bone biopsy may be required in order to provide appropriate treatment. Osteopenia is a radiographically descriptive term indicating only that the skeleton appears visually decalcified on x-ray films (2).

EPIDEMIOLOGY

More than 20 million Americans are affected by osteoporosis, and millions more are at risk for its development. About 1.3 million new fractures attributable to osteoporosis occur annually in people over age 45. Vertebral crush fractures, occurring eight times more frequently in women than in men, are found in nearly 60% of women over age 60. If radiographic evidence of spinal osteoporosis is taken as the diagnostic criterion, 65% of women over age 60 and virtually 100% of women over age 90 are affected. Considered in another way, more than 2% of those over age 65 have an osteoporosis-related fracture each year.

Hip fracture, largely afflicting adults over age 75, affects 32% of women and 17% of men by age 90 (20). The rate of hip fracture quadruples with every decade past age 50 in women. Once the initial hip fracture is sustained, the risk of a subsequent fracture triples, with an incidence of 15% per year thereafter. In the United States there are more than 200,000 new hip fractures per year, costing more than $2 billion annually in acute care services alone. The addition of the cost of long-term care, rehabilitation, and other support services raises this figure to more than $3 billion yearly.

The morbidity of hip fracture continues to be substantial, with mortality rates described as high as 20% at 3 months after fracture (20), largely secondary to the complications of bed rest, immobilization, and hospitalization. A 12% overall difference in survivorship between hip fracture patients and age-matched controls has also been observed. More than half of the survivors of a hip fracture never resume independent walking. Forty percent of persons over age 75 with hip fracture are transferred to nursing homes, and two-thirds of these individuals never return home (12). We can expect these figures to increase, as the group at highest risk (those over age 75 years) is the fastest growing portion of our population.

Age, Gender, and Racial Dimorphism in Osteoporosis

The major demographic characteristics associated with primary osteoporosis are increasing age, female sex, and Caucasian race. Bone loss begins in normal adults of both sexes at about age 25 to 30 with an acceleration in loss occurring at menopause in women and at about age 70 in men. Riggs and colleagues have described two major classes of osteoporosis, distinguished primarily by age of onset (48). Type I osteoporosis is seen almost exclusively in women (female/ male ratio, 8:1) during the decade immediately following menopause and is characterized by disproportionate loss of spinal trabecular bone, predisposing to vertebral crush fractures. The proposed etiology is described in Fig. 1A. Type II osteoporosis is characterized by a more equal loss of cortical and trabecular bone leading to hip, wrist, and vertebral fractures. Most of these patients are over age 75 with a more equal distribution by sex (female/male ratio, 2:1). Measurements of bone mineral content and rates of bone loss in the type II group have not been significantly different from those measured in age-matched controls (Fig. 1B; Table 1).

Patterns and rates of bone loss observed at different ages depend in large part on the type of study undertaken (cross-sectional or longitudinal), the skeletal compartment measured (comprised of largely cortical or trabecular bone), the densitometric technique employed, and the characteristics of the subjects studied (randomly selected, healthy, osteoporotic, etc.). For example, cross-sectional studies of male and female trabecular vertebral bone mineral have demonstrated a linear loss beginning at age 25 to 30. In contrast, cross-sectional studies of proximal radial (largely cortical) bone mineral have demonstrated little or no bone loss in men until about age 70. In women, however, loss of cortical bone begins in an accelerated manner

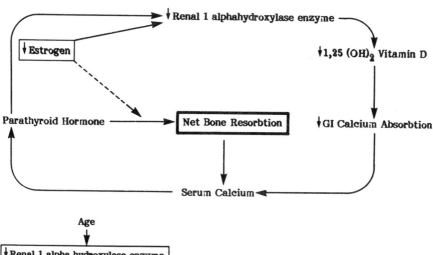

FIG. 1. Top: Type 1 osteoporosis: proposed mechanism. Loss of estrogen's inhibitory effect on PTH-mediated bone resorption and stimulatory effect on 1α,25-(OH)₂-vitamin D synthesis leads to increased bone resorption. **Left:** Type 2 osteoporosis: proposed mechanism. Primary age-related decrease in synthesis of 1α,25-(OH)₂-vitamin D leads to low serum calcium, secondary hyperparathyroidism, and increased bone resorption. (Adapted from ref. 48.)

TABLE 1. *Characteristics of types I and II osteoporosis*

Characteristic	Type I	Type II
Age	51–65	75
Sex (F:M)	6:1	2:1
Loss of skeletal compartment	Trabecular	Trabecular and cortical
Site of fracture	Spine and wrist	Spine and hip
Primary cause	Estrogen deficiency	$1\alpha,25\text{-(OH)}_2$-vitamin D deficiency
Parathyroid hormone	↓	↑
Calcium absorption	↓	↑
Abnormal vitamin D synthesis	Secondary	Primary

Adapted from ref. 48.

for approximately one decade following menopause and then returns to a slower rate thereafter (25) (Fig. 2). Thus age-related bone loss is not a linear or homogeneous process and may have quite different etiologies at various points in the age range.

Reasons advanced to account for the observed gender dimorphism in fracture rate, most marked during the postmenopausal period, include the observation that women have a lower bone mass than men at the time of skeletal maturity and thus start out with less calcium in the skeletal "bank." Therefore even if women were losing bone at the same rate as men, they would approach the theoretical fracture threshold earlier. In fact, women do lose bone at a faster rate than men,

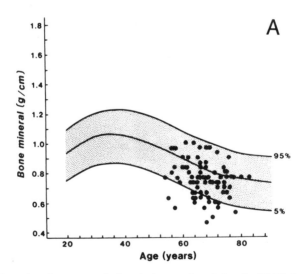

FIG. 2. **A:** Normal and osteoporotic female bone mineral density (BMD) by single-photon absorptiometry (mid-radius). Individual values for BMD of the mid-radius in 76 women with osteoporosis and one or more vertebral compression fractures. Center line denotes age regression for normal women, and upper and lower lines represent 90% confidence limits. (From ref. 51.)

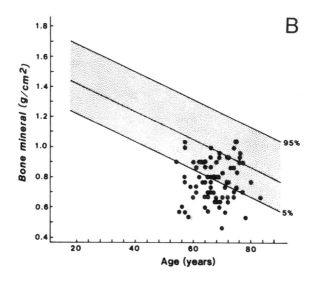

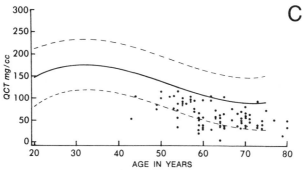

FIG. 2. B: Normal and osteoporotic female bone mineral density by dual-photon absorptiometry (lumbar vertebrae). Individual values for BMD of the lumbar spine in 76 women with osteoporosis and one or more vertebral compression fractures. Center line denotes age regression for normal women, and upper lines represent 90% confidence limits. (From ref. 51.) **C:** Normal and osteoporotic female bone mineral content by quantitative computed tomography (QCT) of lumbar vertebrae in women who have postmenopausal osteoporosis and spinal fractures plotted against the normal female curve (cubic regression with 95% confidence intervals). (From. ref. 24.)

particularly during the immediate postmenopause period, in large part because of the effects of estrogen lack on calcium absorption and bone formation and resorption (Fig. 1A).

Several studies have reported a significantly lower incidence of osteoporotic fractures in Blacks (59), but reasons for this purported racial difference have not been well investigated. Possibilities include higher bone mass at skeletal maturity in Blacks than in Whites, a slower rate of age or menopause-related bone loss, or other factors such as frequency of falls, influence of body weight (higher body mass protects against bone loss), and cohort effects influencing patterns of bone loss. The failure of previous studies to exclude diseases and medications that influence bone homeostasis, to match subjects for body size and weight, to compensate for large biological variability in bone mass and in densitometric technique by studying appropriately large numbers of subjects with repeated measures over time, and to measure both trabecular and cortical bone mineral content has left unanswered the question of why Blacks appear to be relatively protected from osteoporotic fracture, and if there are subgroups of Blacks who are at risk for osteoporosis and who might benefit from preventive measures. For example, lactose intolerance and calcium-deficient diets are prevalent in the North American Black population and, in combination with other risk factors (e.g., low body weight or premature menopause), may pose substantial risks for some Black individuals. Comparison studies of other racial groups (e.g., Hispanic, Oriental) are also needed to clarify the influence of heritable factors on osteoporosis risk.

PATHOGENESIS

Most individuals with metabolic bone disease have primary osteoporosis. This category includes Rigg's type I and II osteoporosis, often referred to, respectively, as postmenopausal and senile (involutional or idiopathic) osteoporosis. Only 5% of all cases of metabolic bone disease are secondary to other disease processes including various endocrinopathies, gastrointestinal diseases, nutritional deficiencies, neoplasias, and drugs (Table 2).

TABLE 2. *Secondary causes of osteoporosis*

Immobilization	Genetic
Nutritional deficiency	Osteogenesis imperfecta
Alcoholism	Homocystinuria
Chronic illness	Drug-induced
Rheumatoid arthritis	Heparin
Kidney failure	Methotrexate
Sarcoidosis	Glucocorticoids
Chronic lung disease	Aluminum-containing antacids
Neoplasia	Diuretics
Multiple myeloma	Vitamin A excess
Lymphoma	Vitamin D excess
Leukemia	Anticonvulsants
Metastatic disease	Gastrointestinal disease
Endocrinopathy	Hepatic failure
Hypercortisolism	Small bowel resection
Hyperthyroidism	Gastrectomy
Hypogonadism	Malabsorption
Hyperparathyroidism	
Diabetes mellitus	

The most important currently appreciated etiological factors in primary osteoporosis include advancing age, low bone mass at skeletal maturity, female sex, Caucasian race and other hereditary components, inadequate calcium intake and bioavailability, sex steroid lack, inadequate vitamin D intake and bioavailability, and other, less clear hormonal parameters (e.g., calcitonin availability and responsivity). The observed associations of age, sex, and race to osteoporosis risk are most likely due to their influence on more proximate variables affecting maximal bone mass and subsequent rates of bone loss.

Calcium Intake and Bioavailability

The effect of dietary calcium intake in bone mass and prevention of bone loss remains controversial. The Yugoslavian study of Matkovic et al. (39) demonstrated that women in regions of higher calcium intake (810–940 mg/day) had a higher metacarpal cortical area and lower rate of hip fracture than women from a comparable region of lower calcium intake (340–445 mg/day). It is of note that higher calcium intake appeared to primarily influence peak skeletal bone mass, as rates of bone loss were similar in the two groups. Other studies have supported this conclusion, suggesting that calcium intake protects not so much by influencing rates of bone loss but by affecting peak bone mass achieved during the third and fourth decades (32). In support of the thesis that dietary calcium primarily affects peak bone mass are several studies that have not demonstrated any improvement in calcium balance or slowing of postmenopausal bone loss after calcium supplementation in adults (22,43). However, studies of dietary calcium consumption during childhood and adolescence have demonstrated a positive association between childhood and adolescent milk consumption and postmenopausal bone density (54). In contrast, Recker et al. and Horseman et al. (30,45) have demonstrated improved calcium balance and slower rates of peripheral cortical bone loss in postmenopausal women on calcium supplementation. Of note, however, is the fact that combined calcium plus estrogen or estrogen therapy alone were more effective in each of these studies for slowing bone loss than increased calcium intake alone.

Further confusing the issue is the increasing debate over which calcium source (dietary versus supplements, type of calcium salt) is more bioavailable or most effective in preventing bone loss.

Despite these conflicting data, a National Institutes of Health Consensus Development Conference on Osteoporosis (NIH Consensus Development Conf., April 1984, Osteoporosis) recommended an increase in calcium intake for premenopausal (1,000 mg elemental calcium/day) and postmenopausal 1,500 mg elemental calcium/day) women, and the National Academy of Sciences is considering revision of the Recommended Daily Allowance for calcium upward (from 800 mg/day to 1,000 mg/day). Because the risk of calcium supplementation is minimal (in persons without a personal or family history of kidney stones) the current standard practice recommends daily calcium intakes in Caucasian women in the ranges noted above.

Definitive longitudinal studies are required before this recommendation can be clearly justified by the available data.

Estrogen Status

The primary importance of changes in sex steroid concentrations in the development of osteoporosis in postmenopausal women has been demonstrated by numerous studies showing that cessation of ovarian function results in an acceleration of age-related bone loss (9).

Theories advanced to account for the effect of sex steroid deficiency on the pathophysiology of bone loss are multiple and include failure of osteoblastic function, increased bone sensitivity to the resorptive effects of parathyroid hormone, inhibition of calcitonin secretion or decreased bone sensitivity to available circulating calcitonin, reduction of gastrointestinal calcium absorption (via estrogen effects on renal synthesis of $1\alpha,25$-dihydroxycholecalciferol), and an increase in urinary calcium excretion (15,17). No estrogen receptors have been located in bone, and so the sex hormone is presumed to affect bone homeostasis through a more indirect mechanism, such as those listed above. Rapid bone loss and fracture have also been demonstrated in young amenorrheic women, athletes, and anorectics (38). Similarly, multiple prospective controlled trials and case–control studies have shown prevention of bone loss from both appendicular and axial sites with sex hormone therapy (35–37,42). Therapeutic response to estrogen results in decreased bone resorption without a significant increase in the rate of bone formation and resulting stabilization of bone mineral content.

Additional evidence in support of the etiological role of sex hormones in osteoporosis may be found in studies of castrate laboratory animals (male and female) showing that osteoporosis is reversible upon replacement of gonadal hormones. Hypogonadal men develop osteoporosis just as do hypogonadal women; and therapeutic trials using testosterone in hypogonadal (Klinefelter's) men with osteoporosis have shown increases in osteoid volume and surface, bone formation, and mineralization (4). Possible mechanisms for testosterone's influence on bone metabolism include direct effects on bone remodeling, as conversion of testosterone to dihydrotesterone in ground spongiosa of bone has been shown (as in other androgen-dependent tissues, e.g., the prostate gland). Second, testosterone could affect bone metabolism by one or more of the indirect mechanisms postulated for estrogen (see above).

Use of Estrogen as a Therapeutic Agent

Despite the indisputably beneficial effect of estrogen in preventing postmenopausal bone resorption, substantial controversy surrounds its use as a therapeutic agent.

First, estrogen replacement therapy must be continued indefinitely in order to prevent accelerated demineralization, as discontinuation of treatment leads to the same rapid bone loss that would have occurred at untreated menopause (37). Second, multiple retrospective case–control studies have shown that the risk of endometrial caricinoma is increased 2 to 18 times that seen in nonusers (56). Some have claimed that ascertainment bias accounts for much of this increase (28), and others (again by restrospective case–control study) have shown no increase in the mortality rate in women with estrogen therapy-associated endometrial cancer (11). In contrast, retrospective case–control reports have suggested that long-term use of postmenopausal conjugated estrogen increases the risk of both localized and widespread endometrial cancer, although no mortality data were given (57). Although the overall 5-year survival rate for endometrial cancer is about 70%, it is an uncommon disease (annual incidence 100 per 100,000), and the risk of estrogen-associated endometrial cancer is less than 0.5% per year. The risk of osteoporosis-related morbidity and mortality is also substantial, and benefits and risks must be weighed for each individual.

Similar concerns regarding the risk of breast cancer from postmenopausal estrogens are not well supported by the available evidence. Multiple retrospective case–control studies have shown no increased risk, and others have demonstrated diminished risk in estrogen users (27,29). Preliminary data suggest that cyclical use of progestins with estrogens may prevent any increase in endometrial or breast cancer associated with postmenopausal estrogen use (62), but the long-term effects of progestin use (particularly on lipid status) are virtually unknown, prohibiting definitive treatment recommendations at this time. Finally, several large retrospective case–control and three nonrandomized prospective studies have shown a decrease in all-cause mortality rates in postmenopausal estrogen users (6,27), possibly due to a beneficial increase in HDL-cholesterol levels.

In sum, although estrogen is of clear benefit in the treatment and prevention of postmenopausal osteoporosis, its ultimate effect on morbidity and mortality remain undetermined; prospective randomized longitudinal studies are needed to resolve these questions.

Vitamin D Intake and Bioavailability

The contribution of vitamin D deficiency to menopause and age-related bone loss remains unclear. Ingested calcium is absorbed from the upper small intestine and regulated by the renal metabolite of vitamin D, $1\alpha,25$-dihydroxycholecalciferol [calcitriol or $1\alpha,25$-$(OH)_2$-vitamin D]. When dietary calcium is inadequate, the intestine normally responds by increasing the efficiency of calcium absorption (5). However, efficiency of intestinal calcium absorption diminishes with age in both sexes, with an accelerated decrease after age 60 (19). Multiple studies have demonstrated lower calcium absorption in osteoporotic subjects than in age- and sex-matched controls (18). Dietary calcium intake also decreases with age, further exacerbating this calcium-deficient state (53).

The 25-hydroxyvitamin D_3 hepatic metabolite of vitamin D has also been shown to decrease with age for multiple reasons, including inadequate dietary intake of vitamin D, decreased exposure to sunlight, and impaired gastrointestinal absorption of dietary vitamin D. Contradictory evidence has demonstrated both diminished (19) and unchanged (44) levels of $1\alpha,25$-$(OH)_2$-vitamin D with age, as well as diminished secretory reserve of $1\alpha,25$-$(OH)_2$-vitamin D in response to provocative testing with synthetic human parathyroid fragment 1-34 (58). Similarly, several studies have shown decreased $1\alpha,25$-$(OH)_2$-vitamin D levels in osteoporotic subjects (58), whereas others have not demonstrated any difference (44). The mechanism of a reduction in $1\alpha,25$-$(OH)_2$-vitamin D levels or responsivity has not been established but may be related to the decreasing renal function associated with increasing age (61).

Similarly, trials utilizing vitamin D in the therapy of osteoporosis have yielded mixed results. Studies by Gallagher et al. have demonstrated transiently improved calcium balance and significantly decreased fracture incidence in treated subjects without evidence of improved trabecular bone mineral content, biopsy morphometry, or any serum measures of bone turnover (21). Riggs and colleagues have shown normalization of gastrointestinal calcium absorption using small doses of calcitriol [$1\alpha,25$-$(OH)_2$-vitamin D] in a 12-month trial, indicating that the etiology of decreased calcium absorption in postmenopausal osteoporosis is at least in part due to a decreasing production of $1\alpha,25$-$(OH)_2$-vitamin D (49).

In contrast, other investigators have demonstrated negative calcium balance and unchanged vertebral, radial, and metacarpal bone mineral measures after variable periods of therapy with $1\alpha,25$- or $24,25$-$(OH)_2$-vitamin D (14,31,46). In addition, therapeutic trials comparing calcium, estrogen, and fluoride combination regimens with and without vitamin D (50,000 units of ergocalciferol once or twice weekly) showed no added benefit and a substantial risk of side effects from the vitamin D therapy (50).

Side effects of therapy with $1\alpha,25$-$(OH)_2$-vitamin D include hypercalcemia, hypercalciuria, and decrements in the glomerular filtration rate (31,49). Thus more definitive evidence of therapeutic benefit in terms of fracture prevention is required before calcitriol becomes an accepted therapeutic modality in the treatment of osteoporosis. That there is a role of vitamin D deficiency in the etiology of osteoporosis is clear: whether the decrease in vitamin D status is a primary event or a secondary consequence of the hypercalcemia of accelerated bone loss remains to be determined (19). Finally, there is some evidence that a primary failure in renal 25-(OH)-vitamin D 1α-hydroxylase enzyme activity is demonstrable in senile (or Rigg's type II) osteoporosis, whereas the decreased enzyme activity shown in postmenopausal osteoporosis (Riggs' type I) appears to be secondary to decreased parathyroid hormone secretion resulting from accelerated bone resorption (61). Thus the heterogeneity of the osteoporosis syndrome precludes a single unifying hypothesis of etiology.

DIAGNOSTIC TECHNIQUES

In order to institute timely preventive measures, a method of measuring bone mineral content is required that is accurate, reproducible, and sufficiently sensitive to permit clear separation of normal individuals from those at risk. At present, such an ideal technology is not available, but intensive research and development directed toward this goal are under way. In the past, a diagnosis of osteoporosis could not be made until a fracture had occurred. The ability to detect low bone mineral content compared to that in age- and sex-matched controls permits institution of preventive measures before a fracture has occurred. The risk of fracture increases as bone mineral content decreases. However, although decreased bone calcium content is associated with decreasing bone strength and increased risk of fracture, the two factors are not identical. Other factors, currently not well defined, may also influence bone strength, but at present measures of bone mineral content are available, are clinically applicable, and correlate reasonably well with available reference standards, e.g., bone ash weight. Thus measurements of bone mineral are performed on patients for one or more of the following reasons.

1. To measure and compare appendicular (largely cortical) or axial (largely trabecular) bone mass for comparison with age- and sex-matched normals.
2. To relate a given bone mineral measurement to a known fracture "threshold" for the site measured and to thus predict an individual's risk of fracture at that point in time.
3. To estimate a rate of bone loss by repeated measurements (3–12 months apart) and to compare this individual rate with known age- and sex-specific normative longitudinal population studies of bone loss rate.
4. To assess rates of bone loss at various skeletal sites that may be differentially affected by distinct osteoporosis syndromes (e.g., vertebral site most affected in postmenopausal type 1 osteoporosis, hip most affected in senile or type II osteoporosis).
5. To monitor rate of loss of bone mineral in individuals receiving therapeutic interventions in order to assess response, identify nonresponders, and thus determine optimal duration and type of therapy.

Evaluation of Available Techniques

Several factors influence the utility and reliability of bone mineral measurements in the diagnosis and therapy of osteoporosis.

Accuracy

Accuracy, or reliability, or a measurement provides an index of the ability of the method to correlate with reference standards. Accuracy is usually described as a percentage indicating the degree of difference between bone mineral content as estimated by the test in question as it compares to the bone mineral content assessed by the reference standard, usually ash weight of bone or total body calcium measurements. A high degree of accuracy is important for diagnostic purposes where a clear separation between normals and osteoporotic persons is required.

Substantial overlap has been observed between bone mineral content measurements at both axial and appendicular sites in normal subjects and those with vertebral fractures, making accurate prediction of fracture risk impossible with currently available methods. It is due not only to machine and technique error but also to the fact that fractures are not solely the result of low bone mineral content but are associated with other factors (e.g., falling) as well.

Reproducibility

Reproducibility, or precision, is a measure of the reproducibility of a test on repeated determinations. It is usually described as a percentage (coefficient of variation) indicating the degree of variation in a result when the test is done several times on the same specimen. Poor reproducibility indicates a substantial degree of machine variation between measurements or suggests that the technique is highly vulnerable to technician error such as patient repositioning. A high degree of reproducibility is necessary to permit utility of serial measurements over time in the same individual: Observed changes can be ascribed to the patient changes only if the technique's coefficient of variation is lower than the measured change (although this limitation can be overcome in part by increased frequency of repeat measurements).

Skeletal Site

The skeleton is made up of cortical (compact) and trabecular (honeycomb-like spongiosa) bone compartments that are distributed differentially in the skeleton and respond somewhat independently to metabolic influences. Cortical bone accounts for 80 to 85% of total bone mass and trabecular bone for only 15 to 20%. However, trabecular bone is responsible for 80% of bone surface area and 70% of metabolic activity, suggesting a possible explanation for the disproportionate vulnerability of sites high in trabecular bone to fracture. The vertebral bodies are largely (66–90%) made up of trabecular bone, whereas the long bones and femur have higher amounts of compact cortical bone (approximate proportions: distal radius 75% cortical, mid-radius 95% cortical, femoral head 50% cortical, femoral neck 75% cortical) (52). Measures of largely cortical bone at appendicular skeletal sites do not correlate well with trabecular bone measures at axial sites (40). Similarly, techniques measuring integral bone (sum of cortical and trabecular) and total body calcium (by neutron activation analysis) correlate poorly with measures of pure trabecular bone by quantitative computed tomography (CT) scanning or iliac crest biopsy (10). Unfortunately, histomorphometric analyses of iliac crest bone biopsy specimens cannot serve as a reference standard with which to compare densitometric techniques because of substantial inter- and intrabiopsy variation (SD 4–6% of total bone volume) and because iliac trabecular bone density is poorly correlated with vertebral trabecular bone density and with appendicular integral bone mineral measures (16). Thus the use of multiple measurement techniques aimed at both peripheral and axial sites and at trabecular, cortical, and integral bone may be necessary to obtain an accurate assessment of what is clearly a heterogeneous spectrum of clinical bone disease (63).

Disease and Skeletal Site Specificity

Diverse metabolic bone diseases appear to affect various skeletal sites and measurement variables preferentially. For example, preferential loss of trabecular bone occurs in the bone loss of immobilization, corticosteroid therapy, and postmenopausal (or Riggs' type I) osteoporosis (51). Endocrine dysfunctions such as primary hyperparathyroidism, hypercortisolism, and hyperthyroidism appear to cause more spinal than peripheral mineral loss, whereas with acromegaly and postsurgical hypoparathyroidism spinal mineral gain is observed, reflecting regional differences in skeletal response to metabolic influences (8,55). Similarly, the response to therapy (of osteoporosis with fluoride and of renal osteodystrophy with vitamin D therapy) is measured earliest at trabecular bone sites.

Temporal Factors, Study Design, and Subject Selection for Densitometry Evaluation

The influence of cohort effects, the high prevalence of subclinical (i.e., prefracture) osteoporosis in so-called normal control groups, the uncertain clinical course of a chronic process such as osteoporosis, and densitometry technique variability requires a study design appropriate to these potential confounding factors. Thus prospective longitudinal studies are superior to retrospective or cross-sectional studies for describing the natural history of bone loss or response to therapy. Similarly, multiple sequential measurements (providing improved precision) taken over time in a small group are preferable to one or two measurements taken in a larger group of subjects. Subject selection for study participation also influences comparability within and between studies. Volunteer studies reflect a different population than a randomly selected cohort. Application of exclusion criteria (i.e., diseases or medications known to affect bone homeostasis) must be consistent in both study and control groups, as well as between studies, if outcomes are to be compared. Finally body mass parameters are a known influence on bone mineral content, as several studies have demonstrated a protective effect of obesity on appendicular bone mass (64). For example, a study by Cohn and associates utilizing total body calcium measurements by neutron activation analysis demonstrated a 7% greater mineral mass in Black women than in White. However, when the measurements were corrected for lean body mass, the differences were no longer significant (13).

Comment

An evaluation of densitometric technique utility requires attention not only to accuracy, reproducibility, the skeletal site measured, and the disease state studied but also to study design because of the substantial limitations of cross-sectional or retrospectively controlled investigations and subject selection.

Densitometric Techniques

Appendicular Cortical Bone Measurements

Peripheral, largely cortical bone mineral content measures are available, inexpensive, and safe but are of limited diagnostic utility because of substantial overlap in values between normals and fracture patients, as well as because of poor correlations with spinal (largely trabecular) bone mineral measurements (47).

Radiogrammetry

Radiogrammetry involves the caliper measurement of cortical bone thickness from a simple radiograph, usually at the metacarpal bone. The technique is highly reproducible when measurements from several bones are averaged (16). However, it reflects only changes in endosteal bone resorption, whereas intracortical and trabecular bone, which are better indices of high turnover states, are not measured. In addition, correlations with axial vertebral bone mineral measurements are poor.

Radiographic photodensitometry

Photodensitometry is a technique that employs an x-ray source, radiographic film, and a standardized wedge. The optical density of a radiographic bone image is approximately proportional to the mineral mass, but substantial error is introduced by nonuniformity of x-ray intensity, beam scatter, beam hardening from the polychromatic radiation source, and variable film sensitivity during processing. These and other difficulties have resulted in accuracy and precision inadequate for *in vivo* clinical measurements on individuals (23).

Single-photon absorptiometry

A widely used and more reproducible technique is photon absorptiometry using an iodine-125 source interfaced with a sodium iodide scintillation detector. The technique measures integral (sum of cortical and trabecular bone) at mid-radius (about 95% cortical) and distal radius (about 75% cortical) sites with a precision of 2% and an accuracy of approximately 6% (7). Errors due to scatter, beam hardening, path length changes, and processing errors are largely eliminated, accounting for the high reproducibility and utility for serial measures of this technique. Radiation exposure is low (2–5 mrad), patient acceptability is high, and the cost is minimal.

A major drawback of single-photon absorptiometry includes its poor correlation with mineral measures at the largely trabecular vertebral site of highest turnover and greatest clinical interest. Attempts to increase the proportion of trabecular bone measured by using the "ultradistal" radial site (where radius and ulna are 5 mm apart and trabecular bone volume is about 50%) yields a correlation coefficient of lumbar spine density (by dual-photon absorptiometry) to distal (5 mm site) radial density of only $r = 0.52$ ($p < 0.0001$) (3). Second, although the high reproducibility of single-photon absorptiometry makes it suitable for serial measurements on individuals, the relatively slow turnover of cortical bone compared to trabecular bone, as well as the preferential involvement of spinal trabecular bone with some types of osteoporosis (e.g., postmenopausal osteoporosis, primary hyperparathyroidism) limit the clinical utility of this technique. Finally, a substantial overlap has been observed between fracture patients and age-matched normals (1 SD, or 15%), thus substantially limiting the diagnostic accuracy of single photon absorptiometry (Fig. 2A).

Axial Trabecular Bone Measurements

Dual-photon absorptiometry

Dual-energy photon absorptiometry is a modification of the single-energy technique using a radioisotope that emits photons at two energy levels. The use of this two-wavelength source, gadolinium (^{153}Gd) permits measurement in areas without a constant path length, e.g., the spine and hip, producing a signal corrected for soft tissue variation. Dual-photon, like single-photon, absorptiometry measures integral bone mineral and cannot separately measure the cortical and trabecular compartments. The radiation dose is minimal (5–15 mrad), the cost moderate (around $250 per scan), and the time required about 45 minutes, but the technique is available at only a few centers nationwide. Reproducibility *in vivo* is about 2.5% (thus requiring multiple serial measurements to assess the rate of change in bone mineral as distinct from machine variability) and the accuracy about 4 to 6%. Overlap of osteoporotic values with normals, although less than that observed with single-photon absorptiometry, is still substantial (Fig. 2B) (51). Ninety percent of vertebral fracture patients have bone mineral density (BMD) values below 0.965 g/cm^2. By age 65 half of a normal (without fracture) female population, and by age 85 all, have BMD values below this value, suggesting that a high percentage of the female population has asymptomatic (i.e., prefracture) osteoporosis. Patients with multiple fractures fall approximately 2 SD below age-matched controls in spinal density, and the number of compression fractures correlates inversely with spinal bone mineral density (40). In contrast, femoral neck bone density as measured by the dual-photon method does not differ between hip fracture patients and age-matched controls (52). Correlations with total body calcium (by neutron activation analysis), measures of bone strength, and ashed bone samples are high (40).

Other drawbacks to the dual-photon method include the fact that paravertebral vascular calcifications, sclerotic degenerative joint disease, and crush fractures are all read by the technique as higher bone mineral content, thereby limiting the utility of the measurement in high-risk middle-aged and older individuals. The presence of an increasing volume of vertebral marrow fat with age also influences the accuracy of the dual-photon assessment of bone mineral content, particularly when measured over time. The magnitude of this problem is under debate, but it also affects other axial (e.g., CT) bone densitometry techniques.

The primary virtues of dual-photon absorptiometry are its high *in vivo* reproducibility, low radiation exposure (important for repeated measurements), and ability to measure spinal (largely trabecular) bone mineral content. Technical difficulties limit its applicability to the elderly population, and the overlap between normals and fracture patients is too substantial to permit accurate prediction of fracture risk.

Quantitative computed tomography

Enhanced by the wide availability of CT scanners, CT vertebral densitometry is increasingly utilized as a noninvasive means of determining purely trabecular spinal bone mineral content. It is the only method able to separately measure cortical, trabecular, and integral bone mineral and is thus of potentially great value in the early detection of bone loss occurring preferentially in the trabecular skeletal compartment. The technique utilizes a lateral scout view for CT positioning and takes four 1-cm slices at the midplane of four vertebrae (T_{12}–L_3). The machine is calibrated by simultaneous scanning of a normalization phantom on which the subject lies during the procedure. Analysis for mineral content is carried out using an oval cursor over the region of interest to determine the mean CT number for a 4-cc volume within the vertebral body. The reproducibility *in vivo* ranges from 1 to 4%, and accuracy is about 8% (accuracy is probably decreased in the elderly with osteoporosis) (24). The radiation dose required is substantially higher (about 250 mrad) than that received during dual-photon absorptiometry and is a limiting factor if frequent serial measurements are to be used. The cost is approximately $350 per scan and the time required about 20 minutes.

Overlap of osteoporotic values with normals is slightly less than that observed with dual-photon absorptiometry but is still significant enough to prevent accurate prediction of fracture risk (Fig. 2C). The "fracture threshold" value below which 90% of fracture patients fall is about 105 mg/cc.

The technique suffers from the same marrow fat-induced inaccuracies as described above for dual-photon absorptiometry. In addition, the repositioning error may be substantial in older persons with scoliosis, degenerative disease, vertebral sclerosis, and crush fracture. Although the confounding factors of paravertebral calcifications and intervertebral sclerosis do not affect CT measures to the same extent as they do dual-photon absorptiometry, intravertebral sclerotic changes and crush fractures falsely elevate the measured value. Technician avoidance of these areas when placing the cursor permits substantial introduction of variation between scans.

Correlations between CT values for trabecular bone mineral and those of other methods for integral bone mineral at multiple sites are poor. This is to be expected, as measures of purely trabecular mineral would be expected to yield lower absolute values for mineral content and higher rates of change over time than would measures of integral bone containing low turnover and comparatively high mineral content cortical bone. Of note is the fact that highly accurate and reproducible CT measures of pure trabecular bone at the distal radial site demonstrate high correlations ($r = 0.92$, $p < 0.01$) with CT vertebral trabecular values, suggesting that peripheral measures of pure trabecular bone may predict axial trabecular mineral content with high accuracy (and less radiation risk, time, and cost to the patient) (41,47).

The singular advantage of CT densitometry is its ability to separately quantitate cortical and trabecular bone compartments, thus theoretically facilitating the early detection and treatment of spinal bone loss. Technical issues involving reproducibility, accuracy, effects of marrow fat, and radiation dose are currently limiting; development of a radial quantitative CT technique may solve some of these problems.

Other Techniques

Neutron activation analysis

Total body calcium assessment by neutron activation analysis (NAA) is a research technique utilizing high-energy neutrons that elevate body calcium from calcium-48 to calcium-49. The decay back to calcium 48 is measured with a gamma radiation counter, providing an accurate assessment of skeletal calcium (99% of total body calcium is sequestered in the skeleton). As an integral measurement (sum of trabecular and cortical calcium) NAA permits assessment and validation of other integral (largely cortical bone) techniques such as single- and dual-photon absorptiometry where correlation coefficients are high. NAA cannot separately assess the trabecular and cortical compartments, and so correlations with CT spinal trabecular mineral are, as expected, poor, and the technique does not reflect early high turnover states located primarily in trabecular bone (40).

The radiation dose is high (ranging from 300 to 500 mrad), thereby preventing the use of this technique for frequent serial measurements. *In vivo* precision and reliability are acceptable (2–3% and 6%, respectively), although substantial inaccuracies are introduced by vascular and other heterotopic calcifications, which are common in the elderly. Overlap between normal and fracture patients is high, preventing prediction of risk. Thus NAA, although useful as a research tool and for validation of other integral bone densitometric techniques, is not applicable to individual monitoring in the clinical situation.

Bone histomorphometry

Quantitative histomorphometric analyses of transiliac double tetracycline-labeled bone biopsies are used in the diagnosis and monitoring of metabolic bone disease; they provide information on both cortical and trabecular bone turnover and dynamics. The technique finds its greatest use in diagnosis of osteomalacia and other rare bone disorders clinically indistinguishable from osteoporosis, as well as in the assessment of high versus low turnover states when choosing therapeutic modalities. The invasiveness, inter- and intra-biopsy variability, observer bias, and lack of general availability of pathologists skilled in the interpretation and handling of undecalcified bone specimens limits the clinical utility of this technique as a quantitative method of assessing bone mineral content (40).

Normative Densitometric Studies

Cross-sectional studies of normal male and female subjects utilizing single- and dual-photon absorptiometry and quantitative CT scanning have revealed different rates of bone loss. Longitudinal studies are rare, and explication of the true natural history of bone loss (e.g., linear loss versus plateaus alternating with periods of rapid loss) await long-term efforts with serial measurements taken over several decades. Cross-sectional single-photon absorptiometric studies in women (Fig. 2A) have revealed fairly stable bone mineral content with only minimal losses after about age 30 to 35 until menopause when an approximate 10-year period of accelerated radial cortical loss occurs. This rate of loss decreases again after age 65, returning to its previous, slower rate. The age regression was best fit by a cubic equation indicating a nonlinear rate of loss. In contrast, studies on the same normal women by vertebral dual-photon absorptiometry (Fig. 2B) revealed a linear bone loss at a rate of about 6% per decade (51). Other workers using dual-photon absorptiometry have demonstrated a menopausal acceleration in bone loss in normal women; similarly, cross-sectional quantitative computed tomographic (vertebral trabecular) studies of normal women (Fig. 2C) revealed a cubic relation with menopausal acceleration (8–10% loss per decade) and slowing of loss after about age 65 (24).

Similar cross-sectional studies in normal men have revealed essentially no change in radial cortical bone mineral content until the eighth decade (41,51), and measures of integral spinal mineral by the dual-photon method revealed a linear loss of about 2.5% per decade. In contrast, cross-sectional studies of normal men by vertebral trabecular CT demonstrate much faster rates of linear loss (8–12% per decade) (24,41).

Thus accumulated evidence indicates that age-related demineralization does not proceed uniformly in all skeletal locations; future studies require a longitudinal approach to a chronic process as well as techniques that permit separate assessment of cortical and trabecular bone compartments. The use of multiple measurement techniques aimed at both peripheral and axial skeletal sites and trabecular, cortical, and integral bone may be necessary to obtain an accurate assessment of the heterogeneous spectrum of clinical bone disease. Currently available techniques have distinctive advantages and limitations, and the choice of methods must be appropriate to the experimental design and disease studied.

PREVENTION AND THERAPY

Problems encountered when studying preventive and therapeutic measures for osteoporosis are multiple and include the fact that the disease is clearly heterogeneous in its severity (e.g., course and rates of loss) and in its responsiveness to various interventions. For example, in a study of sodium fluoride, fully 40% of those treated did not respond, whereas the other 60% demonstrated measurable increases in vertebral bone mass (50).

Second, the disease develops over decades before it becomes clinically evident with fracture. Thus longitudinal placebo-controlled trials over long periods of time are required to establish the efficacy of a preventive measure.

Similarly, side effects of therapies, particularly hormonal therapies, may require decades to appear, thus adding another element of uncertainty to treatment recommendations based on relatively short (i.e., less than a decade) periods of study. The presence of a simultaneously studied and randomly assigned control group is critical to distinguishing a treatment effect from the natural (and heterogeneous) history of the disease. (For example, fractures may occur in groups and then cease for long periods in untreated populations, an observation easy to ascribe to the effects of an intervention if no control group is available.) Blinding of subjects and investigators is the best way to diminish bias. Control and study groups must be as comparable as possible in terms of age, sex, type of fracture, and exclusion of secondary causes of bone disease. Because of the length of time required to measure an effect in a chronic process such as bone loss, group sizes must be large enough and the study period long enough to permit ascertainment of a difference (risk of type II error) and to ascribe that difference to the treatment employed (type I error). Estimates of the natural history of bone loss or fracture rate in the untreated population must be available as well as an assessment of the change expected because of the intervention in order to evaluate statistical power and calculate group size prior to initiation of the study. Finally, low bone mass is a principal determinant of fracture risk. However, many persons with low bone mineral content do not fracture; conversely, some states characterized by high bone mass (e.g., osteopetrosis) present with an increased risk of fracture. Therefore if measures of bone mineral are to be used as indicators of therapeutic efficacy, it must be determined that the agent produces its effect by alterations in the bone itself (and not in some extrinsic factor). Thus simultaneous measures of bone mass with bone histomorphometric parameters, as well as more difficult outcome measures such as fracture rate, should be sought (32).

The ethical (long-term placebo-controlled studies) and practical difficulties inherent in this approach have resulted in few such cohort investigations taking place. Limitations in currently available data must be viewed in this light, and future studies should incorporate as many of these considerations as possible in the experimental design.

Specific Therapeutic Modalities

Once bone loss has occurred, replacement is difficult. Many pharmacological agents have been investigated in the treatment of osteoporosis, including calcium, phosphorus, vitamin D, estrogens and progestogens, sodium fluoride, thiazide diuretics, androgens, anabolic steroids, calcitonin, and parathyroid hormone. Utility of calcium, sex hormone, and vitamin D therapies in the prevention and treatment of bone loss are reviewed in the Pathogenesis section of this chapter. Weight-bearing physical exercise has also been suggested as a preventive and a therapeutic modality.

Physical Exercise

It is clear that the immobility of weightlessness (e.g., space flight) promotes the bone loss of disuse. Increases in physical exertion have therefore been evaluated as a means of increasing bone mass. Correlations have been demonstrated between lean muscle mass and skeletal mass, and athletes develop skeletal hypertrophy in areas of greatest exertion (1). Several prospective controlled studies have demonstrated increases in bone mineral content, calcium balance, and total body calcium in high risk groups of postmenopausal and elderly women (34). Demonstration of decreased fracture risk awaits longer-term follow-up.

Sodium Fluoride

Sodium fluoride is the only currently available agent that stimulates new bone formation. It appears to preferentially increase trabecular bone mass (without affecting total body calcium) and, in some studies, to decrease fracture risk. These investigations have been limited by inappropriate or absent controls and other problems of experimental design. Although trabecular bone mineral clearly increases, the architecture of this new bone is abnormal: The effect of this alteration on bone strength is not yet known. Furthermore, if fluoride is given without adequate supplemental calcium, an osteomalacic mineralization defect is observed. As noted above, a high proportion of those treated with fluoride do not respond, and no clear characteristics predictive of response have emerged. This finding is of great importance because a minimum of 1 to 2 years of treatment is necessary for a therapeutic effect, and fluoride has substantial side effects involving some 40%

of treated subjects (including gastrointestinal irritation and blood loss, and periarticular pain) (50). For these reasons fluoride is still an experimental drug in the United States. Definitive results await completion of a prospective randomized control clinical trial currently under way.

Calcitonin

Calcitonin deficiency has been implicated in the pathogenesis of postmenopausal osteoporosis because of studies showing lower immunoreactive calcitonin levels (a) with increasing age, (b) in women than in men, and (c) in osteoporotic subjects compared to normals. Calcitonin levels appear to decrease at menopause, and calcitonin response to calcium infusion appears to be blunted in postmenopausal osteoporosis, although some investigators have not been able to reproduce these observations (15,60). Data supporting these findings are sparse and contradictory, and studies have been limited by noncomparable case and control selection, small numbers of subjects, prior treatments, and poor sensitivity and specificity of calcitonin assays.

Nonetheless, the Food and Drug Administration approved calcitonin therapy for osteoporosis in 1984, a decision based largely on a 2-year controlled study by Gruber et al. (26) of 24 postmenopausal patients (on calcitonin, calcium, and vitamin D_2) and 21 controls (on calcium and vitamin D). The study demonstrated increased total body calcium by neutron activation analysis and greater percent bone area and decreased resorption area on bone histomorphometry. No differences in fracture rate or improvement in radial bone mass were noted in the treatment group over the period of follow-up. Although side effects are minimal, the cost is substantial and the drug must be self-administered parenterally.

The theoretical mechanism of action of calcitonin efficacy in osteoporosis involves the observed inhibition of osteoclastic bone resorption, resulting in decreased serum calcium and phosphorus, increased parathyroid hormone secretion, a hypothesized increased synthesis of $1\alpha,25$-$(OH)_2$-vitamin D, and increased intestinal calcium absorption. Until this theoretical model is better explicated and contradictory findings in studies of calcitonin levels and responsivity in osteoporosis are resolved, the drug is reserved for patients with contraindications or nonresponsiveness to other forms of therapy for osteoporosis.

REFERENCES

1. Aloia, J. F., Cohn, S. H., Ostuni, J. A., et al. (1978): Prevention of involutional bone loss by exercise. *Ann. Intern. Med.,* 89:356–358.
2. Avioli, L. V. (1976): Senile and postmenopausal osteoporosis. *Adv. Intern. Med.,* 21:391–415.
3. Awbrey, B. J., Jacobson, P. C., Grubb, S. A., et al. (1984): Bone density in women: a modified procedure for measurement of distal radial density *J. Orthop. Res.,* 2:314–321.
4. Baran, D. T., Bergfeld, M. A., Teitelbaum, S. L., et al. (1978): Effect of testosterone therapy on bone formation in an osteoporotic hypogonadal male. *Calcif. Tissue Res.,* 26:103–106.

5. Bishop, J. E., Norman, A. W., Coburn, J. W., et al. (1980): Studies on the metabolism of calciferol. XVI. *J. Mineral Electr. Metab.*, 3:181–187.

6. Bush, T. L., Cowan, L. D., and Barrett-Conner, E. (1983): Estrogen use and all-cause mortality. *JAMA*, 249:903.

7. Cameron, J. R., Mazess, R. B., and Sorenson, J. A. (1968): Precision and accuracy of bone mineral determination by direct photon absorptiometry. *Invest. Radiol.*, 3:141–150.

8. Chalmers, J. (1973): Distribution of osteoporotic changes in the ageing skeleton. *Clin. Endocrinol. Metab.*, 2:203–220.

9. Chestnut, C. H. (1984): An appraisal of the role of estrogens in the treatment of postmenopausal osteoporosis. *J. Am. Geriatr. Soc.*, 32:604–608.

10. Chestnut, C. H., Nelp, W. B., and Lewellen, T. K. (1981): Neutron activation analysis for whole body calcium measurement. In: *Osteoporosis—Recent Advances in Pathogenesis and Treatment*, edited by H. DeLuca, H. Frost, W. Jee, et al. University Park Press, Baltimore.

11. Chu, J., Schweid, A. I., and Weiss, N. S. (1982): Survival among women with endometrial cancer: a comparison of estrogen users and non users. *Am J. Obstet. Gynecol.*, 143:569–573.

12. Cobey, J. C., Cobey, J. H., Conant, L., et al. (1976): Indicators of recovery from fractures of the hip. *Clin. Orthop.*, 117:258–262.

13. Cohn, S. H., Abesamis, C., Yasamura, S., Aloia, J. F., et al. (1977): Comparative skeletal mass and radial bone mineral content in Black and White women. *Metabolism*, 26:171–178.

14. Crilly, R. G., Horsman, A., Peacock, M., and Nordin, B. E. C. (1981): The vitamin D metabolites in the pathogenesis and management of osteoporosis. *Curr. Med. Res. Opin.*, 7:337–348.

15. Deftos, L. J., Weisman, M. H., Williams, G. W., et al. (1980): Influence of age and sex on plasma calcitonin in human beings. *N. Engl J. Med.*, 302:1351–1353.

16. Dequeker, J., (1977): Problems in measuring amount of bone: reproducibility, variability, sequential evaluation. In: *Bone Histomorphometry: Second International Workshop*, edited by P. J. Meunier, Armour Montague, Paris.

17. Furahgelm, M., and Zador, G., (1978): Present status of estrogen treatment in prevention of postmenopausal osteoporosis. *Acta Obstet. Gynecol. Scand.* [Suppl.] 88:97–101.

18. Gallagher, J. C., Aaron, J., Horsman, A., Marshall, D. H., Wilkinson, R., and Nordin, B. E. C. (1973): *Clin. Endocrinol. Metab.*, 2:293.

19. Gallagher, J. C., Riggs, B. L., Eisman, J., et al. (1979): Intestinal calcium absorption and serum vitamin D metabolites in normal subjects and osteoporotic patients: effect of age and dietary calcium. *J. Clin. Invest.*, 64:729–734.

20. Gallagher, J. C., Melton, L. J., and Riggs, B. L. (1980): Epidemiology of fractures of the proximal femur in Rochester, Minnesota. *Clin. Orthop.*, 150:163–171.

21. Gallagher, J. C., Terpbak, C. M., Jee, W. S. S., et al. (1982): 1,25-Dihydroxy vitamin D_3: short and long term effects on bone and calcium metabolism in patients with postmenopausal osteoporosis. *Proc. Natl. Acad. Sci. USA*, 79:3325–3329.

22. Garn, S. M., Rohmann, C. G., Wagner, B., et al. (1969): Population similarities in the onset and rate of adult endosteal bone loss. *Clin. Orthop.*, 65:51.

23. Genant, H. K. (1981): Methods of noninvasive quantitative bone mineral analysis. In: *Diagnosis of Bone and Joint Disorders*, edited by D. Resnick, G. Niwayama, pp. 679–691. Saunders. Philadelphia.

24. Genant, H. K., Gordan, G. S., and Hoffman, P. G. (1983): Osteoporosis. I. Advanced radiologic assessment using quantitative computed tomography—medical staff conference, Univ. of California San Francisco. *West. J. Med.*, 139:75–84.

25. Gordan, G. S., and Genant, H. K. (1985): The aging skeleton. *Clin. Geriatr. Med.*, 1:95–118.

26. Gruber, H. E., Ivey, J. L., Baylink, D. J., et al. (1984): Long term calcitonin therapy in post menopausal osteoporosis. *Metabolism*, 33:295–303.

27. Haber, R. J., (1985): Should postmenopausal women be given estrogen? *West. J. Med.*, 142:672–677.

28. Horowitz, R. I., and Fienstein, A. R. (1978): Alternative analytic methods for case-control studies of estrogens and endometrial cancer. *N. Engl. J. Med.*, 299:1088–1094.

29. Horowitz, R. I., and Steward, K. R. (1984): Effect of clinical features on the association of estrogens and breast cancer. *Am. J. Med.*, 76:192–198.

30. Horsman, A., Gallagher, J. C., Simpson, J., and Nordin, B. E. C. (1977): Prospective trial of oestrogen and calcium in postmenopausal women. *Br. Med. J.*, 2:789–792.

31. Jensen, G. F., Christiansen, C., and Transbol, I. (1982): Treatment of postmenopausal osteoporosis: a controlled therapeutic trial comparing estrogen/gestagen, 1,25 dihydroxy-vitamin D_3 and calcium. *Clin. Endocrinol. (Oxf.)*, 16:515–524.

32. Johnston, C. C., and Norton, J. A. (1981): How can effectiveness of treatment be determined? In: *Osteoporosis: Recent Advances in Pathogenesis and Treatment,* edited by H. F. DeLuca, H. M. Frost, et al., pp. 375–382 University Park Press, Baltimore.

33. Johnston, C. C., Hui, S. L., Wiske, P. S., et al. (1981): Bone mass at maturity and subsequent rates of loss as determinants of osteoporosis. In: *Osteoporosis: Recent Advances in Pathogenesis and Treatment,* edited by H. F. DeLuca, H. M. Frost, W. S. S. Jee, et al., pp. 285–291 University Park Press, Baltimore.

34. Krolner, B., Toft, B., Nielsen, S. P., et al. (1983): Physical exercise as prophylaxis against involutional vertebral bone loss: a controlled trial. *Clin. Sci.,* 64:541–546.

35. Lindsay, R., Hart, D. M., Aitken, J. M., et al. (1976): Long term prevention of osteoporosis by estrogen. *Lancet,* 1:1038–1041.

36. Lindsay, R., Hart, D. M., Forrest, C., and Baird, C. (1980): Prevention of spinal osteoporosis in oophorectomized women. *Lancet,* 2:1151–1154.

37. Lindsay, R., Maclean, A., Kraszewski, A., et al. (1978): Bone response to termination of estrogen treatment. *Lancet,* 1325–1327.

38. Marcus, R., Cann, C., Madvig, P., et al. (1985): Menstrual function and bone mass in elite women distance runners. *Ann. Intern. Med.* 102:158–163.

39. Matkovic, V., Kostial, K., Simonovic, I., et al. (1979): Bone status and fracture rates in two regions of Yugoslavia. *Am. J. Clin Nutr.,* 32:540–548.

40. Mazess, R. B. (1983): The noninvasive measurement of skeletal mass. In: *Bone and Mineral Research Annual 1,* edited by W. Peck, pp. 223–279. Excerpta Medica, Princeton, NJ.

41. Meier, D. E., Orwoll, E. S., and Jones, J. M. (1984): Marked disparity between trabecular and cortical bone loss with age in healthy men. *Ann. Intern. Med.,* 101:605–612.

42. Nachtigall, C. E., Nachtigall, R. M., Nachtigall, R. D., and Beckman, E. M. (1979): Estrogen replacement therapy. I. A 10 year prospective study in the relationship to osteoporosis. *Obstet. Gynecol.,* 53:277–281.

43. Nilas, L., Christiansen, C., and Rodbro, P. (1984): Calcium supplementation and postmenopausal bone loss. *Br. Med. J.,* 289:1103–1106.

44. Nordin, B. E. C., Peacock, M., and Crilly, R. G. (1979): Calcium absorption and plasma 1,25 $(OH)_2$ D levels in postmenopausal osteoporosis. In: *Vitamin D: Basic Research and Its Clinical Application,* edited by A. W. Norman, K. Schaefer, D. V. Herrath, et al., 99–106. Walter de Gruyter, Berlin.

45. Recker, R. R., Saville, P. D., and Heaney, R. P. (1977): Effect of estrogens and calcium carbonate on bone loss in post menopausal women. *Ann. Intern. Med.,* 87:649–655.

46. Reeve, J., Tellez, M., Green, J. R., et al. (1982): Long term treatment of osteoporosis with 24,25 dihydroxy cholecalciferol. *Acta Endocrinol. (Copenh.)* 101:636–640.

47. Reugsegger, P., Anliker, M., and Dambacher, M. (1981): Quantification of trabecular bone with low dose computed tomography. *J. Comput. Assist. Tomogr.,* 5:384–390.

48. Riggs, B. L., and Melton, L. J. (1983): Evidence for two distinct syndromes of involutional osteoporosis. *Am. J. Med.,* 75:899–901.

49. Riggs, B. L., and Nelson, K. I. (1985): Effect of long term treatment with calcitriol on calcium absorption and mineral metabolism in postmenopausal osteoporosis. *J. Clin. Endocrinol. Metab.,* 61:457–461.

50. Riggs, B. L., Seeman, E., Hodgson, S. F., et al. (1982): Effect of the fluoride/calcium regimen on vertebral fracture occurrence in postmenopausal osteoporosis. *N. Engl. J. Med.,* 306:446–450.

51. Riggs, B. L., Wahner, H. W., Dunn, W. L., et al. (1981): Differential changes in bone mineral density of the appendicular and axial skeleton with aging. *J. Clin. Invest.,* 67:328–335.

52. Riggs, B. L., Wahner, H. W., Seeman, E., et al. (1982): Changes in bone mineral density of the proximal femur and spine with aging: differences between the postmenopausal and senile osteoporosis syndromes. *J. Clin. Invest.,* 70:716–723.

53. Rivlin, R. S., (1982): Evidence relating selected vitamins and minerals to health and disease in the elderly population in the United States. *Am. J. Clin. Nutr.,* 36:1083–1086.

54. Sandler, R. B., Slemenda, C. W., LaPorte, R. E., et al. (1985): Postmenopausal bone density and milk consumption in childhood and adolescence. *Am. J. Clin. Nutr.,* 42:270–274.

55. Seeman, E., Wahner, M. W., Offord, K. P., et al. (1982): Differential effects of endocrine dysfunction on the axial and the appendicular skeleton. *J. Clin. Invest.,* 69:1302–1309.

56. Shapiro, M. B., Kaufman, M. S., Slone, D., et al. (1980): Recent and past use of conjugated estrogens in relation to adenocarcinoma of the endometrism. *N. Engl. J. Med.,* 303:485–492.

57. Shapiro, S., Kelly, J. P., and Rosenberg, L. (1985): Risk of localized and widespread endometrial

cancer in relation to recent and discontinued use of conjugated estrogens. *N. Engl. J. Med.,* 313:969–972.

58. Slovik, D. M., Adams, V. S., Neer, R. M., et al. (1981): Deficient production of 1,25 dihydroxyvitamin D in elderly osteoporotic patients. *N. Engl. J. Med.,* 305:372–374.

59. Solomon, L. (1979): Bone density in aging Caucasian and African populations. *Lancet,* 29:1326–1330.

60. Tiegs, R. D., Body, J. J., and Wahner, H. W. (1985): Calcitonin secretion in postmenopausal osteoporosis. *N. Engl. J. Med.,* 312:1097–1100.

61. Tsai, K. S., Heath, H., Kumar, R., and Riggs, B. L. (1984): Impaired vitamin D metabolism with aging in women. *J. Clin. Invest.,* 73:1668–1672.

62. Whitehead, M. I., Townsend, P. T., Pryse Davies, J., et al. (1981): Effects of estrogens and progestin on the biochemistry and morphology of the postmenopausal endometrium. *N. Engl. J. Med.,* 305:599.

63. Whyte, M. P., Bergfeld, M. A., Murphy, W. A., et al. (1982): Postmenopausal osteoporosis: a heterogeneous disorder as assessed by histomorphometric analysis of iliac crest bone from untreated patients. *Am. J. Med.,* 72:193–202.

64. Williams, A. R., Weiss, N. S., Ure, C. L., et al. (1982): Effect of weight, smoking and estrogen use on the risk of hip and forearm fractures in postmenopausal women. *Obstet. Gynecol.,* 60:695–699.

Human Aging Research: Concepts and Techniques,
edited by B. Kent and R. N. Butler.
Raven Press, Ltd., New York © 1988.

The Liver

Hans Popper

Mount Sinai School of Medicine of the City University of New York,
New York, New York 10029

Research on aging of the liver concerns two problems, mainly the specific alterations of the liver during aging and the effect of the liver on the aging process. Most information is found in gerontologic and pharmacologic journals and relatively little in the vast hepatologic literature, including books, journals, and review articles devoted to the liver and its diseases. Particularly in the hepatologic publications, scattered and often contradictory statements are found that contrast sharply with the otherwise characteristic vigor of hepatologic research. The initial survey may therefore best start with four proceedings of conferences on the subject, the first in Germany (18), then in Japan (12,13) and subsequently in Holland (29). They consist of interesting and sometimes challenging presentations but do not provide a comprehensive review. Further reference is made to state-of-the-art reports (6,19).

The following discussion has three goals: (a) to briefly review, as a basis, the available information on aging and the liver; (b) to point out the many questions that may be answered by additional biomedical investigations; and (c) to provide selected background information required for research approaches to the problems of aging and the liver. For coherence, however, the three aspects are frequently combined. Only the processes following maturity are considered here. This area is particularly important in the liver, where precise and not controversial information is available about the development to maturity, in contrast to the changes between maturity and death.

INTRODUCTORY REMARKS

The aging liver shows well-recognizable structural alterations that on the electron microscopic level are somewhat controversial; in contrast to many other organ systems, surprisingly few functional alterations are evident. Therefore if aging is differentiated from senescence—the latter in the sense of significant deterioration leading to natural causes of death (16)—the liver ages but does not suffer senescence. There in only a decrease of its homeostatic efficiency; there is no disease state caused by senescence of the liver, and little suggests that aging of the liver is even a contributory cause of death of patients with nonhepatic diseases. The major practical clinical consequences of aging of the liver are therefore variations in response to drugs, but even there contradictory information prevails.

One question thus concerns the resistance of the function of the liver to aging despite some recognizable structural alterations. One of the causes may be the low turnover of hepatocytes under normal circumstances, which is coupled with increased proliferation on stimulation. Thus injured or degenerated hepatocytes may be replaced. The second is the abundant supply of blood to the liver, which greatly exceeds under normal circumstances the household needs of the hepatocytes and which serves primarily their action on the circulating blood. Only with a severe reduction of the effective hepatic blood flow does it become rate-limiting for hepatic function. Moreover, both the hepatic artery and the portal vein supply blood to the liver. Therefore the secondary effects of vascular alterations, particularly arteriosclerosis, during aging make themselves far less felt in the liver than in the other organ with similar "expanding" cell populations, e.g., the kidney. Third, the liver has a great functional reserve capacity indicated by patients' survival after subtotal hepatectomy.

The subsequent discourse starts from relatively well-documented morphologic observations of the aging liver; it continues with aspects of increasing uncertainty, i.e., the function of the whole organ, its cells, organelles, and molecules in the aging liver. After short reference to liver diseases in the elderly, it concludes with the even more elusive effect of the liver on the senescent organism.

MORPHOLOGIC OBSERVATIONS

There is no question that the major morphologic change of aging of the liver is its brown color; a reduction in weight is usually assumed. Indeed, the liver weight/body weight ratio is significantly reduced, apparently more in women (5). There are, however, great individual variations in both factors quite independent of the duration of life.

Pigmentation

Pigmentation is produced by excess accumulation of lipofuscin pigment in hepatocytes. The biochemical nature of these pigments is not established. They are derived mainly from unsaturated lipids of the various cell membranes that have undergone peroxidation, especially under abnormal circumstances; oxidized polymerized proteins, particularly those cross-linked with glucose, also serve as a source of the brown pigment. The critical factor is the lack of some lipases and other digestive enzymes acting on these substances in the lysosomes to which the pigment precursors are transferred. Moreover, organelles turn over much faster than the cells themselves, and some of their breakdown products become lipofuscin. All these wear-and-tear pigments accumulate therefore in the lysosomes of the hepatocytes as they do in other organs with aging of their cells, but their number is also increased with wasting diseases, some pigment abnormalities, and deficiencies of the antioxidant vitamin E. In addition to endogenous material, exogenous substances (including some metabolites of such drugs as phenacetin or chlorpromazine) may accumulate in lysosomal lipofuscin granules. The brown pigmentation of the aging liver thus reflects the life history of the individual cells as well as of the organism. Regenerated hepatocytes are pigment-free. There is, however, no evidence that the accumulation of this pigmented material has any effect on hepatic function, and there is little reason to believe that additional study of this impressive sign of liver aging should contribute to the understanding of the aging mechanism. Similarly, other gross features in the aged liver, e.g., irregular thickening of its capsule or scattered hepatic cysts, have no functional significance.

Liver Weight

By contrast, the reduced weight of the liver, though less well established, may somewhat influence overall hepatic function. Because the number of the constituent circulatory units, acini or lobules, of the liver is not reduced, the average size of the hepatocytes or their number should be diminished. Extensive Japanese studies (28), so far not yet fully confirmed, suggest that with human malnutrition the hepatocytes are smaller but normal in number, whereas with aging the cell number is decreased and the cells frequently enlarged. This fact is coupled with the claim that higher dietary protein intake, possibly already influential during adolescence, may accelerate progression of these aging changes. If at an older age the overall liver function is indeed reduced under normal and particularly under abnormal circumstances (e.g., stress), and if in turn aging manifestations of the body are influenced by the liver status, additional information is required about the role of nutritional variations, particularly of protein intake. This situation encourages investigations as to the size of the liver and of hepatocytes in old persons of different countries with quantifiable variations in the diet. However, these desirable geographic pathologic investigations present major organizational obstacles.

Morphometric Findings

Information about the morphologic features of the hepatocytes in aged humans and animals is still conflicting, even if quantitative analyses have been applied. In animals there are distinct strain and sex variations that justify the recommendation of using specific strains, e.g., of rats. Moreover, extrapolation from inbred animals to outbred humans may be difficult. Certain features appear to be established. An authoritative presentation by David (5) not only reviewed the available literature but also provided exact morphometric measurements of the hepatic cells and their constituents in Wistar rats. Thus both conspicuous enlargement (macrohepatocytes) and small cells (minihepatocytes) were found in rodents and humans, in the latter even after sudden death (30); the size of nuclei and mitochrondria varied greatly as well. Lysosomes appeared to be increased in number as expected with increasing age, and peroxisomes were said to be smaller but more numerous. Morphometric analysis by some investigators detected a diminution of the smooth endoplasmic reticulum in rats (26), which would be in keeping with the altered microsomal biotransformation, to be discussed below, but others denied such change. The nuclear variations are also reflected in the frequent polyploidy of some hepatocytes, associated with increased nucleoli, observed in several but not all species; at least some hepatocytes move from diploid stage to higher ploidy. Indeed, on routine histologic examination, groups of hepatocytes of variable size and polyploid nuclei were, in addition to the pigment accumulation and intralobular proliferation of bile ductules, the only other indication of old age in human livers. These findings are supported by observations of increased DNA and apparently increased protein content of the hepatocytes, and there are reports of altered chromosomes. The available light and electron microscopic observations, however, provide little evidence for degenerative changes related to a qualitative alteration of the aging liver. Although there is significant discrepancy between the observations of different authors, the present information can best be summarized by stressing increased variability of the hepatocytes and their various constituents.

ALTERATIONS OF HEPATIC CONNECTIVE TISSUE

Despite an extensive literature on the aging changes of the connective tissue, documented in the progeric syndromes, and their role in senescence (14), and despite the rapid advances in knowledge of the connective tissue matrix in the liver and its diseases (22,23), there is little information on the hepatic collagens and matrix in aging. An exception is casual description of increased collagen fibers in the aging liver, presumably explained by reduced collagen breakdown similar to its excess in cirrhosis. Extensive baseline information is available on the various components of the matrix of the normal and abnormal liver. It includes, in addition to elastic fibers: (a) the various interstitial and basement collagens; (b) the proteoglycans, which either form the glycocalix around the cells, are found in the basement membrane, or are within hepatocytes; and (c) the attachment proteins fibronectin and laminin, for which specific receptors exist. Whereas previously the matrix was assigned mainly supporting function, it is now ascribed the ability to modulate the phenotypic expressions of its adjacent epithelial cells (22). Because senescence might affect the liver by altering its matrix, systematic research of the hepatic matrix during aging might be promising.

FUNCTIONAL HEPATIC ALTERATIONS IN AGING

Pertinent problems concern the function of the whole liver, specific metabolic activities, the response to modulating agents, the important question of the drug metabolism, and finally the function of the constituent cells and their organelles.

Function of the Whole Liver

Few of the routine liver function tests indeed measure a specific function of the liver but, rather, indicate an altered status of the organ; that is, they demonstrate one of the major hepatic abnormal reactions such as liver cell injury or cholestasis. Thus the question of whether age itself or abnormal hepatic reactions and therefore diseases in the aged account for abnormal results of the hepatic tests is of major clinical significance. Most reports have failed to establish a definite effect of aging, and abnormal results should therefore be interpreted as in young persons, in that they point to a disease. One must, however, keep in mind that almost all single routine tests render slightly abnormal results in about 10% of seemingly healthy persons. Age-related changes, possibly found in dye clearance determinations, may simply reflect altered hepatic blood flow. Further studies with the routine hepatic tests are not required, and continuous investigations may be justified only if new, more sophisticated tests such as the various breath tests are applied.

Hepatic Blood Flow and Transport

Most but not all investigators report a reduction of hepatic blood flow during aging, mainly on the basis of dye clearance studies. If a diminution of the liver size is accepted, overall hepatic blood flow should be diminished. Moreover, its reduction may simply reflect decreased cardiac output. Because blood flow is an important reference point for other determinations, it should be reinvestigated with the reliable, noninvasive methods now available. At the same time, the ratio of hepatic arterial to portal vein flow during aging should be established. The claim of decreased hepatic blood flow is based mainly on reduced dye clearance of indocyanine green and Bromsulphalein (BSP), the latter of which requires conjugation and is stored in the liver. Earlier it was claimed that BSP storage is reduced during aging, but newer observations indicate delay of transport of conjugated BSP in older rats, particularly male rats. Delay of transport through the hepatocytes in aging rats has also been demonstrated for immunoglobulin A. The number of receptors, at least for low density lipoproteins (LDLs), is reduced (3). Bile flow appears not to be altered.

Alterations of Specific Hepatic Functions

Many papers report reduction of some specific metabolic functions of the liver, whereas others claim it to be unchanged; thus selective disturbances must be assumed. The most convincing human data concern reduced bile acid synthesis and pool with increased biliary cholesterol secretion, which by raising biliary cholesterol saturation favors gallstone formation (7). Animal observations agree in principle; there are variations in the metabolism of individual bile acids. Bile acid uptake by hepatocytes, which is reduced during immaturity, is not diminished by age. So far it is difficult to obtain a clear picture of the changes of the various metabolic activities, and additional studies hardly explain the selectivity of the functional alterations in the aging liver.

Response of the Liver to Modulators (*Adaptation*)

The response of the liver in aged persons to hormones and other circulating modulators acting on its epithelial and mesenchymal cells appears to be somewhat reduced, and some receptor functions seem to be decreased, either as a result of defects in the receptors or after ligand–receptor binding. Moreover, extrahepatic synthesis of hormones may decrease. Today, however, much of the pertinent information is derived from cells other than hepatic cells. As reliable techniques become standardized and baseline data accumulate, it is a promising area of clinical research in the aged to confirm the prevailing notion that hepatic homeostasis and adaptation are impaired, as is known for immunologic surveillance in general. The anatomic position of the liver, which provides it with high concentrations of pancreas- and intestine-derived growth factors, may compensate for defects of hepatic receptors. Because these large numbers of modulating agents are not only important in the variations of phenotypic expression of the hepatic cells but also in the alterations of cell proliferation in aging, reference is made to the general discussion of modulation and regulation under Functions of the Several Cell Types in the Aging Liver on p. 254.

Role of the Liver in Drug Metabolism in the Aged

Alterations of hepatic drug metabolism influence the dosage of drugs to be given to older people. This problem is in part related to alterations in the extrahepatic factors that determine blood level and, with it, bioavailability of the drug in the elderly. There is little evidence for impaired intestinal absorption of drugs, some indications of disturbance of renal excretion, a possibility of altered body distribution of drugs because of variations in the drug-retaining fat compartment of the body, and, probably most important, variations of binding of drugs to blood carriers, particularly albumin. Albumin concentration is not reduced in older individuals in the absence of malnutrition, but impaired binding is a remote possibility because of qualitative changes of albumin (see later).

A reduction of blood flow may play a role in drug metabolism, mostly for drugs such as propranolol, which are readily taken up by the liver on first passage. However, most of the interest focuses on altered metabolic transformation in the liver. It deserves description not only from the point of view of drug metabolism but also from that of oxygen toxicity as a possible cause of aging and therefore is here discussed in some detail.

Biotransformation System

Many endogenous and exogenous substances, including environmental and dietary chemicals as well as drugs, are lipid-soluble and in this form not necessarily bioactive. They undergo biotransformation, often in several consecutive steps, to metabolites with variable biologic activity; eventually they become water-soluble, to be excreted by the cell or by the body in urine or bile. Most of these biotransformation processes occur in the phospholipid membranes of the endoplasmic reticulum, mainly in its smooth portion but also in the nuclear membrane and less so in the cell membrane. The liver is the main site of this biotransformation system (24,27), with lesser amounts in other, predominantly epithelial cells. The key hemoprotein enzymes are the monooxygenases, or mixed-function oxidases, which consist of cytochromes P_{450}, so called because their complex with carbon monoxide has a characteristic absorption spectrum at 450 nm. Chemical analysis and genetic studies indicate several variants of cytochrome P_{450}, often with different substrate specificity. The cytochromes P_{450} act on the lipophilic ligands with the help of a flavoprotein (cytochrome c) reductase which depends on reduced nicotinamide adenine nucleotide phosphate (NADPH) (Fig. 1). In this process one molecule of molecular oxygen (O_2) is reduced to water (H_2O), and the other serves hydroxylation of the ligands or similar oxidative reactions, e.g., formation of epoxides and sulfoxidation. Sometimes reduction of the ligand occurs. In these processes cytochrome P_{450} serves as a terminal component of an electron transport chain, with one electron transferred via NADPH and another added subsequently. Thus a series of reactions are possible, all of which result in activation of the ligand as well as formation of various active and potentially toxic oxygen species. Ligands with hydroxyl radicals may bind to several conjugating enzymes such as glutathione-, glucuronosyl-, or sulfotransferases or to epoxide hydrolases. The reaction product is, as a rule, no longer bioactive (except for some epoxide conjugates) and is removed as a hydrophilic substance by excretion from the cells and from the organism; this process is in effect detoxification. Other active metabolites exert, in part by covalent binding to proteins such as enzymes, their physiological, pharmacologic, and potentially toxic reactions. Binding to other macromolecules, particularly to DNA and less so to RNA, results in their hydroxylation or sometimes alkylation; it leads to mutation or to initiation of carcinogenesis. Finally, in these complex oxidoreductive processes active oxygen radicals may be formed, depending on the number of electrons added. If an additional unpaired electron is added, a superoxide (O_2^-) or the especially toxic active hydroxyl radical OH· forms. An example is cytochrome P_{450}-produced toxic oxygen radical cleavage products of carbon tetrachloride. It is not certain whether metabolite-bound free oxygen radicals (O_2^- or OH·) formed during the biotransformation are active *in vivo*. Moreover, in the reductive form of cytochrome P_{450}-dependent transformation, hydroperoxides develop; some may interact in the presence of iron ions with O_2^- to form additional active hydroxyls (OH·). The several active oxygen species are counteracted by a complex antioxidant system consisting of ascorbic acid, α-tocopherol, radical scavengers (e.g., carotenoids or retinoids), and the enzymes superoxide dismutase or catalases. Finally, reduced glutathione, which is diet-dependent, acts as an antioxidant and in addition may bind toxic metabolites with resulting depletion of its stores. The various oxygen species have essential physiological functions, but they are also incriminated in liver cell injury, e.g., by their relation to the calcium balance or to the destruction of phospholipid membranes and of cytochrome P_{450} itself enclosed in such membranes (21). One theory of aging is based on oxygen toxicity (16); the shorter the life span of a species, the greater is the amount of peroxidable material in tissue (4).

The amount of oxygen production depends also on the specific variant of the cytochrome P_{450}. The alcohol-metabolizing variant produces much toxic oxygen. Another variant, previously designated cytochrome P_{448}, is characterized by a large binding site for lipophilic ligands, e.g., steroids or carcinogens. It interacts with some drugs and is induced by methylcholanthrene and produces more oxygen

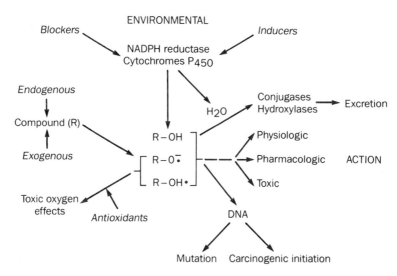

FIG. 1. Microsomal biotransformation of drugs and the formation of toxic oxygen species. Aging potentially influences all steps. *R* = ligand.

than another variant, which is phenobarbital-induced and acts on drugs and lipids. The lower the body weight and the shorter the life expectancy of the species, the greater is the oxygen production in the liver (17). In addition to this relation between hepatic oxygen production on one side and life-span and aging on the other, the increased activity of the cytochrome P_{450} in rodents compared to man accounts also for their greater response to environmental agents in biologic activity, toxification, and detoxification, as well as carcinogenesis.

The microsomal biotransformation processes may be divided into (a) the cytochrome P_{450}-dependent, class I, essentially oxidative reactions, and (b) the conjugating or hydrating, class II reactions. Both are under genetic control but also are greatly influenced by environmental factors, including drugs, alcohol, and smoking. These factors may increase the activity of the system (induction) or inhibit it (blockage) and thus modulate the biotransformation system. Also of major importance is diet, which includes dietary protein content, with deficiency reducing cytochrome P_{450} activity, and amino acid precursors (methionine, cysteine) of glutathione. It also takes into consideration the amount of saturation of dietary phospholipids, as the constitution and fluidity of the phospholipid membranes, particularly the endoplasmic reticulum, influence activity of the enzymes (25), e.g., the monooxygenases, located in the membrane. Thus in the response of the liver to drugs and other environmental agents, in addition to extrahepatic factors, the activity of the constituent drug-metabolizing enzymes and their response to inducing and blocking agents enter the picture. The finely tuned balance of the combined microsomal biotransformation system and the toxic oxygen species metabolism appear to be a promising target of aging research because variations of the balance may be important in: (a) the usually multistep biotransformation of drugs, controlling their effectiveness as well as their potential hepatic toxicity, the latter possibly increased during aging; (b) the explanation of senescence; and (c) the vague possibility of its potential retardation by dietary means.

Variations in Drug Responses by the Aged

Species and sex differences as well as genetic factors (inbred or outbred animals) may account for the many controversial statements in the literature. Particularly observations in humans or other primates and in rats are often contradictory. In brief review, it is not yet established whether hepatic uptake of drugs is impaired because of receptor alterations, and little is known about drug transport within the hepatocytes. In rats there are indications of reduced activity of the NADPH-dependent cytochrome c reductase (26), which seems to be identical for all variants of cytochrome P_{450}. This enzyme appears to have reduced catalytic activity (26). There is no agreement on whether cytochrome P_{450} activity is reduced in rodents; most investigators favor the idea of such a reduction, however, which may also result from age-dependent alterations of the supporting phospholipid membrane, e.g., relative increased cholesterol content or fatty acid saturation. This situation may inhibit the lateral mobility of the monooxygenase complex required in its function (15,25,26). Interestingly, when old-age effects were observed, sex differences disappeared in older rats; the higher monooxygenase activity of younger male rats was explained by a hormonal influence fading in older age rather than by constitutive changes of the endoplasmic reticulum (11). Induction in rats, e.g., by phenobarbital, seems to be reduced or at least delayed.

The reported significant differences in the responses of aged man to the various drugs probably depend on the variants of the cytochrome P_{450} involved and the type of ensuing reaction (e.g., hydroxylation, N-demethylation). Reference is made to the many reviews that record human experiences with various drugs (10,12, 13,19). The metabolism of the now widely used cimetidine appears to be significantly reduced. Similarly, the literature is not unanimous as to the effect of age on induction in man.

There seems to be more agreement on the class II reactions, most of which do not change in the aged and may even show increased activity as they often do with hepatocyte injury. There is a similarity between aging and cirrhosis so far as hepatic drug metabolism is concerned. With both aging and cirrhosis hepatocytic activity is less altered than extrahepatic factors: with cirrhosis the intrahepatic circulation, and in the elderly hormonal and other modulating factors.

The important area of drug metabolism in aging, an area pioneered by two Japanese investigators, Kato and Kitani, does not yet provide reliable general guidelines for dose prescription to the elderly in view of the selectivity of the observed alterations, with the possible exception of drugs taken up by the liver on first passage, e.g., propranolol. Otherwise, observance of tolerance in the individual elderly patient and for each drug is recommended. In view of possible drug interactions, watchfulness is particularly recommended if several drugs are given simultaneously, as is so frequently the case in the elderly. At present, clarification of this important practical problem can best be expected from progress in investigations of the aging effects on the conformation and turnover of proteins, discussed under Macromolecules in the Aging Liver on p. 259.

FUNCTIONS OF THE SEVERAL CELL TYPES IN THE AGING LIVER

Pertinent observations concern the kinetics of renewal as well as of specific cell and organelle functions of the hepatocytes and the other cells of the liver.

Kinetics of Hepatocyte Renewal

The problems of hepatocyte renewal kinetics involve the behavior of the cells in the body and in culture. Some of this area of interest requires reviewing the regulation of differentiation and proliferation or regeneration.

Hepatocyte Renewal and Regeneration

Despite earlier optimistic reports, hepatocytes, either human or rodent, even embryonal, are difficult to keep in continuous culture, in contrast to hepatoma cell lines. Human primary cell lines were maintained for more than 3 weeks only in co-culture with rat epithelial cells, which permits viability up to 2 months. Thus the effect of aging can barely be quantitated; and only the response of the hepatocytes in culture to proliferating stimuli, particularly on DNA synthesis reflected in thymidine incorporation, can be evaluated, as the latter may increase up to 600-fold. However, nonsynchronous DNA synthesis complicates the evaluation.

In contrast to rapidly renewing cells (e.g., bone marrow or intestinal epithelium) and the permanently postreplicative cells (neurons and most muscle cells), the facultatively replicating hepatocytes are renewed only once or twice during the life-span of the individual under normal conditions but turn over more rapidly when stimulated. Such stimulation may be induced by loss of a sufficient number of hepatocytes from necrosis or, more quantifiable, partial hepatectomy. Moreover, reduction of hepatocytic function without cell loss by necrosis also increases the size (hypertrophy) and number (hyperplasia) of hepatocytes. With preserved parenchymal architecture, the increases develop predominantly in the periportal zone. Regenerating hepatocytes are resistant to cytotoxic factors, have fewer receptors, are less capable of fulfilling the specialized cell functions, and are devoid of the lipofuscin of aging cells. There is no agreement as to the factors that induce enlargement and accelerated turnover of hepatocytes. One possibility is the increased demand on the persisting hepatocytes, which is illustrated by the hypertrophy and hyperplasia stimulated by drugs the hepatocytes metabolize. Another explanation, at present more emphasized, are humoral stimulators of proliferation. These hepatotropic factors are either liver-specific agents formed in the liver following hepatectomy (hematopoietins), so far moderately well identified, or not necessarily liver-specific regulators.

Diminished proliferation of hepatocytes during aging after liver cell injury or hepatectomy was described many years ago. Ever since that report a reduction of the regeneratory potential of the aging liver has been postulated, as it has in clinical circumstances. Quantitative studies with hepatectomy reveal reduced mitosis and a reduction in the pool of regenerating hepatocytes, as well as delays in the onset of mitosis or in the formation of hepatocytes and its constituents such as the endoplasmic reticulum. However, because more mitotic cycles may set in, overall regeneration seems not to be significantly impaired, and there is no evidence for its qualitative alteration.

The spontaneous, presumably programmed death of human hepatocytes develops by the morphologic characteristic apoptosis, which is an energy-dependent process different from hepatocyte death following most liver cell injuries. Because the turnover of the hepatocytes is related to the life-span or the maximum life-span potential of the species (the latter in part related to the body weight) the life-span of the hepatocytes in rodents seems to be about ⅓₀ of that in humans. Far less lipofuscin accumulates in rodent hepatocytes, and thus pigment deposition depends more on actual time than on relative age. It is not certain whether the more rapid senescence of rodent hepatocytes results from such factors as increased tissue stores of peroxidable material (4), higher tissue oxygen concentration, and basal metabolism (17) or is directly gene-determined. It has been estimated that about 7,000 of the 100,000 genes of the human species may be potentially significant, with 70 loci deserving the most attention (16). The difference in onset of hepatocyte senescence in various species, e.g., between humans and rodents, not only interferes with extrapolation of results on aging but also explains the greater tendency to hepatic tumors in rodents because the more frequent division of hepatocytes serves as a strong promoting factor.

Tumorous Proliferation with Aging

The higher incidence of many variants of tumors in the elderly is well established, and spontaneous tumors are known to occur more frequently in old animals. It is not certain to what degree it reflects the beginning of tumor formation many years before, as growth of existing tumors is usually slow. Several sequential steps are now assumed in carcinogenesis, (chemical, physical, or viral). The first, initiation, is considered an alteration of DNA, e.g., by chemical metabolites formed by microsomal biotransformation, which, if anything, is less active at older age. Indeed, aging does not have a significant influence on the effect of DNA-altering carcinogens except that possibly the tumors appear earlier. Formation of mutagens seems to be diminished. The subsequent steps involve promotion, implying primarily cell division. Again, aging should retard it, though experimentally more tumors have been found in aging rodents after exposure to the promoting phenobarbital. Whether aging reduces the induction of biotransformation by environmental chemicals is not certain, and it may vary with different agents. In summary, further studies are required to establish whether the susceptibility to carcinogenesis from environmental factors is altered during aging. Adequate technology and baseline data are available.

Renewal of Nonhepatic Cells of the Liver

The life-span of the epithelium of the bile ducts appears to be similar to that of the hepatocytes. By contrast, the half-life of proliferating bile ductules is less than 2 weeks. This short half-life is reflected in the absence of pigments such as hemosiderin when hepatocytes and bile duct cells are loaded in iron overload diseases. The life-span of the sinusoidal cells, particularly of the macrophagic Kupffer cells and endothelial cells, is relatively short; but it is of interest that Kupffer cells that have phagocytosed material live long. Elucidation of this problem may contribute to the understanding of aging. After hepatectomy the proliferation of nonhepatocytic cells begins later than that of the hepatocytes, which indicates delayed stimulation. Bile duct epithelium starts proliferation after the hepatocytes and before the sinusoidal cells. The hardiest cells of the liver are the fibroblasts. In any cell or organ culture of the liver, fibroblasts grow out most readily, followed by myofibroblasts, possibly related to interstitial fat-storing (Ito) cells, endothelial cells, and eventually bile duct cells. Fibroblasts are a long-established model for study of aging (see Hayflick, *this volume*). It is not certain to what degree these observations apply to the resting fibrocytes and to the fibroblasts proliferating in disorders of the liver.

Regulation of Phenotypic Expression, Differentiation, and Normal or Abnormal Proliferation

It has become clear that the phenotypic expressions of the liver cells are determined by regulatory factors acting alone or in sequence in a regulatory chain (20). These factors are either: (a) primary gene products, exemplified by hormones and growth factors for epithelial or mesenchymal cells; (b) the virtually unlimited number of secondary gene products, which include nutrients and intermediary metabolites, the arachidonic acid oxidation products, particularly leukotrienes and prostaglandins, retinol and retinoids, lipoproteins, and ion fluxes; or (c) the matrix substances referred to before. Although both concentration and constitution of all these regulators may also determine aging in a fashion to be explored, of most interest are the modulators that are primary gene products. Many bind to receptors in the cell membrane, the cytoplasm, or possibly the nucleus. Binding to cell membrane receptors mobilizes "secondary messengers" (the cyclic nucleotides), the cytosolic concentration of ionized calcium, and the recently appreciated breakdown of phosphatidylinositol. The latter is a small component of the membrane phospholipids, which in turn interacts with ion fluxes and cytosolic ionized calcium to stimulate cell proliferation. The genes of the various modulators are being identified, and of interest is the information that some of the oncogenes code for some growth factors, receptors, or modulators of cell membrane receptors, linking knowledge derived from carcinogenesis with nontumorous proliferation and other metabolic reactions. Ionized calcium-dependent protein kinase-induced phosphorylation not only initiates and stimulates reversible metabolic processes (e.g., in carbohydrate or lipid metabolism) but also cell proliferation. Phosphorylation of proteins is now considered a main regulatory mechanism in the body. Thus the difference between growth factors (often called mitogens) that induce cells to enter the mitotic cycle and modulators that stimulate metabolic processes is fading. The nonmitogenic modulating effects are far more important in the phenotypic expressions of the slowly dividing hepatocytes. The circulating modulators of epithelial cells are the classic peptide hormones (e.g., insulin or glucagon) and the other epithelial growth factors (e.g., the insulin-like and the transforming or tumor growth factors). The latter group of growth factors differs from the prototype, the peptide hormones, by their activity at much lower concentration, a shorter half-life, and by their having endocrine activity not only via the circulation but also by direct action on neighboring cells or even on the cells synthesizing them. The lipid-soluble hormones, exemplified by steroid and thyroid hormones, are in fact similar growth factors except that they bind to intracellular receptors. The knowledge of the role of the mesenchymal cell growth factors, exemplified by lymphokines or interleukins, in the liver is not only restricted to Kupffer cells.

The various modulators act singly or in concerted fashion to induce the reversible metabolic or irreversible proliferative or transforming (including carcinomatous) reactions. This regulatory chain may eventually terminate in programmed cell death. It is seriously altered in the common abnormal hepatic reactions (disorganization of a network of interacting key events) (21), which may terminate in unscheduled cell death. This chain also responds to environmental demands by adaptation, which during aging may be disturbed by mechanisms not yet explored. Such studies on the hepatocytes are a promising aspect of aging research because, again, much baseline information is available and the process is slower than in shorter-lived cells and probably more reactive than in nondividing cells.

Specific Functions of Individual Hepatocytes

Information on the function of isolated aged hepatocytes includes an increased albumin content and a reduced uptake of BSP, particularly by hepatocytes with polyploid nuclei. These cells with increased nuclear DNA store less BSP. The integrity of their mitochrondria is apparently not changed, and the enzymatic activity of the large hepatocytes may even be increased. Published data suggest that the overall respiratory activity per gram of liver may be slightly reduced, but that of the individual hepatocytes, particularly the large ones, is preserved or even increased.

Specific Function of the Nonhepatocytes in the Liver

Kupffer cells, both isolated and in the body, show reduced phagocytic activity by a variety of testing techniques (2). This reduction is associated with increased activity of most of their lysosomal enzymes. The role of macrophagic Kupffer cells in antigen presentation and complement clearance is an area requiring more aging research. The endocytosis of the endothelial cells also appears to be reduced (2). The width of their fenestrae, which regulates access of circulating substances to the hepatocytes (31) during aging, deserves study, as does the function of the interstitial fat-storing cells, which seem to be involved in fibroplasia and in regulating (by their extensions) the hepatic microcirculation. Because the sinusoidal and perisinusoidal cells participate in immunologic activities, their alterations during aging may be more readily influenced by therapeutic strategies than those of the hepatocytes with far more complex functions.

MACROMOLECULES IN THE AGING LIVER

In view of the few observations on phospholipids, most of the interest concerns proteins and nucleic acids. Although the molecular biology of aging probably represents the cutting edge of biologic aging research, relatively few firm data concern the liver (6,8,19), and therefore this rapidly expanding field is reviewed here only sketchily. Moreover, any information recorded may be outdated by the time this book appears.

Evidence has been presented that selected proteins undergo conformational changes of their three-dimensional structure, possibly from posttranslational events. This change, which is reflected in their reduced enzymatic but preserved immunologic activity, might explain accumulation of "junk" protein, including the excess albumin and altered aldolase B in aging hepatocytes. There is some suggestion of reduced global protein synthesis in the liver. Reliable data indicate impaired formation of some proteins, e.g., α_{u2}-globulin, the major urinary protein in the male rat, synthesized by a specific subpopulation of hepatocytes. However, there seems to be more evidence for diminished protein breakdown during aging, reflected in reduced activity of proteases, but respiratory enzymes appear more reduced than hydrolytic ones. There is also no clear indication of diminished DNA synthesis during aging or of reduced fidelity of transcription; the latter probably because of the large number of available DNA repair enzymes. DNA polymerase in aging mice does not have less fidelity, not even in regeneration. Chromosomes are supposedly altered, including their chromatin and histones. The protein synthetic activity of ribosomes in cell-free preparations has been found uniformly reduced; however, messenger RNA activity of at least one enzyme is induced. In preliminary hybridization studies, albumin messenger RNA was found increased, which might reflect a prolonged life-span of the messenger. Fidelity of translation seems to be impaired. Again, one has the impression that great selectivity prevails in the molecular biologic alterations described so far. The impairment in adaptation seems to result from alterations of assumed translational, posttranslational, or catabolic processes, all of which require clarification.

RESPONSE OF THE LIVER TO INJURY

Experimentally induced liver injury is not necessarily more severe in aging animals than in younger animals. Various results have been recorded; but on balance, aging seems not to exert an effect. Similarly, the available evidence, also presented in various monographs on diseases of the elderly (1,9), does not list liver diseases that are restricted to the elderly and only limited indications of more severe liver disease in aging except where immunologic factors enter the picture (e.g., liver abscess formation, chronic hepatitis, and hypersensitivity reactions to drugs). It is not even certain whether the elderly are more susceptible to these drug reactions, as it appears on first view, or they simply reflect increased drug intake in this group. In general, one might assume that the same liver diseases occur in the elderly as in those who are younger. It is important to remember that alcoholic liver disease and cirrhosis are frequent in the aged, and furthermore that secondary effects of aging, e.g., mental disease and malnutrition, may obscure an existing liver disease.

EFFECT OF THE LIVER ON AGING OF THE BODY

Whether the liver has any influence on the aging of the body is a matter of speculation. If environmental chemicals play a direct or indirect role in the aging process, the hepatic biotransformation system may be protective, and the macrophagic Kupffer cells may prevent injury from microbial and immunologic causes. If oxygen radicals play a significant role in aging (4), the activity of the liver may be important. In addition to the formation of these radicals, which in view of their short life-span do not travel readily and therefore probably do not have a systemic action, the amount of peroxidative material (essentially lipid membranes) and to some degree antioxidant activity are important. In both of these aspects, liver metabolism and the dietary supply, mostly channeled through the liver, may be influential. One might speculate that drugs or diet may, in addition to altering or stimulating sinusoidal cell phagocytosis, influence microsomal biotransformation and thus have an effect on senescence. Such dietary variations may include the type and amount of proteins, the supply of glutathione precursors or antioxidants, and modification of phospholipids (25). Finally, the possibility arises that so far unknown bioactive compounds synthesized in the liver may act as both growth-stimulating and growth-inhibiting agents in aging, as suggested by various parabiosis experiments so far difficult to explain.

SUMMARIZING REVIEW

The effects of aging on the liver are far less dramatic or alarming than those of other organs; as with aging of the spleen, laboratory abnormalities predominate (32). So far, selectivity of effects, as well as increased variations in the hepatic cells and their constituents, seem to be in the foreground, as well as altered response or adaptation to extrahepatocellular factors. Of practical significance is the observation that altered results of liver function tests in the elderly point to a disease rather than to aging, and that the response to drugs may be changed but not in a uniform or predictable fashion except that drugs removed by the liver on first passage remain longer in the blood.

If one would choose priorities in laboratory research on hepatic problems related to liver and aging, it would be to identify the specific defects in three processes: (a) the predominantly microsomal biotransformation and the associated metabolism of toxic oxygen species; (b) the host responses and other adaptations; and (c) molecular biology. The first process not only influences drug bioavailability and therapy in the elderly, it also concerns one of the postulated causes of the body's senescence, i.e., oxygen toxicity. Analysis of the host response has long been attempted, but abundant information is accumulating about new modulators, particularly epithelial or mesenchymal growth factors, arachidonic acid oxidation products, and lipoprotein and ionic mediators. Moreover, the mechanism of their action is being clarified, including their genes, receptors, postreceptor events, and the anatomy of the regulatory chain. Abnormal hepatic reactions are no longer considered to result from a singly abnormal reaction but, rather, from alteration of a network of interacting key events; the effect of aging may be another such alteration. Stress induced by environment is an important example, though the preliminary evidence available at this time fails to suggest increased susceptibility of the aging liver. Even if some depression of biotransformation exists, it may, on one hand, reduce formation of toxic metabolites and carcinogens as well as induction and, on the other hand, diminish detoxification, not to mention the difficult extrapolation from rodents to the far less sensitive humans. Little is certain at this time about the molecular biology of aging, which might eventually explain the first two processes. More speculative would be an attempt to develop therapeutic strategies to improve the status of the aging liver if that would indeed be required and, in the sense of interventional gerontology, to delay senescence of the body via influences of the liver. Finally, study of the aging of the liver may be useful in general gerontology, as the fact that it does not undergo senescence may permit recognition of principles not as readily recognized in organs that wither from secondary effects such as vascular abnormalities. Moreover, general pathobiology may benefit if aging is considered a readily available experiment of nature in which one factor, time, is varied.

REFERENCES

1. Brandt, L. J. (1984): *Gastrointestinal Disorders of the Elderly*. Raven Press, New York.
2. Brouwer, A., Barelds, R., and Knook, D. L. (1985): Age-related changes in the endocytic capacity of rat liver Kupffer and endothelial cells. *Hepatology*, 5:362–366.
3. Daniels, C. K., Schmucker, D. L., and Jones, A. L. (1985): Age dependent loss of dimeric immunoglobulin A receptors in the liver of the Fischer 344 rat. *J. Immunol.*, 134:3355–3358.
4. Cutler, R. G. (1985): Peroxide-producing potential of tissues: inverse correlation with longevity of mammalian species. *Proc. Natl. Acad. Sci. USA*, 82:4798–4802.
5. David, H. (1985): *The Hepatocyte—Development, Differentiation, and Ageing*. VEB Gustav Fischer Verlag, Jena.
6. Dice, J. F. (1985): Cellular theories of aging. *Hepatology*, 5:508–513.
7. Einarsson, K., Nilsell, K., Leijd, B., and Angelin, B. (1985): Influence of age on secretion of cholesterol and synthesis of bile acids by the liver. *N. Engl. J. Med.*, 313:277–282.

8. Frolkis, V. V., and Litoshenko, A. Y. (1982): Aging of the liver cells. *Interdiscip. Top. Gerontol.,* 18:122–134.

9. Hellemans, J., and Vantrappen, G., editors (1984): *Gastrointestinal Tract Disorders in the Elderly.* Churchill Livingstone, London.

10. James, O. F. W. (1985): Drugs and the ageing liver. *J. Hepatol.,* 1:431–435.

11. Kitagawa, H., Fujita, S., Suzuki, T., and Kitani, K. (1985): Disappearance of sex difference in rat liver drug metabolism in old age. *Biochem. Pharmacol.,* 34:579–581.

12. Kitani, K., editor (1978): *Liver and Aging—1978.* Elsevier/North Holland, Amsterdam.

13. Kitani, K., editor (1982): *Liver and Aging—1982: Liver and Drugs.* Elsevier, Amsterdam.

14. Kohn, R. R. (1978): *Principles of Mammalian Aging,* 2nd ed. Prentice-Hall, Englewood Cliffs, NJ.

15. Maloney, A. G., Vessey, D. A., and Schmucker, D. L. (1985): The effects of aging on the fluidity of hepatic microsomal membranes in non-human primates. *Gastroenterology,* 88:1676.

16. Martin, G. M. (1977): Cellular aging—clonal senescence: a review. 1. Some general considerations of the pathobiology of aging: definition of senescence. *Am. J. Pathol.,* 89:484–511.

17. Parke, D. V., and Ioannides, C. (1984): Reactive intermediates and oxygen toxicity in liver injury. In: *Mechanisms of Hepatocyte Injury and Death,* edited by D. Keppler, pp. 37–48. MTP Press, Lancaster.

18. Platt, D., editor (1977): *Liver and Ageing.* Schattauer Verlag, Stuttgart.

19. Popper, H. (1986): Aging and the liver. In: *Progress in Liver Diseases, Vol. VIII,* edited by H. Popper and F. Schaffner, pp. 659–683. Grune & Stratton, Orlando. See also Popper, H. (1985): Relations between liver and aging. *Semin. Liver Dis.,* 5:221–227; and Popper, H. (1987): The liver in aging. In: *Modern Biological Theories of Aging,* edited by H. R. Warner, R. N. Butler, R. L. Sprott, and E. L. Schneider, pp. 219–234. Raven Press, New York.

20. Popper, H., and Acs, G. (1985): Regulatory factors in pathologic processes of the liver: modulators and interacting metabolic networks. *Semin. Liver Dis.,* 5:191–208.

21. Popper, H., and Keppler, D. (1986): Networks of interacting mechanisms of hepatocellular degeneration and death. In: *Progress in Liver Diseases, Vol. VIII,* edited by H. Popper and F. Schaffner, pp. 209–235. Grune & Stratton, Orlando.

22. Popper, H., and Martin, G. R. (1982): Fibrosis of the liver: the role of the ectoskeleton. *Prog. Liver Dis.,* 7:133–156.

23. Rojkind, M. (1982): Fibrogenesis. In: *The Liver. Biology and Pathobiology,* edited by I. M. Arias, H. Popper, D. Schachter, and D. A. Shafritz, pp. 801–809. Raven Press, New York.

24. Sato, R., and Omura, T., editors (1978): *Cytochrome P-450.* Kodansha Ltd., Tokyo, and Academic Press, New York.

25. Schachter, D. (1984): Fluidity and function of hepatocyte plasma membranes. *Hepatology,* 4:140–151.

26. Schmucker, D. L. (1985): Subcellular and molecular mechanisms underlying the age-related decline in liver drug metabolism. In: *The Aging Process: Therapeutic Implications,* edited by R. N. Butler and A. G. Bearn, pp. 117–134. Raven Press, New York.

27. Singer, B., and Grunberger, D. (1983): *Molecular Biology of Mutagens and Carcinogens.* Plenum Press, New York.

28. Tauchi, H., and Sato, T. (1978): Hepatic cells of the aged. In: *Liver and Aging,* edited by K. Kitani, pp. 3–19. Elsevier/North Holland, Amsterdam.

29. Van Bezooijen, C. F. A., editor (1984): *Pharmacological, Morphological and Physiological Aspects of Liver Aging. Topics in Aging Research in Europe, Vol. 1.* Eurage, Rijswijk.

30. Watanabe, T., and Tanaka, Y. (1982): Age-related alterations in the size of human hepatocytes: a study of mononuclear and binucleate cells. *Virchows Arch [Cell Pathol.],* 39:9–20.

31. Wisse, E., de Zanger, R. B., Charles, K., van der Smissen, P., and McCuskey, R. S. (1985): The liver sieve: considerations concerning the structure and function of endothelial fenestrae, the sinusoidal wall and the space of Disse. *Hepatology,* 5:683–692.

32. Zago, M. A., Figueiredo, M. S., Covas, D. T., and Bottura, C. (1985): Aspects of splenic hypofunction in old age. *Klin. Wochenschr.,* 63:590–592.

Human Aging Research: Concepts and Techniques,
edited by B. Kent and R. N. Butler.
Raven Press, Ltd., New York © 1988.

Respiratory Changes of Aging

Michael D. Lebowitz

Department of Internal Medicine, Pulmonary Disease Section, University of Arizona College of Medicine, Tucson, Arizona 85724

Conceptually, one must recognize that aging in humans is associated with decreased performance capabilities, especially exercise capacity and performing at high altitudes. These changes are related predominantly to the capacity of the lungs decreasing with aging, changes based on reduced functioning of lung tissue, anatomical structures, and biochemical alterations. These changes are subtle, occurring over the entire adult age span. Furthermore, not all individuals are affected to the same degree. In general, even with these changes, the respiratory system is resilient, to the extent that the older system adequately supports function. In the absence of major acute and chronic diseases, the aging lung adequately adapts to aging and permits a full range of activities. It is the subtle, gradual changes with age that are explored in this chapter, as well as some specific disease processes that are age-related.

PHYSIOLOGICAL ALTERATIONS

Functionally, the mature adult population exhibits a wide range of normal behavior. Many host and experiential factors have contributed to this great variability. The primary factors are inhalation injury, permanent sequelae of pulmonary infections, host immune system characteristics, and other modulators of lung development (including growth under conditions of high altitude, nutritional support/deprivation, exercise, and endocrine/biochemical activity). Because of the many external insults, it is difficult to distinguish normal from atypical changes with aging (16,24).

In the absence of cigarette smoking, major occupational exposures, and disease, there is a reduction of both volume excursions and instantaneous expiratory flow rates (at different parts of the flow–volume curve) with age. The typical reduction does not reach the level of clinical disease, even in the elderly, for even the lower segment of the distribution in the asymptomatic nonsmoking populati n. The major changes are seen in the vital capacity (VC), which decreases with age after 20 to 35, and the residual volume (RV), which increases with age. Total lung capacity (TLC), which is the sum of the VC and RV, changes little with age. As the VC changes, the forced vital capacity (FVC) and forced expiratory volume in 1 second (FEV_1) decrease with age, as do the flow rates. The functional residual capacity (FRC), which is the resting lung volume at the end of normal respiration, increases with age; it is the balance between chest wall and lung elastic forces. Lung elastic recoil decreases with age as the lung becomes more distensible (13). Chest wall compliance decreases with age (22), and expiratory muscles become weaker (13), both leading to the increase in RV (13). However, changes in the chest wall and respiratory muscles with age are not likely to be responsible for the increased air trapping (hyperinflation) seen on chest roentgenograms (16). The changes in instantaneous flows are related to the changes in lung elastic recoil, the frictional resistance of the airways peripherally, and the cross-sectional area and compliance of the central (larger) airways subject to dynamic compression (13). Changes in lung parenchyma, distribution of ventilation, and airway closure can be observed with aging (16).

The ultimate function of the respiratory system is gas exchange, and arterial oxygen pressures (Pao_2) are reduced with age. The alteration is due to changes in lung mechanics (described above) and increasing ventilation–perfusion imbalances with age (16). Arterial carbon dioxide tension ($Paco_2$) does not appear to be age-related. Diffusion across the alveolar–capillary membranes appears to be affected by age, which is affected by the blood flow to the lung and its distribution, the surface available for gas exchange, and the resistance to diffusion. These factors appear to be affected by aging, along with ventilation changes. The decrease of cardiac output and the changes in capillaries with aging, which influence perfusion and diffusion, are important and distinct topics. The large pulmonary vessels can develop atherosclerotic plaques, and the medium-size ones can develop increased stiffness (16). Fibrosis of small pulmonary artery intima is common, increasing vascular resistance: Although blood flow in the elderly can be uniform, the vascular response to hypoxia appears blunted (16). Smoking appears to accelerate physiological changes seen with aging (12).

BIOCHEMICAL ALTERATIONS

Collagen and elastin are the basic structural components of the lung parenchyma and, along with the proteoglycans, make up the connective tissue components of the lung. Collagen, the predominant protein in the lung (comprising about 10–20% of the dry weight), has been difficult to assay because of its insolubility and its heterogeneous macromolecular structure. As indicated in the review by Krumpe et al. (16), staining techniques have yielded confusing, contradictory results. In general, the ratios of the major types do not appear to change radically with age. Likewise, proteoglycans are not appreciably different with age. Elastin content in the lung does appear to increase with age, and there appears to be a related change in the protease/antiprotease activity with age. An increase in elastin fibers in the lung with age are considered to be a major part of the structural remodeling. The effects of this increase on functional changes in elasticity have not been determined.

Surfactant formation and activity (i.e., preservation of alveolar tension and maintenance of alveolar competence), as measured by lecithin and palmitic acid activity, do not appear to change markedly with aging. Changes in calcium deposition with age are important also in the respiratory system. There appears to be increased calcification of cartilage, as in the trachea, leading to changes in large airway behavior. There appears to be a reduction of calcification of the rib cage and vertebrae, partly responsible for the changes observed in chest wall mechanics. There are decreases in biosynthesis in the lung as well with age, related to protein changes and decreased repair of DNA/RNA lesions.

ANATOMICAL AND MORPHOMETRIC ALTERATIONS

The large airways appear to increase in diameter with aging, thereby increasing the amount of lung not engaged in ventilation (anatomical "dead space"), and the trachea becomes stiffer (21,25). Distally, the bronchioles decrease in diameter, and the alveolar ducts increase in volume (25). Structure, especially changes in alveolar septa, appear to be occurring with aging (25). Even without pulmonary disease, the lungs of the elderly appear to be smaller and flabbier (21,25). Smaller airways do close and appear to relate to the increased air trapping seen radiographically; both progress with age.

In addition to the decalcification of ribs and vertebrae, calcification of costal cartilages occurs, and osteoporosis of the spine with kyphosis or scoliosis occurs with aging. The overall stiffness of the chest wall, accompanied by the configuration of the chest wall, accounts for the greater dependence of abdominal and diaphragmatic contributions to ventilation in the elderly (3). These changes contribute also to the gravity gradient in the lung and the appearance of air trapping in the upper lung zones (3).

NEUROLOGICAL ALTERATIONS

Krumpe et al. (16) reviewed neurological alterations. There appears to be a blunting of the chemoreceptor response to hypoxia related to a decrease in respiratory neuronal outflow or blunted response to mechanical loads; force requirements may be used as cues for ventilation more than volume displacement in the elderly. Ventilatory response to aerobic exercise seems unimpaired despite blunted CO_2 responses, apparently as a compensation for impaired gas exchange and increased dead space.

The leakage of transmitter acetylcholine from diaghragmatic neuromuscular junctions appears to be increased with age (although diaghragmatic neuromuscular coupling is not decreased), influencing neurological activity. Furthermore, the amount of extracellular magnesium needed to block phrenic nerve stimulation of diaghragmatic contraction appears to be less, at least in animal models of aging.

IMMUNOLOGICAL ALTERATIONS

There appears to be a definite change in the host defense mechanisms with aging, leading to increases in the pathogenicity and virulence of microbiological organisms. Pneumonia and influenza are significant infections in the elderly and produce high mortality rates that increase with age; co-morbidity increases the risks. Increased disability and the increased likelihood of aspiration (due to reduced mechanical abilities) increase the risks also. The mucociliary clearance mechanism is affected in aging by loss of cilia, reduced ciliary activity, and atrophy of mucosa and nasal secretory glands (24). Reactivation of granulomatous diseases, e.g., tuberculosis, occurs more frequently in the elderly as well. The presence of immuno-suppressive diseases (diabetes, cancer, renal failure) and the increased likelihood of malnourishment and corticosteroid usage increase the likelihood of reactivation, as well as the adverse effects of new infections (16). Smoking affects these mechanisms, but the accumulated effect of smoking with age has yet to be determined.

Atopic status and associated conditions change with age: Immediate (and delayed) skin test reactivity to antigens decrease with age after midlife, as does immunoglobu-lin E (IgE), the mediator of immediate immunological reactions. However, smokers maintain higher levels of IgE (and lower levels of IgG and IgA) than nonsmokers. Furthermore, there appear to be alterations in mediators, e.g., prostaglandins, and receptors (16). The two functions may be independent; the change in IgE with age may be related to T-cell function, especially in smokers (18). This change in host characteristics appears to play a major role in the pathogenesis and course of acute and chronic respiratory disease. The direct or indirect relation of IgE to obstructive airway function demarcates one large class of airway problems (18).

CHRONIC LUNG DISEASES WITH AGING

The two most common types of chronic lung disease in the aged are the airway obstructive diseases (AODs) and the restrictive lung diseases. AOD is the most common, comprising emphysema, chronic bronchitis, bronchiectasis, occasionally bronchiolitis obliterans, and asthma; the first three have been called the chronic obstructive lung/pulmonary diseases (COLD/COPD). They increase with age during adulthood, reaching a maximum in different populations in the sixties or seventies, after which the prevalence decreases because of mortality. As most cases of disabling chronic lung disease in the elderly is AOD, it is the focus of most attention. [The restrictive diseases, e.g., pneumoconioses, are a result primarily of occupational exposures. There are other chronic lung diseases, such as the alveolitides/pneumonitides, the collagen-vascular diseases, and others; they are much more infrequent and occur as often in the younger adult (7,21).]

Emphysema is a disease of anatomical destruction; it is dependent on biochemical changes and morphological alterations (3,25); it is marked by destruction of alveolar septa. Chronic bronchitis is noted by morphological changes in the airways, related most frequently to changes in mucosal lining and hypertrophy of the mucosal gland (25). Bronchiectasis is an inflammatory disease of bronchi (7). Asthma is marked by variable airflow obstruction (7). The latter are simplified statements, as the diagnoses of these diseases are confused frequently, and the disease states overlap (2,7,15). The many epidemiological studies conducted have not clarified the prevalence rates, the rates of new cases (incidence), or the factors that differentiate them (2). The therapy and prognoses of the AODs have been even more confused by the realization of their communality. Diagnoses are different by gender as well as by smoking habits and allergic status.

Nevertheless, it is becoming clearer that there are two very different basic processes operating: One has a gradual onset and an insidious course, and one is much more variable in both characteristics. The former is more the classical emphysematous disease, with biochemical and anatomical alterations operating more clearly. The latter gives more the picture of asthma, with its strong immunological component. (Chronic bronchitis is more frequently a confused picture, and bronchiectasis is rarely diagnosed alone.) Skeletomuscular abnormalities, some produced by chest surgery, need to be separated from the picture. The occurrence of pulmonary hypertension, cor pulmonale, and congestive heart failure can complicate any of these conditions, though they are frequently associated with chronic bronchitis. Furthermore, it is not uncommon in working men with significant occupational exposures to dusts, fibers, or chemicals to see both AOD and restrictive diseases. Other co-morbidity, abnormalities in other organ systems, and acute conditions can alter the signs and symptoms as well.

AOD is the major cause of long-term disability, especially in the aged, and of all the chronic lung diseases; and it must be studied as such. In the process, one can differentiate restrictive lung diseases, other chronic lung diseases of importance, and, by necessity, lung cancer, acute lung conditions, and lung conditions secondary to other chronic processes.

METHODS FOR STUDYING RESPIRATORY ALTERATIONS OF AGING

As discussed in other sections, studies can be clinical or community epidemiological studies of pulmonary changes in aging. They can be retrospective (e.g., case–control) or, even better, prospective (e.g., cohort). They can be cross-sectional, as in a survey, or longitudinal. In a clinical or laboratory setting, they can be experimental or take the form of a clinical trial. Often the basic techniques used are the same. These techniques are discussed and modifications described, as suitable for the somewhat different designs.

Physiological Techniques

The most useful technique in the pulmonary armamentarium is the standard pulmonary function test using a spirometer or a pneumotachograph. The technique has been extensively standardized (8), is relatively easy to administer, and provides the most reliable and valid measurements (8). The most useful measure so obtained is the FEV_1, and it and the FEV_1/FVC ratio distinguish obstructive from restrictive complaints (3). Because of the nature of obstructive diseases, as previously described, the FEV_1 and the FVC are reduced—but the FEV_1 more than the FVC, such that the FEV_1 and the ratio of the two are low (3). In restrictive diseases with fibrosis and a "tight" lung, both measurements are reduced, but the ratio is normal (3).

Spirometric measures of volume and flows are significantly correlated with age and body size; during adult life these parameters decrease with age, as described previously. Within each age group there is a direct correlation of these measures with body size; the best correlation is with height (14). The height-corrected measures decrease nonlinearly, in an accelerating fashion, with age; this nonlinearity is difficult to see cross-sectionally. The acceleration is greater with increased duration and intensity of smoking (15,21) and occupational exposures, with some effect from general environmental exposures. Lower respiratory illnesses (LRIs) decrease the FEV_1 and the flows, though transiently, in most normal and AOD patients; but major LRIs can precipitate a rapid decrease in function in those predisposed, which in turn may lead to a series of transient and large downward excursions, corrected somewhat for awhile but relentless over time (18). Those with variable airflow obstruction have a variable course of functional change with age and time, affected by therapy, infections, etc. They may return to normal after each remission; often at older ages they develop an irreversible component, frequently linked to concomitant AOD diagnoses (18).

Even cross-sectionally, the age- and height-corrected volumes and flows show a skewed distribution with smoking and respiratory symptoms/syndromes/diagnoses, with a greater proportion than expected toward the lower end (14,15). This skewness can occur as well in the asymptomatic never-smoker (the "normals" or reference population) with age alone (14). As one examines the size-corrected trends of pulmonary function with age, one sees also a survival effect in men over age 70 and in women over age 75 (12,14). It is because of a higher age-specific mortality due to pulmonary and cardiopulmonary conditions starting in those in their fifties; it can lead to higher predicted values in these older groups than in those slightly younger. Cross-sectionally, this effect is due as well to a cohort effect, especially in women, as fewer in the older cohorts smoked, but it is present longitudinally as well (6).

Longitudinal studies show a different trend of pulmonary function with age, partly due to the effect of following cohorts over time (6). There is a reduced annual reduction in the decrease of function, especially in normals, but the accelerating decrease of function with age, smoking, and disease can be seen more clearly, related to the cumulative effects of these factors and other insults (11). Mortality is increased also in those with a low FEV_1 or FEV_1/FVC ratio and is not just due to respiratory or cardiovascular problems (4). Even after adjusting for smoking, a major risk factor for mortality from many causes, patients with poorer function have higher age-specific mortality from a variety of causes (4). It has been hypothe-sized that it is an outcome of the role of the respiratory system through life. The lungs are the primary defense against external toxic agents, are the primary deposi-tory for many toxic particles and fibers, and are important for eliminating various metabolic byproducts and wastes. Whatever enters the lung, and from there enters the circulation, may well affect the lungs in the process. The relation between the respiratory and cardiovascular systems may accelerate the effects of other chronic diseases (4).

Thus clinically, the status of pulmonary function of a patient is important, even if the patient does not have a cardiopulmonary complaint, especially as he becomes aged. The obvious abnormal function of the chronic bronchitic or emphyse-matic patient is prognostic of his continued morbidity and eventual mortality. Even the asthmatic, who may have normal function at diagnosis (2), shows a variability with time and age and often an abnormality of function in time associated with these other diagnoses, which represents a poorer prognosis (2). Though the flow rates may detect reductions or fluctuations related to these diseases processes earlier, the FEV_1 and FEV_1FVC ratio are the best prognostic factors (6). For restrictive diseases, interstitial/fibrotic diseases, and other allergic pulmonary dis-eases, these measures are important for the prognosis as well; they often show the benefit of therapy also, even if/when transient.

In addition to these measures of volumes and flows, for large and small airway function, and as affected by uneven distributions of ventilation, parenchymal changes, skeletal–muscular changes, and elastic recoil, there are studies of diffusion, ventilation–perfusion inequalities, and more specific indicators of respiratory muscle and cardiovascular effects. The diffusing capacity (DLco), mentioned previously, does decrease with age and disease; it can be a relatively standard and reliable test in the pulmonary function laboratory. Though it is of use for AOD, it shows greater differentiation of restrictive diseases. It can be used with exercise to determine the course of various other lung problems, including collagen-vascular diseases (8). Used in its multiple-breath form, it, like the nitrogen washout and helium dilution tests, can be used to estimate total lung capacity. The single-breath nitrogen test can provide measures of small airway, lung parenchymal, and ventilation homogeneity measurements (using the slope of phase III) as well as airway closure measures, especially the closing capacity/total lung capacity (TLC) ratio. The test provides information on possible effects of loss of elastic recoil with age, gravity dependence, and hyperinflation (which increases with age as well) (16). The single- and multiple-breath nitrogen tests and the helium dilution test are relatively standard in most clinical pulmonary function laboratories. They can be used in conjunction with spirometry, including the timed vital capacity and the diffusing capacity, when applicable. A plethysmographic determination of TLC and other volumes may be useful on occasion for determining these volumes instead, depending on the objectives and processes being evaluated (as discussed previously). None of these other techniques is considered a screening technique per se; the extended spirometric evaluation (for AOD and restrictive diseases) and the DLco (especially for restrictive/interstitial diseases) are the basic techniques for screening.

The plethysmographic studies of the pressure–volume relation, which provide measurements of lung elastic recoil, are useful in studies of aging, but less so as screening procedures; swallowing an esophageal balloon is not necessary for most screening purposes. The loss of elastic recoil (as previously discussed) occurs with aging but is not the major contributor to lost function, chronic lung diseases, or mortality.

One of the most useful developments in the pulmonary function testing area has been the development of microcomputers that help perform many of these tests and provide values on almost all variables that can be determined from each test. A good example of a beneficial use is the provision of the whole flow–volume loop (inspiratory and expiratory) from such equipment: The shape of the expiratory curve indicates slowing and a scooped-out appearance in AOD, and the inspiratory–expiratory differences highlight problems that may be related to the disease process and site of action. However, there is a common fallacy that an abnormality of any kind is indicative of serious clinical disease; thus the results are often overinterpreted. The likelihood of at least one test being "abnormal" increases with the number of variables mentioned, even in "normals" (12). Other useful advantages of the microcomputers are that they help in the performance of some of the more difficult tests, e.g., the DLco and the nitrogen test. Unfortunately, results may not be comparable from one set of equipment to another, as different software and different standards (for providing predictions) are used by different manufacturers. The standard use of microcomputers and interpretations therefrom require further work.

There are physiological tests that are restricted in their usefulness. Arterial blood gases are useful in serious disease, and the Pao_2 does decrease with age, but they are not determined commonly in all outpatient clinic patients. Methacholine challenges are useful for detecting disorders marked by bronchial hyperreactivity, but they are not specific for studying the aged; a bronchodilatory change after use of a β_2-agonist is useful for evaluating reversibility of airflow obstruction and is common as part of the work-up in the clinical pulmonary function laboratory but, again, is not a specific tool for studying the effects of aging. The use of electromyography (EMG) especially in sleep apnea laboratories (along with electroencephalography, etc.) is useful for studying sleep problems and muscle physiology (especially diaphragmatic behavior), but it is not a common technique for screening or for studying effects of aging in the typical setting.

There are some cardiopulmonary techniques worth mentioning and commonly used. They include the electrocardiogram (ECG), which is found in most outpatient clinics; it has been shown that ECG results indicating right ventricular hypertrophy (especially type C) are important in chronic lung diseases and do relate to pulmonary function status, disease status, and age (20). Furthermore, perfusion scans, along with ventilation scans, are used commonly, especially for specific events such as pulmonary emboli determinations; they are not used commonly, though, outside of these clinical applications.

Abnormal coronary findings on ECG and hypertension appear to be associated with abnormal pulmonary function, indicating an interaction of cardiovascular and pulmonary systems, which increases with age. Evaluation of one system without evaluation of the other appears unwarranted in the aged.

Biochemical Techniques

The measurement of elastin and collagen in the lung would be useful, but better and easier assays are needed. The activity of elastin-derived peptides are being assayed at present, and they appear to increase with age, smoking, and obstructive lung diseases (17). Also, it would be of benefit to study the proteoglycans in the lung and their mechanism of change with age. Although proteoglycans appear to increase with aging, and some appear to decrease within cartilage content, their activity requires further elaboration. At present, these techniques are experimental and deserve further work (16).

Decreased biosynthesis has been studied, as described previously; protein synthesis appears to be a function of increased DNA and RNA lesions (16). These lesions and the ability of the lung to repair them require further research. Definition of other intracellular activities in the 40 cell types of the lung, especially as they are affected by aging, is a goal in the pulmonary community. A primary area of study has been of cyclic nucleotides intra- and intercellularly, of which much is already understood (1) but little related to the effects of aging. The biochemical and pharmacological release of chemical mediators from cells has been studied extensively as well (1,23) but not gerontologically. Other cellular activities, e.g., calcium transport and lipid metabolism, are under study as well (16). The production of surfactant and its predecessors, activity, and degradation are under careful scrutiny as well (16). At present, these areas are research problems.

A major area of research has been in the protease inhibitors (Pi), especially the α_1-antitrypsin deficiencies. The co-dominant genotype Pi Z is associated with early-onset emphysema but does not appear to change the course of the disease once present (5). The homozygote SS and the heterozygote SZ appear also at increased risk of abnormal pulmonary function, but all these Pi types are uncommon in the population and have their effect earlier in adult life (5). The heterozygote MZ does not appear to be at greater risk. Because these Pi types have their effect, if any, earlier in adult life, it is not recommended specifically to screen for them in the elderly (even though the technique is in use in many locations).

Anatomical and Morphometric Techniques

The chest radiograph is the most useful technique by which to look at the living lung and its structure, and clinicians use it widely and wisely. It is a primary tool in the differential diagnoses of pulmonary and cardiopulmonary disease. It helps differentiate the type of pulmonary process, the acute and chronic changes, and the interaction of pulmonary and cardiovascular processes (7,9,10). With aging, one can see also the skeletal changes on the radiograph that imply a change in function, e.g., kyphoscoliosis, that produce an abnormal pulmonary function test. Other major changes visible on the radiograph are the markings of increased calcification, pleural thickening, changes in the diaphragm, increased vascular markings, and frequent hyperinflation/air trapping seen with aging.

The radiograph is more likely to show changes due to restrictive, fibrotic, interstitial, collagen-vascular, granulomatous, neoplastic, and chronic and acute inflammatory diseases than it is to demonstrate obstructive diseases. Allergic processes such as hypersensitivity pneumonitides, B-P allergic aspergillosis, and inhalation damage due to some fibers (e.g., asbestos) are likely to be visible on the chest x-ray film as well.

The reading of the chest radiograph for pneumoconioses has been standardized, but the readings for obstructive diseases have not (8). Nonradiologists have relied on instructions from their radiological colleagues to view the chest radiograph and interpret its likely meanings (9,10).

Image-enhanced and enlarged radiography has been used with certain disease processes and for certain research endeavors. It has helped in the visualization of changes in airways of different caliber with changes induced by disease processes, aging, and experimental insults. These techniques are useful research tools for physiological–morphological–radiological correlational studies but are not commonly in use clinically at present. Computed tomography (CT) scanning has become widely used, appropriately, and newer tests likewise.

With certain disease processes, biopsy material is available for morphometric analysis. The larger the piece of lung, the more sensitive and accurate the description; larger specimens from pneumonectomy, lobectomy, and wedge resection permit evaluation of morphometric changes potentially associated with disease processes and aging (in addition to serving the purpose for which the surgery was performed). Transtracheal and needle biopsies are useful on occasion only, and other bronchoscopic sampling is not usually done for reasons beyond the original purposes. The most likely changes seen with aging per se are emphysematic (25). One may see also interstitial and fibrotic changes, both acute and chronic, and neoplastic changes. Granulatomatous and inflammatory changes can be detected for diagnostic purposes as well. For the purposes of gerontological studies, these samples can provide material for intra- and intercellular function as well. On occasion, one can also obtain sufficient bronchial and vascular samples to evaluate changes therein induced by disease or aging (described previously).

Neurological Techniques

Knowledge of the functions of the vagas nerve and the cholinergic system continues to progress, but further work vis-à-vis aging is worthwhile. Receptors, which appear to decrease with aging, are under intensive study now. Neuromuscular control, as described previously, requires further work as well. Except for cholinergic/anticholinergic activity studies (1,23) and some studies of CO_2 responsiveness (16), studies useful for gerontology are still needed.

Immunological Techniques

Clearance Mechanisms

Mucociliary clearance appears to decrease with aging (24), but the effects of age on mucous composition, mucous physical properties, the number and mechanical behavior of cilia are insufficiently understood (24). Likewise, the effects of age on alveolar macrophages (motility, phagocytosis, bactericidal capabilities) are unknown. The use of bronchoalveolar lavage (BAL) should benefit the study of macrophages, in both their quantity and quality, with aging. Furthermore, the number and activity of neutrophils as key ingredients of host defense mechanisms can be studied more with the further use of BAL (including the secretion of proteases) in aging studies. At present, these studies are entering the realm of clinical activity, mostly for evaluating disease processes.

Cellular Immunity

There appears to be a functional depression of lymphocytes in the elderly; and reactions to delayed skin tests, a measure of cell-mediated immunity (CMI), appear to be fewer and smaller in the elderly (24). It has been reported that those who are hyporesponsive to these CMI skin tests have significantly higher age-specific (over age 80) mortality (24). The incidence of malignancy also increases with age, possibly related to attrition of host defenses, including impairment of immune surveillance (24). The increase of infections that are more pathogenic and virulent in the elderly may be partly a response to these changes (as well as to humoral changes, described below).

Humoral Immunity

Despite increases in major immunoglobulins (IgG, IgM, IgA) with age, the antibody response to foreign antigens is reduced with age; some assume that the increased immunoglobulins are busy with autoantigens, e.g., from nuclear, gastric, and thyroid sources (24). IgE, which among its other attributes mediates immediate hypersensitivity (i.e., allergy) decreases from age 10 from an average of about 100 IU in mid-life to less than 20 IU in those over age 65 in the nonatopic nonsmoker (18). Atopy, defined as immediate hypersensitivity as measured by skin tests to aeroallergens, decreases from a high in mid-life and is lower in the smoker (18). The atopic smoker maintains a high IgE level throughout life, associated with respiratory symptoms and lower lung function (even in the elderly with reduced IgE) (18). The major effect of this immunological state is seen in the nonatopic smoker; in those aged 55 and older, the prevalence rate of diagnosed chronic bronchitis increases with increased IgE from 8.8% (in those with < 10 IU) to 18.8% (in those with 40+ IU) and the percent predicted FEV_1 under 80% goes from 30.3% to 42.3%, respectively (18). Asthma prevalance increases throughout all ages with increasing age-specific IgE, and the communality of asthma and chronic bronchitis increases in the smoker with a high IgE level, indicating the occurrence of what we call "asthmatic bronchitis" (2,18). This disease is characterized by more variable airflow obstruction, a greater role of eosinophils, and greater contributions by both infections and allergies (2,18). It is marked by a more variable and rapidly descending course in many patients after a later onset. Smoking appears to be the epitome of bronchial irritation that promotes this immune status through several potential mechanisms (including greater airway permeability leading to more neuronal and mast cell stimulation, bacterial/viral-specific IgE production, T-helper-suppressor cell changes); the IgE so produced does not appear to be aeroallergen-type IgE (18). The presence of both high IgE levels and increased eosinophils in these smokers is associated with greater reductions of pulmonary function (FEV_1), which requires further exploration as well (18). It is possible that BAL will allow investigation of the eosinophil's role and the localized T-cell ratio and functioning.

Intracellular Antibody

Several antibodies within the cell are under clinical investigation at present. They include antinuclear antibody, anti-mitochondrial antibody, and anti-DNA antibody. They are proving interesting in interstitial and collagen-vascular diseases, but they have not been studied in sufficient normal individuals to evaluate the effects of aging.

Other Techniques

The questionnaire remains a key technique in clinical and community epidemiology. The respiratory questionnaire has been standardized (8) and is in wide use. It provides the basic respiratory history, diagnoses, symptoms, and more recent events. It has been designed to provide the basic anthropometric and demographic information (necessary for adjusting pulmonary function values as well as for investigating age trends), smoking habits, occupational exposures, history of chest surgery, other co-morbidity, and family respiratory history. It does not take the place of a thorough history and physical, but it provides similar information on respiratory symptoms compared to a typical checklist (19). It can be administered or self-administered. Standardized questionnaires on sleep apnea and occupational and environmental exposures are under development.

The physical examination and routine blood work are typical elements of a pulmonary evaluation, as they are in most organ systems. Community epidemiological studies can perform typical blood tests, such as white blood cell counts, hemoglobin, hematocrit, eosinophil smears, as well as other specific assays, e.g., immunoglobulins, Pi, elastin-derived peptide assays, genetic markers.

FUTURE RESEARCH NEEDS

Specific goals are considered important now for evaluation of the effects of aging on the pulmonary system. The cellular biology activity in pulmonary research is now beginning to be productive. Other biochemical assays need to be developed for wider usage, e.g., for measurements of elastin and collagen, receptor studies (especially adrenergic, cholinergic), and muscarinic), localized prostaglandin and mediator activity (through the use of BAL), and T-cell and other immune functioning within the lung itself. More whole-human studies are needed as well: the role of hyperreactive airways with age and in disease, the better characterization of "end-stage" disease in the elderly, the various effects of smoking cessation longitudinally with aging, and the differentiation of survivor versus cohort effects in longitudinal epidemiological studies of the elderly.

ACKNOWLEDGMENT

This work was supported by NHLBI SCOR grant HL 14136.

REFERENCES

1. Austin, K. F., and Lichtenstein, L. M. (1973): *Asthma: Physiology, Immunopharmacology and Treatment*, pp. 29–38, 55–71, 111–210, 251–279. Academic Press, New York.
2. Barbee, R. A., Dodge, R., Lebowitz, M. D., and Burrows, B. (1985): The epidemiology of asthma. *Chest*, 87(Suppl.):21S–25S.
3. Bates, D. V., Macklem, P. T., and Christie, R. V. (1971): *Respiratory Function in Disease*, 2nd ed. Saunders, Philadelphia.
4. Beaty, T. H., Newill, C. A., Cohen, B. H., Tockman, M. S., Bryant, S. H., and Spurgeon, H. A. (1985): Effects of pulmonary function on mortality. *J. Chronic Dis.*, 38:703–710.
5. Bruce, R. M., Cohen, B. H., Diamond, E. L., Fallat, R. J., Knudson, R. J., Lebowitz, M. D., Mittman, C., Patterson, C. D., and Tockman, M. S. (1984): Collaborative study to assess risk of lung disease in Pi MZ phenotype subjects. *Am. Rev. Respir. Dis.*, 130:386–390.
6. Burrows, B., Lebowitz, M. D., Camilli, A. E., and Knudson, R. J. (1986): Longitudinal changes in FEV_1 in adults: methodologic considerations and findings in healthy non-smokers. *Am. Rev. Respir. Dis.*, 133:974–980.
7. Cherniack, R. M., Cherniack, L., and Naimark, A. (1972): *Respiration in Health and Disease*, 2nd ed. Saunders, Philadelphia.
8. Epidemiology standardization project (1978): *Am. Rev. Respir. Dis.*, 118(Suppl.).

9. Fraser, R. G., and Paré, J. A. P. (1971): *Structure and Function of the Lung: With Emphasis on Roentgenology.* Saunders, Philadelphia.
10. Freundlich, I. M. (1979): *Diffuse Pulmonary Disease: A Radiologic Approach.* Saunders, Philadelphia.
11. Glindmeyer, H. J., Diem, J. E., Jones, R. N., and Weill, H. (1982): Noncomparability of longitudinally and cross-sectionally determined annual change in spirometry. *Am. Rev. Respir. Dis.*, 125:544–548.
12. Knudson, R. J., Burrows, B., and Lebowitz, M. D. (1976): The maximum flow-volume curve: its use in the detection of ventilatory abnormalities in a population study. *Am. Rev. Respir. Dis.*, 114:871–880.
13. Knudson, R. J., Clark, D. F., Kennedy, T. C., and Knudson, D. E. (1977): Effect of aging alone on mechanical properties of the normal adult human lung. *J. Appl. Physiol.*, 43:1054–1062.
14. Knudson, R. J., Lebowitz, M. D., Holberg, C. J., and Burrows, B. (1983): Changes in the normal maximal expiratory flow-volume curve with growth and aging. *Am. Rev. Respir. Dis.*, 127:725–734.
15. Knudson, R. J., Slatin, R., Lebowitz, M. D., and Burrows, B. (1976): The maximum expiratory flow-volume curve: normal standards, variability, and effects of age. *Am. Rev. Respir. Dis.*, 113:587–600.
16. Krumpe, P. E., Knudson, R. J., Parsons, G., and Reiser, K. (1985): The aging respiratory system. *Clin. Geriatr. Med.*, 1:143–175.
17. Kucich, U., Christner, P., Weinbaum, G., and Rosenbloom, J. (1980): Immunologic identification of elastin-derived peptides in the serums of dogs with experimental emphysema. *Am. Rev. Respir. Dis.*, 122:461–465.
18. Lebowitz, M. D., and Burrows, B. (1985): Risk factors in induction of lung disease: an epidemiologic approach. In: *Mechanisms of Lung Injury,* edited by G. Weinbaum and P. Kimbel. Stickley, Philadelphia.
19. Lebowitz, M. D., Burrows, B., Traver, G. A., McDonagh, D. J., Dodge, R. R., Barbee, R. A., Glover, J., Kennedy, T., Clark, D., and Resar, R. (1985): Methodological considerations of epidemiological diagnoses in respiratory diseases. *Eur. J. Epidemiol.*, 1(3):188–192.
20. Lebowitz, M. D., Phibbs, B., Robertson, G., Holberg, C., Knudson, R. J., and Burrows, B. (1985): Vectorcardiographic and blood pressure correlates of obstructive pulmonary diseases in a community population. *Chest*, 89:78–84.
21. Macklem, P. T., and Permutt, S. (1979): *The Lung in the Transition Between Health and Disease.* Marcel Dekker, New York.
22. Mittman, C., Edelman, N. H., and Norris, A. H. (1965): Relationship between chest wall and pulmonary compliance and age. *J. Appl. Physiol.*, 20:1211–1216.
23. Morley, J. (1982): *Bronchial Hyperreactivity,* pp. 53–68, 99–122, 187–206, 219–234. Academic Press, London.
24. Murray, J. F. (1976): *The Normal Lung.* Saunders, Philadelphia.
25. Thurlbeck, W. M. (1976): *Chronic Airflow Obstruction in Lung Disease.* Saunders, Philadelphia.

Human Aging Research: Concepts and Techniques,
edited by B. Kent and R. N. Butler.
Raven Press, Ltd., New York © 1988.

Neurochemistry of Human Aging: Conceptual and Practical Problems

Peter Davies

Departments of Pathology and Neuroscience, Albert Einstein College of Medicine, Bronx, New York 10461

Neurochemical studies of the effects of aging on the human brain seem simple in design, execution, and interpretation. All that is apparently needed are samples of brain tissue from humans of various ages and a series of assays for neuronal markers. Once the assays are complete, if the variables measured increase or decrease with the age of the subjects, a paper can be written. Both human and animal studies performed in this way are being reported in increasing numbers in the literature, and a superficial reading of these papers suggests that many neuronal markers show a decrease in activity or concentration with age. These data tend to support the popular notion that the brains of old individuals do not function as well as those of young adults. Some of the publications claim to provide partial explanations for the functional decrease.

With the expansion of interest in neurochemical studies of human aging, it seems appropriate to examine some of the assumptions and theoretical points that underlie the work being performed. Conceptual and practical problems are illustrated with examples from the author's published and unpublished work, as well as with highly selected examples from the literature. To examine the conceptual issues, a critical approach is taken to the available data. It should be emphasized that such criticism is intended only to highlight the difficulties of studies on human aging. No direct criticism of specific pieces of work is intended, either by citation or omission of citation.

HUMAN AGING: WHAT IS NORMAL?

In Western society almost everyone carries some preconceptions about the decrease in function suffered by the elderly. Asked to describe a typical 80-year-old, many of us would use the term slow, feeble, forgetful, etc. Although such expressions might be applicable to a large number of the elderly, it is still not clear that they accurately describe most individuals reaching the age of 80 years. Even if most of the individuals do not suffer such problems, there are enough examples of frail, forgetful elderly people for us to speak of this situation as common. However, it is also increasingly common to encounter individuals well over 80 years in whom there is little or no evidence of functional decrease, especially in cognition. We must face the difficult question of what is *normal:* to be 80, feeble, and forgetful, or to be 90 and in good shape? It is an important question. If it is held that the neurochemical parameters to be measured have some direct relation to the behavior of the individual (and as a neurochemist I hope it is the case), one would expect to obtain different results in studies of frail and feeble elderly compared to highly functional individuals of the same age.

What is surprising is how rarely the level of function of the older human (or indeed animal) is considered in neurochemical studies. Almost all the neurochemical studies that have been reported note that there is a high degree of variability in the data on old animals or humans (usually reflected in increasing standard deviations or standard errors of the mean as the population ages). Rarely is it acknowledged that the ability of older humans or animals to perform complex tasks is also variable. We seem to accept that the older individuals display a wide variety of levels of ability, with the *average* individual performing less well than the average younger individual.

There are semantic problems here that need to be explored if we are to understand the effects of age on the human brain. The terms that are used almost interchangeably in the literature are *common, average,* and *normal.* It seems likely that the average elderly individual shows a decrease in performance when compared to the average younger individual, and it is common to find rather extreme examples of functional decrease. Is it normal? Not necessarily. In mid-February in New York, it is common to find primary school children with upper respiratory tract infections, and the average 10-year-old suffers at least one such infection during the winter. It does not mean that it is a part of the normal physiology of children; the infections are a pathologic process that is found with high frequency and occasionally can be severe. It seems worth considering the possibility that the decrease in function in the elderly is also the result of pathology, pathology that is common and sometimes severe but not normal to the species. Following this line of reasoning, the normal human would maintain high levels of function throughout life unless some pathologic process were to intervene. This pattern would suggest that age alone was not sufficient to cause changes in level of function or in neurochemical parameters. This line of argument might change the way we regard studies of normal aging of the brain. At least it calls for some definition of what aging means.

The variable of greatest concern in aging studies is the passage of time. Strictly speaking, a study of the effects of aging on the brain should be a study of the effects of the passage of time on components of the brain. In practical terms, there are two facets to this study: The first is to attempt to determine the intrinsic stability of different elements of the brain, and the second is to determine the nature of extrinsic factors that disrupt this stability.

INTRINSIC STABILITY OF THE NERVOUS SYSTEM

In mammals it seems unlikely that significant numbers of neurons are added after birth. Thus the neuronal population present at birth must last for the lifetime of the individual if normal functioning is to be maintained. It is remarkable that extremely complex cells, e.g., anterior horn motor neurons with axons many centimeters long, can indeed survive and maintain function for more than 100 years in some individuals. In exchange for the ability to divide, neurons presumably gain a high degree of stability. From the point of view of aging studies, the important question seems to be whether the life-span of specific neuronal populations is intrinsically limited. Because of data apparently showing that the number of dopaminergic neurons in the substantia nigra decreases with age (7–9), it has been suggested that all humans would develop Parkinson's disease if they lived long enough. This point effectively argues that the life-span of these neurons is limited, and that the limit of survival is close to the average human life-span. Similar data on ventral forebrain cholinergic neurons have been published (2,3,7,10) suggesting that dementia is inevitable if the individual lives long enough to exceed the life-span of this neuronal population.

The idea that specific populations of neurons have a finite life-span is attractive from a cell biology point of view. There is a substantial body of data suggesting that fibroblasts have a limited life-span or capacity for division, and that it seems to be genetically determined (5,6). However, it does not seem that the data available at this time support this hypothesis in regard to neurons in the mammalian central nervous system, largely because of the failure of most workers to adequately exclude individuals who might lose neurons as a result of extrinsic factors. Such exclusion is extremely difficult in human studies, as it is not known what factors might affect different cell populations.

The author's work on the neurochemistry of normal aging began as an offshoot of work on Alzheimer's disease. For comparison with cases of Alzheimer's disease, brains were collected at autopsy from apparently nondemented individuals; those found to be free of pathologic changes were used as controls. In these early studies the neuropathologist's report was considered the only important criterion for selecting material for study, and little attention was paid to the clinical history, except that there was no evidence of neurologic or psychiatric disease. Because the brains of Alzheimer patients were from individuals ranging in age from 46 to 95, controls covering this age range were also obtained. When analyzing the results of these studies, it was apparent that the activity of choline acetyltransferase was significantly and negatively correlated with the age of the control patients (Table 1). Others have published similar results (7,10). These data seem to support the notion that as normal individuals age they begin to look more and more like patients with Alzheimer's disease. Over a 7-year period a chance to expand this study came from a large collaborative effort in which neuropsychological, neuropathologic, and neurochemical data could be correlated. In a preliminary analysis of the data obtained in this study, correlations between age and choline acetyl-

TABLE 1. *Correlations between choline acetyltransferase and age in early studies*

Brain region	r	n	p
Study 1 (Davies, 1978)			
Mid-temporal gyrus	−0.773	20	<0.01
Hippocampus	−0.847	19	<0.01
Study 2 (Davies & Terry, 1981)			
Inferior parietal cortex	−0.654	12	<0.02
Occipital cortex	−0.561	12	<0.05
Inferior temporal gyrus	−0.559	12	<0.05

The r values listed are Pearson correlation coefficients, with the number of cases providing tissue samples indicated by *n*. The two studies from which these results were taken were independent in that two populations of cases were studied.

transferase were sought. The relation between age and choline acetyltransferase in hippocampus and frontal cortex in the whole population studied (112 cases) is shown in Fig. 1. It is obvious that there is no decrease with age in this population.

While attempting to determine why this study was at variance with earlier published data, the relation between neuropsychological, neuropathologic, and neurochemical data were examined. Initially, a group of elderly individuals were selected who were judged to be normal on the basis of clinical data, neuropsychological test scores, and neuropathologic criteria. The mean choline acetyltransferase activity in the cerebral cortex of these patients, as well as other data, is presented in Table 2. These truly normal elderly (normal in terms of intact cognitive function and free of brain pathology) had choline acetyltransferase activities that did not significantly differ from those found in much younger individuals who were also free of pathology (Table 2). Thus age alone did not appear to be a major factor in determining the choline acetyltransferase activity. It was also of some interest to note that the level of cognitive function was not a major factor, suggesting that dementia did not result in reduced activity. A number of elderly demented individuals were found to have mean levels of activity in the same range as the young controls. On the other hand, several individuals also had low activity, and not all of them had the pathologic signs of Alzheimer's disease: Some had no pathologic findings at all.

All these results suggest that, if aged subjects are selected for normal levels of cognitive function and lack of brain pathology, markers of ventral forebrain cholinergic neurons do not decrease with age. However, the results also suggest that reductions in markers are commonly found in elderly people, sometimes associated with the pathology of Alzheimer's disease, sometimes with other pathologies, and sometimes without evident pathology. Again, the distinction between what is *normal* and what is *common* or *average* is important. This study suggests that there are numerous factors that can affect the survival or function of cholinergic

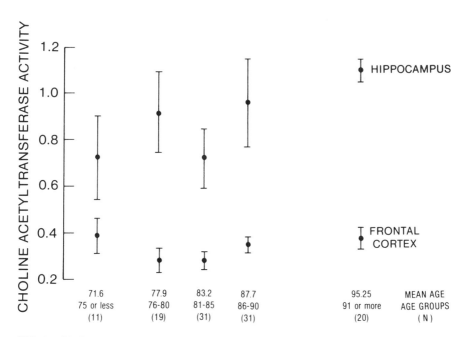

FIG. 1. Choline acetyltransferase activity as a function of age. The figure displays the mean (± standard error of the mean) choline acetyltransferase activities of five groups of patients of increasing age. The upper five data points are for samples of hippocampus, and the lower five are for frontal cortex. There is clearly no tendency for the activity to decrease as a function of age. In fact, the hippocampal value for the oldest group of patients is significantly higher than that for the youngest group ($p < 0.05$). Units for choline acetyltransferase activity are micromoles of acetylcholine produced per hour per 100 mg protein.

TABLE 2. *Choline acetyltransferase activity in the cerebral cortex of elderly people selected on the basis of normal performance on neuropsychological test scores and free of significant neuropathology*

Brain region	Acetylcholine (nmol/hr/100 mg protein)		
	Group 1 ($n = 11$)	Group 2 ($n = 13$)	Group 3 ($n = 12$)
Frontal cortex	516 ± 61	470 ± 90	531 ± 91
Parietal cortex	552 ± 118	360 ± 50	420 ± 82
Mid-temporal gyrus	595 ± 56	450 ± 40	520 ± 65

Group 1 cases had a mean age of 82.5 ± 2.6 years (mean ± SEM), group 2 a mean age of 58.1 ± 6.0, and group 3 a mean age of 57.2 ± 5.6. Group 1 cases made four or fewer errors on the Blessed Dementia Rating Scale and were judged to be free of dementia on clinical examination. Such data were not available for the two other groups of patients. All cases were free of significant neuropathology. Data are mean ± 1 SEM.

neurons, one of these being Alzheimer's disease and many of which we have yet to identify. Age alone does not seem to be a significant factor.

SURVIVOR EFFECT

One of the major problems with attempts to study the neurochemistry of normal human aging is that virtually all the subjects who might be included in such investigations are normal except they are deceased. Detailed neurochemical studies can be performed only on tissue removed at autopsy, which of course requires the death of the individual. This seemingly trivial point is actually a serious problem. In animal studies, extensive behavioral or performance testing can be used to determine the level of functional ability, and the animal can then be sacrificed while still in good health (it is appalling how rarely it is done). In humans this situation is clearly not possible, and there are few occasions when the effects of terminal illness can be avoided. We do know that the effects of the "agonal" state can have pronounced effects on the brain: The exemplary work of Bowen and colleages (1) on the effects of prolonged hypoxia prior to death on glutamic acid decarboxylase activity is an excellent example of what can be done. However, it is still true that we know far too little about the effects of mode of death on neurochemical parameters and still less about the possible changes in mode of death with aging.

The important point here is that there seems likely to be a "survivor" effect in much of the aging research on both humans and animals. In general, individuals who do not suffer a decrease in nervous system function seem more likely to survive to advanced age than those who experience such a decrease. There are numerous obvious exceptions to this statement, but it is likely that an individual with a high level of cognitive function would be better able to avoid a variety of potentially fatal problems than an impaired individual. Death may in fact be a sign that the individual has lost the ability to avoid such problems. Thus it is difficult to know if studies of the neurochemistry of normal human aging are possible. It is noteworthy that the one study of the effects of aging on the cholinergic system that employed samples of brain tissue removed at biopsy (usually to gain access to tumors) failed to reveal any correlations between either choline acetyltransferase activity or rates of acetylcholine synthesis and age (11).

CONCLUSIONS

There should be no doubt that attempts to study the effects of age on the neurochemistry of the human brain are considerably more difficult than is initially apparent. The survival potential of neuronal systems is illustrated by those individuals who achieve advanced age without signs of decrease in intellectual or other function. Whether these people have intrinsically more stable neuronal populations or are simply lucky enough to avoid the insults that can devastate specific cell groups we do not yet know. There can be little doubt that there are complex interrelations between the effects of age on the brain and on the rest of the body, and that they are reciprocal. Physical illness has the potential to affect the brain, and brain changes seem likely to result in physical problems. Although we might not yet be in a position to understand all facets of these interrelations, we must at least begin to recognize that they exist.

ACKNOWLEDGMENTS

The author's research is supported by NIH grants MH32678 and AG02478, and by grants from the Joyce Mertz-Gilmore Foundation, the McKnight Foundation, and the Commonwealth Fund. The collaboration of Drs. Robert D. Terry, Robert Katzman, and Paula A. Fuld in some of the work reported here is acknowledged.

REFERENCES

1. Bowen, D. M., Smith, C. B., White, P., and Davison, A. N. (1976): Neurotransmitter-related enzymes and indices of hypoxia in senile dementia and other abiotrophies. *Brain,* 99:459–495.
2. Davies, P. (1978): Loss of choline acetyltransferase activity in normal aging and in senile dementia. In: *Parkinson's Disease. II. Aging and Neuroendocrine Relationships,* edited by C. E. Finch, D. E. Potter, and A. D. Kenny, pp. 251–256. Plenum Press, New York.
3. Davies, P. (1979): Neurotransmitter-related enzymes in senile dementia of the Alzheimer type. *Brain Res.,* 171:319–327.
4. Davies, P., and Terry, R. D. (1981): Cortical somatostatin-like immunoreactivity in cases of Alzheimer's disease and senile dementia of the Alzheimer type. *Neurobiol. Aging,* 2:9–14.
5. Hayflick, L. (1965): The limited in vitro lifetime of human diploid cell strains. *Exp. Cell Res.,* 37:614–636.
6. Hayflick, L. (1976): The cell biology of human aging. *N. Engl. J. Med.,* 295:1302–1308.
7. McGeer, E. G. (1978): Aging and neurotransmitter metabolism in the human brain. In: *Aging, Vol. 7: Alzheimer's Disease: Senile Dementia and Related Disorders,* edited by R. Katzman, R. D. Terry, and K. L. Bick, pp. 427–440. Raven Press, New York.
8. McGeer, E., and McGeer, P. L. (1976): Neurotransmitter metabolism in the aging brain. In: *Aging, Vol. 3: Neurobiology of Aging,* edited by R. D. Terry and S. Gershon, pp. 389–404. Raven Press, New York.
9. McGeer, P. L., McGeer, E. G., and Suzuki, J. S. (1976): Aging and extrapyramidal function. *Arch. Neurol.,* 34:33–36.
10. Perry, E. K., Perry, R. H., Gibson, P. H., Blessed, G., and Tomlinson, B. E. (1977): A cholinergic connection between normal aging and senile dementia in the human hippocampus. *Neurosci. Lett.,* 6:85–89.
11. Sims, N. R., Bowen, D. M., and Davison, A. N. (1981): (^{14}C)Acetylcholine synthesis and (^{14}C)carbon dioxide production from (U-^{14}C)glucose by tissue prisms from human neocortex. *Biochem. J.,* 196:867–876.

Human Aging Research: Concepts and Techniques,
edited by B. Kent and R. N. Butler.
Raven Press, Ltd., New York © 1988.

Research in Human Neuropsychology: Issues of Aging

Nancy S. Foldi

*Department of Geriatrics and Adult Development, Mount Sinai Medical Center, New York,
New York 10029*

Members of the lay and scientific communities are still struggling with the belief that aging is inextricably linked to the decrease of mental processes. The image of mental deterioration seems even more hopeless when one adds that the rate of decrease of psychological function accelerates beyond the seventh decade (20). Perhaps these images were a reflection of the pervasive downhill slopes of other biological and physiological functions. Perhaps, too, these beliefs have grown out of psychologists' use of the intelligence quotient (IQ), which in the tradition of American psychology was designed to represent some correlate of general "mental capacity." In either case, these facts combine to leave a bleak image of growing old.

This theme of pervasive decrease of cognition warrants a careful look, however. As we are at the infancy of aging research in cognition, we need to ensure that what is being looked at and how the measurements are made will yield a fruitful direction of research. For instance, the concept of an IQ score, which represents some global intelligence, may not be an appropriate metric; or perhaps the standardization of this test for the 40- and 74-year-old may not be an appropriate application of the psychological test.

We are at a point where we need to ask the right questions about cognition and aging. The questions need to be theoretically informative, experimentally accessible, and not necessarily motivated to assuage our own fears of aging. In this vein, two important questions face this field of neuropsychology: How does the older brain change, and what does the behavior of the older person teach us about cognitive processing or development? The inquiry is twofold. One is to learn about the neurobehavioral mechanisms, and the second is to advance a sound theoretical foundation for adult development. This chapter surveys how the various approaches of neuropsychological research are answering these questions. Because reviews (28) have expertly covered the content areas of the neuropsychology of aging, this chapter approaches the challenges of techniques and principles in conducting studies in this field.

Perhaps the single most important influence in current research is flouting the concept of a "general" decline. Indeed, much work focuses on differentiating those functions that change from those that do not, establishing different rates of change among different tasks, or determining which functions may decrease and which may improve with age. Even the early work on the IQ projected this theme of differentiating different tasks and subtests (20): With increased age, performance scores decreased more than verbal subtests. Another approach to distinguish the overall performance was offered by Horn (29) and Cattell (11) in the theory of crystallized versus fluid intelligence. What is lacking in these approaches is that there is no inference about an underlying structural change, and it is this relation between structure and function that is the heart of neuropsychological research.

Neuropsychology is the study of the relation between brain and behavior. Certainly, it is an area that has benefited from the multidisciplinary involvement (i.e., linguistics, developmental and experimental psychology, and behavioral neurology) and in that way foreshadows the type of work employed in the study of aging. Human neuropsychology is particularly challenged because of the limitations of adapting animal models to human activities (e.g., higher cortical functions such as problem-solving or language). As a result, neuropsychology has relied on two sources of investigation: brain-damaged subjects or persons without neurological impairment. The premise of research with brain-damaged subjects is that behaviors are revealed that otherwise would not be observable and thus shed light onto the mechanism of the behavior itself. In addition, important links between structure and function can be drawn when impaired behaviors coexist with discrete, circumscribed lesions. In order to draw inferences about structure and function in normal individuals, neuropsychologists have resorted to careful manipulations of tasks. This point is seen in tachistoscopic visual presentation, which, given the nature of the visual architecture, allows the images to be projected to each hemisphere. Similarly, dichotic listening procedures allow one to infer information about the brain mechanism as a function of the nature of stimuli. Thus by manipulating the mode of presentation or the type of stimuli, nonneurologically impaired subjects can serve as informative resources in the quest for understanding brain–behavior relations.

How do these techniques lend themselves to the study of aging, and how does this approach serve to differentiate the types of cognitive changes that occur with age? Are the methods that have been applicable in the past in neuropsychological research appropriate for this age group? These questions are the methodological challenges of this research. Importantly, the question to ask is whether there are new ideas about aging that can contribute to the knowledge base of neuropsychology. I think so. First, there needs to be a close examination of the traditional methods used and an assessment to determine if and when these methods are appropriate and informative in an aging population. Second, the neurological changes in the older brain have to be brought into the overall picture. The maturation of the neuroanatomy, neurophysiology, and neurochemistry must then be thought of in terms of its functional repercussions. Third and last, disease models must be reexamined. Neurological diseases in the elderly manifest differently than in younger individuals, and certain diseases may be age-specific to the latter years of life. Each of these three areas is discussed. From these observations, I have surveyed some of the directions where aging research can offer new ideas for the fundamentals of brain–behavior relations.

NEUROPSYCHOLOGICAL METHODS WITH THE ELDERLY

There are several methodological issues that plague most aging research, and psychology is equally vulnerable. The area of design is such an instance, and criteria for subject selection, procedural problems, and selection of materials raise more specific issues in psychological research. As a result, some modification of our present techniques may be warranted in the work with the elderly.

Design

The drawbacks of longitudinal versus cross-sectional versus cohort sequential has been the topic in many critiques of aging research and need little repetition here. The biases of each design should not be underestimated. Indeed, each brings with it certain partiality to the data (2). Where longitudinal designs favor the dependent measures because of subject survival, cross-sectional designs bias group means unfavorably either because of cohort effects or other intergroup differences. Left with cohort sequential methods, it is not clear that these two biases automatically cancel one another out.

Subject Selection

Perhaps the most embittered thorn in this type of research is that of subject selection. Two issues stand out. The first is the lack of normative data. The second is the challenge to select homogeneous groups. Psychological tests are developed at first for experimental purposes but frequently with the hope of being more generalizable for the larger population. Important in this process is the standardization of the test (17), which should follow strict criteria of validity and reliability testing. In order for this standardization to occur, or for that matter even in early experimental phases of test development, it is essential to be able to make some predictions on a normal sample. However, who the "normal" older person is is not clear. First, there is the consideration of general health, which is not promising, as 78% of persons older than 65 years have at least one systemic disease (53). Naturally, the influence of the disease can easily affect the cognitive performance, and thus investigations are now opting to search for "optimally healthy" individuals (10), thereby veering away from the traditional concept of "normal." There is therefore a tricky methodological line to travel: On the one hand, one wants to select a "representative" group of elderly, but they would be representative in that they have some chronic ailment. On the other hand, selection of the optimally healthy biases the data to represent a less generalizable group of elderly. However, because disease processes can and do interfere with the cognitive correlates, investigators are forced to opt for the healthy individuals for the sake of being able to make statements about cognitive performance and aging, but they similarly need to recognize that their sample may have limited generalizability to the population at large.

Second, as individuals age and the likelihood of disease increases, the homogeneity of the group becomes less likely over time. Thus (see Lakatta, *this volume*) the downward slope of the longitudinal or even cohort sequential data may then be a reflection of a wide variance around the mean, resulting from the disparate, heterogeneic group, rather than a true downhill course of the aging, homogeneic sample.

Both of these issues address the problems of subject selection in traditional psychological experiments. Perhaps, however, we can learn about "normal" aging by focusing on those gifted individuals. Developmental neuropsychologists (24) have investigated the gifted child precisely for this purpose. It is the exceptional case that can shed light on normal functioning, and thus there is room for, and reason to study, the aging Picassos and Casals.

Lastly, another aspect of selecting groups among the elderly is the issue of age itself. Several studies have standardized tests with "older" adults around 55 years (6,23), 65 years (55), or even up to 74 years of age (20). Yet clinical situations today and certainly more in the future will be faced with persons well beyond these years. Although the subdivisions of early adulthood tend to follow decades, and those of childhood and infancy are divided more finely, it remains unclear what age subdivisions are appropriate in the elderly. The concept of "young old," "old," and "old old" has been introduced; but although it begins to address the differentiation of the elderly, it is unclear what the motivations for these subdivisions are. Perhaps there will be certain physiological milestones that could be used as indices on which the scientific community can agree, or perhaps certain tests sensitive to different types of function will each require their own individualized age subdivisions.

Another more practical aspect of group selection, particularly in those experimental groups with brain disease, is the need to establish strict criteria for group admission. In doing so, however, the yield is small (34). The criteria need to be principled, yet the inclusion of multiple criteria diminishes the subject pool. Despite these frustrations, the selection of groups is time-consuming and costly but should remain one of the highest priorities in these early stages of aging research in psychology.

Procedures

New procedural problems arise when testing elderly subjects. First, there are the inherent problems of the cohort effect. An 85-year-old immigrant who may have been a successful provider for his family is not necessarily successful with standard American multiple choice tests. In contrast, most Americans since the late 1940s have grown up with this system of testing. When working with computers, the cohort effect may not even span a full generation. Here the difference between the 50-year-old and the 35-year-old may already be noteworthy, even though both could be found in a similar work force. It is not to say that these procedures should be avoided. Rather, they highlight the need for methodological procedures that can avoid confounds because of the technique used. Specifically, baseline threshhold performance measures and practice items need to be standard fare to ensure familiarity with the test protocol for all groups.

More important procedural issues need to be considered in psychological work with the elderly. Specifically, methods that demand speed performance (44) require careful consideration. The older person has slower nerve conduction in the peripheral nervous and central nervous systems (12) and so, based on physiological grounds, has slower reaction times. Any speed test that penalizes performance simply because of a time limit puts the elderly at a disadvantage. The inferences about central cognitive processes based on reaction time must be drawn carefully. Alternate approaches are perhaps more advisable, at least in conjunction with reaction time or speed performance. To this end, qualitative methods successfully employed in other research of neuropsychology can yield important supplemental information and affect how timed studies are interpreted.

The second area of caution in terms of methods is the use of dependent variables that could place large demands on the peripheral mechanisms in the elderly patient. It is precisely the changes in hearing (13), vision (32), and motor dexterity (52) that are compromised with age. If the procedure of the experiment uses a variable that depends on the intactness of these functions, these subjects are disadvantaged not because of any underlying central processing deficit but simply because of the peripheral decrements. Therefore at least the impact of peripheral changes must be ruled out as any source of variance in the elderly group, particularly when comparisons are being made with younger subjects. While not performed in all psychological research, and trite as it may seem, it is important to test for visual and hearing acuity and to account for arthritic changes on a regular basis.

Lastly, some of the methods used in psychological procedures require lengthy periods of testing, and fatigue must be considered. The elderly tire easily, and the older individual is likely to show decreased attention or increased error rate over time. Shorter tests may need to be developed, or procedures for multiple testing periods can be introduced. In those situations where it is possible, i.e., when administering experimental versus more strict standardized tests, it is equally advisable to account for the fatigue factor (much like a learning or practice effect) by invoking strict counterbalancing measures between subjects.

UNDERLYING NEUROLOGICAL CHANGES

Numerous neuroanatomic and neurochemical changes occur in the aging central nervous system. Reviews covering these changes (16) have detailed alterations in both normal and pathological contexts. Three issues become apparent. First, a number of frequently observed changes that have been documented do not necessarily change equally throughout all areas of the brain. For example, such changes include loss of brain weight and evidence of gyral atrophy, neuronal cell loss, decreased distal dendritic growth, and accumulation of lipofucsin. Again, the direction of differentiation is increasingly prominent in this research. That is, be it atrophy or cell loss, certain areas of the brain may be more vulnerable to change as a function of age.

Second, the processes of brain changes must be differentiated into those that are "eugeric" and those that are "pathogeric" (22). To the extent that changes can occur similarly in normal older brains and disease processes (e.g., the presence of neurofibrillary plaques and tangles), it has always been important to determine when a process represents disease and when it is part of the aging pattern. Importantly, this distinction needs to be correlated with behavioral abnormalities in order to further substantiate the manifestation of what is disease and what is "normal" aging. Do pathological findings that affect different brain regions selectively (51) show a corresponding selective behavioral change? What are the implications of changes such as prominent cortical sulci that are observed in the demented individual as well as in the individual without documented behavioral abnormalities? In such an instance, visualized atrophy on computed tomography (CT) scans simply cannot be used as a pathognomonic sign. At this point, while basic changes in the aging brain are still being investigated, the meaningful distinction between the normal processes and the disease processes remain somewhat murky.

Both of the above issues—distribution of change and distinguishing between normal and disease processes—must be put into the context of a third issue: the effect on higher cortical function. Specifically, is there any impact on the behavior of the individual as a result of these changes? This area is where the important link between brain and behavior relations must take place. If certain cortical areas are more susceptible to degeneration (41) or even synaptic growth (14), are there predictable neuropsychological functions that could be determined based on these neurological changes? For example, are the behavioral changes observed in what is referred to as "frontal system" effects (28) a reflection of underlying changes in the frontal regions or frontal projections in the elderly brain? These questions are broad and difficult to answer. First, they require fine-tuning of our neuropsychological assessments of the optimally healthy elderly, a sample that, as discussed above, is not easy to designate. Costly and time-consuming screening procedures are unavoidable precursors necessary for establishing a clean cohort of subjects. Second, the use of available diagnostic techniques such as CT scans (21), electroencephalography (EEG) (31), positron emission tomography (PET) (19), and evoked potentials (43) can provide important data about underlying neurological processes. These tools—neuropsychological assessments and diagnostic techniques—must be used in an integrative fashion: When methods address only one aspect of the changes, be they psychological or neurological, they fail to consider the critical interdependent relation that exists between the aging neural mechanisms and behavior. The difficult and pragmatically demanding step is to continue to accrue behavioral data of subjects who have full neurological work-ups or pathological investigations in order to establish the correlational or even causal relations between brain and behavior.

DISEASE MODELS IN THE ELDERLY

The use of disease models in neuropsychology has been extensive. Clinical/pathological findings provided early researchers with brain behavior correlates. Gunshot wounds (35) and careful examinations of individuals with cerebrovascular insults (3) or neurosurgery (7) have similarly been fruitful sources of information of structure and function relations. To this end, inferences about the function of a specified area of the brain can be gleaned based on its dysfunction or absence. Such localization of function, however, has had to be carefully assessed. Anatomical destruction of a site, e.g., Broca's area, does not automatically indicate the subsequent behavioral syndrome characteristic of Broca's aphasia (27,37). Thus although differentiation of neural substrate is recognized, the one-to-one correlation of structure and function warrants cautious consideration.

The use of focal lesion data during aging similarly requires careful assessment. One cannot necessarily assume that the localization of function remains constant and static throughout the life-span: Neural development progresses from early fetal weeks (47) through the aging years and must be thought of as a dynamic process throughout the life-span. A demonstration of this phenomenon can be seen when looking at the distribution of aphasias from childhood through old age (40). Brain damage in children frequently results in a Broca's-like, nonfluent aphasia, whereas fluent aphasias are rarely seen in the young child. In contrast, the older the subject, the more likely he is to exhibit the fluent aphasias typical of posterior lesions. Therefore the location of the lesion in and of itself is not a determinant of the behavioral disorder; not only for the reasons referred to above regarding the limitations of predicting the behavioral symptoms based solely on the lesion site but also that the manifestation of damage differs in the brain as a function of the age of the individual.

Another facet of using disease models for aging research is the existence of age-related diseases specific to the elderly. For neuropsychology, the question is how these diseases (e.g., the senile dementias) can provide a new source of information for the understanding of brain and behavior. In part, the dementias present a different behavioral paradigm than focal lesion study, not only in terms of the late-onset presentations but also in terms of the progressive nature of the illness. The neuropsychological changes in geriatric dementias (1) demonstrate that specific functions are affected. Yet unlike the data from focal lesions, the neuropsychological inferences from the dementias underscore a radically different disease process. Diseases due to neurotransmitter alterations invoke changes along complex pathways, with intricate interrelations among several neural systems. Unlike a section through single-fiber pathways or damage to circumscribed neural tissue, alterations in neurotransmitters are less likely to involve only one dimension of behavior. Thus although neuropsychology and behavioral neurology has advanced from a tradition of correlations of behavior with focal lesions, progressive idiopathic dementias in particular do not necessarily share the same kind of method of one-to-one associations. Yet neurologists are wont to continue in this tradition: Distinctions of cortical versus subcortical dementias (18) is one such example. Such a distinction is clinically useful only insofar as it mimics what is known about focal damage in these areas. The term has come into question, however (50), as it does not accurately represent the effects of an underlying disease process. First, neurochemical changes involve both cortical and subcortical areas of the brain; and second, the process progressively deteriorates increasing regions of neural tissue. Thus in neuropsychological work with the dementias, investigators can benefit from an approach that not only incorporates data learned from focal lesion studies but also takes into consideration the fundamentally different kind of process underlying these diseases.

EMERGING PRINCIPLES ON THE NEUROPSYCHOLOGY OF AGING

Neuropsychology of aging is following several directions of research. The common goal, however, is to use the changes of aging as a new source of data to further the understanding of brain–behavior relations. As mentioned before, there are difficulties because of methodology and lack of standard norms on the one hand and only the relatively primitive knowledge of underlying neuroanatomical changes in aging humans on the other. At this point, there appear to be three general themes emerging that begin to make sense of the neuropsychological data: the neurologically, the cognitively, and the developmentally based models. These three models are by no means mutually exclusive, and by no coincidence they parallel the route that neuropsychological research has been taking in the course of the past 40 years.

Neurological Model: Laterality

One hypothesis about aging is that the hemispheres age differentially. This subject has been reviewed by some authors (28,33) and derives from the observations that tasks traditionally mediated by the right hemisphere seem to be more compromised in the elderly. One hypothesis is that the right hemisphere, in particular, is more vulnerable to the aging process. As suggested in the aforementioned reviews, several types of data fit this pattern. The distinction between verbal and performance subtests on the Wechsler IQ (20), differences in strategy of task performance (2), and memory of visual material are all suggestive indicators. The concept of differential aging of the hemispheres is not without precedent. The developmental literature, on the levels of psychological performance (36) and neurological maturation (25), has already documented differences in hemispheric growth. Whether growth rates develop asymptotically during adulthood or the growth rates of the hemispheres level off only to mature differentially in old age remain important unanswered questions. To add a further variable, the issue of sex differences of hemispheric growth has been well documented on the neurological and psychological levels: The predominance of language disorders in boys compared to girls and performance versus verbal IQ score differences during early childhood are but two examples. The effect of aging on these early sex differences is not known, but some suggestion of differences (4) would not be surprising. Hemisphere by sex interactions may emerge during old age much like ones observed during childhood. Thus the patterns seen during aging would then be a reflection of the continuing hemispheric maturation that has been at play throughout the life-span.

Perhaps the alleged decrease of right hemispheric functions could be explained by other hypotheses. The decrease of these functions may be a reflection of how functions are represented in the brain. The tests used for right hemisphere functions are unlike those of language in that they are not always as detailed and theoretically well defined. Perhaps as a result psychologists still perceive certain right hemispheric functions to be represented in the brain in a more diffuse, less localized fashion— unlike the language functions attributed to the dominant hemisphere. One corollary of this perception is that a small lesion in the right hemisphere does not produce the kind of specific behavioral deficit that can be seen with similar-sized damage in the left hemisphere; thus the right hemisphere lesions are more apt to produce the "silent strokes." In contrast, a large global deterioration puts the diffusely represented functions at greater risk compared to functions with discrete focal representation. Such would be the scenario in the course of aging: the observed changes in right hemispheric tasks and the relative preservation of language functions.

To complicate the picture further, one must take into account the impact of our culture on psychological tasks. The visual-spatial tasks tend to be novel and unrehearsed. In contrast, language and verbal tasks are well practiced and used throughout everyday conversations and activity. Another hypothesis by Whitaker (39) suggests that verbal skills are less likely to be vulnerable to a global process such as aging because they are highly automatized. Because language function is localized in the dominant hemisphere, nondominant functions look relatively more impaired. It is worth noting here that Horn (29) did not equate his fluid/crystallized distinction (which also implicates overlearned materials) with this hypothesis of hemispheric differentiation, as Horn's theory is not based on an underlying neurological process.

Lastly, the hypothesis of laterality in aging and depression deserves some attention. In the depression of younger persons, the neuropsychological profile is not unlike that of patients with right hemispheric damage (48,54). Moreover, the prevalence of depression also increases with age (5). It is not clear if there is a relation between these two phenomena. Specifically, could the increase in depression in the elderly be a reflection of the decrease in right hemispheric functions, thereby making this group more susceptible to depression? Alternatively, are the laterality changes seen in depression independent of the changes observed in aging? Careful future comparisons of these groups, with attention to strategies of cognitive function, could help determine the nature of this relation and would hopefully shed light onto the underlying neurological mechanisms.

In short, the observed laterality distinction in aging is extremely complex and warrants considerable reworking. There are many confounding variables at play, not the least of which is our need to understand cognitive processes mediated by the right hemisphere. Application of these more refined tests need to be applied to the aging and depressed populations before this issue is resolved.

Cognitive Model

Neuropsychology has advanced because of the input of two areas of study. One, as discussed above, has been the benefits of new techniques and approaches in behavioral neurology. The second has stemmed from the theoretical advances in cognitive psychology, which has proved to be of singular importance for understanding brain–behavior relations. The interplay of theory and neurobehavior is not new, as exemplified by the advances of aphasiology based on developments from linguistic theories. The study of memory has traveled a similar route. The early information-processing theory (8) has progressively provided a way to study memory that could be both clinically and theoretically useful (9). Here the integration of observations from different amnesic states, be they from Wernicke-Korsakoff syndrome, degenerating dementias, trauma, or neurosurgical treatment, has given the field of memory a foundation and direction of research. Aging provides still another category to use in memory research, not only to enhance what transpires in the course of aging but also to provide additional details to our understanding of memory function. Thus changes in aging should figure into the current theory and methodology. For example, in an elegant experiment using the sensitive delay matching to sample, Oscar-Berman and Bonner (42) compare young, middle-aged, and old-aged normals to young, middle-aged, and old-aged alcoholics and to patients with Korsakoff's syndrome. Their results negated the concept that alcoholism presents a neuropsychological equivalent to aging, or that alcoholism is merely a form of accelerated or premature aging. Thus the task of delayed matching to sample, as used in this experiment, provided a method to separate the theoretical entities of selective attention and short-term memory demands, which could then subsequently capture the similarities and differences among these groups.

Psychologists have used the information-processing theory in innovative ways for both disease models and patterns in normal aging. Another instance is that the theory of memory storage models has been deemphasized in favor of models that stress the encoding strategies: Aging paradigms have followed this trend. Although the early focus of aging changes highlighted the difference between long-term and short-term memory, current research plays with concepts devoted to the changes of the encoding processes throughout the life-span. From the theoretical distinction between two types of encoding, effortful versus automatic processing (26,46), some psychologists have suggested that aging affects these processes differentially, i.e., that the volitional, effortful skills do decrease with age, whereas the automatic processes that can occur without any demands on attentional resources do not change with age. This hypothesis is still undergoing investigation (15) and refinement. Whatever the outcome, it is relevant that these models stimulate the questions that psychologists ask about aging and thereby determine the direction of the research. What these investigations can do is integrate the basic theories of the experimental literature with the neuropsychological and neurobehavioral advances of brain mechanisms.

Developmental Model

In earlier writings, Schaie (45) suggested that developmental models of psychology are not applicable to the study of late life development. Specifically, he stated that the works of developmental theorists such as Piaget are not transferable to aging, and that a developmental theory of aging requires an entirely new approach with new constructs and even new methods. If psychologists are trying to avoid concretizing the proverbial "second childhood" of old age, which in an ageist way denigrates the years of acquired experience, it is understandable why a psychologist dealing with adults veers away from literature having to do with childhood. However, in the hope that psychologists do not "throw the baby out with the bathwater," the progression of life-span developmental psychology should take a close look at what developmental theory has already spawned and what it can offer.

The first emphasis in incorporating developmental theory into the older years is to draw on theoretical principles, rather than being tied to concrete similarities observed during childhood and old age. Aphasia and language acquisition are not exactly paralleled: the language of an aphasic never dissolves to a form of infant babbling. Yet similarities can be drawn if the theory of psycholinguistics is used as a basis of comparison, e.g., phonemic simplification. In aging the same kind of analysis can be made. One fruitful example is provided by Moscovitch (38), where the theoretical categories of infancy memory stem from the piagetian model and are used to explain behaviors of older amnesics. As Moscovitch pointed out, the piagetian framework is not without critique: The developmental model addresses memory and retrieval before the infant has a fully developed symbol system, and therefore the model for older adults demands some sort of modification for individuals who have already acquired language. The point is that Moscovitch capitalized on the theoretical formulation of the piagetian model and applied it to the memory system in later disease states.

Another application of this principle is drawn from use of the organismic-developmental model of Werner (49). Kaplan and her associates (2,28,30) have invariably drawn parallels between developmental sequences and those observed in instances of deterioration in brain damage. The application of this paradigm in aging research is ready for the asking. The principles are not to seek the exact behaviors in children and old adults, but to use the wernerian method of following a process/ strategy approach to the neuropsychology of aging. Again, the theoretical foundation of change during adulthood can be thought of in terms of the theoretical levels of differentiation and hierarchical integration proposed by Werner. The expectation of changes would follow a reversal of these levels at the theoretical level, but the manifestation of the changes would be different in early and late development.

In short, although cognitive psychology has ample room for additional theory for late life development, the prior work of developmental cognitive psychologists provides an important contribution to the foundation of future research.

CONCLUSIONS

The study of aging provides an exciting new arena for neuropsychology. Hopefully, however, psychologists can learn from the history of early developmental literature. Comparisons can be made between young and old, but it is not enough to say that the older person is "worse" than his or her younger counterpart or even in comparison with himself or herself of earlier years. It is not only not enough, it is uninteresting: The comparison fails to elucidate the basics of brain–behavior relationships.

This chapter has attempted to address the hurdles that neuropsychology must face in order to avoid that direction. There are clearly methodological problems inherent in the research. The need for normative data, careful group selection, distinction among later decades into separate groups, and adaptive procedures and materials for the elderly are but a few such problems. However, the key challenge is in the realm of theory. There is no comprehensive cognitive theory of aging, and psychologists are in search of a route to follow. The prominence of the information-processing theory reflects the current trend in much of the literature of cognitive psychology. The neurological changes in the older brain certainly do not parallel the expansive growth experienced during childhood, but changes will nonetheless be revealed. With that information will come the neurological foundation that motivates the cognitive decrease or compensatory mechanisms of normal aging. The combined neuropsychological and developmental approach that has influenced much of our understanding of brain–behavior relations promises to offer an important contribution to aging research. Investigators may draw on or modify existing developmental theories, or they may need to create a new theory. However, it will be the infusion of the developmental approach that will yield an insightful understanding of the relation of behaviors and the older brain.

REFERENCES

1. Albert, M. S. (1981): Geriatric neuropsychology. *J. Consult. Clin. Psychol.*, 49:835–850.
2. Albert, M. S., and Kaplan, E. (1980): Organic implications of neuropsychological deficits in the elderly. In: *New Directions in Memory and Aging: Proceedings of the George Talland Memorial Conference,* edited by L. Poon, J. Fozard, L. Cermak, D. Ehrenberg, and L. Thompson, pp. 403–432. Erlbaum, Hillsdale, N.J.
3. Benson, D. F., and Geschwind, N. (1975): Psychiatric conditions associated with focal lesions of the central nervous system. In: *American Handbook of Psychiatry: Organic Disorders and Psychosomatic Medicine,* edited by S. Arieti, pp. 208–243. Basic Books, New York.
4. Berg, S. (1980): Psychological functioning in seventy and seventy-five-year-old people. *Acta Psychiatr. Scand.* [Suppl. 288], 62:5–47.
5. Blazer, D., and Williams, C. D. (1980): Epidemiology of dysphoria and depression in an elderly population. *Am. J. Psychiatry,* 137:439–444.
6. Blessed, G., Tomlinson, B. E., and Roth, M. (1968): The association between quantitative measures of dementia and senile changes in cerebral gray matter in elderly subjects. *Br. J. Psychiatry,* 114:797–811.
7. Bogen, J. (1979): The callosal syndrome. In: *Clinical Neuropsychology,* edited by K. Heilman and E. Valenstein, pp. 308–359. Oxford University Press, New York.
8. Broadbent, D. E. (1958): *Perception and Communication.* Pergamon Press, London.
9. Butters, N., and Cermak, L. (1980): *Alcoholic Korsakoff's Syndrome: An Information Processing Approach to Amnesia.* Academic Press, New York.
10. Butters, N., Albert, M., Sax, D., Milliotis, P., Nagode, J., and Sterste, A. (1983): The effect of verbal memory mediators on the pictorial memory of brain-damaged patients. *Neuropsychologia,* 21:307–323.
11. Cattell, R. B. (1963): Theory of fluid and crystallized intelligence: a critical experiment. *J. Educ. Psychol.,* 54:1–22.
12. Cerella, J. (1985): Information processing rates in the elderly. *Psychol. Bull.,* 98:67–83.
13. Corso, J. (1977): Auditory perception and communication. In: *Handbook of the Psychology of Aging,* edited by J. Birren and K. W. Schaie, pp. 535–553. Van Nostrand Reinhold, New York.
14. Cotman, C., and Scheff, S. (1979): Synaptic growth in aged animals. In: *Physiology and Cell Biology of Aging,* edited by A. Cherkin, C. Finch, N. Kharasch, T. Makinodan, F. Scott, and B. Strehler, pp. 109–120. Raven Press, New York.
15. Craik, F., and Rabinowitz, J. (1985): The effects of presentation rate and encoding task on age-related memory deficits. *J. Gerontol.,* 40:309–315.
16. Creasey, H., and Rapoport, S. (1985): The aging human brain. *Ann. Neurol.,* 17:2–10.
17. Cronbach, L. (1970): *Essentials of Psychological Testing.* Harper & Row, New York.
18. Cummings, J., and Benson, D. F. (1984): Subcortical dementia: review of an emerging concept. *Arch. Neurol.,* 41:874–879.
19. Cutler, N. R., Haxby, J., Duara, R., Grady, C., Kay, A., Kessler, R., Sundaram, M., and Rapoport, S. (1985): Clinical history, brain metabolism, and neuropsychological function in Alzheimer's disease. *Ann. Neurol.,* 18:298–309.
20. Doppelt, J. E., and Wallace, W. L. (1955): Standardization of the Wechsler Adult Intelligence Scale for older persons. *J. Abnorm. Social Psychol.,* 51:312–330.
21. Duffy, E. H., Albert, M. S., and McAnulty, G. (1984): Brain electrical activity in patients with pre-senile and senile dementia of the Alzheimer type. *Ann. Neurol.,* 16:439–448.
22. Finch, C. E. (1972): Enzyme activities, gene function, and aging in mammals. *Exp. Gerontol.,* 7:53–67.
23. Folstein, M., Folstein, S., and McHugh, P. (1975): "Mini-mental state": a practical method for grading the cognitive state of patients for the clinician. *J. Psychiatr. Res.,* 12:189–198.
24. Gardner, H. (1980): *Artful Scribbles: The Significance of Children's Drawings,* Basic Books, New York.
25. Geschwind, N., and Galaburda, A. (1985): Cerebral lateralization. *Arch. Neurol.,* 42:428–459.
26. Hasher, L., and Zacks, R. T. (1979): Automatic and effortful processes in memory. *J. Exp. Psychol.,* 108:356–388.
27. Henderson, V. W. (1985): Lesion localization in Broca's aphasia: implications from Broca's aphasias without hemiparesis. *Arch. Neurol.,* 42:1210–1212.
28. Hochanadel, G., and Kaplan, E. (1984): Neuropsychology of normal aging. In: *Clinical Neurology of Aging,* edited by M. L. Albert, pp. 231–244. Oxford University Press, New York.

29. Horn, J. L. (1982): Aging of fluid and crystallized intelligence. In: *Advances in the Study of Communication and Affect: Aging and Cognitive Processes,* Vol. 8, edited by F. Craik and S. Trehub, pp. 237–278. Plenum Press, New York.

30. Kaplan, E. (1968): Gestural Representation of Implement Usage: An Organismic-Developmental Study. Doctoral dissertation, Clark University, Worcester, MA.

31. Katz, R., and Harner, R. (1984): Electroencephalography in aging. In: *Clinical Neurology of Aging,* edited by M. L. Albert, pp. 114–138. Oxford University Press, New York.

32. Kline, D., and Schieber, F. (1985): Vision and aging. In: *The Handbook of the Psychology of Aging,* edited by J. Birren and K. W. Schaie, pp. 296–324. Van Nostrand Reinhold, New York.

33. Lapidot, M. B. (1983): Is there hemi-aging? In: *Hemisyndromes: Psychobiology, Neurology, Psychiatry,* edited by M. S. Myslobodosky, pp. 193–212. Academic Press, New York.

34. Levy, M. I., Mohs, R. C., Rosen, W., and Davis, K. L. (1982): Research subject recruitment for gerontological studies of pharmacological agents. *Neurobiol. Aging,* 3:77–79.

35. Luria, A. R. (1962): *Higher Cortical Functions In Man.* Basic Books, New York.

36. Matarazzo, J. D. (1972): *Wechsler's Measurement and Appraisal of Adult Intelligence.* Williams & Wilkins, Baltimore.

37. Mohr, J. P. (1976): Broca's area and Broca's aphasia. In: *Studies in Neurolinguistics,* Vol. 1, edited by H. Whitaker and H. A. Whitaker. Academic Press, New York.

38. Moscovitch, M. (1985): Memory from infancy to old age: implications for theories of normal and pathological memory. *Ann. N. Y. Acad. Sci.,* 444:78–96.

39. Obler, L., and Albert, M. L. (1985): Language skills across adulthood. In: *Handbook of the Psychology of Aging,* 2nd ed., edited by J. Birren and W. K. Schaie, pp. 463–473. Van Nostrand Reinhold, New York.

40. Obler, L, Albert, M. L., Goodglass, H., and Benson, D. F. (1978): Aphasia type and aging. *Brain Lang.,* 6:318–322.

41. Obrist, W. D. (1976): Problems of aging. In: *Handbook of EEG and Clinical Neurophysiology,* Vol. 6A, edited by G. E. Chatrian and G. Lairy, pp. 275–292. Elsevier, Amsterdam.

42. Oscar-Berman, M., and Bonner, R. T. (1985): Matching and delayed matching-to-sample performance as measures of visual processing, selective attention, and memory in aging and alcoholic individuals. *Neuropsychologia,* 23:639–651.

43. Polich, J., and Starr, A. (1984): Evoked potentials in aging. In: *Clinical Neurology of Aging,* edited by M. L. Albert, pp. 149–177. Oxford University Press, New York.

44. Salthouse, T. (1985): Speed of behavior and its implications for cognition. In: *Handbook of the Psychology of Aging,* edited by J. Birren and K. W. Schaie, pp. 400–422. Van Nostrand Reinhold, New York.

45. Schaie, K. W. (1977): Toward a stage theory of adult cognitive development. In: *Adult Development and Aging,* edited by K. W. Schaie and J. Geiwitz, pp. 227–233. Little, Brown, Boston.

46. Shiffrin, R., and Schneider, W. (1977): Controlled and automatic human information processing. *Psychol. Rev.,* 84:127–190.

47. Truex, R. C., and Carpenter, M. B. (1969): *Human Neuroanatomy.* Williams & Wilkins, Baltimore.

48. Tucker, D., Stenslie, C., Roth, R., and Shearer, S. (1981): Right frontal lobe activation and right hemisphere performance: decrement during a depressed mood. *Arch. Gen. Psychiatry,* 38:169–174.

49. Werner, H. (1937): Process and achievement: A basic problem of education and developmental psychology. *Harvard Educ. Rev.,* 1:353–368.

50. Whitehouse, P. (1986): The concept of subcortical and cortical dementia: another look. *Ann. Neurol.,* 19:1–6.

51. Whitehouse, P., Price, D., and Struble, R. (1982): Alzheimer's disease and senile dementia: loss of neurons in the basal forebrain. *Science,* 215:1237–1239.

52. Williams, M. E., Hadler, N. M., and Earp, J. A. (1982): Manual ability as a marker of dependency in geriatric women. *J. Chronic Dis.,* 35:115–122.

53. Wilson, L. A., Lawson, I. R., and Bross, W. (1962): Multiple disorders in the elderly. *Lancet,* 2:841–847.

54. Yazowitz, A., Bruder, G., Sutton, S., Sharpe, L., Gurland, B., Fleiss, J.,and Costa, L. (1979): Dichotic perception: evidence for right hemisphere dysfunction in affective psychosis. *Br. J. Psychiatry,* 135:224–237.

55. Yesavage, J., Brink, T. L., Rose, T. L., Lum, O., Huang, V., Adey, M. B., and Leirer, V. O. (1983): Development and validation of a geriatric depression screening scale: a preliminary report. *J. Psychiatr. Res.,* 17:37–49.

Human Aging Research: Concepts and Techniques,
edited by B. Kent and R. N. Butler.
Raven Press, Ltd., New York © 1988.

Immunology

James E. Nagel and William H. Adler

Clinical Immunology Section, Gerontology Research Center, National Institute on Aging,
National Institutes of Health, Baltimore, Maryland 21224

The field of immunology has contributed to aging research in many ways. On a clinical level it is well documented that the incidence and severity of infectious diseases and some neoplasias increase with age. The mechanisms that underlie this age-related decrease in host defenses have been the focal point of most clinical studies of immune function in the elderly. However, there are also basic research projects involving the study of human cells. These projects are concerned with the function of cells, the ability of cells to make antibody, the control mechanisms in an immune response, the transcription of genes that control the synthesis of bioactive proteins, influence cells, and alter cell membranes, and projects that detail the ability of cells to divide and replicate their genome. There are also a large number of investigations in the area of research about aging that use experimental animal models in which immunization procedures, genetic studies, nutritional influences, transplantation, and reconstitution experiments are more appropriate and more easily accomplished. There is also a hypothesis that the breakdown and change in immune function during aging causes aging itself.

This chapter focuses on the various facets of clinical studies of immune function used to outline the changes seen in the elderly population. These studies are both clinical diagnostic procedures as well as research procedures whose significance at this time is as yet undetermined.

LYMPHOCYTES

The first consideration in a clinical appraisal of the immune function of an individual is determination of the lymphocyte count. The finding of a lymphopenia and a drop in lymphocyte count from previously determined levels both have clinical significance. Studies utilizing nursing home and hospitalized elderly show that a drop in lymphocyte count is correlated with an imminently grave prognosis. These changes in lymphocyte count also have significance in healthy elderly subjects in whom death is associated with a decrease in lymphocyte count that occurs up to several years prior to death. Longitudinal studies in a large population have

299

shown that the lymphocyte count does not decrease with age (2). The reason may be that those individuals with a drop in their count die, which then removes them from the study—in effect a selection process.

Using several different monoclonal antibodies that identify and quantitate T-lymphocytes and T-cell subsets, one can find age-associated changes (11). In general, however, these changes have yet to be shown to have any clinical significance. Some investigators have reported changes in helper ($T4^+$) or suppressor ($T8^+$) T-cell subpopulations with aging, but it is not a consistent finding. These differences may relate more to the health of the study subjects than to their age. A comparison of the ratio of helper and suppressor cells (4:8 ratio) reveals either no change from young adults or a slight increase (due to decreased suppressor cells) with age. In short, there are no clinically important major losses of any particular type of cell represented in the peripheral blood (Table 1). However, there are important changes seen in the functional abilities of lymphocytes from the elderly. The systems that have been developed to study T-cell and B-cell function are mostly *in vitro* assays. However, there are *in vivo* tests that are not only important but that have clinical significance. The foremost test in this category is the delayed hypersensitivity skin test for tuberculosis. Although this disease occurs mainly in the elderly, the pathogenesis is still in doubt. It was previously thought that tuberculosis in the elderly was the reactivation of dormant disease, but studies suggest that an age-related immunodeficiency results in the elderly being more susceptible to infection. The skin test becomes important not only for detecting those individuals who are positive and require additional studies to rule out active disease but also to detect the level of T-cell and macrophage function *in vivo*. A general anergy is more common in the elderly, so tuberculin is usually administered in combination with other skin test antigens to which most individuals respond. In this way it is possible to test *in vivo* the level of the individual's cell-mediated immunity.

TABLE 1. *Monoclonal antibodies*

Function	Antigen	Peripheral blood (%)	Age-associated change in number
T-lymphocytes	T3 (OKT3, Leu4, T3)	76 ± 6	No change
T-helper lymphocytes	T4 (OKT4, Leu3a, b, T4)	46 ± 8	No change
T-suppressor/cytotoxic	T8 (OKT8, Leu2a, b, T8)	32 ± 8	Sl. decrease
T-lymphocytes, SRBC-receptor associated	T11 (OKT11, Leu5, T11, Lyt3)	83 ± 5	No change
NK cells	Leu7 (HNK-1)	20 ± 7	No change
B-lymphocytes	Leu12	10 ± 5	No change

There are many *in vitro* assays of lymphocyte function available; however, many are complex and therefore are not available as routine laboratory tests. The first and still most widely used assay of lymphocyte function is the proliferative response to mitogen stimulation. This assay measures the ability of lymphocytes to respond to an activating signal by quantitating the cells incorporation of tritiated thymidine into newly synthesized DNA. The level of radionuclide incorporation is dependent on the number of responsive cells in the cell culture, as well as the ability of those cells and their daughters to divide in culture. In both animal models and humans, cell proliferative ability decreases with age; however, there is large individual variation within age groups in the degree of this impairment. Some old people have lymphocytes that display good proliferative potential, and there are young people whose cells respond poorly to mitogens. The mitogenic activating signals that are the least able to drive lymphoid cells from the elderly are those that stimulate T-cells. Commonly used T-cell mitogens include phytohemagglutinin (PHA), concanavalin A (Con A), staphylococcal enterotoxin B (SEB), and the OKT3 anti-T-cell antigen receptor monoclonal antibody. Mitogens such as pokeweed (PWM) and staphylococcal protein A, which affect mainly B-cells, have less or no age-related decrease in their ability to stimulate cells. The other stimuli to which there is an age-related decrease are the histocompatibility (HLA) antigens on allogeneic cells in a mixed lymphocyte reaction, again a T-cell response (8).

Interleukin

Stimulated T-cells release factors that can augment the level of proliferation of T-cells. These factors can also up-regulate the receptors on the T-cell membranes for these factors. In cell culture, interleukin-2 (IL-2) is primarily responsible for the continued proliferation of the daughter cells after the initial T-cell response to a mitogenic signal. Several investigators have now shown that the ability to produce IL-2 decreases with the age of the cell donor. Furthermore, the ability to express cell surface receptors for IL-2 also decreases with age (5). Of major interest, however, is the finding that the *in vitro* addition of exogenous IL-2 can boost the proliferative ability of cells from old people and induce additional cell surface receptors for IL-2. This finding suggests that IL-2 may be a useful agent for reconstitution of an impaired immune response. To date, several short-term clinical trials examining the *in vivo* effects of IL-2 on various age-related immune defects have been conducted. The results, however, have generally been inconclusive or irrelevant to clinical gerontology. Although IL-2 is the object of most research in aging and immune function, it is well to consider that other factors also regulate IL-2 levels. For example, IL-1 can induce IL-2 release, and interferon can augment the transcription of the IL-2 gene. Because all these substances are interrelated, a defect in the synthesis of one may affect the others (16).

Functional T-cell Studies

One function of the helper T-cell population is to promote the induction of antibody synthesis by B-cells. The T-cell receptor (the cell surface molecule that recognizes and binds foreign antigens) triggers a chain of events that culminates in T-cell activation and proliferation. Activated T-cells release lymphokines, which influence B-cell gene rearrangements necessary for the synthesis and release of complete antibody molecules. It is possible to study this helper function *in vitro* using either an antigen-specific response or a polyclonal response induced with PWM. To study a specific response, the donor of the peripheral blood lymphocytes must have been immunized with the antigen within a period of about 6 weeks prior to obtaining the blood sample. In most studies the antigen used is tetanus toxoid. Because this procedure requires immunization and a period of time before the cells can be used, it is seldom practical to utilize this assay in the usual clinical setting. As such, the polyclonal response to PWM is often used, as no immunization procedure is necessary and no time need elapse before blood collection. Both assays have shown that there is a loss of helper T-cell function with the increasing age of the cell donor. The decrease in the antibody-forming ability of cells from elderly individuals is not totally but almost completely due to a defect in helper T-cell function. This has been shown using experiments in which T- and B-cells from old and young people are mixed *in vitro*. The T-cell defect is associated with a decrease in IL-2 release by the helper T-cells (8). Another consideration concerning individuals whose cells have poor or negligible antibody-forming ability is an association between this lack of cell function and certain histocompatibility genetic types. It means that chronological age as well as genetic considerations may be associated with faltering immune function.

Summary

T-cell function, in particular helper T-cell function, shows the most decrease in functional levels with age. However, other T-cell studies, especially in animals, have shown that other systems in which IL-2 is important, e.g., the generation of cytotoxic T-cells, also have an age-related decrease in function. It appears that all functions of T-cells that require IL-2 for full expression show the greatest decrease with age. Therefore IL-2, IL-2 receptors, and IL-2 inducers are of great interest in aging research at this time. Coupled with the observation that exogenously added IL-2 can reconstitute normal functional levels in T-cells from old people in some *in vitro* assay systems, one can understand why this interest exists. Analysis of the receptors that mediate immune responses reveals that virtually all belong to a single gene superfamily. Future studies will be concerned with the structure of the IL-2 gene as well as the promotor and enhancer elements that regulate its expression. The structure of these genes and their regulatory elements in cells from old people and animals will contribute a great deal to the understanding of the nature of the age-associated immune defects.

CYTOTOXIC CELLS

Natural killer (NK) cells, first described about a decade ago, are lymphoid cells from normal individuals that mediate spontaneous cytolytic activity against many types of tumor and virus-infected cells. Because NK cells do not require prior exposure to antigen, they appear to function as the primary effectors of a broad surveillance system to prevent tumor growth (7). Although the precise role of NK cells in immunosurveillance, especially as related to primary *in vivo* tumor resistance, remains uncertain, considerable evidence exists that NK cells play important roles in allograft rejection, regulation of hematopoiesis, and resistance to some infections, and are effector cells in several pathological conditions. Not only are NK cells cytolytic killers, they are also capable of producing IL-2, IL-1, B-cell growth factor (BCGF), colony-stimulating factor (CSF), and interferon. Like polymorphonuclear leukocytes and macrophages, NK cells rapidly (< 24 hours) mediate spontaneous cytolytic activity—in contrast to unsensitized cytotoxic T-cells, which display virtually no spontaneous cytolytic activity and must be activated by exposure to an antigen. Unprimed cytotoxic T-cells require a week or more of antigen exposure before they can mediate a cytolytic response.

Most NK activity is associated with a population of lymphocytes that have a large, granular morphology. These large granular lymphocytes (LGLs) comprise 5 to 10% of the peripheral blood lymphocytes; however, fewer than half of the LGLs display functional NK activity. The enumeration of NK cells is most easily accomplished using a panel of monoclonal antibodies and flow cytometry. A number of monoclonal antibodies that identify NK cells have been developed; however, none alone is unique for NK cells or distinguish NK cells from other cytotoxic effector cells.

The first monoclonal antibody to identify a large proportion of human NK cells was HNK-1 (Leu-7). It combines with an antigen of approximately 110,000 molecular weight and reacts with 20 to 70% of peripheral blood NK cells. It also reacts with some T- and pre-B-cell lines, as well as myelin-producing oligodendrocytes of the central nervous system. Although it was initially reported that the representation of Leu-7$^+$ cells increases with age, further studies have demonstrated that after approximately 20 years of age there is no appreciable change in the percentage or absolute numbers of Leu-7$^+$ cells.

There has been considerable interest in classifying NK cells by multiple cell-surface antigens. Using this technique, several groups of investigators have identified subpopulations of NK cells that have differing phenotypes as well as functional cytolytic capabilities. Two-color immunofluorescence indicates the existence of three distinct subpopulations (11^+7^+, 11^+7^-, 11^-7^+) of NK cells defined by their expression of Leu-11a and Leu-7 antigens. Data from our laboratory indicate that the Leu-11a$^-$,7$^+$ subpopulation, which accounts for 40 to 50% of peripheral blood NK cells, decreases in both relative and absolute numbers in individuals over 60 years of age. It should be noted, however, that this subset displays weak cytolytic activity compared to the Leu-11a$^+$,7$^+$ or Leu-7$^+$,7$^-$ subsets (1).

Quantitation of cytotoxic cell function is most often done using a chromium release assay. A constant number of ^{51}Cr-labeled target cells are incubated with serial dilutions of effector cells, after which the amount of radioactivity in the supernatant that was released from the lysed target cells is measured. Most studies of human NK cell function use tumor cells (the most popular being the erythroleukemia cell line K562) as targets because most normal cells, unless infected by a virus, are generally resistant to NK lysis and difficult to label with chromium. Several studies have examined the effect of age on NK function and have concluded that little or no change in peripheral blood NK activity occurs throughout adult life.

Early studies of NK cells have concentrated on their antitumor activity, but it has also been shown that there are important roles for these cells in resistance to infectious diseases and in allograft rejection, as well as a possible role in the pathogenesis of medically important diseases such as multiple sclerosis. These activities provide areas for future research.

ANTIBODY

Corresponding to the diminished *in vitro* production of both specific and polyclonal antibody, age-related changes in the amounts and types of serum immunoglobulins have been reported in several studies. The pathogenesis of these changes and the relative effect of age are difficult to determine because of concurrent medical problems in many elderly individuals and a general lack of longitudinal data. The levels of immunoglobulin M (IgM) and IgD decrease with age, and salivary and serum IgA levels increase (3). Although there are conflicting data, IgG levels appear to modestly increase in the elderly. IgE levels decrease markedly with advanced age in atopic individuals but remain stable in nonatopic subjects. The wide range of normal values for IgG, IgA, and IgM make the subtle age-related changes in immunoglobulin levels of limited practical use in clinical gerontology. Specific serum antibody levels such as antitetanus toxoid antibody decrease in concentration with age, especially in women. The ability of individuals over 70 years of age to respond to this antigen is markedly compromised. Therefore even though serum immunoprotein levels remain about the same with age, specific antibody levels decrease.

Autoimmunity

Many studies have noted that serum from 10 to 15% of normal elderly individuals contains immunoglobulin with autoantibody activity. Autoantibodies are more commonly found in women of all ages. The presence of serum autoantibodies in elderly individuals who lack the typical clinical manifestations of autoimmune disease has generally been interpreted as indicative of a loss of self-recognition and attributed to defective helper/suppressor immunoregulatory mechanisms (13).

These antibodies also form the basis for the autoimmune theory of aging in which autoantibodies are implicated as being causative of aging phenomena through the production of immune complexes and their resultant tissue damage. The autoantibody most frequently found in old people is IgM rheumatoid factor (RF), although an increased incidence of anti-gastric and anti-thyroglobulin antibodies has also been reported. Antinuclear antibodies are generally not found. Several reports suggest that the incidence of autoantibodies other than RF in the elderly is actually no different than the level found in young individuals (15). This result is thought to be due to the use of more rigorous criteria in the selection of "normal" healthy elderly subjects for study. Because of a lack of understanding of the precise role of RF, it is unclear whether an increased amount of RF is pathologic or physiological, but in the elderly it is not necessarily associated with the presence of rheumatoid arthritis. Because RF increases the antigen-binding ability of low-avidity IgG antibody, it has been suggested that increased RF may actually enhance humoral antibody activity and therefore may be a mechanism for improving host resistance.

Monoclonal Gammopathy

Whereas the presence of a monoclonal immunoglobulin (M-component) in young individuals is generally indicative of a malignant process, serum from 3% or more of individuals over 65 years of age contains an M component (10). Measurement of immunoglobulin light-chain kappa/lambda ratios also demonstrates that elderly individuals have reduced immunoglobulin heterogeneity (14). Approximately one-third of older individuals with an immunoglobulin or immunoglobulin fragment of discrete mobility and size in their serum or urine have no underlying disease. This condition is generally referred to as "benign" monoclonal gammopathy (BMG). Whether this condition is truly benign remains controversial, as the diagnosis of BMG is largely one of exclusion and careful follow-up to eliminate individuals who develop malignant lymphoreticular disease. Clinical differentiation of BMG from multiple myeloma and Waldenström's macroglobulinemia, which also appear with increased incidence in the elderly, is frequently difficult or impossible. One useful observation is that if the monoclonal immunoglobulin remains stable and no clinical findings develop within 1 year, malignant disease is unlikely (< 5% incidence) to occur. Mono- or oligoclonal immunogammopathies are also found in association with liver and cold agglutinin disease, systemic lupus erythematosus, and subacute bacterial endocarditis. The spectrum of defects, from monoclonal immunoglobulinemia to restricted antibody heterogeneity, are considered to be the result of impaired T-cell regulation of B-cell function.

GRANULOCYTES

The morbidity and mortality of bacterial infections are markedly increased in the elderly. A major host defense mechanism against bacterial infection is the polymorphonuclear leukocyte (PMN). There are presently few data available about PMN function in the elderly. Studies from our laboratory indicate that PMN oxidative metabolism, as quantitated by the nitroblue tetrazolium dye reduction test, does not differ between young and elderly subjects. We also found no difference in *in vitro* staphylococcal killing, although others have reported defective killing of *Candida*. Despite a daily turnover of approximately 10^{11} PMNs, there is no indication that the level of maturity (as judged by nuclear lobation) or the number of circulating PMNs decreases in the elderly. There is information suggesting that the rate of PMN release and the size of the neutrophil storage pool in the bone marrow of elderly individuals are diminished. An important discovery is that PMNs from individuals over 60 years of age demonstrate a phagocytic defect. A subpopulation of the PMNs from old people have a markedly decreased ability to phagocytose latex beads. This finding means that despite normal numbers of circulating PMNs there is a functional granulocytopenia present in the elderly (12). One rather consistent finding in studies examining age-related changes in PMN function is that few or no changes are observed in PMNs from individuals under the age of 60 to 70 years.

CONCLUSION AND CLINICAL RECOMMENDATIONS

One frequently heard statement regarding immunologic evaluations of elderly adults is that they are useless or unnecessary as little or nothing can be done to improve any of the deficits that might be identified. At the present time this assessment of the situation is generally correct. There are, however, exceptions. One area of medical therapeutics largely ignored by physicians dealing with adult and elderly patients is immunization. Clearly adults through the fifth decade of life are capable of responding equally as well as younger persons to immunization and can be effectively immunized with several vaccines. At the present time, it is recommended by the Centers for Disease Control and the American College of Physicians that individuals over age 65 be immunized with tetanus–diphtheria toxoid (Td) and influenza and pneumococcal vaccines (Table 2). Certain life styles or occupations may subject a person to an increased risk of exposure to some vaccine-preventable diseases, and these persons should receive additional vaccines (4). The rationale for the administration of these vaccines is clinically based.

The age distribution of tetanus cases in America is essentially bimodal, with most occurring in the neonatal and elderly age groups. The incidence of tetanus in the over-60 age group is 8 to 10 times that seen in young adults, and mortality is 25 to 50 times higher. Many cases of tetanus among the elderly are associated with injuries not generally considered tetanus-associated. Elderly patients may be too old to have received pediatric immunization, which has been routine only since the 1940s, or they may not have had a booster immunization for a long time. Tetanus is more common in men of all ages despite the fact that many men were routinely immunized while in military service. Data indicate that there

TABLE 2. *Adult immunization program*

Vaccine	Dose	Recommendations
Tetanus and diphtheria toxoids, adsorbed (Td)	0.5 ml i.m.	
Primary series		Two doses 4–6 weeks apart; one dose 6–12 months later
Booster	0.5 ml i.m.	Every 10 years
Pneumococcal vaccine	0.5 ml i.m. or s.q.	One dose; booster not recommended
Influenza vaccine, either whole or "split" virus	0.5 ml i.m.	Yearly

is adequate recall ability with tetanus toxoid for as long as 25 years after immunization. Verbal immunization histories are notoriously unreliable, and adults of any age with unknown or uncertain histories of receiving tetanus toxoid should therefore be considered unimmunized and receive a three-injection primary series of Td vaccine. Immunized individuals should receive a booster dose every 10 years. The combined adult-type Td vaccine should be used, as diphtheria titers diminish at a rate similar to those of tetanus. Should diphtheria arise in a community, as it has done several times during the last two decades, unvaccinated elderly individuals would be unprotected.

Mortality from pneumococcal pneumonia increases in incidence among individuals over 40 years of age. By age 60 this rate is approximately twofold greater than that observed in younger persons. Several medical conditions commonly found among the elderly, e.g., diabetes mellitus, chronic pulmonary disease, and congestive heart failure, are generally thought to increase the risk of contracting pneumococcal disease as well as its severity. At present *Streptococcus pneumoniae* is the most common cause of community-acquired pneumonia, being responsible for 30 to 78% of cases. Bacteremia is a complication in approximately 20% of patients with pneumococcal pneumonia and is associated with a 20 to 40% mortality rate.

Studies have demonstrated that pneumococcal vaccine confers substantial protection against systemic pneumococcal infection in the elderly. Immunization of this age group with pneumococcal vaccine, previously only encouraged, is now recommended (6). There is now a newly licensed pneumococcal vaccine available that contains antigens to 23 serotypes, representing approximately 85% of the pneumococcal types responsible for bacteremic disease. The dose of each antigen in the 23-serotype vaccine has been reduced from 50μg to 25μg to diminish the incidence of local transient side effects. Because of a marked increase in serious adverse reactions following reimmunization, a second, or booster, dose should not be given even if the individual previously received the earlier 8- or 14-serotype pneumococcal vaccines. It has been observed that approximately two-thirds of patients with serious pneumococcal disease have been hospitalized within the preceding 5 years, leading to the recommendation that all elderly persons be immunized during a hospitalization or at the time of their discharge (9).

Influenza develops twice as frequently in individuals over age 60 as it does in younger adults. Morbidity is highest at both ends of the age spectrum, but mortality is confined almost exclusively to the older age groups. Approximately 20% of a nursing home population can be expected to develop influenza during an epidemic. Although some studies show that early treatment of nursing home residents with amantadine can reduce the severity of influenza infection, many practitioners are hesitant to use this drug in the elderly because of its expense and side effects, e.g., confusion and drowsiness. During recent epidemics most of the deaths from influenza among the elderly occurred in individuals with underlying chronic disease. Although the administration of influenza vaccine to the elderly has been recommended for at least a decade, estimates indicate that fewer than 20% of the target population are actually immunized (4). In addition, many elderly individuals, especially those in their eighth and ninth decades, have poor antibody responses to the single 0.5-ml dose now recommended. A booster 4 to 6 weeks after initial administration improves antibody responses, but more research is needed before this approach can be generally recommended.

One goal of research on aging is to decrease the morbidity and hospitalizations associated with care of the elderly. By changing age-related disease patterns, one may be able to decrease utilization of medical facilities and lessen the economic burden on both the individual and the society related to health care of the elderly. Changes in the therapeutic approaches to the care of the elderly based on a sound understanding of the mechanisms underlying age-related alterations in host defenses are critical to accomplishing this goal. A number of age-related changes in immune function are summarized in Table 3; however, at present no therapy exists to

TABLE 3. *Changes in immune function with aging*

1. No change in number of peripheral blood lymphocytes except in individuals within 3 years of death
2. Decreased responses to T-cell mitogens
3. Decreased helper T-cell activity
4. Decreased levels of specific antibody (i.e., anti-tetanus)
5. Increase incidence and diversity of "autoimmune" antibodies
6. No change in number of peripheral blood B-lymphocytes
7. Increased incidence of monoclonal immunoglobulins in serum
8. Decreased heterogeneity of antibody response and decreased avidity of immunoglobulin molecules produced
9. Diminished synthesis of mediator IL-2
10. Increased production of anti-idiotype antibodies
11. No change in NK cell function
12. Diminished *in vivo* cutaneous delayed hypersensitivity
13. No significant change in serum immunoglobulin levels
14. Enhanced cellular responsiveness to prostaglandin E_2
15. Increased numbers of auto rosette-forming cells
16. Slightly decreased numbers of peripheral blood suppressor cells

correct these deficits. If common mechanisms are found to be associated with a number of immune deficiencies, it may be easier to rejuvenate or augment certain areas of the immune system than is now thought. Clearly, additional investigations, including studies of immunoadjuvants or immunostimulants are needed to develop improved therapeutic algorithms for treatment of the elderly patient.

REFERENCES

1. Bender, B. S., Chrest, F. J., and Adler, W. H. (1986): Phenotypic expression of natural killer cell associated membrane antigens and cytolytic function of peripheral blood cells from different aged humans. *J. Clin. Lab. Immunol. (in press)*.
2. Bender, B. S., Nagel, J. E., Adler, W. H., and Andres, R. (1986): A sixteen year longitudinal study of the absolute peripheral blood lymphocyte count and subsequent mortality of elderly men. *J. Am. Geriatr. Soc. (in press)*.
3. Buckley, C. E., III, and Dorsey, F. C. (1970): The effect of aging on human serum immunoglobulin concentrations. *J. Immunol.*, 105:964–972.
4. Committee on Immunization (1985): *Guide for Adult Immunization*. American College of Physicians, Philadelphia.
5. Gillis, S., Kozak, R., Durante, M., and Weksler, M. E. (1981): Immunological studies of aging: decreased production of and response to T cell growth factor by lymphocytes from aged humans. *J. Clin. Invest.*, 67:937–942.
6. Health and Public Policy Committee, American College of Physician (1986): Pneumococcal vaccine. *Ann. Intern. Med.*, 104:118–120.
7. Herberman, R. B., and Callewaert, D. M., editors (1985): *Mechanisms of Cytotoxicity by NK Cells*. Academic Press, Orlando, FL.
8. Jones, K. H., and Ennist, D. L. (1985): Mechanism of age-related changes in cell mediated immunity. In: *Review of Biological Research in Aging*, Vol. 2, edited by M. Rothstein, pp. 155–177. Alan R. Liss, New York.
9. Klein, R. S., and Adachi, N. (1983): Pneumococcal vaccine in the hospital: improved use and implications for high-risk patients. *Arch. Intern. Med.*, 143:1878–1881.
10. Kyle, R. A., and Bayrd, E. D., editors (1976): *The Monoclonal Gammopathies. Multiple Myeloma and Related Plasma Cell Disorders*. Charles C Thomas, Springfield, IL.
11. Nagel, J. E., Chrest, F. J., and Adler, W. H. (1983): Monoclonal antibody analysis of T-lymphocyte subsets in young and aged adults. *Immunol. Commun.*, 12:223–237.
12. Nagel, J. E., Han, K., Coon, P. J., Adler, W. H., and Bender, B. S. (1986): Age differences in phagocytosis by polymorphonuclear leukocytes measured by flow cytometry. *J. Leuk. Biol.*, 39:399–407.
13. Pandey, J. P., Fudenberg, H. H., Ainsworth, S. K., and Loadholt, C. B. (1979): Autoantibodies in healthy subjects of different age groups. *Mech. Ageing Dev.*, 10:399–404.
14. Riesen, W., Keller, H., Skvaril, F., Morell, A., and Barandun, S. (1976): Restriction of immunoglobulin heterogeneity, autoimmunity and serum protein levels in aged people. *Clin. Exp. Immunol.*, 26:280–285.
15. Silvestris, F., Anderson, W., Goodwin, J. S., and Williams, R. C., Jr. (1985): Discrepancy in the expression of autoantibodies in healthy aged individuals. *Clin. Immunol. Immunopathol.*, 35:234–244.
16. Thoman, M. (1985): Role of interleukin-2 in the age-related impairment of immune function. *J. Am. Geriatr. Soc.*, 33:781–787.

Human Aging Research: Concepts and Techniques,
edited by B. Kent and R. N. Butler.
Raven Press, Ltd., New York © 1988.

Biochemical Aspects of Aging

Diana S. Beattie

*Department of Biochemistry, West Virginia University, School of Medicine,
Morgantown, West Virginia 26506*

The reader may wonder at the decision to include a chapter on the biochemistry of aging in a book such as this one. It should be noted, however, that the biochemist studies age-related changes at the molecular level whose sum total is what others, i.e., physiologists, physicians, statisticians, and epidemiologists, are observing at a more complex level. Our hope is that an increased understanding of these fundamental aging processes at the molecular level, e.g., in a protein, may be applied to the study of changes in cell function during senescence and eventually may help to define useful approaches to the study of organ and whole animal aging processes.

This chapter first includes a brief description of the major theories of biochemical aging originally proposed during the 1950s and 1960s. Subsequently, available experimental models for the study of biochemical aging are discussed followed by a brief survey of experimental results of aging research obtained by biochemists over the past 20 years. Data from the author's laboratory on the effects of aging on the key regulatory enzyme (5-aminolevulinic acid synthase) of the heme biosynthetic pathway are included. Finally, some suggestions are offered about where research in the biochemistry of aging may (or should) be headed, in the author's opinion.

THEORIES OF AGING

Three major theories to explain aging at the biochemical or molecular level have been proposed and continue to form the basis of much research on the biochemistry of aging. These theories include the free radical theory initially proposed by Harmon, the error catastrophe hypothesis usually credited to Orgel, and the cell senescence theory (or genetic programming theory) of Hayflick (see refs. 4, 7, 14 for reviews).

According to the *free radical theory* of aging, free radicals produced either within the cells as a consequence of the usual metabolic pathways or by events occurring external to the cell, e.g., ionizing or ultraviolet radiation, cause irreversible damage to the cells during the life-span of the organism, leading to senescence and eventual death. For example, free radicals may be generated during electron transport by the mitochondrial electron transport chain as a consequence of the transfer of a single electron to oxygen, forming the superoxide anion. Subsequently, the superoxide anion in a series of reactions may lead to formation of the hydroxyl radical, an active free radical that may be the actual damaging agent (Fig. 1). Alternatively, oxygen in the presence of either a metal ion or certain enzyme systems may cause damage by the peroxidation of the double bonds in unsaturated fatty acids present in intracellular membranes. The eventual production of free radicals by this process may cause cross-linking of biological molecules, especially polymers such as proteins or DNA with the subsequent accumulation of damage. As is discussed in more detail later in the chapter, a relation between lipid peroxidation and the appearance of the so-called age pigment, lipofuscin, during aging has been observed. Furthermore, certain protective systems to remove these potentially damaging free radicals, e.g., superoxide dismutase, catalase, and glutathione peroxidase, have evolved in most organisms.

The *error catastrophe hypothesis* suggests that mistakes may occur during biosynthetic processes such that proteins with an incorrect primary structure are produced. Possibly these errors are amplified, especially if the proteins (enzymes) involved in either DNA, RNA, or protein synthesis are among those synthesized incorrectly. It is clear today that the information necessary for the correct sequence of all the proteins in the body is encoded in genes present in DNA (in the nucleus of the cell). The information contained in DNA is transcribed into RNA, which provides the message for subsequent synthesis of the proteins. All of these processes, e.g., replication of DNA during cell division, transcription of DNA into RNA, and translation of RNA into protein, require a large number of enzymes as catalysts for the process. As a consequence of a mistake in the primary sequence of any of these enzymes, it is possible that the initial error may be amplified severalfold such that eventually a catastrophe occurs within the cell, leading to irreversible changes and death. Considerable research efforts during the 1970s were directed to establishing differences in the primary structure of proteins from senescent animals. The results obtained have indicated that errors in the primary sequence of proteins do not commonly occur during the aging process. Some of the altered proteins observed during senescence have been shown to result from posttranslational changes in the protein.

$$O_2 + e^- \longrightarrow O_2^{\cdot -} \quad \text{(superoxide radical)}$$
$$2H^+ + O_2^{\cdot -} + O_2^{\cdot -} \longrightarrow O_2 + H_2O_2 \quad \text{(hydrogen peroxide)}$$

Superoxide Dismutase

$$O_2^{\cdot -} + H_2O_2 \longrightarrow O_2 + OH^- + OH^{\cdot}$$

Haber-Weiss Reaction

FIG. 1. Basis of the free radical theory of aging.

The third major theory of aging is the *genetic programming theory,* which suggests that the mechanism of senescence is built into the genetic material as another aspect of differentiation and development. Aging of any organism, according to this view, is built into the genetic program. Several observations lead to the formulation of this view of aging, viewed by many as fatalistic and hence somewhat frightening. It is clearly obvious that different species of animals have different and fixed life-spans that encompass every member of the species. Most important were the observations of Hayflick, who reported that diploid human fibroblasts in tissue culture had a finite number of doublings. Although all of the cells in the culture appeared identical and a constant number was maintained prior to doubling, after a certain number of doublings the number of cells in the culture began to decrease noticeably owing to cell death. Further studies of fibroblasts obtained from different organisms suggested that the maximum number of doublings correlated reasonably well with the maximum life-span of the species. For example, fibroblasts from humans divide 40 to 60 times, whereas those from the tortoise with an estimated mean maximum life-span of 175 years double 90 to 125 times. By contrast, cells from the mouse with a mean maximum life-span of 3 to 5 years double 14 to 28 times. Of even greater interest was the report that the number of doublings observed in the cultures of human fibroblasts correlated well with the age of the donor from which the fibroblasts were obtained. The major question raised by this theory is whether cells differentiate to a terminal type that is destined to die.

METHODS TO STUDY THE BIOCHEMISTRY OF AGING

One of the major problems in the literature describing biochemical changes during aging is the lack of consistency in the reports from different laboratories. For many metabolic processes, reports of decreased activities in cells of an aging organism have appeared along with reports of no age-related changes from other equally reputable laboratories. Undoubtedly, a contributing factor to the lack of agreement in research on the biochemistry of aging is the experimental system used to obtain tissues for study. A popular model for the study of aging is a whole animal, especially rodents (rats or mice). An often overlooked problem with whole animals is the possibility that the "old" animal is diseased, causing related changes in various biochemical parameters unrelated to senescence. In addition, the diet of these animals may not be consistent among different suppliers, and hence some of the changes observed in the aging animals may actually reflect nutritional changes. These problems can be avoided by using animals maintained in a pathogen-free environment with a standard diet in colonies such as those supported by the National Institute on Aging. Unfortunately, animals raised in this manner are expensive for the individual researcher who cannot always afford to purchase a sufficient number of animals to perform an adequate statistical analysis of the data obtained.

Cells in tissue culture form a second major system for studying the biochemistry of aging. As discussed earlier, fibroblasts in tissue culture have been shown to have a definite life-span (expressed as cell doublings) that is correlated to the longevity of the donor species as well as to the age of the donor. One major advantage of the tissue culture system is that the experimental variables such as environmental effects and nutritional requirements can be carefully controlled. A question that arises when examining the biochemical data obtained as cells age in tissue culture is the relevance of this system, consisting of isolated cells, to an entire animal, consisting of different organs in an interrelated system. For example, the effects of hormones as regulators of the functioning of different organ systems and their relation to each other is lost in tissue culture. Another question is whether late-passage cells are indeed analogous to tissues aging *in vivo*. To date, few biochemical data have been obtained to characterize the aging cells in tissue culture due in part to the difficulty of obtaining sufficient material to do biochemical experiments. It is clear that biochemical comparisons of cells *in vitro* and animals *in vivo* are necessary before the reliability of data obtained in either system is established.

Another popular system to study the biochemistry of aging is the use of small animals with a short life-span, e.g., nematodes or insects. The question may arise as to the relevance of biochemical data obtained from aging insects to humans. In response to this query, data obtained from studies of whole animals during aging still provide an integrated approach to the various organs within a reasonable period of time because of the short life-span of these animals. Any novel or important discoveries can then be applied to "higher" organisms with longer life-spans with which better questions can be asked with a greater chance of obtaining meaningful results. In this context, note that some of the initial data demonstrating changes in enzyme structure during senescence were obtained with nematodes.

Certain important considerations must be kept in mind when the data obtained in experiments on the biochemistry of aging are evaluated. First, it is important to distinguish between primary and secondary effects of aging. For example, if a change in a given parameter, e.g., the activity of an enzyme, is observed during aging, this change may be a consequence of the senescent process rather than a cause. For example, a biochemical change that is a primary cause of aging should be observed in all organs of the species and in all species examined. Some experimenters have tried to avoid this problem by examining key enzymes that are known to regulate important metabolic pathways in the cell. In our laboratory, we observed an age-related decrease in the activity of 5-aminolevulinate synthase (the enzyme catalyzing the rate-limiting enzyme of heme biosynthesis) in the liver, brain, and heart but not the kidney of rats (11). It thus became clear that any changes in this enzyme must not be a primary cause of aging. Undoubtedly, changes in the activity of an enzyme in one tissue during aging may be important physiologically to that cell and organ as well as consequently to the overall functioning of the animal; however, such a change cannot be the causative agent responsible for aging of the animal.

A second important point that any biochemical theory of aging must explain is that longevity is species-specific. Every species from mouse to man has a given maximum and average life-span. Hence any theory of biochemical aging, whether based on a genetic program or on the presence of external pressures, must explain how agents such as ionizing radiation may result in a shorter life-span in one species relative to another.

RESULTS OF STUDIES ON THE BIOCHEMISTRY OF AGING

Free Radicals: Formation of and Possible Protection Against Them

The major source of free radicals in organisms living in an oxygen environment comes from endogenous sources, mainly the mitochondrial respiratory chain but also from other electron-transferring enzyme systems in the cell. During the transfer of electrons from substrates to oxygen, eventually four electrons and protons interact with oxygen to form water. Certain of the respiratory chain carriers, i.e., the flavins, the ubiquinones, and the iron catalysts, have the ability to transfer one electron to oxygen, forming the superoxide anion radical (O_2^-). It has been calculated that under normal circumstances about 6% of the total oxygen uptake by mitochondria results in the formation of superoxide rather than water (8).

Superoxide anions formed in the mitochondria are generally removed with some efficiency by the mitochondrial enzyme superoxide dismutase, leading to the formation of oxygen and hydrogen peroxide. The hydrogen peroxide is also capable of forming the reactive hydroxyl radical in the presence of iron via the Haber-Weiss reaction (Fig. 1). Several protective devices have also evolved to remove the potentially harmful hydrogen peroxide, including catalase, peroxidase, and glutathione peroxidase. Furthermore, the antioxidant vitamin E has been shown to be present in the mitochondrial membrane where it reacts with peroxides and oxygen radicals and thus protects the membranes.

Once formed, the hydroxyl radical is extremely active in abstracting hydrogens from the double bonds present in the polyunsaturated fatty acids of biological membranes. The radical, thus formed, may eventually become a peroxide radical, which initiates a chain reaction leading to the formation of compounds such as malondialdehyde. Malondialdehyde can react with amines, leading to cross-linking of different molecules and resulting in the formation of fluorescent compounds generally termed lipofuscin. A more dangerous consequence of the formation of free radicals and malondialdehyde may be the cross-linking of macromolecules, especially DNA and proteins, with consequent damage to their function. Furthermore, the peroxidation of the polyunsaturated fatty acids in membranes may result in damage to the intracellular membranes thus affected.

Before examining the data, a question that must be addressed is whether the formation of these free radicals ever occurs to excess in the living organism with the presence of the protective reactions described above. According to Kanungo (7), there is no evidence that the level of free radicals increases in older animals. This statement is in apparent contradiction to the observation that the amount of lipofuscin increases with age in all types of cells and animals including invertebrates. Indeed, the increase in these age pigments in human hearts was observed in the absence of any obvious myopathies (8). Furthermore, the accumulation of lipofuscin in dog hearts occurred more than five times faster than that in human hearts as the animals aged, a value corresponding to the difference in life-span of the dog and the human. In the housefly, whose life-span is proportional to its metabolic rate, the life-span of the organism can be prolonged by slowing down the metabolic rate. When the metabolic rate was slowed by lowering the temperature, the appearance of lipofuscin was also delayed to the same extent that the life-span was prolonged (14). Hence, if the formation of lipofuscin is used as a measure of lipid peroxidation *in situ,* there is no question that free radicals are formed during the lifetime of the cell and not always removed efficiently, resulting in pigment formation.

Although it appears clear that lipofuscin accumulates during aging of all species, the question remains as to whether these pigments are toxic to the cell. Experiments have demonstrated that the feeding of vitamin E or other antioxidants to mice leads to a significant decrease in the amount of lipofuscin accumulated intracellularly; however, it has been stressed repeatedly by various experiments (8) that the feeding of these antioxidants does not prolong the life-span of the animals. Lipofuscin accumulation can thus be retarded by the antioxidants reacting with free radicals without any permanent changes in longevity.

The question also remains as to whether these are indeed deleterious consequences to the cell because of the formation of free radicals. First, there is almost no evidence to indicate that there is increased cross-linking of DNA during senescence, as would be predicted from the presence of more free radicals (14). In more recent studies it was concluded that there are no age-related changes in DNA polymerase fidelity, no change or a decrease in replication rate, and no change in DNA methylation among other parameters studied (6). It should be noted that all of the above studies indicate that there are no gross changes in total DNA, and the results do not preclude changes in gene expression, as is discussed later in the chapter.

Several changes in biological membranes, e.g., those of the mitochondria and microsomes, have indicated that increased free radical formation does occur during aging. For example, a marked decrease in the number of polyunsaturated fatty acids in the membranes of these organelles has been observed in the aged compared to that in young animals. The loss of unsaturated fatty acids may have resulted because of peroxidation of the lipids due to the accumulation of free radicals. Similarly, the NADPH-dependent lipid peroxidative system in both isolated mitochondria and microsomes has been shown to increase with age. It thus appears that changes in the membranes accumulate with age and become permanent despite the dynamic exchange of fatty acids and phospholipids in membranes.

Changes in the lipid composition of the membranes of mitochondria and other intracellular organelles may render them more susceptible to destruction. Consequently, fewer organelles may be present in the senescent cells. Studies in our laboratory have indicated that the specific content of hepatic mitochondria decreased approximately 25% with age in the rat (16). This conclusion was based on using two mitochondrial enzymes as markers (a membrane-bound and a soluble matrix enzyme) for the organelle and measuring enzymatic activity in whole liver homogenates. Furthermore, the possibility that a more "fragile" population of mitochondria might accumulate in the aging liver was examined by measuring the release of a known mitochondrial matrix enzyme into the cytosol of the cell. No increase in the release of citrate synthase was observed in aging rat liver, suggesting that a fragile population of mitochondria do not accumulate during aging. One explanation for this phenomenon may be the interesting hypothesis proposed by Luzikov (9) that nonfunctional mitochondria are eliminated by degradative processes in the cell. Either the synthesis of incomplete respiratory assemblies during mitochondrial biogenesis or the selective destruction of part of the respiratory chain by external sources such as ionizing radiation would lead to nonfunctional mitochondria targeted for destruction. For example, the autophagocytosis of old organelle components by lysosomes has been suggested to lead to the formation of lipofuscin (8).

Changes in the protective devices against free radicals described above may also occur during aging. For example, an age-related increase in superoxide dismutase has been observed in rat heart mitochondria, suggesting that more protection may be afforded as the animal becomes senescent. Similar age-related increases in the activity of both hepatic and cardiac catalase have been reported, suggesting that levels of this protective enzyme also increase during senescence (12). By contrast, lowered levels of glutathione were observed in blood, kidney, and intestine of aging rats, suggesting that the enzyme glutathione peroxidase may be less efficient as a scavenger of peroxides during aging.

Other possible protection devices that have been shown to increase in species with greater longevity include the concentrations of uric acid and carotene. Both of these compounds can act as antioxidants. Interestingly, primates with a longer life-span than many other species do not contain the enzyme uricase and hence excrete uric acid as the end-product of purine catabolism. Similarly, carotene accumulates to a much greater extent in humans than in the deer mouse and not at all in rodents. These data correlate well with the longevity of the species.

In conclusion, aerobic cells contain membranes with a high concentration of polyunsaturated fatty acids necessary to maintain membrane fluidity. The normal by-products of oxygen metabolism, e.g., the superoxide anion, hydrogen peroxide, and the hydroxyl radical, have the ability to attack these double bonds, leading to peroxidative damage. In addition, by-products of this lipid peroxidation, e.g., lipofuscin, have been shown to accumulate with age in many postmitotic tissues, e.g., heart and brain. More well-designed experiments on the molecular level are needed to demonstrate how lipid peroxidation affects cell function and related aging processes.

DNA, RNA, and Protein Synthesis

Age-related changes in the metabolism of the genetic material, DNA, would obviously be detrimental to the organism. Three distinct aspects of DNA metabolism have been investigated in aging animals and cells: DNA replication and transcription into RNA, repair mechanisms that maintain the accuracy of the DNA, and gene expression. It is clear from the studies described earlier that cell replication does decrease with aging, expressed as the number of doublings in tissue culture. Furthermore, we are all aware of a decreased rate of cellular replication, as we observed that the time necessary for wound healing increases with age. Whatever may be the cause of the decrease in the rate of cellular replication, little evidence has been accumulated to indicate a decrease in DNA replication at the molecular level as a consequence of changes in DNA polymerase. In addition, an age-related decrease in the fidelity of DNA replication has not been observed. Obviously, if mistakes were made in the replication of DNA during aging, deleterious consequences to the organism would result.

DNA repair mechanisms have evolved either to correct synthetic mistakes or, more importantly, to excise damaged bases produced because of external causes such as ionizing radiation. Initially, certain workers claimed that the efficiency of the excision repair system correlated with the life-span of an organism; however, as usual, certain exceptions were observed. For example, the turtle with a life-span of 115 years has no appreciable excision repair, whereas the nematode has a high rate of excision repair and a life-span of 40 days. More careful experiments *in vitro,* in which cell cultures from 21 mammalian species were irradiated with ultraviolet light and DNA repair measured, indicated that no relation existed between the size of the repair regions and the life-span of the animal from which the cells were obtained (6).

RNA synthesis has also been reported to decrease in aging rat livers, although it has been diffficult to correlate these changes to enzymes such as RNA polymerase. Unfortunately, little information has been obtained on age-related changes in the synthesis of specific messenger RNAs. One can predict that with the application of the new recombinant DNA technology such information will be forthcoming.

Similarly, decreases in the rate of protein synthesis as a function of age have been reported. Richardson (13) has described some of the problems of measuring protein synthesis in whole organisms using radioactive amino acids as precursors. The incorporation of labeled amino acids into proteins not only is a function of the rate of protein synthesis (or in any of the individual steps of this process) but also depends on the transport of amino acids across cellular membranes to the site of synthesis. Furthermore, the observed rate of incorporation of exogenous labeled amino acids into protein is affected by the presence of amino acid pools in the tissues, which in turn may be affected by changes in protein degradation in the aging animal. More recent studies have focused on specific steps of the protein synthetic pathway, which may be affected by age, and have indicated that certain reactions show an age-related decrease. Again, little information as to the rate of synthesis of a particular protein as a function of age has been obtained, although it seems clear that such information is invaluable to understanding the molecular basis of age-related changes in the protein composition of the cell. Furthermore, no information is available as to the effect on the organism of a decreased overall rate of protein synthesis.

In conclusion, the changes observed in DNA, RNA, or protein synthesis during aging have not yet been correlated with changes in specific proteins and their regulation at the genetic level. Further studies in this area should be dramatic and hopefully will lead to a more unifying theory of the biochemistry of aging that can be tested experimentally.

Changes in Enzymes and Proteins During Aging

Alterations in proteins as a consequence of aging appear self-evident, as proteins form the basis of the structure of all cells as well as acting as intracellular catalysts for all metabolic pathways. One of the most productive areas of research in the biochemistry of aging has been the measurement of enzymatic activity during senescence. The ease with which enzymes can be assayed and compared in tissues and animals as a function of age has contributed to the proliferation of knowledge in this area. Furthermore, the large amount of information on various enzymes, including their catalytic mechanisms, regulation, and induction, has made it easy to make comparisons between young and aging animals.

Two problems are immediately apparent when the data obtained are examined critically. First, as biochemists examine the catalytic activity of an enzyme, conditions are always established so the enzyme itself is rate-limiting for the reaction. The maximum turnover of some enzymes, e.g., cytochrome c oxidase, the terminal enzyme of the mitochondrial respiratory chain, when assayed under optimal conditions may be 20 times higher than the rate ever observed for substrate oxidation by the whole chain. A good analogy is an automobile that has the capacity to go more than 100 miles per hour, but with current speed limits and traffic conditions it is never driven faster than 60 miles per hour. Hence a decrease in enzymatic activity during aging of 20 to 30% (under optimal conditions) may have no effect in an intact cell where the enzyme might never approach maximum catalytic activity.

The second problem with research on enzyme activity during aging is the lack of consistency of the data obtained. For example, various enzymes have been observed to have decreased activity with aging, whereas others have increased or no change in activity with aging. Furthermore, some enzymes may have decreased activity in one tissue of the animal during aging but remain the same in another tissue. As mentioned earlier, the activity of 5-aminolevulinate synthase (ALAS) decreased dramatically in several tissues of the aging rat, including brain, heart, and liver, but was unaffected in the kidney, indicating a tissue-specific regulation of this enzyme protein (11). Consequently, no clue as to the mechanism of aging is gained from studies of this type, although information about changes in the functional activity of the cells involved is obtained and may be useful for understanding subsequent age-related changes.

The activity of certain enzymes has been shown to increase in specific tissues in response to an external stimulus to the animal. Such enzyme induction, when investigated at the molecular level, is often associated with an actual increase in the amount of protein due to regulation at the gene level. A gradual decrease in adaptability to the environment is generally observed during aging and is reflected in changes in enzyme induction. The initial experiments of Adelman's group (10) indicated that after administration of a hormone to an aging animal a longer lag was observed before the enzyme activity increased compared to that in a young animal; however, with time the same maximum activity was obtained in both young and aged animals. In many cases of this type of induction, the actual age-related defect occurred because the number of hormone receptors on the cell membrane decreased with age, thus leading to an initial slow response after treatment with hormone.

Studies on the induction of other enzymes in aging animals indicate that some enzymes are never induced to the same level in the aged as in young animals. The suggestion could be made that this group of enzymes represents age-related changes at the gene regulation level resulting in a lack of complete induction of these enzymes. In a third group of enzymes, a longer lag was observed before the enzymatic activity began to increase after administration of the inducer, *and* the enzymatic activity never reached the same maximum as in the young animal. One example of this type of enzyme studied in our laboratory is ALAS, the rate-limiting enzyme of the heme biosynthetic pathway, which can be induced by drugs causing experimental porphyria (11). In addition, ethanol has been shown to lead to a four- to fivefold induction of hepatic ALAS in young animals. Ethanol administration to aged rats resulted only in a twofold induction of hepatic ALAS after a longer lag. This response is probably due to a complicated series of changes in gene expression, protein synthesis, and perhaps the movement of proteins within the cell from their site of synthesis in the cytosol to their final locus.

One important and exciting area of research in cell biology and biochemistry today is protein trafficking, or the mechanism by which proteins move from one part of the cell to another. For example, ALAS, an enzyme localized in the matrix of the mitochondria, is synthesized in the cytosol on free ribosomes and transferred into the mitochondria in a subsequent step. In noninduced control animals, about 5 to 6% of the total enzymatic activity can be assayed extramitochondrially, a value probably representing leakage from broken mitochondria during preparation. After treatment with allylisopropylacetamide, a drug that induces ALAS and leads to experimental porphyria, the percentage of ALAS observed in the cytosol increased until it represented 18% of the total activity (16). The explanation for these results is that the enzyme is synthesized so rapidly after administration of the inducer that the transport process by which these newly synthesized proteins are transferred across the mitochondrial membrane is saturated. Interestingly, the induction of ALAS, when assayed in isolated mitochondria from old rats, was decreased compared to that in young animals; however, the total induction was not so affected, as more than 30% of the total ALAS activity had accumulated in the cytosol. These results suggested an age-related change in the process by which cytosolic ALAS is translocated into the mitochondria. Perhaps these changes are hormonally related, as it has been reported that insulin and perhaps glucagon are necessary for the translocation process by which ALAS crosses the mitochondrial membrane (5).

A potentially important observation in aging-related research on proteins and enzymes is that altered proteins accumulate during senescence. For example, a decrease in enzymatic activity with age might result from the presence of fewer enzyme (protein) molecules or from lowering the catalytic activity of the enzyme (altered protein). In many cases, once an enzyme has been purified and its content in the cell measured using immunoassay, it is shown that there is a decrease in the amount of enzyme protein with age leading to the lower activity. By contrast, several enzymes with lowered activity have been purified, initially from senescent nematodes and subsequently from rat liver and muscle, and have been shown to be present in the cell in the same quantities in the aged animal as in the young animal (1,14,15). Analysis of the purified protein by sophisticated biochemical techniques capable of determining a single amino acid change in the protein revealed that the primary sequence of the protein was unchanged. Hence the lowered catalytic activity of the protein did not result from "errors" in the synthesis of the protein. The changes observed in these "senescent" proteins included heat sensitivity, specific activity, spectral properties, inactivation by proteases, and immunotitration. Rothstein (15) has proposed that altered enzymes result from a slower turnover (degradation) of proteins during aging such that the increased "dwell" time of proteins in the cell allows them to be subtly denatured. Some enzymes might have a more stable conformation, which would be less suceptible to these subtle alterations leading to the varying results obtained with different enzymes. The question to be addressed experimentally is thus: Does protein turnover slow with age? Some evidence has suggested that protein turnover may indeed slow with age.

In conclusion, age-related changes in enzymatic activity due to changes in synthesis of the enzyme protein have been observed. Furthermore, lowered induction of certain enzymes in response to external stimuli have been observed as a function of age. Some of these effects appear to be a consequence of changes in gene activity or gene regulation. The accumulation of enzymes with lowered activity owing to the formation of an altered protein during aging may result from environmental influences such as free radicals and not be a gene-directed phenomenon.

FUTURE DIRECTIONS OF RESEARCH ON THE
BIOCHEMISTRY OF AGING

Several observations about aging and the process of senescence must be restated before a productive approach to further research directions can be suggested. First, all multicellular organisms show a gradual decrease in adaptability to the environment after attaining sexual maturity. Second, as mentioned earlier, all members of a given species have a fixed life-span. Furthermore, each of these individuals in a given species reach sexual maturity at the same time and have the same reproductive life-span, suggesting a relation between the processes of development and longevity. For example, those species that take longer to reach sexual maturity have a longer life-span. Finally, all organisms have similar deteriorative changes with age despite the differences in their life-span (e.g., their susceptibility to various diseases). The changes just occur sooner in species with a shorter life-span.

The major question for researchers studying the mechanism of biochemical aging is to differentiate between aging caused by by-products of essential living processes (e.g., oxygen metabolism) and aging caused by processes involved in differentiation at the genetic level. Considerable evidence was presented earlier in the chapter to establish the possibility that free radicals arising during normal oxidative pathways might contribute to aging. In addition, the existence of a multitude of protective devices that remove the dangerous oxygen radicals has been discussed, including the possibility that long-lived species may contain higher levels of these protective mechanisms. The remainder of the chapter considers the role of gene expression with aging.

It has always been obvious that genetic mechanisms play a role in the longevity of individuals, as families with long-lived parents tend to have children with longer lives. This observation is not exclusive to humans but is also true for rats and insects such as *Drosophila*. The scientist can thus consider aging as a developmental process at the genetic level. Development of an individual from the fertilized egg to the adult results from the sequential activation and expression of specific genes at the molecular level. A good example of the expression of different genes during development is hemoglobin. This protein in adult humans contains four polypeptide chains consisting of two α chains and two β chains. This structure is termed hemoglobin A, and its subunit structure is designated α_2, β_2. During fetal life two types of hemoglobin have been described. In the early months of gestation, an $\alpha_2\epsilon_2$ hemoglobin has been detected followed by hemoglobin F, which has the subunit structure $\alpha_2\gamma_2$. Shortly after birth the expression of hemoblogin A is observed. It can be noted that the α chain is common to all of these hemoglobins, but the β, ϵ, and γ chains differ. All of these polypeptides have about the same molecular weight with rather similar amino acid sequences but are indeed different proteins encoded on unique genes. During the genetic expression of these hemoglobin subunits, α, ϵ, γ, and β chains are activated sequentially. Once the γ gene is activated the ϵ gene is repressed, and once the β gene is activated the γ gene is repressed. The product of expression of one gene regulates the expression of the next gene.

Applying this model to the aging process, senescence might also begin by the activation of certain genes in a sequential manner. The question then arises: How, when the differentiated stage of the organism is reached, is the functional status of the genome altered? In other words, what causes the expression of genes that result in the observed effects of aging? Indeed, are there specific aging genes present in the genome? Furthermore, what causes activation of these genes?

One model for genetic aging suggests that gene products of the reproductive phase may, in turn, *repress* some genes required for differentiation and growth. This situation would lead to dysdifferentiation or dedifferentiation. Thus cancer and aging might result from similar losses of the ability to differentiate because of changes at the genetic level. Another thought has been that during reproduction various factors necessary for expression of certain genes are depleted and cannot be replenished as fast as they disappear, leading again to a lack of differentiation.

In support of this model are the aging disease syndromes such as progeria and Werner's syndrome. Individuals with these syndromes age prematurely, showing the same age-related changes as the rest of the population, only much earlier in their lives. These syndromes, which are genetic diseases, undoubtedly arise from the mutation of an autosomal gene or perhaps from a defective chromosome (2). Fibroblasts, isolated and cultured from individuals with these syndromes, do not divide well in tissue culture. Perhaps the mutation leading to the premature aging has occurred in a developmental gene. If the product of this mutated gene is necessary to activate other genes in a sequential manner, the lack of such a product would lead to a chain reaction of deleterious events.

The suggestion has also been made that biochemists should study the biological basis of longevity rather than aging. In principle, aging may be a consequence of a few genetic alterations involved in regulatory genes that result in a change in timing and the level of expression of a common set of genes determining longevity. Further knowledge of gene activation during development should be forthcoming with the research explosion in molecular biology and genetic engineering. Eventually, further research at the genetic level appears to be the most promising if the primary cause of aging is to be elucidated. To date, most of the aging research has been data collecting, as is generally true of the initial stages in any scientific field. The data thus accumulated forms the basis on which subsequent scientists will unify the field with perceptive insights.

Increased knowledge of the biological aspects of aging may aid in the development of means to treat the undesirable physical and behavioral aspects of aging. This long-range goal should be foremost whether the biochemical mechanism of aging is shown to be due to environmental causes such as free radicals, changes in gene expression, or, even more probable, a combination of these processes.

ACKNOWLEDGMENTS

The experiments described from the author's laboratory were performed in the Department of Biochemistry at the Mount Sinai School of Medicine of the City University of New York and were supported in part by a grant from the National Institutes of Health (AG-00099).

REFERENCES

1. Adelman, R. C., and Roth, G. S. (1983): *Altered Proteins and Aging.* CRC Press, Boca Raton, FL.
2. Brown, W. T., and Wisniewski, H. M. (1983): Genetics of human aging. In: *Review of Biological Research in Aging,* Vol. 1, edited by M. Rothstein, pp. 81–91. Alan R. Liss, New York.
3. Comfort, A. (1979): *The Biology of Senescence,* 3rd ed. Elsevier, New York.
4. Cutler, R. G. (1984): Evolutionary biology of aging and longevity in mammalian species. In: *Aging and Cell Function,* edited by J. E. Johnson, pp. 1–148. Plenum Press, New York.
5. DeLoskey, R. J., and Beattie, D. S. (1984): The effects of insulin and glucose on the induction and intracellular translocation of δ-aminolevulinic acid synthase. *Arch. Biochem. Biophys.,* 233: 64–71.
6. Eichhorn, G. L. (1983): Nucleic acid biochemistry and aging. In: *Review of Biological Research in Aging,* Vol. 1, edited by M. Rothstein, pp. 295–303. Alan R. Liss, New York.
7. Kanungo, M. S. (1980): *Biochemistry of Aging,* Academic Press, London.
8. Lippman, R. D. (1983): Lipid peroxidation and metabolism in aging: a biological, chemical, and medical approach. In: *Review of Biological Research in Aging,* Vol. 1, edited by M. Rothstein, pp. 315–342. Alan R. Liss, New York.
9. Luzikov, V. N. (1985): *Mitochondrial Biogenesis and Breakdown,* translated by A. V. Galkin. Consultants Bureau, New York.
10. Obenrader, M. F., Sartin, J. L., and Adelman, R. C. (1981): Enzyme adaptation during aging. In: *Handbook of Biochemistry in Aging,* edited by J. R. Florini, pp. 263–267. CRC Press, Boca Raton, FL.
11. Paterniti, J. R., Jr., Lin, C-I. P., and Beattie, D. S. (1978): δ-Aminolevulinic acid synthetase: regulation of activity in various tissues of the aging rat. *Arch. Biochem. Biophys.,* 191:792–797.
12. Paterniti, J. R., Jr., Lin, C-I. P., and Beattie, D. S. (1980): Regulation of heme metabolism during senescence: activity of several heme-containing enzymes and heme oxygenase in the liver and kidney of aging rats. *Mech. Age Dev.,* 12:81–91.
13. Richardson, A. (1981): The relationship between aging and protein synthesis. In: *Handbook of Biochemistry in Aging,* edited by J. R. Florini, pp. 79–101. CRC Press, Boca Raton, FL.
14. Rothstein, M. (1982): *Biochemical Approaches of Aging.* Academic Press, New York.
15. Rothstein, M. (1983): Detection of altered proteins. In: *Altered Proteins and Aging,* edited by R. C. Adelman and G. S. Roth, pp. 1–8. CRC Press, Boca Raton, FL
16. Scotto, A. W., Rinehart, R. W., and Beattie, D. S. (1983): Aging-related decreases in hepatic mitochondrial and cytosolic aminolevulinic acid synthase during experimental porphyria. *Arch. Biochem. Biophys.,* 222:150–157.

Human Aging Research: Concepts and Techniques,
edited by B. Kent and R. N. Butler.
Raven Press, Ltd., New York © 1988.

Pathology and Aging

Donald West King

Department of Pathology, The University of Chicago, Chicago, Illinois 60637

Aging is defined as a genetic physiological process associated with morphological and functional changes in cellular and extracellular components aggravated by injury throughout life and resulting in a progressive imbalance of the control regulatory systems of the organism, including the hormonal, autocrine, neuroendocrine, and immune homeostatic mechanisms. Fries and Crapo (7) suggested that the maximum life-span of humans is in the 80- to 100-year range, and their rectangular survival curve (Fig. 1) postulated this millennium. We believe, as did Schneider and Brody (16), that one does not die from the physiological aging process but from a distinct pathological event. With age, the accompanying increased susceptibility and decreased resistance to injury of cells makes the organism fragile and more vulnerable to injury. The principal precipitating injurious factor in death is often trauma and resultant infection, leading to cardiovascular collapse (Table 1).

In general, the basic morphological lesions of aging, programmed at birth but accelerated by the environment, are atrophy (e.g., decrease in number and size of cells), a compensatory hyperplasia (an increase in the number of those cells able to divide, e.g., liver, kidney, lung, endocrine), and hypertrophy (an increase in the size of those cells unable to divide, e.g., heart). Compensatory hyperplasia

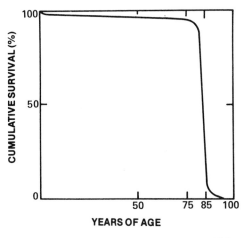

FIG. 1. Rectangular survival curve.

325

TABLE 1. *Death rates and percent of total deaths for the 15 leading causes of death: United States, 1983*

Rank[a]	Cause of death[b]	Rate[c]	Percent of total deaths
—	All causes	862.8	100.0
1	Diseases of heart	329.2	38.2
2	Malignant neoplasms, including neoplasms of lymphatic and hematopoietic tissues	189.3	21.9
3	Cerebrovascular diseases	66.5	7.7
4	Accidents and adverse effects	39.5	4.6
	Motor vehicle accidents	19.0	—
	All other accidents and adverse effects	20.5	—
5	Chronic obstructive pulmonary diseases and allied conditions	28.3	3.3
6	Pneumonia and influenza	23.9	2.8
7	Diabetes mellitus	15.5	1.8
8	Suicide	12.1	1.4
9	Chronic liver disease and cirrhosis	11.7	1.4
10	Atherosclerosis	11.3	1.3
11	Homicide and legal intervention	8.6	1.0
12	Certain conditions originating during the perinatal period	8.3	1.0
13	Nephritis, nephrotic syndrome, nephrosis	8.1	0.9
14	Septicemia	5.7	0.7
15	Congenital anomalies	5.6	0.7
	All other causes	99.3	11.5

[a] Rank based on number of deaths.
[b] Ninth Revision, International Classification of Diseases, 1975.
[c] Per 100,000 population.

sometimes progresses to nodules, adenoma, polyps, and occasionally cancer. There is also disorganization of the surrounding extracellular matrix and progressive changes in the vascular system. Most organs show classic lesions that lose cells that are replaced by mesenchymal supportive structures such as collagen, elastin, or lipid, often with an infiltration of chronic inflammatory cells. The resulting disorganization and malfunction of parenchymal tissue is partially due to distortion of the architecture (Fig. 2).

RESEARCH METHODS FOR STUDY OF HUMAN AGING

Past morphological research in human aging has involved descriptive qualitative changes in various cells and tissues, as well as quantitative changes in fluids and secretions from samples obtained immediately before or at the time of death. Numerous physiological and biochemical studies have been carried out on patients in aging cohorts (18) (Fig. 3). When immediate autopsy material has been available, enzymatic studies of various tissues have been done (22). In most instances, unless

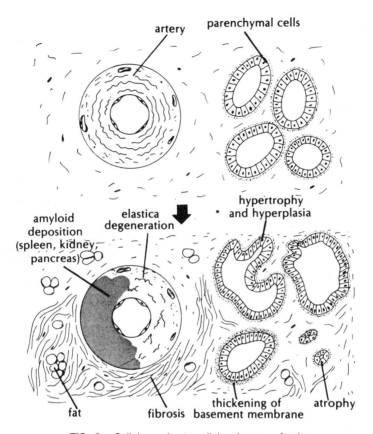

artery

parenchymal cells

hypertrophy
and hyperplasia

amyloid
deposition
(spleen, kidney,
pancreas)

elastica
degeneration

fat

fibrosis

thickening of
basement membrane

atrophy

FIG. 2. Cellular and extracellular changes of aging.

directly associated with a medical examiner's office, permission to perform autopsies of bodies within less than 4 hours is not possible, and by this time enzymatic and metabolic analyses of various internal organs are not satisfactory for quantitative studies.

Clinical pathological laboratories supply biopsy specimens and fluid samples at various ages during life. White blood cells have been particularly useful for studying a variety of markers. They include not only typical B- and T-lymphocyte and macrophage immune markers but a variety of other receptors as well. Numerous studies in these areas have been reported in previous chapters in this book and in the literature (19,20).

A largely untapped source of tissue samples is the surgical pathology service. Here tissue is available within a few minutes after removal from the body. It can either be frozen, immediately prepared for a variety of histochemical and biochemical analyses, or placed in tissue culture for study. Later in this chapter studies are presented that utilized tissues obtained from the surgical pathology service.

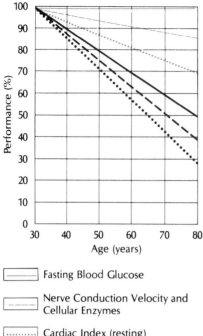

FIG. 3. Physiological changes in the aged. In a study by N. W. Shock, cross-sectional data on physiological functions in adult men of various ages were analyzed using mean values in 20- to 35-year-olds as baseline. Idealized linear projections from age 30 to age 80 showed no aging change in fasting blood glucose; but nerve conduction velocity and cellular enzymes fell about 15%, resting cardiac index 30%, vital capacity and renal blood flow 50%, maximum breathing capacity 60%, and maximum work rate and oxygen uptake 70%.

Finally, tissues from the autopsy itself can also be utilized in a variety of ways. The analytical problems are largely technical, with the reservation that most studies should exclude those metabolic parameters that are undergoing catabolic reactions. Of great importance is the design of a standard written protocol in which procedures are carried out in as identical fashion as possible on each case. The protocol determines from where samples are taken: often a variety of sites usually not examined in great detail. It is essential to properly label samples from appropriate areas of the heart, lung, kidney, and other organs prominent in the aging process and to ensure that the preparation of tissues (fixation, approximate thickness of specimen, and staining procedures) is uniform (10).

Although enzymatic and metabolic studies were not found to be useful for most autopsy tissue, there are a variety of other studies from which considerable data can be obtained. In a more detailed follow-up of the size and weight of organs, the size and number of cells in a particular site can be examined by morphometric means. These sites include specialized structures of endocrine glands, the central nervous system, the immune system, and other parenchymal cells within a stated geographic area. The use of immunoperoxidase stain with purified antibodies allows identification of a considerable number of antigens. The size, shape, and number of cells containing hormones, immunoglobulins, or receptors can be easily assayed. There is, of course, no indication of rates of synthesis, assembly, release, transport in the bloodstream, or receptors on target cells. Similarly, basement membranes of capillaries and organs, size of medullary follicles in lymphoid tissue, particular structures in the liver (portal areas) or kidney (juxtaglomerular apparatus) can be analyzed in great detail. An appreciation of extravascular matrix disruptions and abnormalities of ligaments and tendons can be noted and quantitated.

Considerably more data can be obtained but with significant increase in cost of both materials and personnel. It is generally acknowledged that metaplastic lesions often precede neoplastic lesions in the bronchus (1). There has been no careful study of these lesions related to specific age cohorts. There have been numerous studies relating Barrett's esophagus to carcinoma and colonic polyps to carcinoma of the bowel (6), as well as studies describing prostatic hyperplasia and occult carcinoma (8). A controlled study of young, middle, and old age groups utilizing serial sections of prostate, bladder, bowel, and bronchi to detect the earliest premalignant changes in all these organs is highly desirable.

In addition to neoplasia, another example of a needed study is one that explores the relation of osteoporosis, vitamin D, calcitriol, parathormone, kidney function, and intestinal absorption. As more information is gained concerning the dementias, particularly Alzheimer's and Parkinson's diseases, it will be highly desirable to correlate the morphological changes at autopsy with documented behavioral patterns while living.

The best way to correlate detailed morphological changes with the metabolic physiological changes in the kidney, heart, lung, liver, and other major organs is to do a combined study before and after death in various age cohorts. Usually the history and laboratory findings in the chart immediately preceding death are sketchy, deficient, and not uniform enough to provide a meaningful statistically valid analysis. Unfortunately, the longitudinal studies in Baltimore and Framingham (9) have not included autopsy findings along with the physiological and historical data necessary to give an integrated picture.

DISEASES AND LESIONS OF AGING

The spectrum of diseases usually encountered during life is presented in Table 2. Two true diseases of aging that occur consistently in 90% of all individuals over the age of 80 are osteoporosis and osteoarthritis. Osteoporosis may occur with hyperparathyroid adenoma, metastatic carcinoma, and chronic renal disease, but it is most common in postmenopausal women. Although partially alleviated by progestin therapy, the mechanism of osteoporosis development is unknown.

Other lesions found in older individuals include atherosclerotic heart disease,

TABLE 2. *Spectrum of disease*

Age	Cause
0−5	Allergy Infection Neoplasia (leukemia, Wilms' tumor, medulloblastoma, retinoblastoma)
5−15	Allergy Diabetes (juvenile) Infection Accidents
15−30	Allergy (asthma) Accidents (suicide) Venereal disease Endocrine disorders (women) Acne
30−40	Complications of pregnancy Ulcer Hypertension Suicide Homicide
40−60	Heart disease (infarct, hypertension, rheumatic fever) Liver disease (cirrhosis) Kidney disease (glomerular nephritis) Neoplasia (lung, colon, breast, ovary)
60−80	Neoplasia (lung, colon, prostate) Cardiovascular disease
80−100	Neoplasia (leukemia, lymphoma, prostate) Dementia (Alzheimer's, Parkinson's) Osteoporosis, osteoarthritis Accidents (fractures) Infection Cardiovascular disease

Modified from King, D. W. (1979): Health problems. *In: Young Adulthood,* edited by J. Scanlon. Academy for Educational Development, New York.

hepatic cirrhosis (resulting from viral, chemical, or drug injury), and nephritis associated with end-stage kidney disease (arteriolosclerosis, glomerular nephritis, or pyelonephritis). Alzheimer's disease occurs in 12% of the population over the age of 65 and in 20% over the age of 80. Neoplasia occurs in 38% of the population, with a 22% death incidence. Minimal essential hypertension occurs in 50% of the population over the age of 50, but hypertensive heart disease is considerably less frequent. Maturity-onset type II diabetes occurs in 10% of the population, and moderate senile emphysema and terminal pneumonitis are present in a high percentage of cases at autopsy (Table 3).

In addition to the cellular changes of atrophy, hyperplasia, and hypertrophy, lipofuscin deposits are found commonly in the adrenals, heart, and central nervous system. Extracellular vascular lesions include atherosclerosis (commonly seen in

TABLE 3. *Diseases and lesions associated with aging*

Disease of aging	Diseases associated with aging	Lesions associated with aging
Osteoporosis	Without specific pathogenesis	Cellular lesions
Osteoarthritis	Maturity-onset diabetes	Lipofuscin
	Alzheimer's disease	Atrophy
	Parkinson's disease	Hyperplasia
	Neoplasia	Hypertrophy
	Emphysema	
	Hypertension	Extracellular lesions
		Arteriosclerosis
	With known pathogenesis	Amyloid deposits
	Septicemia	Immune deposits
	Pneumonia (bacterial, viral)	Fractures
	Cirrhosis (hepatitis)	Intervertebral disk disease
	Nephritis	Cataracts, presbyopia
	Myocardial or pulmonary infarct	Increased cross-linkage of collagen
		Disorganized extracellular matrices
		Pulmonary thrombosis or embolism

the aorta, coronary, and cerebral vessels), arteriolosclerosis (found in the pancreas, spleen, and kidney), Monckeberg's medial sclerosis (in the peripheral arteries), and varicosities (in the legs and rectum). Amyloid is present consistently in vessels and sometimes in extracellular deposits.

Extracellular spinal lesions may result in rupture of the intervertebral disk, myositis, or osteoarthritis. Presbyopia in the eye, which occurs at age 40 to 45, is without an apparent lesion; but obvious cataracts in the sixties and seventies age group are both common and demonstrable. Immune deposits are seen in all obsolescent glomeruli at autopsy, with both anti-idiotypic antibodies and other antigen–antibody–complement complexes being present. The replacement of extracellular organized ground substance with disorganized collagen, elastin, and muscle may result in diaphramatic and inguinal hernias, cystocele, rectocele, retroversion of the uterus, diverticula in the bowel, and mesenchymal degeneration of the ligaments and tendons on the extremities. These lesions of atrophy and degeneration and repair are the mesenchymal counterparts of adenoma to polyps as well as focal hyperplastic and hypertrophic lesions in the parenchymal organs.

A 50% thickening of the basement membrane of capillaries not related to diseases of the arteries or veins and unassociated with inflammation of tumor has been documented in the older age groups (23) (Fig. 4).

It is well recognized that a variety of agents accentuate and accelerate the physiological aging process. They include industrial, urban, and rural pollutants (coal, pesticides, herbicides), infectious agents (in the past, *Mycobacterium tuberculosis* and syphilis; now, commonly viral agents), physical injury associated with ultra-

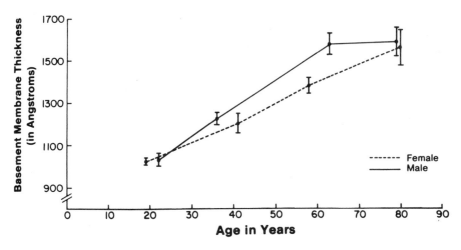

FIG. 4. Age-related changes in normal human basement membranes of capillaries in psoas muscle.

violet sunlight and therapeutic x-radiation, and autoimmune complex injury resulting from a variety of altered antigens induced by injury by various agents. Two principal chemical age-accelerating environmental agents are the hydrocarbons of alchohol and tobacco.

GENETICS—SIGNIFICANCE IN AGING

True genetic diseases associated with aging in the human are discussed elsewhere in this volume. They include Hutchinson's, Gilbert's, Werner's, Pick's, and Down's syndromes. These early-aging syndromes are often associated with the classic maturity-onset type II diabetes and neoplastic lesions, both benign and malignant. Genetics play a large role in susceptibility in many diseases with documented correlations between HLA groups and disease processes. A prime example is ankylosing spondylitis in which 70% of the patients have HLA haplotype B27 (15).

Of most importance is the fact that individual variations of aging have been documented in several studies (5) (Fig. 5). The wide spectrum of the number of pituitary cells containing thyroid-stimulating hormone (TSH), particularly in those over age 40, is noted. It is the result of both individual genetic programming and different susceptibility and resistance to environmental influences, resulting in varying rates of deterioration of the homeostatic endocrine processes.

The response to injury is governed by both the heritable genetic state and the somatic genetic changes accumulated during the life of the organism. Intracellular organelle regeneration is largely dependent on effective DNA repair. We have previously shown that fusion of L-cells with 82-year-old fibroblasts reactivates

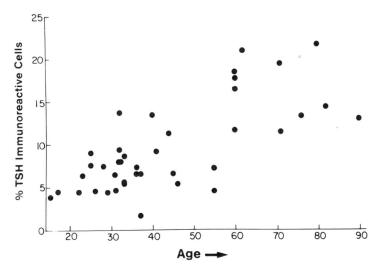

FIG. 5. Percentage of thyrotropin (TSH) immunoreactive cells in the pituitary versus age.

DNA synthesis (12). In a later study, we showed that with increasing age the percentage of epidermal cells able to repair DNA remained relatively stable (Fig. 6). However, the efficiency of this repair, or the number of competent repair sites measured by thymidine incorporation following injury by irradiation during a given length of time, was markedly reduced (13) (Fig. 7).

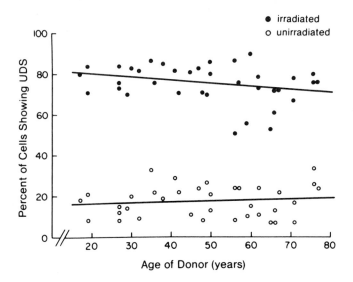

FIG. 6. Percentage of irradiated epidermal cells incorporating radioactive thymidine following uniform ultraviolet irradiation.

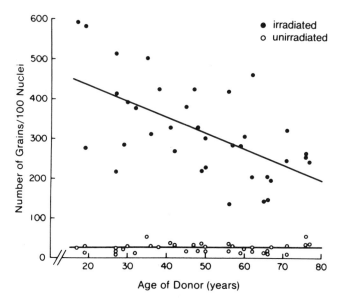

FIG. 7. Quantitative evaluation of radioactive thymidine incorporation (grains per 100 hundred nuclei) following irradiation correlated with age.

The inability of DNA to repair efficiently as well as mistakes in other control mechanisms result in disorganization of cell structure. This situation is seen pathologically in many cells as increased free ribosomes, abnormal mitochondria, distorted cytoskeletal structures, irregularities in nuclear and cytoplasmic membranes, and abnormal chromosomes. On the tissue level, as a result of cellular and extracellular changes, there is an increase in fibrosis, immune deposits, amyloid deposition, disorganization of the extracellular matrix, lipid infiltration, and cyst formation. It may result in altered architecture, with reduced function. A lack of proper substrates and an increase in toxic metabolites can produce an inability for cells to function well in the surrounding environment (11).

HOMEOSTATIC MECHANISMS REGULATING THE AGING PROCESS

Cellular and extracellular abnormalities associated with lack of repair in aging are also present in endocrine, neural, and immune cells and are reflected by an accentuation of degeneration and a breakdown of the homeostatic, regulatory control mechanisms. The marked degeneration of cells of the forebrain in Alzheimer's disease produces first a lack of acetylcholine transferase enzyme and later a lack of acetylcholine neurotransmitters (3). It is typified by neurofibrillary degeneration (Fig. 8).

The decrease in cells in the substantia nigra producing the neurotransmitter

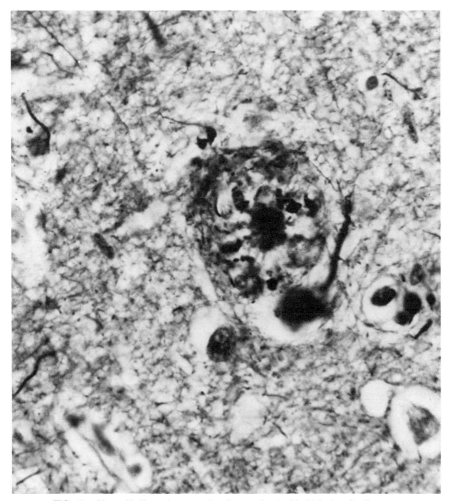

FIG. 8. Neurofibrillary degeneration in a patient with Alzheimer's disease.

dopamine and the inability to repair this deficiency either by cellular hyperplasia of appropriate cells or by hypertrophy results in Parkinson's disease, typified by the Lowy body (Fig. 9). This degenerative process in Alzheimer's and Parkinson's diseases is later expressed in motor and behavioral functions.

Little is known about aging of the autocrine hormonal system. The imbalances in epithelial and other growth factors and their receptors are important factors in the development of neoplasia, both benign and malignant. The disorders in the paracrine system in reproductive glands must be related to the genetically programmed reduction in fertility in both men and women. Atrophy of endocrine tissue sometimes results in compensatory hyperplastic and hypertrophic changes, e.g., leiomyomas in the uterus, cysts and solid tumors in the ovary, cystic disease

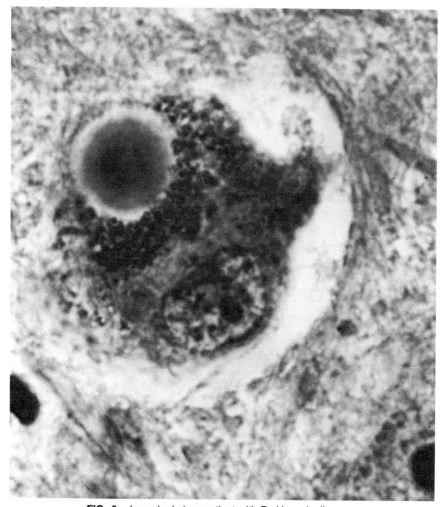

FIG. 9. Lowy body in a patient with Parkinson's disease.

and fibroadenoma of the breast, a wide variety of hyperplastic lesions in the endocrine glands (chromophobe adenoma, nodular goiter, parathyroid hyperplasia and adenoma, islet cell hyperplasia, and adrenal adenoma or hyperplasia). Studies on the aged pituitary gland have shown a decrease in the size and number of cells producing growth hormone and prolactin (21) (Fig. 10), and there appears to be increased TSH in pituitary cells (5) and increased calcitonin in the "C" cells of the thyroid (14). Hypofunction or hyperfunction occurs with the appropriate morphological changes but remains an individual characteristic of the organism.

Similarly, in the immune system there appears to be no absolute degeneration in hematopoietic stem cells. Stem cells can be transferred from an old mouse

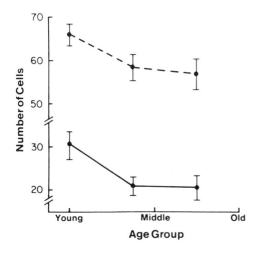

FIG. 10. Number of pituitary cells containing growth hormone in different age groups.

into a young mouse with subsequent growth and maturation, indicating the importance of the surrounding environment. Nevertheless, it is well recognized that the thymic tissue after puberty atrophies and disperses. With disorganization of the normal cortical medullary function, there is disappearance of epithelial cells and appearance of Hassel's corpuscles (2). Gradual fibrosis and atrophy of lymphoid nodules is seen in lymph nodes and tonsils. Hypoplasia and focal hyperplasia in the bone marrow may result in blood abnormalities and, not uncommonly, chronic leukemia in the elderly. The change in the patterns of the B- and T-cells and their subsets has been documented (Table 4). It is well recognized that serum immunoglobulin levels may be increased, as are immune deposits, but the primary immune response to new antigens is markedly reduced.

Correlative relations between the immune, endocrine, and neuroendocrine systems are increasingly well documented. Somatostatin is found in the islet cells of the pancreas and nerve cell sheaths, and it acts in both the endocrine and neuroendocrine systems (4). Thymosin acts as paracrine hormone to mature the T-cells of the immune system. A variety of autoimmune diseases affect the central nervous system, e.g., subacute panencephalitis and probably amyotrophic lateral sclerosis. Endocrine disorders such as thyroid Hashimoto's disease produce a disturbance in both cellular and immune systems; type 1 diabetes is known to cause endocrine dysfunction as a result of accelerated autoimmune disease.

SUMMARY

Aging is a physiological process that progresses steadily to a maximum lifespan of 80 to 110 years. It has a programmed genetic basis in which cells in elderly individuals, when compared to those of younger age groups, poorly repair cellular and extracellular constituents. This repair deficiency is accentuated by a

TABLE 4. *Changes in the immune system with age*

Component	Change
Lymphocytes	No change in total number Decrease in B-cell maturation Increase in suppressor (T) cells Decrease in helper (T) cells
Complement	Deficient complement levels associated with age, neoplasia, and infection
Antibody	Lack of thymic-dependent antibody response Decrease in primary response to new antigens Increase in globulins associated with secondary response and autoimmunity (benign monoclonal gammopathies) Increase in idiotypic antibodies to receptors
Immune complexes (antigen, antibody, complement)	Presence in all obsolescent glomeruli Presence in many vessel injuries Presence in many tissues previously injured Presence as amyloid either as light chains or in complexes with other protein and carbohydrates
Tolerance	Decrease in natural and acquired tolerance
Lymphoid tissue	Involution of thymus Loss of thymic hormones Atrophy, hypertrophy of some lymph nodes Hyperplasia of selected lymphoid elements, particularly in bone marrow Infiltration of lymphoid tissue in various organs (e.g., thyroid)

variety of environmental factors and injury throughout life that affect the genome and other constituents of the cells and extracellular components. The defect in intrinsic repair of individual cells may result in degeneration and imbalance of homeostatic control mechanisms of the immune, neuroendocrine, and autocrine systems, which indirectly hinder cellular repair processes.

Aging is a completely individual phenomenon as seen initially by the extreme variation in individual loss of the senses—smell, taste, touch, sight, and hearing—and the extrinsic anatomical characteristics noted by Shakespeare: "Have you not a moist eye, a dry hand, a yellow cheek, a white beard, a decreasing leg, an increasing belly? Is not your voice broken, your wind short, your chin double, your wit single, and every part about you blasted with antiquity?" (17).

The susceptibility and resistance to trauma, drugs, and environmental insult are individually determined. When coordinating control systems fail to function properly, an individual succumbs in a rapid fashion to a relatively minor insult. Even when the two major causes of death, cardiovascular disease and cancer, are cured, the life-span increases only some 12 years (Table 5). Modern human aging research demands a correlation of historical, biochemical, physiological, and morphological data before and after death.

TABLE 5. *Estimation of life-span*

Cause of death	Gain (years) in expectation of life if cause was eliminated	
	At birth	At age 65
Major cardiovascular and renal diseases	10.9	10.0
Heart diseases	5.9	4.9
Vascular diseases affecting CNS	1.3	1.2
Malignant neoplasms	2.3	1.2
Accidents, excluding motor vehicle	0.6	0.1
Motor vehicle accidents	0.6	0.1
Influenza and pneumonia	0.5	0.2
Infectious diseases (excluding tuberculosis)	0.2	0.1
Diabetes mellitus	0.2	0.2
Tuberculosis	0.1	0.0

Adapted from life tables published by the National Center of Health Statistics, U.S. Public Health Service, and U.S. Bureau of the Census: *Some Demographic Aspects of Aging in the United States*, February 1973.

REFERENCES

1. Auerbach, O., et al. (1962): Changes in bronchial epithelium in relation to sex, age, residence, smoking and pneumonia. *N. Engl. J. Med.*, 267:111–119.
2. Makinodan, T. (1980): Changes in immune function with age. *Adv. Pathobiol.*, 7:160–168.
3. Davies, P., and Maloney, A. J. F. (1976): Selective loss of central cholinergic neurons in Alzheimer's disease. *Lancet*, 2:1403.
4. Fenoglio, C. M., and King, D. W. (1983): Somatostatin: an update. *Hum. Pathol.*, 14:475–479.
5. Fenoglio, C. M., Zegarelli-Schmidt, E., Yu, X. P., O'Toole, K., Pushparaj, N., Kledzik, G., and King, D. W. (1985): Endocrine changes associated with the human aging process. II. Effects of age on the number and size of thyrotropin immunoreactive cells in the human pituitary. *Hum. Pathol.*, 16:277–286.
6. Fenoglio-Preiser, C. M., and Hutter, R. V. (1985): Colorectal polyps: pathologic diagnosis and clinical significance. *CA*, 35:322–344.
7. Fries, J. F., and Crapo, J. M. (1981): *Vitality and Aging.* W. H. Freeman, San Francisco.
8. Harbitz, T. B., and Haugen, O. A. (1972): Histology of the prostate in elderly men. *Acta Pathol. Microbiol. Scand.*, 80:756–768.
9. Kanell, W. B., Sorlie, P. D., and McNamara, P. M. (1979): Prognosis after initial myocardial infarction: the Framingham Study. *Am J. Cardiol.*, 44:158–161.
10. King, D. W., Pushparaj, N., O'Toole, K., and Gross, E. M. (1982): The value of human tissue in studies of aging. *J. Am. Geriatr. Soc.*, 30:539–545.
11. Kohn, R. R. (1978): *Principles of Mammalian Aging.* Prentice-Hall, Englewood Cliffs, NJ.
12. Nette, E. G., Sit, H. L., and King, D. W. (1982): Reactivation of DNA synthesis in aging diploid human skin fibroblasts by fusion with mouse L karyoplasts, cytoplasts and whole L cells. *Mech. Ageing Dev.*, 18:75–87.
13. Nette, E. G., Xi, Y., Sun, Y., Andrews, A. D., and King, D. W. (1984): A correlation between aging and DNA repair in human epidermal cells. *Mech. Ageing Dev.*, 24:283–292.
14. O'Toole, K., Fenoglio-Preiser, C., and Pushparaj, N. (1985): Endocrine changes associated with the human aging process. III. Effect of age on the number of calcitonin immunoreactive cells in the thyroid gland. *Hum. Pathol.*, 16:991–1000.
15. Sasazuki, T., Grumet, F. C., and McDevitt, H. O. (1977): The association of genes in the major histocompatibility complex and disease susceptability. *Ann. Rev. Med.*, 28:425.

16. Schneider, E. L., and Brody, J. A. (1983): Aging, natural death and the compression of morbidity, another view. *N. Engl. J. Med.,* 309:854–856.
17. Shakespeare, W.: *Henry IV, I, ii.*
18. Shock, N. W. (1977): Systems integration. In: *The Biology of Aging,* edited by C. E. Finch and L. Hayflick. Van Nostrand Reinhold, New York.
19. Suciu-Foca, N., Rohowsky, C., Kung, P., and King, D. W. (1982): Idiotype-like determinants on human T lymphocytes alloactivated in mixed lymphocyte culture. *J. Exp. Med.,* 156:283–288.
20. Suciu-Foca, N., Reed, E., Rohowsky, C., Kung, P., and King, D. W. (1983): Anti-idiotypic antibodies to anti-HLA receptors induced pregnancy. *Proc. Natl. Acad. Sci. USA,* 80:830–834.
21. Sun, Y. K., Xi, Y., Fenoglio, C., Pushparaj, N., O'Toole, K., Kledzik, G., Nette, G., and King, D. W. (1984): The effect of age on the number of pituitary cells immunoreactive to growth hormone and prolactin. *Hum. Pathol.,* 15:169–180.
22. Trump, B. F., McDowell, E. M., and Arstila, A. U. (1980): *Principles of Pathology,* 3rd ed., edited by R. B. Hill and M. F. LaVia. Oxford University Press, New York.
23. Xi, Y. P., et al (1982): Age related changes in normal human basement membrane. *Mech. Ageing Dev.,* 19:315–324.

Human Aging Research: Concepts and Techniques,
edited by B. Kent and R. N. Butler.
Raven Press, Ltd., New York © 1988.

Funding Process

Robert N. Butler

*Department of Geriatrics and Adult Development, Mount Sinai Medical Center,
New York, New York 10029*

Understanding how to raise money through grants and other means is a fundamental part of academic medical training. Whether one has clinical interests and is seeking support for service activities or is interested in a research career, it is important for medical students and fellows in training to learn how to evaluate the literature, create and refine their ideas, and undergo peer review. Moreover, to understand geriatrics, one needs to have some appreciation of research gerontology and research geriatric medicine, two distinguishable concepts.

Geriatrics is still in its rudimentary stages, and descriptive studies are needed. Thus learning to make solid observations ("reproducible facts") of unexplained clinical behavior and findings in geriatrics is desirable. The understanding that comes from astute observation may also be useful to others as we learn more about the potential for intervention to reduce the debilitating processes of aging. We need to study varied older populations over time. We need to develop common protocols for assessment in all settings where outpatients and inpatients are seen.

This chapter presents a "nuts and bolts" review of funding sources for the support of aging research.[*] It provides some idea of how one goes about seeking support, i.e., raising money through the presentation of ideas. Ideas in the arts and sciences have always depended on patronage, whether private or governmental. The relatively modest amounts of money that are available for intellectual activities compared with other human activities yield rewards in the form of gratifying results of discovery and application.

Few medical schools teach scientific research concepts and methods. Yet science education is necessary so the United States can compete effectively in the world economy. The United States requires increasing productivity which, in turn, depends on ideas that can come about only through research, development, and education. In medicine we have lamented the "disappearance of clinical investigators," to use a phrase of James Wyngaarden, Director of the National Institutes of Health. There are few physicians pursuing research careers, and yet we recognize the

---

[*] An excellent overall guide to sources of funding for research and other projects in the field of aging is *National Guide to Funding in Aging,* Weiss D. M., Mahlmann D. E., eds. Available from the Foundation Center, 79 Fifth Avenue, New York, N.Y. 10003.

vital connection between the bedside clinical problem and basic science, one example being neuroscientists seeking proximity to clinical populations with Alzheimer's disease.

SOURCES OF GOVERNMENTAL FUNDING

Federal Government

National Institutes of Health

The National Institutes of Health (NIH), begun in 1887 under a different name in Bethesda, Maryland, are located on approximately 400 acres donated by the Wilson family to the government. (There the National Cancer Institute began in 1935). The NIH was the successor to the National Hygienic Laboratory of the U.S. Public Health Service, where remarkable work such as the understanding of pellagra by Goldberger was accomplished. The U.S. Public Health Service began during the administration of John Adams, the second president of the United States.

The NIH has 12 institutes, with about 12 to 13% of its budget being used for intramural support (where there have been a number of Nobel Prize winners in outstanding laboratories). About 80% of NIH funds goes to grantees and the remaining 7% to administrative costs. NIH funds account for some 30% of the support of biomedical research in the United States. The remainder comes from other sources, especially industry. The directors of the institutes at NIH are not political appointees but are selected by search committees similar to those that operate within universities. The search committees usually have outside members as well as members of the NIH community. The overall director of NIH, however, is a presidential appointee.

What does the intellectual leadership of an NIH institute do? Plan and set priorities following identification of the opportunities and needs for research. Sometimes announcements of these initiatives do not work out well. Such was the case for pharmacology of aging at the National Institute of Aging. One would think that such an announcement would be a "natural" because everybody realizes that distinct changes occur in the effects of medication in our bodies as we grow older. Yet there were few responses to a program announcement related to pharmacology of aging, and it remains an undeveloped field today. Nobel prize winning concepts are not necessary in order to understand the pharmacokinetics and pharmacodynamics of aging.

There are dangers involved in establishing a fund "set aside" to provide a certain amount of money to encourage people to pursue a specific topic, e.g., $2 million for the pharmacology of aging. The Institute would be committed to the expenditure of the $2 million even if poor projects came in, and therefore $2 million of taxpayers' money would be spent wastefully. It was found that floating an announcement first, without a "set aside," enables the Institute to evaluate the quality of proposals that come in and then make decisions as to whether there are ideas, animal models, etc. out there to provide support for a particular field.

Institutes that fund research in aging

The National Institute on Aging (NIA) and other institutes of the National Institutes of Health obviously have specific interests in aging where the aging–disease interaction is appropriate. For example, the National Institute of Allergy and Infectious Diseases supports work concerning the possible etiology of an unconventional slow virus in Alzheimer's disease. The National Heart, Lung and Blood Institute and the NIA collaborate in the study of systolic hypertension in the elderly. The new National Institute of Arthritis and Musculoskeletal and Skin Diseases, spun off from the National Institute of Arthritis, Diabetes, and Digestive and Kidney Diseases, undoubtedly supports research helpful to older persons. Other agencies outside the NIH—the Alcoholism, Drug Abuse, and Mental Health Administration (ADAMHA), most particularly the National Institute of Mental Health, and the National Institute of Alcohol Abuse and Alcoholism—support studies on aging.

There already have been useful conjoint efforts among institutes, which is healthy and important to the field of aging. For example, the NIA and the National Dental Institute created the Geriatric Dentistry Academic Award, and the NIA and the Allergy and Infectious Disease Institute issued the infectious diseases announcement.

National Institute on Aging

The NIA celebrated its 10th anniversary in 1985. Established in 1974 as part of NIH through the Research on Aging Act, its mandate was to carry out "the conduct and support of biomedical, social, and behavioral research and training relating to the aging process and the diseases and other special problems and needs of the aged." Prior to the establishment of the NIA, aging research within NIH was conducted at the National Institute of Child Health and Human Development (NICHD) and represented only about 10% of NICHD's budget from 1962 to 1973. Aging research programs were also dispersed among other NIH institutes, but most focused on categorical diseases rather than on aging processes. The impetus for creating a separate institute came from recommendations from the 1961 and 1971 white House Conferences on Aging, as well as the Gerontological Society of America, American Association of Retired Persons, National Retired Teachers Association, and National Council of Senior Citizens. The overall goal of the NIA is to "promote health and well-being by extending the vigorous and productive years of life."

Priorities. Leadership in geriatric research should encourage work on topics that are thought to be unglamorous. The three major antecedents to institutionalization are mobility problems, memory impairments, and incontinence—not the most attractive topics, but alleviating them would make an enormous difference to the health and well-being of the elderly.

In 1980 the National Research on Aging Planning Panel was organized to assist the NIA in the development of a long-range plan for research. It involved 203 consultants from academic life who collaborated in thinking through the needs and opportunities in the field of aging. The plan is divided up similar to the organizational structure of the NIA: basic biology and molecular biology, cellular biology, clinical medicine or geriatrics, and social and behavioral research. There is great interest in fostering linkages between biology and behavior, e.g., healthy, effective functioning, which is certainly important for older people. The interrelation of the aged and society is directed to social science.

The list of NIA announcements includes infectious diseases in the elderly, minority aging, and bereavement, which provides an opportunity to study the interrelation of biology and behavior. Some studies have found some interesting relations between bereavement and immune function changes. Two NIA priorities concern "the oldest old" (the frail elderly, the 85-plus age group, is the fastest growing) and the molecular biology of aging.

How awards are made

1. *Announcements.* There are two kinds of NIH announcements. One is the request for applications (RFA) and refers to grants, and the other is the request for projects (RFP) and relates to contracts. For example, a contract mechanism is appropriate for a project that involves finding nonlethal biomarkers of aging. It requires construction and support of long-term efforts over a 10-year period.

2. *Review process.* NIA health science administrators review drafts and budgets of proposals but can only do so well in advance of deadlines (more than 60 days before) because it takes time to review carefully, make notes, and respond.

Grant reviews for NIH are accomplished by one central office called the Division of Research Grants (DRG). Each institute transfers funds from its budget to support this key entity, which manages some 50 study sections (e.g., pathochemistry, neurology) and covers all fields in medicine. The DRG reviews 18,000 applications per year and has only 12 readers. Therefore they can read only the abstract. Thus it is important for the applicant to (a) use key words in the abstract to be certain the proposal is understood, and (b) refer it to the appropriate institute and study section. A new investigator often has a better chance of getting funded than does an established investigator, so new applicants should not become discouraged.

There is no NIH–DRG study section that covers aging per se. There was great pressure on the new NIA when it came into being in 1975 to create special study sections on aging. As NIA director at the time, I resisted and argued that aging research is complex and cuts across many study sections so that one would have to create 50 additional study sections, which would be expensive. Moreover, eventually aging must come into its own and compete with all other fields of medicine. Aging research does not require special solicitude. Each study section should become acquainted with the special mission of each institute.

Study sections are not made up of government employees but peer scientists from around the United States who properly resist federal intrusion. The NIA director, like any institute director, has the opportunity from time to time to address study sections on the fundamental issues of the NIA, e.g., aging research, opportunities for unraveling the biological mechanisms of senescence (e.g., how immune incompetence rises with age), and, comparing one institute with another, how various grant applications have fared.

There is a two-tier review, not only a review in the study section but also in the institute's advisory council. Every institute has a national advisory council, which is important because it can determine relevance; for example, a famous scientist can conceive a brilliant project in terms of fundamental biology only vaguely connected with aging and be voted down by the council's second review. The advisory council is usually made up of outstanding citizens from science and society.

Although there is no specific NIH–DRG study section on aging, there is an NIA Aging Review Committee. Each institute can have special committees. The Aging Review Committee of the NIA provides a creative opportunity to support program project grants, the program, or multidisciplinary projects.

Grants

At the NIH most support is correctly intended for investigator-initiated research— the *individual research project* called the RO1. This type of grant is central to the support of science in America. It allows an investigator not only to respond to program announcements—ideas that have been thought up by the central government—but to submit original research projects. Any idea should and does receive a hearing at the NIH.

Interdisciplinary or multidisciplinary research is supported through a *program project grant* called a PO1. It is especially useful because of the complexity and multiplicity of problems that arise in the field of aging. This conventional mechanism has been used to support the idea of the "teaching nursing home." (Teaching hospitals have been "flagships" in the development of academic medicine over the last 70 or 80 years. So, too, we need to have the counterpart, the teaching (academic or research) nursing home, so that we can begin to understand better the types of clinical and biomedical challenges that reside within nursing homes, territory that is still virtually unexplored. The teaching nursing home makes it possible for medical students, scholars, and researchers to enter an institution that has been outside the mainstream of medicine.)

Another conventional NIH mechanism is the *center grant*. The history of growth of funding for the NIH has been shaped by the efforts of health science administrators and health science advocates to develop the center concept with emphasis on a disease such as cancer or arthritis. When the NIA came into being in 1975, the problem was how to take an institute that is related to a stage of life or life processes and make use of the historic catalytic importance of the disease-mission approach and the center mechanism. Members of the public do not become ill, or suffer or die, from basic science. They suffer and die from specific diseases such as cancer or polio or heart disease, and these diseases become the focus of their fear. Through the politics of anguish, it was possible to build constituent pressure on Congress and its authorization and appropriation committees to get funding for each of the institutes related to diseases. What about those programs that are not specifically related to diseases, however, such as the National Institute of Child Health and Human Development or the National Institute on Aging?

In order to present the traditionally effective disease-oriented approach to Congress, it was decided to select some of the common, devastating diseases of old age that are costly to individuals, families, and society for funding under the Center Grant Category. One was Alzheimer's disease. The Alzheimer's Disease Research Centers grant program, which took a number of years to build, was introduced and properly coordinated with other institutes that had related missions, such as the National Institute of Neurological and Communicative Disorders and Stroke and the National Institute of Mental Health. There are now ten such centers.

Clinical trials are still another important NIH mission. The NIA and the National Heart, Lung and Blood Institute support the Systolic Hypertension Elderly Program (SHEP), for example, which seeks to better understand how one should treat isolated systolic hypertension in older persons.

The NIA supports various *training awards* to help individuals in biomedical, clinical, behavioral, and social science fields prepare for or advance their careers in research and teaching in aging and geriatrics. These awards include the Clinical Investigator Award and the Academic Award. The Clinical Investigator Award is called a KO8 and is for people within 4 to 7 years of their total professional postdoctoral, clinical, and research experiences. The Academic Award (formerly called the Teacher–Investigator Award) is meant to recruit and prepare future investigators in research and teaching.

The *First Independent Research Support and Transition (FIRST) Award (R-29)* replaces the New Investigator Award. Offered by NIH and the Division of Nursing in the Health Research and Services Administration, the new award was established to provide a sufficient initial period of research support for newly independent biomedical investigators to develop their research capabilities and demonstrate the merit of their research ideas. The awards generally provide funds for 5 years to allow newly independent investigators with promising proposals to make significant and innovative contributions to biomedical research.

Training awards of the NIA are in the following categories.

National Research Service Awards: Individual fellowship (F-32); Senior Fellowship (F-33); Institutional Research Training Grant (T-32); Complementary Training Award for Research on Aging (T-32); and Short-term Training for Students in Health Professional Schools (T-35).

Research Career Award: Research Career Development Award (KO-4); NIA Academic Award (KO-8); Clinical Investigator Award (KO-8); Special Emphasis Research Career Award (behavioral sciences only) (KO-1); Individual Physician Scientist Award (K11); Institutional Physician Scientist Award (K12); and Geriatric Leadership Academic Award (KO-7).

Minority Program: Minority Biomedical Research Support (SO-6); also Minority Access to Research Careers, incorporating Faculty Fellowships (F-34), Visiting Scientists Program (F-36), Honors Undergraduate Research Training Program (T-34), and Predoctoral Fellowship Program (F31).

Intramural Training Programs: Staff Fellow and Medical Staff Fellow: training in NIA's biomedical research laboratories.

Problems and Thoughts on Federal Funding

Initially, there was considerable negativism toward studies on aging. It was fascinating to find that a study on growth and differentiation in the appropriate study section would pass and receive a fundable priority score, whereas a virtually identical aging study would not. The other problem we discovered at the NIA was the voting of poor priority scores even when an outstanding scientist was recruited. The "pink" sheet would read he/she "had no track record in aging." Such responses are partly due to the perception that aging is negative and not promising. Yet scientifically studying and measuring aging are no less interesting or important endeavors than studying and measuring growth. It is important to help study section members understand that aging research is part of developmental biology and, of course, how people and biological functions change over time.

In 1978 NIH Director Donald Fredrickson supported the view that there ought to be a basic number of new grants funded annually, a policy called "stabilization." The "magic number" picked originally was 5,000 with about 11,000 continuing commitments. When a minimum is set it often becomes a maximum. For example, rules and regulations in nursing homes—minimum standards—soon become the maximum standards. In February 1985, however, there was a breakthrough to 6,500. Even so, outstanding proposals go unfunded each year, and there are many wasted scientific opportunities.

Research on aging should be supported through heightened revenues, e.g., tobacco and alcohol excise taxes, and should bear some relation to health expenses, e.g., some percentage of Medicare expenses ($71 billion in 1985). If science is not maintained with new dollars, a new generation of investigators may be lost. If a continuing flow of money is unavailable, it is impossible to keep laboratories active.

The power of leadership that exists at NIH is the power of ideas: identifying issues, developing workshops, commissioning studies, making certain there is a strong science base. Secretary Joseph Califano tried to sharpen the way in which science is supported through the articulation of five "health research principles":

fundamental research, clinical applications and health services research, health regulation and promotion, research capability, and unifying concepts. Five committees were formed, one for each principle, and NIH directors and leadership as well as outstanding U.S. scientists convened for several days in October 1978 to wrestle with the problem of how science could be supported.

Other Public Health Service Agencies

The *National Institute of Mental Health* (NIMH), which is not part of NIH, is a component of the Alcoholism, Drug Abuse and Mental Health Administration (ADAMHA). The NIMH Branch of Aging supports studies on various aspects of aging, including family stress and care of Alzheimer's disease victims, and it supports geriatric psychiatry training programs.

The *Administration on Aging* (AOA) is part of the Department of Health and Human Services in downtown Washington and is not part of the medical scientific establishment. However, the AOA does support work related to health, such as health promotion, long-term care, community-based services, and management information systems.

In 1986 the Administration on Aging Division of Research and Demonstrations gave 96 new awards totaling $11 million and spent $2 million to continue 17 research and demonstration programs. The individual grants of the AOA vary in size up to $200,000 annually, usually for 1 or 2 years. The AOA is somewhat vulnerable to the political whims of Congress and the administration in office. The head of the Administration on Aging, the Commissioner on Aging, is an appointee in the executive branch of government.

The *Health Resources and Services Administration* (HRSA) of the Department of Health and Human Services supports regional Geriatric Education Centers (GECs) in order to strengthen and coordinate multidisciplinary training in geriatric health care involving several health professions. The first four GECs were funded in 1983 at Harvard University, University of Michigan at Ann Arbor, SUNY–Buffalo, and the University of Southern California at Los Angeles. By 1986 there were 22 GECs nationwide.

The AOA and the Health Resources and Services Administration have a different political base or discretionary power. The Commissioner on Aging or his/her boss (the Assistant Secretary of Human Development Services) can serve the particular objectives and goals of the Administration, a power not given to NIH directors or institute directors.

The *National Science Foundation* (NSF) supports work related to aging, e.g., speciation (the evolutionary formation of new species) and the role of aging in evolution. NSF normally does not fund clinical research, including research on the etiology, diagnosis, or treatment of physical or mental disease, nor does it normally support research about such conditions in animal models or the development or testing of drugs. Funding is available for group research proposals and for research equipment.

At the *Veterans Administration* (VA), which is an important source of research funding, scientific investigators compete for merit money and special funds. The major focus of the VA's research programs, which were initiated following World War II, has been on projects with direct applicability to patient management. The VA's Geriatric Research, Education and Clinical Centers (GRECC) program was conceived in 1973 to stimulate the involvement of new practitioners, teachers, and researchers in geriatrics. One of its specific objectives was to study the relation of aging to a variety of problems, to demonstrate the utility and importance of this approach, and to create a focus and visibility for geriatric research. The first GRECCs were established in 1975; as of 1985 there were ten located around the United States, each of which focuses on a different set of priorities.

World War II veterans are approaching the average age of 60 and in 1990 will number as many as 9 million elderly. The VA must plan domiciliary care, nursing home care, and a whole range of services for them. There is a lot of interest from Congress, the American Legion, and organized medicine in VA funding for education, research, and services for aging veterans.

Although *Medicare* provides support for graduate medical education (about $2 billion in 1985), it has not supported the development of geriatrics, even though Medicare beneficiaries are principally persons over 65. Efforts were under way in 1986 to change that fact.

The *National Center for Health Services Research and Health Care Technology Assessment* (NCHSR), a branch of the Public Health Service, funded more than $9.8 million in fiscal 1986 in grants for extramural research projects. It has identified four areas that are likely to be of primary importance during the present decade: (a) primary care/health promotion and disease prevention; (b) technology assessment; (c) role of market forces in health care delivery; and (d) studies relevant to operational and policy issues faced by state and local governments. Proposals in other areas are also encouraged.

State-Funded Programs

It is not within the scope of this chapter to describe in detail the opportunities for research funding in all 50 states. Few states, in fact, support research in aging. However, a few pioneering programs deserve mention.

California

Using the NIA concept of the Geriatric Resource Center, the State of California began in 1985 to provide funding to the University of California's (U.C.) medical schools and health science centers, six in all. The University established an advisory committee comprised of faculty in geriatrics and gerontology that reports to the U.C. president and sets up criteria for funding utilization. At the end of the project year, the six schools must submit a report to the legislature through the advisory committee. The committee decides, depending on the proposal, how the money will be divided; $20,000 per year was allocated for planning and start-up, following which $100,000 per school was provided; $225,000 was then apportioned on a competitive basis.

The proposals can focus on any one or combination of the following categories:

1. Undergraduate professional, including preclinical and clinical; graduate professional, including house staff; graduate and continuing education
2. Multilevel settings including nursing homes for multidisciplinary geriatric training
3. Education for the general public on health-enhancing behavior for the elderly, their special health care needs and resources available to meet these needs
4. Research in aging

Ohio

The Ohio legislative budget provides on a biennial cycle about $1.5 million per year to be divided among the state's seven medical schools. Currently, each school has a division of geriatrics, and three of the divisions are headed by an associate dean of the medical school. The fiscal appropriations are seed money and administrative money. They guarantee that special attention is paid to geriatrics in curricula and residency programs. Although each school has latitude in deciding how they spend the money, there is an incentive program. The criteria include 13 categories, and the money is divided among the schools depending on their points from the criteria. This system emphasizes that the programs in geriatrics should be comprehensive and guides the schools in that direction. Ultimately, the money tends to be divided evenly among the seven schools. As a result of this legislation, the geriatric divisions have the proper administrative support, and other support has been attracted, e.g., NIA and Robert Wood Foundation grants.

Massachusetts

The Massachusetts state legislature funds a Gerontology Institute at the University of Massachusetts in Boston. The Institute focuses on statewide policy and research and is linked to the College of Public and Community Service, which has both undergraduate and graduate programs. The Institute, now in its third year, is strongly supported by the state government, but its support must be voted on each year.

NONGOVERNMENTAL SOURCES OF FUNDING

The medical enterprise cannot depend on government alone; therefore it is essential to develop other sources of funding. Donations from private individuals constitute

90% of all philanthropic gifts and those from foundations and corporations 10%. On the average, Americans give about 2% of their income to charity. According to W. A. Neilson's book *The Golden Donors: A New Anatomy of the Great Foundations* (Dutton, New York, 1985), of some 4,000 foundations and 28,468 philanthropic funds with total assets of $50 billion in the United States, only 50 have any staff. Frequently small family foundations simply respond to requests made by a family friend or physician. Foundations as a whole give away more than $4 billion each year, and variation in that figure depends on the economy in a particular year. Foundations and corporations each gave $4.3 billion in 1985.

Private Philanthropy

Because a great deal of money comes from private sources, and it is possible to find oneself in the company of potential donors, one should always have ready what I call "vest pocket proposals" and back-up information. Philanthropists, who are often entrepreneurial individuals who have worked hard and made their own fortunes, want ideas, and they want to share in their development. You must meet them on their own ground, not be arrogant, and be willing to accept their suggestions. Entrepreneurs are intelligent people who ask provocative questions. When presenting an idea or a proposal, it is important to emphasize the positive and not ask them to make up a deficit. You have to give a sense that there is a "light at the end of the tunnel." I was once introduced at a governor's conference on aging, by a governor who meant well, as someone who has "given his life to a field that you can do nothing about." The *proper* message is: We *can* do something about aging. Often we find it difficult to give a positive message because we are overwhelmed by the complex problems we face. There are effective interventions available, however, and we *can* make the quality of late life more decent through better understanding and action.

Foundations

Foundations have traditionally given little money to research on aging. Just a few years ago, according to the Foundation Clearing House, less than 0.01% of all aspects of aging service, research, and education was supported by foundations. Yet this situation is changing. For instance, the *Florence V. Burden Foundation* in New York, although a modest foundation, has tried to emphasize aging and has provided seed money for several useful projects including a Well Elderly Program at the 92nd Street "Y." The *Edna McConnell Clark Foundation* provided support for a national survey by the Harris Organization, which helped put aging on the map some years ago. The new *Villers Foundation,* a self-liquidating foundation that will end in 20 years, will give $43 million to the field of aging. Half will be spent to develop advocacy and grassroots support to meet the needs of older people. The remaining $23 million will be spent on grants related to advocacy.

The *John A. Hartford Foundation* has been generous in initiating and supporting the Geriatric Faculty Development Award, which supports 1-year training programs for mid-career physicians at four sites: Mount Sinai Medical Center in New York, Harvard University, Johns Hopkins University, and UCLA. It is also supporting other programs in aging, such as pharmacology and gait and mobility problems.

The *Commonwealth Fund* is primarily concerned with improving the health care of Americans, one major area being improvement of the health and well-being of the elderly. By 1985 the Commonwealth Fund had elected to spend one of every three of its new dollars in the field of aging for the next several years. It supports an osteoporosis program, three Alzheimer's disease fellowships, and a urinary incontinence program. The Commonwealth Fund takes great pride in its brokering; that is, for every dollar it provides it may obtain an additional two or three dollars from other foundations. One of its new programs is called "Living at Home." A one-time competition open to the 100 cities in the United States that have the highest concentrations of older people, the Living at Home Program provides support for innovative ways to bring together various agencies, institutions, and organizations within the community to help people stay at home. This program is an unusual multifoundation effort sponsored by the *Commonwealth Fund* with the *Arthur Vining Davis Foundation,* the *Pew Memorial Trust,* the *Cleveland Foundation,* the *New York Community Trust,* the *John A. Hartford Foundation,* and the *Duke Endowment.*

The second Commonwealth Fund program is the "Commission for the Elderly Living Alone," announced in 1986. The Commission is spending 3 years and $5 million to identify the needs of the elderly who live alone and develop model programs to meet those needs.

The *Robert Wood Johnson Foundation* has a program that is relevant to geriatrics: a research and development program to improve patient functional status, which is the heart of geriatrics. Another philanthropic effort from the same family—*The Robert Wood Johnson Junior Charitable Trust*—supports a neurobiology chair, fellowships, and research in Alzheimer's disease at Mount Sinai Medical Center in New York. The *Mathers Foundation,* a private family foundation, supports a molecular biology chair at Mount Sinai.

In 1985 the *Brookdale Foundation* announced a $5 million National Fellowship Program in the field of aging in medicine, the humanities, and social sciences. The medical fellowships provide support for 2- or 3-year stipends for Board-eligible physicians in the first stage of postdoctoral development or those who are junior faculty. The individual's institution must have established credibility in research and training in the field of geriatrics. The program also supports social scientists.

The *MacArthur Foundation* does not accept unsolicited proposals but has developed an important program chaired by Dr. John Rowe of Harvard and devoted to understanding "successful aging."

The *AARP Andrus Foundation,* sponsored by the American Association of Retired Persons, awards research grants in the field of aging twice a year. The Washington-based foundation makes these awards of up to $50,000 per year to universities.

Nonprofit Organizations and Agencies

Major nonprofit organizations include the Alzheimer's Disease and Related Disorders Association (ADRDA), which has provided grants for projects ranging from patient care research to fundamental neurochemistry. ADRDA funded around $13 million in research grants in 1985. The NIH provided about $47 million in 1985.

The *American Federation of Aging Research* is the "American Heart Association of The National Institute on Aging," that is, the NIA's counterpart in the private sector. (The Heart, Lung and Blood Institute and the National Cancer Institute are supported by the American Heart Association and the American Cancer Society, respectively. These organizations provide organized constituency pressure on congressional offices, participate in hearings, issue pronouncements, and sponsor dinner dances, which can raise substantial sums of money.)

There is a new foundation called the *National Aging Foundation* (NAF) founded by a Tucson, Arizona businessman, Robert Gibson, who decided that aging is one of the great social problems of this century and the next, and that it needs a national charity with income in the range of $150 million a year. Gibson helps develop the public charity and uses direct mail and other means of fund-raising. Collaborative Universities for Research on Aging (CURA), composed of Mount Sinai, USC, Baylor, Arizona State, University of Arizona, Emory, Duke, and Johns Hopkins, have given their endorsement to NAF and will be, along with the American Federation of Aging Research (AFAR) among the beneficiaries of the money raised.

Another new organization is the *Alliance for Aging Research,* a Washington-based nonprofit foundation that unites scientists, business leaders, and federal officials in support of research that seeks to understand and affect the human aging process. It is working toward adoption of a national science policy that places greater emphasis on understanding funadmental processes of human aging in order to intervene in those processes for human benefit. Senior corporate and foundation executives serve with scientists on its board of directors. The Alliance is advised in its relations with Congress by a bipartisan committee of U.S. Senators and Representatives.

Corporations

Corporations have not provided much support for aging research, although they have had the privilege under the Internal Revenue Service of donating up to 5% of their profits to various forms of giving. Stockholder suits have claimed that it is not the business of corporations to be benevolent but to make profits. If stockholders want to give their money away it is fine, but the corporations have no right to do so. Atlantic Richfield, Morgan Guaranty, and Exxon are among the most generous corporations. It remains to be seen what effects the 1986 tax reform will have on future donations by the corporate sector.

The pharmaceutical industry must be interested in the extraordinary demographic change that is occurring and needs to develop geriatric clinical pharmacology programs. The *Merck Corporation* has held a major symposium on aging. *Pfizer Pharmaceuticals* and the *American Geriatrics Society* are supporting postdoctoral fellowships specifically for research in geriatric medicine. *Sandoz Pharmaceuticals* has supported research and educational programs related to aging.

An example of research support from the life and health insurance industry is the *Travelers Life Insurance Company,* which has sponsored a Professorship and a Center on Geriatrics at the University of Connecticut.

Beverly Enterprises, a major organization in the proprietary nursing home industry, co-sponsored a major symposium on the teaching nursing home in April 1984 through its *Beverly Foundation,* along with the NIA. Participants shared information on existing programs, and the proceedings were published in *The Teaching Nursing Home: A New Approach to Geriatric Research, Education, and Clinical Care* (Raven Press, New York, 1984).

There is an important "longevity lobby" not only in the United States but in the world that includes some powerful people in industry and public policy. There is an enormous market for Pritikin and the "maximum life-span" books, which sell millions of copies yearly. There are clearly many people who are interested in living longer.

On the other hand, some people are worried that successful aging research will lead to a larger number of older people and, consequently, great financial burdens such as increased social security and health care costs. They use these fears to lobby against aging research. Perhaps the following fictional anecdote will convince them otherwise.

Imagine that it is 1900 and Teddy Roosevelt is president. He has interesting visitors, Robert Koch and Louis Pasteur, who tell him about the germ theory. They tell him about someone named Paul Ehrlich who has the idea of a "magic bullet," an antibiotic, which destroys pathogens without harming the patient. They predict a fundamental historical change that will dramatically increase survivorship. There will be massive reductions of maternal, childhood, and infant mortality rates.

The President calls in an epidemiologist and the Director of the Office of Management and Budget. They tell the President that the average life expectancy is now 47. "If you support this kind of research," they say, "and give more money to the National Hygienic Laboratory [the precursor of NIH], and if the wine industry in France continues to support Pasteur and the Germans keep supporting Koch, we are going to have a problem because the average life expectancy we project by 1986 will be 74 instead of 47. Instead of 3%, we will have nearly 12% of our people over 65. We cannot afford all those old people." Fortunately, President Roosevelt replies: "Full speed ahead. We must support ideas and help progress. We are not going to hold back the clock."

Thanks to dedicated scientists and policymakers who are not afraid to support new ideas we have been able in this century to achieve a 26-year gain in average life expectancy—nearly equal to the gain that took some 5,000 years (3,000 BC to 1900 AD) to achieve. It is important to remember, however, that our mission is not only to extend the life-span but to enhance the quality of life.

Subject Index